The Full Severity of Compassion

STANFORD STUDIES IN JEWISH HISTORY AND CULTURE

EDITED BY *Aron Rodrigue and Steven J. Zipperstein*

The Full Severity of Compassion

The Poetry of Yehuda Amichai

Chana Kronfeld

STANFORD UNIVERSITY PRESS

STANFORD, CALIFORNIA

Stanford University Press
Stanford, California

Publication of this book has been supported in part by a UC Berkeley Mellon Faculty Research Grant, the Taubman Chair at UC Berkeley and the Press Humanities Fund.

Permission to reprint the Hebrew original of Yehuda Amichai's poems granted by Schocken, Israel; permission to print archival materials and previously untranslated poems by Yehuda Amichai granted by Hana Amichai; permission to reprint translations from *The Selected Poetry of Yehuda Amichai* and poems translated with the author for this volume granted by Chana Bloch; permission to reprint translations from *Yehuda Amichai: A Life of Poetry, 1948–1994* granted by Barbara Harshav; permission to reprint the translation of "To Yehuda Amichai" by Zbigniew Herbert granted by Alissa Valles.

Printed in the United States of America on acid-free, archival-quality paper

Library of Congress Cataloging-in-Publication Data

Kronfeld, Chana, author.
   The full severity of compassion : the poetry of Yehuda Amichai / Chana Kronfeld.
      pages cm. — (Stanford studies in Jewish history and culture)
   Includes bibliographical references and index.
   ISBN 978-0-8047-8295-1 (cloth : alk. paper)
   1. Amichai, Yehuda—Criticism and interpretation. 2. Israeli poetry—20th century—History and criticism. 3. Jewish poetry—20th century—History and criticism. I. Title. II. Series: Stanford studies in Jewish history and culture.
   PJ5054.A65Z696 2015
      892.41'6—dc23
                                    2015017615
ISBN 978-0-8047-9721-4 (electronic)

Typeset by Bruce Lundquist in 10.5/14 Galliard

In Memoriam
Yehuda Amichai ז"ל *(1924–2000)*
and
Amichai Kronfeld ז"ל *(1947–2005)*

Contents

Acknowledgments

When Yehuda and Hana Amichai spent a sabbatical at the University of California, Berkeley (UC Berkeley) in the late 1970s—and in later years, whenever they would return for shorter visits—notes and phone messages meant for them would regularly end up being delivered, by mistake, to me and my husband, whose first name was Amichai (Kronfeld). In a book dedication, Yehuda scribbled: "For Chana and Amichai, with a closeness beyond names." We lost both Amichais almost exactly five years apart, in September 2000 and 2005. This book is dedicated to their memory, with unending love. My Amichai, a philosopher of language who was an extraordinarily sensitive reader of Yehuda's poetry and thought, helped me articulate the philosophical contours of Yehuda Amichai's poetics, integrate theory with close reading, and develop an appreciation for the ways in which this poetry paradoxically intensifies pathos by always restraining and keeping it in check. I have included here a couple of Amichai Kronfeld's translations of the early quatrains, the exquisitely terse poems he would always turn to for sustenance. Now they sustain me.

I am grateful to Hana Amichai who, despite the tough years following her loss, found the wherewithal to generously share vital research sources and recollections with me, and to grant me permission to cite archival materials and publish translations of Amichai poems that appear here for the first time, both those by me and those by Chana Bloch and myself.

I am reminded of the way Yehuda would joke about being supported by three camps (*machanot*). He was punning again on the coincidence of names—in this case, the Hebrew name חנה (pl., *Chanot*) shared by his wife Hana and us, his translators, "the two Chanas."

Ever since Yehuda proposed in 1997, during what would turn out to be his last visit to Berkeley, that Chana Bloch and I prepare a translation of his book *Open Closed Open*, Chana has been a most cherished collaborator and soul sister. Her profound understanding of Amichai's poetry and keen sense of English style combined in her insightful comments on every page of the manuscript draft. These comments proved immensely helpful to me in the revision process. Galit Hasan-Rokem read a very early draft of the book and provided encouraging feedback. Two other dear friends and colleagues read and commented in detail on the entire manuscript. Sidra DeKoven Ezrahi, whose innovative and nuanced studies of Amichai's poetry have been an inspiration for years, read the draft of the book with extraordinary care and provided both much-needed validation and a critique that guided me throughout. My dialogue with Sidra takes place on every page of this book. Daniel Boyarin read the manuscript draft as well, always getting exactly what was at stake for me, even when I did not. I am grateful to Daniel for filling in lacunae in theoretical argument and textual allusion, while always providing a real friend's emotional support (*pleytzes*, in our Yiddish idiolect).

This book could not have been completed without the collaboration of two brilliant research assistants, whom I am proud to count among my students. Shaul Setter worked with me on every aspect of the book's composition, from completing my bibliographic research to fleshing out the negotiations between points of theory and close reading. He made it possible for me to submit the manuscript to Stanford University Press under strict time constraints—all this while completing his own Ph.D. dissertation. I could always count on Shaul to let me know when things were working and when they were not, and his sharp critical eye saved me from quite a few blunders. After Shaul returned to Israel, he handed over the baton to Eyal Bassan, who worked closely with me throughout the extensive process of revising, editing, and preparing the manuscript for publication. Not only did Eyal resolve a seemingly endless number of technical and technological problems; he also helped me create a more cohesive structure for the book chapters and, most importantly, showed me ways to sustain the book's commitment to being accessible to poetry lovers and a nonspecialist readership while keeping up critical rigor.

Throughout this process, I have been helped by my personal assistant, Ani Mac, who has kept bringing light and poetry into my life as she's been making it possible for me to write; and by Eliyah Arnon, whose expert skills at bilingual research and technical support have been invaluable. Arnon was always ready to set all else aside to provide me with materials I needed. Paul Hamburg, Judaica Librarian at UC Berkeley, has gone out of his way on numerous occasions to make materials available to me from far and wide. Giddon Ticotsky, archival scholar extraordinaire, shared with me his discovery of a correspondence between the young Amichai and poet Leah Goldberg even before he published these findings himself. He later provided me with other hard-to-find materials, as well as a searchable electronic copy of the entire Amichai holdings in the Gnazim Literary Archives in Tel Aviv. I am in awe of Giddon's boundless intellectual generosity. I am grateful to Ayelet Kahn for transcribing my interviews with Amichai, and to Oren Stier and Azzan Yadin for help with translating them into English. Robert (Uri) Alter has provided encouragement and mentorship over the years, and I am thrilled that this book, informed by the many insights he has shared with me on Amichai and his literary generation, goes to press at the same time that his comprehensive anthology, *The Poetry of Yehuda Amichai*, is scheduled to be published by Farrar, Straus & Giroux. It is our hope that our books end up on many shelves together. Michael Gluzman has been my main intellectual interlocutor for two decades now. I have benefited greatly from his work on the need to reconfigure the historiography of Statehood Generation poetry, a fact that's especially evident in chapters 1 and 6. I am thankful to George Lakoff and Eve Sweetser, who share my love of Amichai, of metaphor—and of Amichai's use of metaphor—for the ongoing dialogue over many years. Special thanks also to Sasson Somekh of Tel Aviv University, Abdul-Rahim Al-Shaikh of Birzeit University, and Kareem Abu-Zeid of UC Berkeley for their generous help with research into the literary contacts between Yehuda Amichai and Mahmoud Darwish, contacts I hope to explore further in the future with my colleague Margaret Larkin, in a joint project on intertextuality in the work of these two great poets. Margaret's thoughtful feedback on chapter 3 was extremely valuable as well. Along with Margaret, Ma'ayan Sela and Carol Redmount provided helpful input on the translation of some challenging passages.

Rabbi Naomi Levy's and Yiskah Rosenfeld's input helped me with chapters 1 and 3. Vered Karti Shemtov provided a wonderful framework at a number of Stanford workshops for me to test out ideas in a friendly, collaborative atmosphere. I am grateful to Naomi Lowinsky for her support and her input on the direction of the Introduction. Caroline Brickman, Mandy Cohen, Rebecca Whittington, and Marina Zilbergerts shared important insights that helped me revise chapter 4. David Hertz gave me helpful feedback on an earlier version of chapter 5. The late William Hallo helped me with the history of the term *turgeman* (translator) in chapter 4. Both Bill Hallo's and Na'ama Rokem's work on the German materials in the Amichai Archives has been very helpful. Naomi Seidman's work on translation theory has greatly informed my discussion in chapter 4.

As this book goes to press, I am mourning the loss of my beloved mentor, Benjamin Harshav, who taught me how to read and how to think, and in whose seminars at Tel Aviv University I first studied Amichai's poetry. My teacher Ziva Ben-Porat introduced me to the systematic study of literary allusion, and her work continues to inform my own.

My editors at Stanford University Press (SUP) have been extraordinarily helpful. Norris Pope first saw the promise of the book, and Eric Brandt made its publication possible. Series coeditor Steve Zipperstein was a source of stalwart support throughout. I am grateful to the editorial, production, and marketing team at SUP for their expertise and dedication: Anne Fuzellier Jain, Bruce Lundquist, Friederike Sundaram, David Jackson, Mary Kate Maco, Linda Stewart, and to Kay Kodner for her copyediting, Michelle Kwitkin-Close for her careful proofreading, and Barbara Roos for her expert indexing.

I wish to thank the staff of the Beinecke Rare Book and Manuscript Library at Yale University for their help with accessing and reproducing materials from the Amichai Archives, during three separate research trips to Yale. I am grateful to Nanette Stahl, Judaica Curator at Yale, for her help in facilitating this research. Research and publication of this book has been supported in part by a Mellon Faculty Research Grant, the Taubman Chair at UC Berkeley, the Center for Middle Eastern Studies at UC Berkeley, and a Beinecke Fellowship from Yale University.

This book was written through some difficult times, but the love and support of dear friends and family has kept me going: Chana Bloch and Dave Sutter, Diane Wolf and Frank Hirtz, Carol Redmount, Ma'ayan Sela, Racheli and David Biale, Margaret Larkin and Mohammed Hussein, Bluma Goldstein, Rutie Adler, Naomi Seidman and John Schott, Gail Holst-Warhaft and Zellman Warhaft, Nanette Stahl, Hanne and Ben Weisbort, Daniella Weisbort-Andreassen, Sionah Kronfeld Honig, Tikva Parnass, Sivan Parnass and Yuval Parnass-Mader, Miki Gluzman, Michal Arbell and Ronni Tor, Ora and David Rawet, Sidra DeKoven Ezrahi and Bernard Avishai, Avidov Lipsker and Rachel Albeck Gidron, Rela and Elisha Mazali, Esti Mitzenmacher, Orit and Zach Adam, Ilana Pardes and Itamar Lurie, Zehavit and Shimon Friedman, Ruth Berman, Yael Greenfeld, and Tova Rosen.

Last but not least, my beloved daughter Maya Kronfeld, whom Yehuda Amichai named *Mayalon yaldat balon* (Maya-loo balloon-girl) when he first saw her as a baby twenty-nine years ago, holding a purple balloon tight in her hand: This book has benefited immeasurably from her soaring mind, her discerning eye—and ear. And she has made it all doable.

The Full Severity of Compassion

Introduction   "Be an Other's, Be an Other"
A Personal Perspective*

What is left for one
to do except renounce oneself in joy
donate one's blood and kidneys
donate one's heart and soul to others
be an other's, be an other.

Yehuda Amichai, "Deganya"[1]

I. A Personal Perspective

My first meeting with Yehuda Amichai, in the fall of 1970, was what we call in Hebrew a *chavaya metakenet*, a "corrective" or "healing experience," one that mends (brings a bit of *tikkun* to) a messy or unpleasant earlier experience. Overeager and all too young, I was trying to put together a series called "Rendezvous with an Author" (*Pgisha im sofer*) for Israeli Educational Television, which would allow high school students to meet with "cutting-edge" Hebrew writers in a relaxed round-table discussion of the writers' work. I was still reeling from a failed attempt to produce the series' pilot: an author whose stories I adored was so sadistically cruel to the young students that we had to stop the taping! And then it came to me—Yehuda Amichai, of course. Having gotten into the habit of reading his poetry daily for my own emotional sustenance since age fifteen, I was sure: Yes, Amichai would be the one to start with. He would know how to connect with the students and put them at ease; he would be able to talk about the most complex poetic issues with utter simplicity and without egocentric affectation. I had never met him before, but from everything I heard, he was invested in *not* playing the role of the Great Poet—even though by 1970 his status as the most revolutionary, indeed the most important poet of the Statehood Generation (*dor ha-mdina*) had solidified and he was

1

* I am grateful to Naomi Lowinsky for her invaluable input into this Introduction.

acquiring an international reputation. He was synonymous with unpretentiousness. And indeed, in his Everyman appearance and unaffected manner, Amichai proceeded to treat the students as his equals, joking his way into all our hearts, and thus the series was off to an exciting start. That experience was the beginning of my lifelong friendship with the man and dedication to study and teach the work of the poet.

Over the years, as I became increasingly engaged in literary theory, I discovered that almost every theoretical issue in which I found myself interested—from intertextuality and metaphor, through modernism and gender, to larger questions such as the principles underlying literary historiography and the ontological status of aesthetic categories in poetry—all these issues large and small were ones on which Amichai's poetry, in its subject matter or rhetoric, articulated a profound, indeed often a *revolutionary* position. I would try to theorize from— rather than into—his poetry. More often than not, I found that the aesthetic, philosophical, and political insights embedded in his verbal art compelled me to rethink quite a few of the views dominant in various changing critical fashions and trends.

I wanted to start with this personal story in order to situate clearly and openly what is at stake for me in this study. To put it bluntly: the revolutionary Amichai has been occluded by his very canonicity, even though his work—its apparent simplicity notwithstanding—presents a coherent poetic system, not unlike the work of Blake, Yeats, and Stevens. Amichai's oeuvre—like Brecht's and Auden's—offers an unrelenting critique of the dominant ideology of its time. Because for him a critique of ideology engenders a deeply empathic affinity for "the lonely people" or "the lovers,"[2] who regularly fall victim to the manipulations of institutional power, Amichai's oppositional stance has been all too easily ignored by defenders and detractors alike. It is important for me, therefore, to show that this empathy itself must not be mistaken for some vague, universalizing neoliberalism. Through a close reading of his poetry I have come to see the relational, empathic mode of Amichai's poetry, the commitment to "be an other's / be an other," as a direct complement of his sustained struggle against historically specific dehumanizing systems of privilege and exclusion.

Ironically, Amichai's great popularity and success also brought about an odd marginalization. In Israel especially, I now encounter many young progressive intellectuals who have come to reject the appropriated, co-opted, and watered-down Amichai they were raised on. For them, Amichai's poetry is no longer readable independent of the context in which they were introduced to it: poems that had to be memorized and shallowly interpreted for matriculation exams, recited at assemblies, and declaimed with great pathos at any number of official celebrations and commemorations, in total disregard for their complexity, irony, and uncompromising critical edge. In fact, Amichai's poetic egalitarianism itself may have resulted in the ambivalent, at times even begrudging critical reception of his work among Israeli literati, despite (or perhaps because of) his immense popularity among common readers, his profound influence on three generations of Hebrew writers, and his unprecedented international acclaim. Somewhat differently, but ultimately with a similar result, I find that the great popularity of his poetry in the United States has been accompanied by some readerly obtuseness to what this poetry actually says and does. Amichai has often found his way into the Jewish American prayer book and rabbinical sermon, but not because of a prevailing interest in his iconoclastic engagement with Jewish sacred texts—although, thankfully, that type of countertraditional reading is becoming increasingly "kosher," leading a growing number of "alternative" Jewish American congregations and their rabbis to read Amichai's poetry *for* its irreverence, feminism, and critique of the establishment tout court. All too frequently, however, have I seen Amichai's poems embraced by American readers who, knowing very little about the sacred texts he takes apart, remain unaware of—and uninterested in—his resistant, anticlerical poetics and are lulled into complacency by the apparent simplicity of his poems' surface. The mere reference to prayers, God, and the Bible in his poetry has qualified him for the role of a religious Jewish poet laureate for the Jewish American community. Thus, Amichai's poetry is not infrequently used to provide readers in the United States with something textual to hold onto, either as a marker of some fuzzy, feel-good Jewish identity or, more generally, for its pleasantly vague sense of Old World tradition.

For both Israeli and American audiences, I want to make the experimental, iconoclastic, and critical Amichai readable again, without marginalizing his empathic "postcynical humanism"—his own poignant term.[3] The Amichai I started reading daily in my teens wrote about topics that had never before been considered worthy of poetry in the Holy Tongue, from housing projects to one-night stands. In his philosophical explorations of the quotidian, he was one of the first to boldly make poetic use of newly minted Hebrew slang and to invoke intertextually not only the Bible but also "subcanonical" popular culture—from children's language to bureaucratese and legalese, and from movie captions to pop songs. What's more, he would often—Heaven forfend!—juxtapose these lowly expressions with allusions to sacred texts, refusing to privilege the latter over the former. Thus, for example, the early poem titled "Jacob and the Angel" (first published in 1963) uses a stylistic collage of children's Hebrew, military slang, and an allusion to a pop song from the 1956 Sinai Campaign to transform a single night of intimacy between a man and a woman into a contemporary equivalent of the sacred encounter between the human and the divine. And it is—horror of horrors—the woman who is the angel in this encounter![4] The outrage early critics expressed toward his work had as much to do with his irreverent style as with his thematics and his critique of ideology, be it clerical or nationalist (ideology that in those days—as again in our own—went by the name of "values," *arakhim*).

II. The Book: An Overview

How then did this revolutionary poet, described by critics and politicians as heretical, even dangerous, in the first two decades of Israeli statehood, become identified with the establishment a mere decade after writing poems such as "Jacob and the Angel"? Arguing that revolutionary poetry is indeed too "dangerous" to be left alone to do its work, the first chapter of this book deals with the appropriation of Amichai's work by the same institutions of authority that his poetry struggles against.[5] I analyze some of the ways he has been misread both in Israel and in the United States in order to rigorously interrogate these misreadings not simply as mistakes that should be corrected, but as symptomatic expressions of the processes of institutional appropriation and readerly interpellation[6]—processes that are always at work in canon formation and in the hegemonic taming of canonical writers.

The Amichai I wish to reclaim in this study is the poet for whom simplicity and accessibility are serious *ethical* principles, guidelines for a poetic effect and a verbal art that can be part of the fabric of everyday life, not simply the mark of "a playful poet" writing "easy," "unstructured" verse who has "no worldview," as some scholars have argued, mistaking his *egalitarian imperative* for a lack of philosophical gravitas in his work. This is the poet who insisted that all his books in Hebrew have the same small format (10 × 18 centimeters) so they would fit in a reader's back pocket—something ordinary people could take along on their arduous journey through workaday reality. He practices an ethics and aesthetics of what he calls "the wisdom of camouflage," since flaunting "the splendor" of artistic vision is as dangerous as leaving the lights on during an air raid.[7] Hence, the commitment not to "stand out," to write "Not Like a Cypress" (the title of one of his most famous early poems) "but like the grass, in thousands of cautious green exits."[8]

In chapter 2, I outline the major principles that underlie Amichai's poetics, principles that focus on the state of *beynayim* or "in-between-ness" as the privileged yet endangered site of poetic subjects–cum–ordinary human beings. These are often metonymically represented by the lovers, or by a nonnational "we" made up of "self" and "other" (man and woman, Jew and Arab) who try to break down socially constructed binary divisions and become "an other's" without erasing the self.[9] For when one donates blood or a kidney (as in the first two images cited in the epigraph), one's embodied self lives on, even as it sustains the life of another; and when one becomes an organ donor after death (a fresh figurative take on the poems' afterlife as part of the life of future readers), one's body (of work) vicariously continues to live through the other. Note that linguistically in Hebrew, body and soul—of which only the first can of course be literally donated—are both perceived as embodied: *nefesh* (soul) in biblical Hebrew is the soul-as-throat. And indeed for Amichai, "what is not of the body will not be remembered" (*ma she-lo shel guf lo yizakher*), as he says in the last line of his poem "Hayi shalom" (translated by Stephen Mitchell as "Farewell").[10] This central intersubjective—and metapoetic—principle is wryly encapsulated by the title of Amichai's early poem (turned popular hit in Israel) "The Two of Us Together and Each of Us Alone," which makes philosophical poetry out of the legalese of a rental contract (the Hebrew equivalent of "the party of the first part and the party of the second part").[11] Though they are invariably crushed between "the grindstones" of world and national history,[12] or between the forces of politics and religion,[13] these subjects continue to try to make a life for themselves in that tight, pressured space, or in the brief temporal interim Chana Bloch has brilliantly rendered as the "twilight betweenlight" (*beynayim arbayim*).[14] For Amichai this spatial and temporal *beynayim* ("in-between-ness") is not only—or even mainly—a theme. Throughout the book I describe an array of systematic correlations between liminality as the governing feature of his poetic worldview and many of his signature rhetorical practices such as juxtaposition, intertextuality, and metaphor, all of which map two domains together without ignoring their distinctness. Liminality as the product of perfect or imperfect rhetorical and intersubjective mapping is thus an organizing principle that permeates all levels of the text, but it also extends to the relationship between poet and reader, and between the contemporary writer and his textual precursors, which—in Amichai's case—are often traditional Jewish sources, their interpretive legacies, and their diverse literary or exegetical genres.

Chapter 3 thus takes on the radical intertextual ethos that forms an important part of both Amichai's stylistic signature and his view of poetry and the poet. His intertextual practices famously consist of iconoclastic allusions to sacred texts and parodic uses of traditional Jewish genres, from biblical poetry and narrative to rabbinical exegesis, and from midrash to liturgy. I ask: What makes it possible for Amichai to use these sources so extensively, subjecting them to irreverent close-readings-as-rewritings without producing a hermetic and exclusionary poetic surface, even when these sources are no longer familiar to many of his readers? How, in other words, does his complex practice of intertextual collage coexist, in contradistinction to Eliot's, with an ever-increasing commitment to lucidity and readerly accessibility? I then proceed to retheorize intertextuality through Amichai's rhetorical practice and its thematization in his work, both of which call into question contemporary Western theories in the field. Using Amichai's unique combination of Jewish and matrilineal notions of literary tradition and (inter)textual exegesis, I engage critically with Harold Bloom's model of "the anxiety of influence," a model that focuses on a bourgeois-individualist, male-Oedipal struggle between "strong poets." But I also critique the poststructuralist view of intertextuality as an anonymous tissue of citations through Amichai's reinscription of a historically inflected human agent as central to any process of recycling and recasting a culture's precursor texts. This agency, though "censored and pasted and limited,"[15] offers a possibility of resisting interpellation by the mere act of changing the words of its subjugating command, as Judith Butler has taught us. Through Amichai's poetics, I read Butler's critique of Althusser as a theory of Jewish radical intertextuality.[16]

One of the most intriguing intertextual practices privileged in Amichai's poetry is translation, a practice I am personally implicated in for better or worse as the cotranslator—with Chana Bloch—of his last book, *Open Closed Open*. In chapter 4, I examine Amichai's theorizing of the work of translation as a model for the poet's own in-betweenness, as well as for the translator/poet's inescapable secondariness. For Amichai, I argue, the fact that the poet, like the translator, holds an immanently mediational position, always recycling the words of others, "words [that] accompany my life,"[17] is a source of comfort rather than anxiety. This view of the poet's role sheds a new light on contemporary theories of translation as cultural negotiation and its attendant focus on the asymmetrical power relations between source and target language. I read closely Amichai's early and late poems about translation as celebrating the imperfect "recycling of words," in which translation is described as the epitome of all poetic intertextuality and, ultimately, of the creative process itself. Through Amichai's ecology of language, I interrogate the cultural and ideological blindspots behind the numerous mistranslations that Amichai has been subjected to— again, not in order to advocate some correct or perfect rendition, but rather to suggest the ways in which they function as meaningful symptoms of what Gayatri Spivak has termed "the politics of translation."[18]

Metaphor (and figurative language tout court) is another articulation of Amichai's principle of in-between-ness, which has a vital significance within his poetic system, far exceeding its rhetorical role. Metaphor, for Amichai as for Wallace Stevens, provides a tenuous yet necessary bridge across semantic and conceptual distances, creating a tentative rapport between reality and the imagination. In chapter 5 my discussion focuses on the ways in which novel poetic metaphor acts as the central marker of liminality, the hyphen of survival and resistance: "The pressure of my life brings my date of birth closer / to the date of my death, as in history books / where the pressure of history has brought / those two numbers together next to the name of a dead king / with only a hyphen between them. // I hold onto that hyphen with all my might / like a life line, I live on it."[19] Metaphor for Amichai must never erase that hyphen, the marker of the disparate domains that it brings together (hence his preference for simile!), even while it strives to make the gap between these domains productive of meaning. In highlighting the ways Amichai's metaphors resist the erasure of difference, I enlist his poetry to critique some poststructuralist views of figurative language that still have purchase today, especially Paul de Man's attack on metaphor. Retheorizing metaphor from Amichai's poetic practice, I present an alternative model based on a historicized, context-sensitive reworking of prototype semantics, which builds upon the work of Eleanor Rosch, George Lakoff, and Eve Sweetser and focuses on the cognitive-linguistic notion of an "image schema." I explain how Amichai's images, while as novel and surprising as those of any seventeenth-century Metaphysical poet, nevertheless strike us as completely "right," as visually and experientially familiar, because of their perceptually primary basis as well as the extensive and rigorous mapping they provide for the distant source and target domains.

"My divided fate [*gorali ha-mefulag*] has willed it so that I should be planted in between two generations, a sort of double agent [*meragel kaful*],"[20] Amichai declared in a 1968 lecture. In chapter 6 I discuss the ways in which Amichai extols the poet's freedom to oscillate between generational trends and poetic styles, while cherishing his outsider role and calling into question the underlying assumptions behind the generational model itself. His self-description as an intergenerational "double agent" has presented a real problem for normative Hebrew literary historiography, with its teleological, unidirectional notions of a literary lineage, and has occasioned an impassioned debate. Far from being just a poetico-political joke, this literally subversive statement also articulates Amichai's post-Marxist critique of teleological historicism; his aversion to chronological order, represented by the "Gods of Order [*elohey ha-seder*] of the *Seder* night" (the Seder is the Passover meal but literally "seder" is the ordinary Hebrew term for "order," hence: "the night of order")[21]; and his preference for a simultaneous

representation of personal and collective temporalities either as a fragmentary "archaeology of the self" or as a fault-line geology (*Now in
the Earthquake* [*Akhshav ba-ra'ash*] is the title of his 1969 book). This
is the background against which I explore Amichai's resistance to the
normative historiographic narrative of Hebrew literature, as well his
refusal to reject his literary predecessors, a rejection prescribed in the
manifestos of the self-proclaimed leader of the Statehood Generation,
Natan Zach, who famously led a rebellion against the "Troika" of the
moderna poets of the 1930s and 40s, Avraham Shlonsky, Leah Goldberg, and especially Natan Alterman. In this context I tease out the
tensions between Amichai's centrality for Israeli and Western consumers of literary culture and his self-consciously marginal association with
established literary movements of Israeli and international modernism.
I examine in some detail the group poetics of *Likrat*, the first Statehood Generation modernist circle in Israel, its belated affiliation with
Anglo-American imagism, and Amichai's ambivalent position toward
and within it. This leads me to reexamine critically some common
views of the concepts of a literary period or movement, developing
further a project I undertook in my earlier work.[22] Amichai's poetry
is then discussed in its troubled (multiple, yet partial) affinities with a
variety of transnational literary and cultural "isms." How, I ask, does
the critique of trend affiliation, as theorized by Amichai's explicit and
implicit poetics, make us rethink Zach's largely accepted account of
Statehood Generation poetry? Ultimately, if it is acknowledged that
Amichai is not alone in rejecting Zach's normative account but is in
fact joined by the other major poets of *dor ha-mdina*, Dahlia Ravikovitch, Dan Pagis, and David Avidan, both in inscribing the political in
their work and in refusing to reject their modernist predecessors, what
alternative historiographic narrative of this generation's poetics is then
allowed to emerge?

III. An Aside on Amichai's Fiction and the Writing of the Shoah

Although Amichai published two novels, a collection of short stories,
and numerous dramatic works (both for the stage and radio), as well as
children's books and translations (most notably of works by Else Lasker

Schüler and Rolf Hochhuth), my book focuses exclusively on the poetic oeuvre.[23] Amichai's avant-garde lyrical fiction still awaits the scholarly attention it so richly deserves. I can only hope that serious research will be done sooner rather than later, especially on his challenging 1963 *Lo me-akhshav, lo mi-kan* (*Not of This Time, Not of This Place*), the first postmodernist Hebrew novel.[24] This book remains an extraordinary, wide-ranging work of experimental fiction, featuring two parallel plots—and the same protagonist—and taking place simultaneously in Jerusalem and in Germany. It provides one of the first challenges in Hebrew fiction to the then-dominant belief that the Shoah can only be represented in the documentary or realist mode. In that sense, *Not of This Time, Not of This Place* is the precursor that provides the conditions of possibility for David Grossman's great antirealist Shoah novel, *Ayen erekh ahava* (*See Under: Love*).[25] Furthermore, as Michael André Bernstein has pointed out, Amichai's novel—like his poetry—refuses to fetishize the Shoah through either the theological model of apocalyptic history[26] or "backshadowing"—the tendency to blame in hindsight the victims who didn't see it coming.[27]

Unlike Nili Scharf Gold, I find that Amichai's poetry and fiction from their earliest moments engage profoundly both with the Jewish trauma of the Shoah and with the Germans' willingness to surrender power to the institutional "super-organism" of the fascist state, which made the genocide possible.[28] These, in fact, are some of the central ethical and political concerns that unify Amichai's poetry with his fiction and motivate his unrelenting critique of ideology. These concerns are often expressed stylistically and structurally rather than through direct statement or in the linear, documentary fashion characteristic of writing on the Shoah up until the 1980s; but the Shoah informs every aspect of his verbal art, poetics, and ethics.

IV. Amichai's Life in Poetry[29]

Amichai's poetry has left its mark not only on Hebrew and Anglo-American literature, for it has been translated into forty languages so far, frequently via the English translation. While I have had to limit my study to his poetry's Hebrew and English receptions and articulations,

there is work to be done on the various "Amichais" these many translations have produced.

Amichai has been described by Robert Alter as one of the greatest
poets of our time,[30] and he is widely considered the greatest Jewish poet
since Paul Celan (with whom he developed a friendship and exchanged
a couple of important letters).[31] Interestingly, despite his Everyman persona, internationally renowned poets often use rarified regal terms to
describe Amichai's achievement. His contemporary, the noted Polish
poet Zbigniew Herbert, wrote in a poem dedicated to Amichai: "You
are a king, and I'm only a prince."[32] And Pulitzer Prize–winning American poet Anthony Hecht proclaimed: "Amichai's splendid poems, refined
and cast in the desperate foundries of the Middle East . . . exhibit a ma-
jestic and Biblical range of the topography of the soul. . . . He is a psalm-
ist utterly modern, yet movingly traditional."[33] A poet's poet in spite of
his populist poetics, Amichai's work won the admiration of many major
poets when they were first introduced to it in the mid-1960s at international poetry festivals in Spoleto and London, where he read alongside
Auden, Neruda, Pound, Ginsberg, Berryman, Ungaretti, and others.[34] In
their 1976 anthology of late-modernist international poets, Charles Simic
and Mark Strand include Amichai among a select group of "mythologi-
cal poets" and single him out—alongside Vasko Popa—as a poet who
has been more influential "on young poets in the United States . . . than
Stevens, Eliot, or any other of their American forbearers [sic]."[35] Former British Poet Laureate Ted Hughes, a longtime friend of Amichai's,
declared, in a year-end poll in the *Times Literary Supplement* in 1997,
taken less than a year before his own death: "I've become more than ever
convinced that [Amichai] is one of the biggest, most essential, durable
poetic voices of this past century. . . . One of the real treasures."[36] While
Hughes is often credited with making Amichai's work known to English
and American readers,[37] it was actually Hughes's second, common-law
wife, Assia Gutmann, whose brilliant translations of Amichai's early poetry first presented him in English in book form, shortly before she too,
like Sylvia Plath, committed suicide.[38] Amichai's international reputation,
which—as I have suggested—began to solidify during the 1960s, was expressed, inter alia, in numerous prestigious titles and awards, from honorary doctorates to induction into the American Academy of Arts and
Letters (1986) and the American Academy of Arts and Sciences (1997), all

of which he accepted with his characteristic mixture of delight, humility, and a heaping dose of self-deprecating humor. At the time of his death on September 22, 2000, after a heroic struggle with lymphoma,[39] Amichai had been a perennial finalist for the Nobel Prize in Literature and had won numerous international awards, a sampling of which includes the Malraux Prize (France, 1994), the Literary Lion Award (New York, 1994), an Honor Citation from Assiut University (Egypt, 1996),[40] and the Bjørnson Prize (Norway, 1996). He was awarded all the major Israeli literary prizes, including the Shlonsky Prize (1961), Brenner Prize (1969), Bialik Prize (1976), and Agnon Prize (1986), and most notably in the Israel Prize, the highest national honor (1982).[41]

None of these international and national honors made Amichai less personally available to his readers. The Yehuda Amichai Papers at Yale University's Beinecke Rare Book and Manuscript Library are filled with letters from ordinary people who shared their troubles and joys with him. On more than one occasion I heard him take phone calls on his publicly listed home line from readers who never hesitated to contact him. And many people who would run into him in the streets of Jerusalem have stories about friendly conversations with the poet they did not personally know.

Yehuda Amichai (né Ludwig Pfeuffer) was born on May 3, 1924 in the town of Würzburg in southern Germany to an Orthodox Jewish family. The German Jewish state school he attended fostered bilingual and bicultural education, allowing him at an early age to engage in the textual study of Hebrew, which he would pursue and deepen even after he renounced religious life as an adult. Amichai would always wistfully emphasize that his childhood Hebrew studies were sponsored by the German state, invoking the tragic gap between pre-1933 Jewish existence in Germany and the horrors that were to follow. In an interview with me, Amichai described it as follows:

> I learned to read and write Hebrew in the first grade, even though it was a German-speaking school. I had already learned a bit how to speak Hebrew in kindergarten, but the language of play was German. . . . My elementary school was a German public school which Jewish children attended, not a Jewish school.[42]

His father, Friedrich, was a farmer's son, who made a living as a notions merchant. Friedrich was a decorated World War I veteran of the

German army and a Jewish community activist, but he also acquired a knowledge of German poetry despite the family's strict orthodoxy. The father's love is one of the strongest sources of inspiration for Amichai's poetry, and a central motif in his work. Indeed, the father's tenderness becomes a model for what Amichai describes in a late poem as the traces of the female in the male and "the yearning of a woman in a man."[43] This figuration of the father provides the poetry with a decidedly diasporic ideal of an alternative, "soft" masculinity that is very different from the normative Israeli one. Dan Miron describes Amichai's rejection of militantly Oedipal models of literary lineage as related to the fact that this is "a revolutionary with a father" (*mahapekhan im aba*).[44] But the father, despite being an active, affiliated Orthodox Jew and—until Hitler's rise to power—a devoted German army veteran, also instilled in his son a profound suspicion about any institutional power. In another interview with me Amichai describes this as "something very paradoxical." He explains:

> My father . . . always warned me about the establishment and it made no difference whether it was the rabbis—the religious establishment— or the political one. "Don't take those speechifiers seriously . . . question them; question anything that claims to be in the name of Great Ideas." He simply didn't realize how far I would take this dictum (I took him too seriously . . .), because for him there was just a single Great Idea which he never questioned, and that was God.[45]

Despite his family's generations-long roots in Germany, Friedrich decided to move the family to Palestine in 1936, when harassment by the Nazis became increasingly threatening. Amichai's childhood love, Ruth Hanover, daughter of the local rabbi, remained behind: because she was disabled, she was refused an affidavit by the British and U.S. immigration authorities even though her father and his family were granted entry to the United States in 1940.[46] Ruth perished in the Sobibor death camp in Poland in 1943, after numerous failed attempts by her father as well as by Amichai's father to rescue her.[47] Amichai's poetry consistently resists making political capital of the Shoah, as Israeli politicians are wont to do ("I Wasn't One of the Six Million" is the title of one of the sections in his last book).[48] The figure of "Little Ruth" (*Ruth ha-ktana*), however, remains a haunting presence throughout his poems and fiction, and is the subject of some of his most poignant *kinot* (the Jewish genre of the lament), culminating in the alliterative *kinot* in *Open Closed Open* that explicitly—though metonymically—link the genocide with the "Othering" of one group of human beings by another: "Ruth Ruth Ruth, little girl from my youth— / now she's a stand-in for Otherness" (*Ruth Ruth Ruth, ha-yalda min ha-yaldut / akhshav hi netzigat ha-acherut*); "Otherness killed Ruth" (*ha-acherut harga et Ruth*); and finally, Amichai's own irreverent and poignant version of the *Kaddish* prayer for Ruth: "Ruth Ruth, who died in my youth, now the two giants, / Yitgadal and Yitkadash, Magnified and Sanctified, / will watch over your death / in place of the two other giants, May He Bless and May He Keep, / who failed to watch over your life" (*Ruth Ruth, she-hikdamt le-fanay la-mut, akhshav / shney ha-anakim, yitgadal ve-yitkadash yishmeru al motekh / bi-mkom shney ha-anakim, yevarekhekha ve-yishmerekha, / she-nikhshelu ve-lo shamru al chayayikh*).[49]

Arriving in 1936 in the mostly secular and predominantly socialist Jewish *Yishuv* in Palestine as a religious preteen from a petit bourgeois German Jewish home, Ludwig Pfeuffer had not only a name that was distinctly "uncool," but an appearance that stuck out like a sore thumb. Amichai describes the grotesque figure that he cut with a mixture of self-irony and compassion in the opening lines of his great surrealist autobiographical *poema*,[50] "The Travels of the Last Benjamin of Tudela" ("Mas'ot Binyamin ha-acharon mi-Tudela"), which moves nonlinearly among the speaker's childhood memories; his present sense of a post-1967 Middle Eastern apocalypse; and a fragmentary collage of historically important characters, from Josephus to Bialik, and of biographically significant figures, from his protective parents to the God of his childhood. The speaker addresses the child that he was in the second person, drawing a tragicomic analogy between the arrival of the pathetic-looking boy and the world poised on the brink of disaster both in the 1930s and in his own present moment:

> . . . you came
> in your twelfth year, in the Thirties
> of the world, with short pants that reached down to your knees,
> tassels dangling from your undershawl
> sticky between your legs in the sweltering land.

— — — — — — — — — — — — —

Clocks were set, according
to the beats of the round heart, train tracks
according to the capacity of children's feet.

— — — — — — — — — — — — —

Tanks from America, fighter planes from France, Russian
jet-doves, armored chariots from England, Sisera's regiments
who dried the swamps with their corpses, a flying Massada,
Beitar slowly sinking, Yodfat on wheels, . . .
Massada won't fall again, won't fall again,
won't fall again, Massada, won't . . .

— — — — — — — — — — — — —

M.I.R.V., S.W.A.T., I.C.B.M., I.B.M.,
P.O.W., R.I.P., A.W.O.L.,
S.N.A.F.U., I.N.R.I., J.D.L., L.B.J.,
E.S.P., I.R.S., D.N.A., G.O.D.
Sit down. Today is the day of judgment. Today there was war.[51]

בָּאתָ . . .
בִּשְׁנָתְךָ הַשְּׁתֵּים עֶשְׂרֵה, בִּשְׁעוֹת הַשְּׁלֹשִׁים
שֶׁל הָעוֹלָם, מִכְּנָסַיִם עַד הַבִּרְכַּיִם,
צִיצִיּוֹת שְׁרוּכוֹת מִתּוֹךְ אַרְבַּע הַכְּנֵסִיּוֹת
נִדְבָּקוֹת בֵּין רַגְלֶיךָ בָּאָרֶץ הַלּוֹהֶטֶת.

— — — — — — — — — —

שְׁעוֹנִים הָיוּ מֻכְוָּנִים לְפִי
דְּפִיקוֹת הַלֵּב הֶעָגֹל, פַּסֵּי רַכֶּבֶת
לְפִי יְכֹלֶת רַגְלֵי יְלָדִים.

— — — — — — — — — —

טַנְקִים מֵאֲמֶרִיקָה, מְטוֹסֵי קְרָב מִצָּרְפַת, יוֹנֵי סִילוֹן
רוּסִיִּים, רֶכֶב מֵאַנְגְלִיָּה בְּלִי פָּרָשָׁיו, גְּדוּדֵי סִיסְרָא
שֶׁיִּבְּשׁוּ אֶת הַבִּצּוֹת בִּגְוִיּוֹתֵיהֶם, מַסָּדָה מְעוֹפֶפֶת,
בֵּיתָר צוֹנַחַת לְאַט, יוֹדְפַת עַל גַּלְגַּלִּים, . . .
. . . שֵׁנִית מַסָּדָה לֹא תִפֹּל, לֹא תִפֹּל,
לֹא תִפֹּל, שֵׁנִית מַסָּדָה, לֹא. . . .

— — — — — — — — — —

מַטָל־רִים, רַרְבַ־ט מַרְבַ־ט, מָרָבָן
וְרַבָּבָן, נון טֵית, נון מֵם, לָמֶד וָו,
חֲרֶמֶ־ש, דְּצָ־דְּ, אַצָ־ג, מַבָּר מְמֻבָּע
רַק־מַלַט, לַהַבְיוֹר, קַבְיָר, מְכָמָש, תוֹב־בָא.
שֵב. הַיוֹם הֲרַת עוֹלָם. הַיוֹם הָיְתָה מִלְחָמָה.

Stephen Mitchell's translation from the last quoted strophe is an ingenious attempt to find American correlatives for Amichai's sarcastic and iconoclastic juxtapositions of rabbinic acronyms with military
ones, drawing in the process an implicit causal chain between religious
dogma, nationalism, and war. Autobiographic poetry, then, as I will argue below, is the occasion for Amichai's "archaeology of the self," as
Robert Alter has called it,[52] which is always also the archaeology of the
world. The autobiographical for him is both the subject of the (necessarily accessible, quotidian) poem and an occasion for the disruption of
linear chronology and orderly history, whether personal or collective.
Thus, various way-stations in Amichai's life become material for poetic
contemplation, part of what Michael André Bernstein has cogently described as Amichai's "prosaics of a history figured in terms of its most
quotidian exigencies."[53] At the same time, life events—both personal and
historical—are imaginatively refigured through the kaleidoscopic multiple perspectives of his verbal art, resisting simple, coherent narration.

After about a year of living in Petach Tikva, where Ludwig—who
was now using his Hebrew given name, Yehuda—attended the Orthodox grade school Netzach Israel, the Pfeuffer family moved to Jerusalem, the city that was to become Amichai's home for the rest of his life.
While his education continued to be Orthodox (he attended the religious high school Ba-Ma'ale), by the time he volunteered for the Jewish Brigade of the British army in 1942 in order to join the fight against
fascism, he had become thoroughly secular. Being secular, however,
never involved for Amichai—as it did for many Israelis of his generation—an antireligious stance. It was clericalism and the political trade
in the sacred, not textual or even ritualistic traditions themselves, that
elicited his most sarcastic critique.

During his service in the brigade, Amichai discovered Anglo-
American modernist poetry[54] and published his first poem,[55] a sonnet

titled ambiguously "Be-motza'ey ha-chofesh" (translated as either
"The Night after Liberty" or "At the Ends of Liberty"—the first word
of the title plays on the term for the end of a holy day or the Sabbath,
as in the expression *motza'ey shabbat*; the second puns on the double
sense of "leave [from the army]" and "freedom"). Between serving in
the British army (1942–1946) and enlisting in the Palmach, the strike
forces of the pre-State army during the 1948 Arab-Israeli War, Yehuda
Pfeuffer studied in a teachers' college. Because it was a condition of
his first teaching position in Haifa, he Hebraized his last name, choosing "Amichai" ("my folk lives"). In the immediate aftermath of the
Shoah, this choice unmistakably asserted both his own Jewishness and
the survival of his people or folk (*am*), as distinct from the nation
(*uma*).[56] As an infantryman in the Palmach, Amichai took part in some
of the toughest battles in the Negev, on the southern front, during
the 1948 war. Here he lost his close friend and commander, Dicky
Lucksberger (1920–1948) from Kibbutz Giv'at Brenner, whom he described in many conversations with me as "a father figure, although he
was only four years my senior." Dicky appears in several of Amichai's
poems, most notably in the dedication of the powerfully minimalist
"Geshem bi-sde krav" (Rain on a Battlefield).[57] Amichai served as well
in the 1956 and 1973 wars. As Chana Bloch suggests, these war experiences shaped him just as much as his father's love did.[58] Indeed, in his
best-known sonnet cycle, "Ahavnu kan" (We Loved Here),[59] Amichai
connects these two shaping influences, explicitly linking the father's
loving efforts to spare his son the horrors of war with his attempt to
develop in the son—even before he was born—an empathy for the
victims of war, regardless of which side they are on. But, as the speaker
concludes in the sonnet's volta, the father did all this in a way that
ultimately cannot work: no war in the present can prevent war in the
future. The father "spent four years inside their war," the war to end
all wars, although—like Yeats's Irish Airman[60]—he "did not hate his
enemies, or love" them. The father "filled his eyes" with all "the nameless dead" (the Hebrew *mile eynav ba-hem* has the sense of "stuffing"
his eyes with the dead) in a tragically ineffectual form of future inoculation meant to make his unborn son "recognize" and "love" those
dead when he sees them years later in his father's eyes, and thus not
treat other human beings as killing objects. This empathic gaze, the

ability to recognize the eyes of the dead "others" in his own father's eyes, was supposed to prevent the son from dying like them "in the horror" (*ba-zva'a*). But the father was wrong: the son still goes out to all his wars (*el kol milchamotay yotze ani*). There is, however, another profound sense in which the father's lesson in empathy did succeed: it provided a model for the war-weary poet, already evident in the other poems in this early sonnet cycle, molding him into the antiwar poet he was to become, a poet who would systematically refuse the notion of a meaningful or redemptive war. As Michael André Bernstein poignantly suggests, Amichai "saw enough combat and bloodshed to be thoroughly repelled by the thematics of a redemptive violence as the catalyst of higher truths."[61]

In 1949, immediately after the war, Amichai married Tamar Horn, with whom he had one son, Ronny, born in 1961. They separated in the early sixties. On March 22, 1949, Amichai mailed—still from his military postal address even though the war was over—a sampling of his poems to Leah Goldberg, the major woman poet of the previous modernist generation, the *moderna*, who was to become his poetic mother of sorts (see chapter 3). In this letter he tells Goldberg that up to that point he had been writing "more or less continuously for about four years."[62] While we are not sure how Goldberg reacted, the fact remains, as Giddon Ticotsky observes, that about three months later a grouping of poems by Amichai was published in the literary supplement of the socialist paper, *Al Ha-Mishmar* (On Guard), where Goldberg had a regular column. And when his first book of poems was met with the unbridled wrath of the old guard, including descriptions of his poems as "paper cockroaches" and "ape-like feats" of "trickery," Goldberg was one of the first to write in enthusiastic defense of his poetic achievement.[63]

Thus, by the time Amichai started his studies of Hebrew literature and the Bible at the Hebrew University in Jerusalem in the winter of 1952, he was already a published poet. This was in advance of the formation in the summer of that same year of the modernist group centered around the journal *Likrat* (Towards), whose first issue appeared in June 1952 and whose second issue, in August of that year, featured two poems by Amichai. As we shall see in chapter 6, Amichai preferred to remain on the margins of the group and its literary politics, although he was to become one of its major poets.⁶⁴ His first book of poems, *Akhshav u-va-yamim ha-acherim* (Now and in Other Days), was indeed published by *Likrat* in 1955, even though by then the group had officially disbanded.⁶⁵ The book was thus both the group's swan song and its crowning achievement.

During his studies at the Hebrew University, Amichai deepened his erudition in Hebrew and world literature and supplemented his early religious Bible study in Würzburg and in the religious high school in Jerusalem with the (then mainly German-inspired) secular biblical scholarship in Israeli academia. It was then also that Amichai fell in love with medieval Hebrew poetry from Spain (Al Andalus) during the Golden Age of Hebrew-Arabic poetic coexistence; and it was then that he started modeling his own quatrains on the Persian and Arabic traditions of the *Rubaiyat* and their medieval Hebrew rearticulations. "The quatrain actually plays the role here [in the Middle East] which the sonnet played in Western culture," he told me in an interview.⁶⁶ He was particularly fascinated by the work and life of the eleventh-century poet Rabbi Shmuel Ha-Nagid, whose influence he freely acknowledges. In the same interview with me he attributes his fascination with Ha-Nagid to the latter's "forthright and blunt . . . encounter with the real." He adds: "[Ha-Nagid's] poem revolves around the world of quotidian reality the way the Oral Torah [*torah she-be-al-pe*, the Talmud and rabbinical exegesis in general] revolves around the [biblical] verse" (Berkeley, 1986). Thus, Ha-Nagid is for Amichai such a powerful early paragon because, though writing within a traditional Jewish world that Amichai no longer inhabits, he offers a model for textualizing and thus sanctifying the mundane. In the Amichai archives at the Beinecke Library I found a seminar paper on the poetry of Shmuel Ha-Nagid, which Amichai wrote for a course at the Hebrew University taught by Professor Chaim Shirman, then the leading authority on the subject and editor of the standard annotated medieval Hebrew *Diwans*.⁶⁷ The paper focuses on Ha-Nagid's war poetry and calls for a modernist, "stereoscopic co-interpretation" of his poetry alongside the historical reality of the period.

Amichai is not alone among the Israeli modernists to recover medieval poetry for a post-theological age. The numerous connections between the poetry of the Statehood Generation of the 1950s and 60s

and the Andalusian Hebrew and Arabic models remain to be fully explored. A particularly interesting aspect to study would be the analogy
between Anglo-American modernism's rediscovery of English Metaphysical poetry as a legitimizing poetic precursor and the Israeli poets'
turn toward medieval poetry in Spain. Ironically, not only were the
modernist English models intertextually important for the Israeli ones,
but seventeenth-century Metaphysical poetry itself may have had its
manneristic style shaped in part—via the mediation of Provençal—by
its medieval Andalusian precursors. Tova Rosen has taken important
steps in recovering those links, analyzing the structural and generic
affinities of Amichai's poetry with Ha-Nagid's unique form of poetic
meditation on the mundane.[68] Not coincidentally, the other main mav-
erick of the Statehood Generation, the poet Dan Pagis, would become
one of the major scholars of medieval Hebrew poetics.

An experienced elementary and high school literature teacher by
the time his first books of poetry were published, Amichai went on—
from the mid-1960s—to teach both overseas students and prospective
teachers at the Hebrew University in Jerusalem. To his work at the
Hebrew University he brought the same relaxed dialogic style and an
erudition tempered with wit that I first witnessed in his TV roundtable
with teenage pupils. This continued to be his signature teaching style
in the various visiting lectureships he held over the years in graduate
Hebrew literature and creative writing programs at major American
universities, from New York University to the University of California,
Berkeley, where I was fortunate to study the fiction of Agnon with him
in the late 1970s. Till his retirement, Amichai continued to describe
teaching rather than writing poetry as his real work. Poetry, he would
say, is neither a vocation nor an avocation. He writes because it is the
easiest, most pleasurable thing for him to do. At other times he'd say,
only half-joking, that he writes poetry because he's too lazy to do real
work. Labor, ordinary work, is hard and important, not poetry. These
statements were, of course, an integral part of his poetics: a principled
refusal to privilege poetry and the poet, and an ethical commitment to
foreground the quotidian struggles of workaday human beings.

From 1964 till his death in 2000, Yehuda Amichai's life partner was
Hana (Sokolov) Amichai, who was born in 1938 in Petach Tikva, the
same town where Amichai's family first lived when they immigrated to

Palestine a couple of years earlier. With Hana, Yehuda had two more children, David (Dadi), born in 1973, and Emanuela, born in 1978. All the dedications in his poetry books from *Akhshav ba-ra'ash* (1969) on are either to Hana or to his children, and there are numerous poems expressing romantic or paternal love, usually in the shadow of history, war, or death—even when the tone appears playful and witty— a shadow that makes the love in these poems all the more poignant. "Love," Amichai said in an interview with me, "is the material that holds everything together, the glue."[69] For me the most powerful expression of this sensibility is the poem "Inside the Apple," where the speaker is metaphorically the little worm inside the apple, hanging on to his beloved who has come to be there with him. As together they hear "the knife / paring around and around" them, he knows that she will stay with him "until the knife finishes its work."[70]

"I have never written a war poem that does not mention love in it, and I have never written a love poem without an echo of war," Amichai said in an interview.[71] This mutual implication of love and war is not just a reiteration of 1960s peace slogans, for throughout his poetry the lovers—and in the later poetry the children as well—are described as always in that hazardous in-between space, surrounded by the threatening forces of death and war: inside the apple with the paring knife coming closer and closer, or in the arena, compelled by the powers-that-be to perform before the warring camps and provide them with distractions of bread and circuses. The unbearable pressure sometimes requires comic, if poignant, relief. For example, when his son Dadi is drafted into the Israeli army, Amichai writes, "I want my son to be a soldier in the Italian army / with a crest of colorful feathers on his cap, / happily dashing around with no enemies, no camouflage."[72]

Amichai writes about many of the major events in his family life, from his wedding to his mother's death, and from the birth of his daughter to his son's aforementioned conscription into the army.[73] These life events are clearly not only part of an autobiographical poetics but also express very genuine and personal feelings; indeed, they occasion some of the most moving poems in Amichai's oeuvre. Yet in reading his personal love poetry we must not reduce them, as some critics have done, simply to biographical gossip. As in the poetry of Ha-Nagid on which Amichai's autobiographical poems are modeled, the personal often serves as an opening narrative *exemplum* taken from familiar life events, which functions in the course of the text as a springboard for poetic, metaphorical elaboration and far-ranging philosophical meditation.[74] Amichai thus draws on his own biography throughout his oeuvre as a source of philosophical reflection, creating in the process the poet's Everyman persona. This move presents, I believe, a self-conscious violation of the *impersonal imperative* typical of Anglo-American modernism that Zach's version of Statehood Generation poetics aimed to emulate. This *rhetoric of autobiography* is an important component of Amichai's egalitarian poetics, and at the same time it engenders a radical reconsideration of the nature of personal and collective history: it reinscribes the personal *as* political. Autobiography under conditions that Amichai describes as a national and universal earthquake can only result in an archaeological simultaneity of the various layers in the ruins of self and history, and in a shifting geology of fragments that repudiates the possibility of both a coherent personal narrative and a linear collective chronology.

The genre of autobiography undoubtedly occupies a privileged position in Amichai's rearticulation of the avant-garde lyric as both revolutionary and egalitarian, for it is never what we now take to be the solipsistic, romantic, lyrical "I" that we encounter in his poetry. In creating the rhetorical impression that poetry is simple autobiography, Amichai's work also subverts traditional distinctions between the poetic and the prosaic, fiction and nonfiction, written text and oral discourse. In similar fashion, his fiction—which lies outside the purview of this study—privileges the lyrical and presents one of the first postmodernist critiques of novelistic notions of representation in Hebrew literature. This insistence on a nonromantic prosaics of autobiography has far-reaching consequences for Amichai's rejection of Western models of high culture. In particular, it takes the form of a sustained aversion to the perception of poets as unique "individual talents" who possess some special gifts that separate them from ordinary human beings, granting them the privilege of being difficult (as Eliot did) or singling them out as spiritually chosen or inspired (as Yeats did). But Amichai's rhetoric of autobiography is also part of his self-conscious alignment with the discursive practices of women's modernism on the one hand, and with the situation of a minor literature on the other.

I will explore these dimensions of Amichai's writing in terms of his explicit acknowledgment of a poetic matrilineage and his identification with great women poets who were on the margins of their literary trends (especially the German Jewish expressionist Else Lasker Schüler and the Hebrew *moderna* poet Leah Goldberg).[75]

But it is precisely this type of valorization of the autobiographical that has led to a critical tendency to reduce Amichai's lyric to the personal, a tendency that is most common in the reception of women's writing. More recently this critical biographism has reached a new extreme, with the demand that Amichai's lyric needs to be nothing short of documentary in its narration of the poet's personal history.[76]

Because Amichai's poetry has become for so many ordinary Hebrew and English readers an essential part of their own lives, I am committed not to reduce it to the specifics of his own biography. This integration of Amichai's work into the daily lives of human beings validates my own "religious" belief in the power of poetry. And the strength of this belief lends a special urgency to my attempt in this study to reclaim Amichai's poems from their—very different—Israeli and American institutional appropriations, and to read them closely and seriously as parts of a coherent yet open-ended aesthetic and ethical system. This book aims, therefore, to open up a dialogue between the Hebrew and the English reading communities about Amichai's epoch-making poetry, and through this dialogue to offer a theoretical and textual interrogation of some crucial issues in the contemporary poetics of culture.

One

Beyond Appropriation

Reclaiming the Revolutionary Amichai

> Authentic art of the past that for the time being must remain
> veiled is not thereby sentenced. Great works wait.
> —Theodor W. Adorno, *Aesthetic Theory*[1]

I. Useful Poet

In the fall of 1999, when the seriousness of Yehuda Amichai's final illness was already public knowledge, and the Israeli media was filled with
tributes by critics, fellow writers, and politicians, it was the outpouring
of love from common readers that Amichai found truly overwhelming.
"It's amazing," he told me in the hoarse whisper that had replaced his
steady voice, "real love.[2] And the poems are useful to them." "The
main thing is to be useful [*ha-ikar li-hyot shimushi*]," Amichai would
often say, in his inimitable mixture of irony and consent, invoking perhaps the socialist mindset of an earlier time, when being useful to one's
community was considered the highest virtue. Providing useful poetry
was indeed something he was always proud of, especially when it was
ordinary human beings, not the mechanisms of state or institutional
religion, that would find some practical application for his words. And
it didn't matter if the context of use was sublime or ridiculous: from
wedding vows and eulogies to lawsuits and hair salon ads.

The advertising poster on page 26 illustrates quite vividly the absorption of Yehuda Amichai's poetry into the fabric of the quotidian,
a fabric that in Israeli culture still includes poetry.[3] The refrain of Amichai's beloved early poem "Balada al ha-se'ar ha-arokh ve-ha-se'ar ha-
katzer" ("A Ballad on the Long Hair and the Short Hair") starts with
the lines: "His hair was shaved off when he got to the base, / Her
hair remained long and without a response."[4] By the end of the poem,
the lovers—separated by an antiheroic, alienating modern army rather
than a tragic Shakespearean family feud—can no longer hear one another, and the third line leading into the refrain and rhyming with it,

is broken in two: "'*ma at omeret?*' / '*ma ata omer?*'" ("What are you [fem.] saying?" / "What are you [masc.] saying?").

The fragmentation of the dialogue in the poem's refrain (dialogue and refrain being the very features that the ballad genre marks as most salient) thematizes the ultimate impossibility of communication between the young lovers once the man is drafted into military service: "*se'arekh ha-arokh, na'ara. / se'arkha ha-katzer*" ("Your long

Figure 1. Storefront Poster: *Your Long / Hair / Girl / Your [masc.] Hair / I Will Cut Short / Midnight Hair Salon* (Arlozorov Street, Tel Aviv).

hair, girl / Your [masc.] short hair").[5] The hair salon ad puns on this refrain, neutralizing in its commercial appropriation the poem's mournful protest against the emasculation brought about by conscription, as well as the military crew-cut's allusion to the Samson story that carries this meaning. The ad replaces this nuanced symbolism and intertextuality with the literal promise of a fashionable and fetching co-ed salon cut. It supplants the dialogue between the lovers with the hairstylist's offer to shorten (*le-katzer*) both men's and women's hair: "Your long hair, girl / Your [masc.] hair **I will** cut short" (*se'arkha* **akatzer**). In modern colloquial Hebrew pronunciation, which assimilates most *ha* sounds to an *a*, the ad's pun produces a virtual homophone between the poetic form of the definite adjective "the short" (**ha-katzer**) and the hairdresser's promise "I will cut [it] short" (**akatzer**). When I showed Amichai my photograph of the poster and asked him if he didn't mind having his poem mangled like that, he answered, smiling: "On the contrary [*le-hefekh*]! I love to be used, to be exploited." And so he was. But not always as he would have liked.

Amichai's poetic system differentiates throughout between two forms of exploitation that his work treats as profoundly distinct: on the one hand, those largely spontaneous, populist processes that have resulted in the incorporation and assimilation of his poetry into the fabric of everyday life, processes his work thrives on, indeed explicitly asks for; and on the other, the hegemonic mechanisms of cultural appropriation, leading to an official reception that constructs him as a national poet and politically neutralizes his sustained critique of institutional nationalism, state bureaucracy, and clericalism. Though I do not necessarily share the rather idealistic view that the two mechanisms can so clearly be distinguished, it is important to me to suggest the ways in which this distinction is crucial to Amichai's poetic ethics. In the process, I will also argue that no matter how powerful the mechanisms of appropriation become, the poetry—in its absorption into the practice of quotidian existence—continues to have a radical and radicalizing effect.

Liron Bardugo has suggested, in a perceptive article, that within all strata of Israeli culture "Yehuda Amichai is quoted almost inadvertently, as part of the sounds of everyday life and the noises of the street,"[6] and this despite what he describes as Amichai's rejection of a poetics of nationalism and collectivity. Becoming an inadvertent quotation is indeed the ultimate fulfillment for the verbal artist who places a high value on the complete integration of poetry into the lives of ordinary people.[7]

One of Amichai's most famous early poems, "Lo ka-brosh" ("Not Like a Cypress"),[8] rejects traditional elitist conceptions of the poet as lone giant or unique genius and offers a series of alternative populist and utilitarian models for the poet's social and cultural usefulness. In negating the tall, visually salient cypress and its towering human stand-in, King Saul, as models for the poet and offering instead, for example, the image of small and dispersed raindrops that are absorbed "by many mouths," Amichai opts for inconspicuous usefulness over a socially useless prominence (the cypress produces no edible fruit). Indeed, this poem rejects the notion that the poet is entitled to any privileged elite position or granted any aesthetic chosenness that would free him or her from the need to be of use to their society.[9]

Less than a year before Amichai's death, it was the novelist David Grossman who articulated with the most poignant simplicity the source of Amichai's great popularity with the common reader over a period that spanned close to half a century. In an interview in *Ha'aretz*, Grossman talks about Yehuda Amichai's poetry as a constant companion:

> This poetry, in its great intimacy, provides us with first names with which to address life situations where, having run out of words, we'd normally be whittled down to clichés [*mitradedim li-klisha'ot*]. Along comes an Amichai line and gives us words [*ve-notenet lanu milim*]. . . . Because he reaches all the way inside the everyday, you suddenly feel that each moment, even the most banal, is shot through with light. . . . [Amichai's] words have become part of my interior monologue, and not mine alone.[10]

Grossman adds, "He has accompanied me both as a teenager and during army service—in my loves, in courting girls, as well as in my daily family life." This ordinary description masks in fact an allusion to an important metapoetic line from an Amichai poem ("Summer Rest and Words"), *milim melavot et chayay* ("Words accompany my life"), which describes the integration of intertextuality into daily experience.[11] And when Grossman says that thanks to Amichai's words, even the most banal moments become—literally and figuratively—shot through with light, he's again invoking a foundational Amichai image: the ordinary beloved woman as the embodiment of—and substitute for!—divine glory, as she is "standing by the wide-open fridge door, revealed / from head to toe in a light from another world."[12] Grossman's allusively charged yet misleadingly simple diction may be the ultimate homage to the increasingly Amichaiesque poetics of usefulness and accessibility that Grossman himself has been pursuing in the years after publishing his novel, *See Under: Love.*

II. The Politics of Verbal Art

In the next chapter I will explore what goes into making Amichai a usable, or simply useful, poet. Here, however, I would like to focus on the other half of the equation: his poetry's systematic co-optation and appropriation by hegemonic discourses of state and institutional religion. Amichai's poetry, despite its oppositional stance, has been thoroughly appropriated in two systematic ways, each corresponding to a different geographic center of readership: for nationalist official ceremonies and commemorative functions by various Israeli state-apparatuses (e.g., the Ministry of Education and the Ministry of Defense); and for religious ritual by the organized Jewish American community, as part of its investment in *Yiddishkayt*-lite.[13] Both types of appropriation require, as I argue in section III below, that central aspects of Amichai's poetry be rendered invisible. In both cases, Amichai's sardonic deflations and critique of these very ceremonies and institutions must be ignored in order for his appropriations as National Poet or Religious-Bard-for-Secular-Jews to be as thoroughly successful as they have been.[14] This is, ultimately, the most cynical distortion of Amichai's egalitarian ideal of the useful poet.

What I find most disturbing is that generations of progressive young Israeli readers have been turned off from Amichai's poetry because they came to identify it with its various official commemorative and ritualistic reifications—to all of which they were exposed from their earliest school years. What I wish to do, then, is peel away a few of the many layers of interpellation in order to make Amichai freshly readable again. I am motivated, above all, by my passion for his poetry and the sense that its prominence has, paradoxically, rendered it illegible. In reclaiming Amichai for a new/old reading and by reconstructing some of the shock value it had when he first appeared on the scene, I do not delude myself that any of his systemic co-optations can be fully undone or, for that matter, that my proposed rereadings are not in themselves expressions of my own political, aesthetic, and even academic-institutional situatedness. But I do hope, in laying bare my own positionality, to avoid some of the mystification that characterizes Amichai's ideologically driven appropriation by the "establishment."[15]

That Amichai was not always received in Israel as the National Poet of Celebratory Statism is brought vividly home by a fascinating recent piece of archival detective work. Rafi Man, as part of his doctoral research, uncovered the minutes of two powwows held at David Ben-Gurion's office in March 1961.[16] Among those present were the young kibbutzniks Amos Oz, who would become one of the major novelists of the Statehood Generation, and Muki Tzur, who would later emerge as a central historian of the Zionist labor movement. During one of these meetings, while the participants complain to their political father-figure about "the nihilism" and "loss of values" (*ovdan arakhim*) typical of the Hebrew literature of their time, Amnon Barzel, then the youth coordinator of the centrist-labor kibbutz movement (Ichud), brings up the poetry of Yehuda Amichai and adds: "He is an excellent poet but extremely dangerous [*mesukan ad me'od*]."[17] He then offers to send Ben-Gurion a copy of Amichai's book. I propose that we take seriously the fact that in March 1961 these young intellectuals, seeking access to the seat of power, felt the need to report the danger of Amichai's poetry to the authorities. "Excellent poetry" is indeed too "dangerous" to be left alone to do its work; hence the need for what eventually became Amichai's massive hegemonic appropriation.

But what exactly was it about the poems of the first two volumes that Amichai had published by 1961—*Akhshav u-va-yamin ha-acherim* (Now and in Other Days) (1955) and *Be-merchak shtey tikvot* (Two Hopes Away) (1958)—that made Amos Oz insist in that meeting that Ben-Gurion must read Amichai not, God forbid, because he is important, "but because he is expressive of something [*Tzarikh li-kro oto. Lo mipney she-hu chashuv, ela mevate mashehu*]"? It is clear from the minutes of those meetings that the budding literati in attendance did not yet have a cohesive sense of a generational poetics in line with what Israeli critics have come to first take for granted and then critique as the distinctive poetics of *dor ha-mdina* (the Statehood Generation). Thus, the participants "reported" to Ben-Gurion on a hodge-podge of writers of all ages and styles whom we associate in hindsight with different literary generations and trends.

No generational sense emerges from the conversations in Ben-Gurion's office simply because in 1961 the Statehood Generation had not as yet acquired the status of a full-fledged literary trend or become fully identified with the poetic avant-garde in the Israeli "republic of letters." Such a sense was not to be consolidated until 1966, when Natan Zach published a series of manifestos and programmatic essays, as well as a book-length attack on the previous generation, the *moderna* poets of the prestate period, and especially Nathan Alterman, who by then had replaced the more leftist and experimental Avraham Shlonsky as the *moderna*'s leading figure. Zach's pronouncements aimed, among other things, to liberate concrete and personal poetic expression from the collectivist abstractions of the past, which were associated both with the socialist realism of the 1948 Palmach Generation and the heavily symbolist nationalism of Alterman's topical poetry. In fact, what we have come to identify since the mid-1960s as the political disengagement—or, in later critical reassessments, the luxury of a privileged individualism that only writers who are citizens of an established state can afford—fits perfectly the explicit poetics (but not necessarily the implicit poetics embedded in the poetry) of just one poet of the Statehood Generation, namely, the early Natan Zach. It fits none of the other poets who have since come to be seen as representative of that literary trend. Any close reading of the work produced in the 1950s and 1960s by Statehood Generation poets such as Dahlia Ravikovitch, Dan Pagis, David Avidan, and indeed Yehuda Amichai reveals that their poetry violates not only many of the famous "Fifteen Commandments" of Zach's manifesto "On the Stylistic Climate of the 1950s and 1960s in Our Poetry" (*Le-akliman ha-signoni shel shnot ha-chamishim ve-ha-shishim be-shiratenu*) but also the group's purported taboo on writing political poetry.[18] Hamutal Tsamir has already shown that this is the case with respect to Ravikovitch and other women poets of the 1960s.[19] I would add that before historiographical labels and hegemonic mechanisms of appropriation came between us and Amichai's work, it was often perceived as political to its very core and as having in its politics something palpably dangerous.

Furthermore, the human toll of the 1948 war (the Israeli War of Independence and the Palestinian *Nakba*) on both Israelis and Palestinians, and more generally the perspective of the defeated, forms a constant presence in Amichai's early poetry, albeit as a shadow of that which is no longer there. Space does not permit a detailed discussion of the fifteen or so poems in Amichai's 1963 collection *Shirim 1948–1962* (*Poems 1948–1962*) in which this shadowy presence is felt even on the thematic surface of the text. But a few salient examples are in order. See, for example, the previously untranslated sonnet "U-veyt sira haya bli sira" (And a Boathouse Was Left without a Boat), a poem in which the absence of the boat whose house this was (and, via metonymy, the home [*bayit*] of the local fisherman), functions as an "echo of another world" (*hed olam acher*, line 14). This absence haunts both the place and the lovers who go through it "whispering as in a house of mourning" (*kemo she-lochashim be-veyt avel*, line 10). The ghost-like rattling of the rusty chains that lead to the boat which is no longer there is like the "empty hand of Tantalus / that hasn't come to terms / with having naught . . . and keeps on grabbing" for what has been taken from him. Unable to forget who and what was in this place before them, the young Israeli lovers in the sonnet cannot rejoice in their sunny present even as the passing cars declare: "This time is ours" (*ze yomenu*, line 12).[20]

Another previously untranslated poem from the same collection, "Mi-zman lo sha'alu" ("It's Been a While Since They Asked"), starts: "It's been a while since they asked, / Who lives in between [*beyn*] these houses, / And who was he . . . / Why didn't he flee [*lama lo barach*]?"[21] The unasked question that Amichai dares to pose is, as contemporary Israeli readers would know, about the 1948 Palestinians who stayed behind in Israel but lost their homes to new Jewish inhabitants. Furthermore, he situates these displaced Israeli Palestinians subtly in that liminal space of *beynayim*, in-between-ness, which, as I will argue, is the endangered yet sacred space of the poetic subject in Amichai's oeuvre in all its phases.

Another example is a well-known poem, but one whose political valence—like that of many of Amichai's other poems—has rarely been critically observed: "Be-khol chumrat ha-rachamim" ("To the Full Severity of Compassion"), the title poem of this book.[22] Like so much of Amichai's poetry, it gives voice to those whom Walter Benjamin has described as the vanquished of history,[23] rather than to the universal, national subject, as most critics have claimed with regard to Statehood Generation poetry in general and to Amichai's work in particular.[24] This poem has the poetic subject issue a call—to the reader or to himself—to observe, identify with, and take responsibility for those people, described in the poem's first stanza, whose houses have been turned to roofless ruins (*churvot*). That rooflessness makes them ironically closer to the sacred—and at the same time more capable of calling divine justice into question—for "thanks to" the demolished roofs of their houses they can look critically and in an unmediated manner at the heavens and their unfulfilled promise to post-diluvian humanity. The poem's addressee or reader is commanded (through the second-person singular imperative verb forms that recur throughout) not to turn a blind eye to the displaced victims' anguished gaze at the heavens. Thus, the Israeli reader is directed to "see them seeing [*re'eh otam ro'im*]" the sky through the ruined houses. Given that the poem was published in the first decade after 1948, the ideological blinders would have needed to fit pretty tightly over those readers' eyes in order for them *not* to read "the ruined houses [*batim harusim*]" and "the few people [*anashim bodedim*]" who didn't "flee" and remained behind at least *also* as Palestinian citizens of Israel.

Before zeroing in on a particularly influential poem from the first decade of the state, let me draw the reader's attention to one last station in this brief tour of the early collection *Shirim 1948–1962*: the poem "Elegya al kfar natush" ("Elegy on an Abandoned Village"), where the loss of what even Israeli Jews now refer to as "the *Nakba*"[25] is described most directly from the Palestinian point of view, which in the poem's present invades the speaker's consciousness and compels him to see and hear what was there before.[26] Scholarly work has focused on "Elegya al ha-yeled she-avad" ("Elegy on the Lost Child"), Amichai's famous lament for the loss of an individual child—and of childhood tout court—which is also the last poem in the volume.[27] But the elegy that immediately precedes it in the book, and that mourns the collective Palestinian loss, has been largely ignored by scholars and critics, as has the significance of Amichai's placing these elegies next to each other.[28] The title, translated by Stephen Mitchell as "Elegy on an Abandoned Village,"[29] cannot but fail to capture the specific code name *natush* for the places from which Palestinians were expelled during the 1948 war (throughout that period and beyond, this code name was closely associated with the ghastly bureaucratic rhyme *rekhush natush*, designating the Palestinians' "abandoned" houses and lands). Furthermore, the term *kfar* (rural village) of the poem's title refers in the Hebrew of the 1950s and 60s primarily to Palestinian villages; and the fragments of the cultural and agricultural landscape encountered or hallucinated by the elegy's speaker (in a modernist stream-of-consciousness collage) are also distinctly Palestinian. The wind reminds him of the ululating women (*yelel nashim*) who once raised their voices there; the ruined houses (*churvot ha-batim*) are described in the poem's opening lines as part of a sober and calculated process of destruction (*ha-heres haya mefukach*). In this process the life history (*korot*) of forgotten human beings (*bney adam nishkachim*) was replaced by its inanimate homophone, the "wooden beams" (*korot etz*) of romantic ruins, where Israeli lovers now sip a glass of summer wine. The fig trees and the azure paint of the rooms are unmistakable metonymic traces of the village in which, just over a decade before the poem's first publication in 1961, Palestinians lived their normal daily lives. Haunted by the past that others wish to forget or erase, the speaker asserts, in a blatant reversal of Hamlet's command to Horatio, "The rest is *not* silence. The rest is a scream" (*Ha-yeter eyno shtika. Ha-yeter tze'aka*).[30] The poem ends with a surrealist depiction of the ruined Palestinian quotidian as a ghostly apparition that will not go away. In a characteristically dry, scientific image, Amichai describes it as part of the water cycle in nature: "And still / girls are hidden among the wash hanging in the air / which will also turn into rain" (*va-adayin ne'arot / mustarot beyn ha-kvasim ha-tluyim ba-avir / she-gam hu yehafekh le-geshem*).[31]

This elegy insists—via an intertextual dialogue with Rilke's modernist rearticulation of the genre, as well as with the Jewish tradition of the collective, often female-centered *kina* (lament)—on the obligation to acknowledge the truth of that which is "half-destroyed" (*he-charev le-mechetza*). Such an acknowledgment is the condition of possibility for the subject having any epistemic claim or retaining the option for an ethical inner life: *Ki rak be-charev le-mechetza navin* ("For only in [or: by means of] the half-destroyed do we understand").[32]

But since this difficult modernist elegy—in the Rilkean style—does not articulate its ethical message via a linear, realist narrative, it has been easy enough for critics either to ignore or to universalize it. Amichai himself insisted, however, on the specificity of the poem's reference, reminding his readers, for example, in an interview given over a quarter century later—during the first Intifada!—that already in the wake of the 1948 war he "was writing poems about abandoned villages [*kfarim netushim*]."[33]

Indeed, the elegy constructs a subtle but unmistakable analogy between the immigrant speaker's loss of his snowy homeland left behind in the distance—*Ha-sheleg ha-gadol hunach harchek* (in Mitchell's translation: "The enormous snow was set down far away")—and the Middle Eastern wind or ghost (*ru'ach*) that must be hired (*li-skor*) as a professional female mourner (utilizing the fact that *ru'ach* is grammatically feminine) for the Palestinian loss and displacement. The hot summer wind[34] is a disembodied metaphorical stand-in for the "ululating women."[35] More than any other aspect of this poem perhaps, that analogy between Jewish and Palestinian displacement, expressed most radically and consistently in the poetry of Avot Yeshurun (1904–1992), had to be disavowed by Amichai's critical reception.[36]

When politics "reentered" the Hebrew poetic scene in the late 1970s—as the normative historiographic narrative goes—and a new generation of poets and critics would from time to time accuse Amichai, by then fully appropriated as "the national poet," of not being political enough, he would respond by saying that from the very start he had always been a political poet. In an interview with me, Amichai situates himself explicitly in opposition both to the collectivist nationalism of *dor ha-palmach* (the writers of the 1948 Palmach Generation), and to the supposedly universalizing "a-political" stance of *dor ha-mdina* (the modernists of the 1950s and 60s Statehood Generation): "In the fifties, when everyone was enraptured with the soil of the homeland [*admat ha-moledet*] or with 'The Wooden Horse Michael' [*Sus ha-etz Michael;* Natan Zach's paradigmatically "apolitical" poem—CK], I was already writing 'I Want to Die in My Bed.'"[37]

Benjamin Harshav corroborates Amichai's emphasis on "I Want to Die in My Bed" as a paradigm for the political critique and even the *refusenik* sensibility that inform Amichai's early work: "If the poem were written in the framework of political discourse [*maba politi*], it would be a call for desertion from the army [*la-arok me-hatzava*]." In the English version of the same article, Harshav goes on to describe "I Want to Die in My Bed" as "memorized by a generation."[38] It bears mentioning that during that first decade of the state, both the actions of the Israeli Defense Forces (IDF) in battle and the expulsions of the Palestinians were still subject to open debate within the Zionist consensus.[39] Those who recited the poem by heart would have most likely been Jewish—but perhaps also Palestinian?[40]—Israelis, members of the post-1948 generation, for whom these words were "expressive of something," to recall Amos Oz's charged comment to Ben-Gurion. But expressive of what, and where might we find "it"?

Amichai's early political poetry brings into relief a theoretical issue that is of central importance in literary and cultural studies today. A brief theoretical aside may be in order here. In a brilliant article about Yitzhak Laor's thematically blunt political poetry, Shaul Setter insists that even in this much later, post-1982 "action writing"[41] or "*J'accuse* poetry,"[42] the question should be: "how is this oppositional stance inscribed within the language of poetry, namely as a position *of* the language of poetry?"[43] As Theodor Adorno argues in his 1957 lecture "Lyric Poetry and Society," "language mediates lyric poetry and society in their innermost core."[44] In *Aesthetic Theory,* Adorno famously claims that what is socially determinant in works of art is "content that articulates itself in formal structures."[45] Lyrical poetry and verbal art in general "reflect" history and social conditions only as a negative mimesis. Adorno uses the term "negative" (with a typical but infrequently acknowledged playfulness) in both the oppositional and the photographic sense. Years earlier Adorno already offered a cogent example of the negative critical capacity of verbal art in his "Notes on Kafka," where—riffing on the photographic sense of "negative"— he suggested that what we have in Kafka's texts is "a cryptogram of capitalism's highly polished, glittering late phase, which he excludes in order to define it all the more precisely in its negative," scrutinizing "the smudges left behind . . . by the fingers of power."[46]

As part of a recent move to vindicate the political in Adornian aesthetics, Robert Kaufman focuses on the connection between lyric's expression and critical agency (Amos Oz's *mevate mashehu*, "expressive of something"). Kaufman exposes what he sees as the erroneous collapse of the aesthetic and the aestheticist in progressive postmodern ideology critiques and rejects the mobilization of Frankfurt School critical theory (in particular, the work of Benjamin and Adorno) for a wholesale "critique of aesthetic ideology" à la Fredric Jameson.[47]

In another recent Adornian study, C. D. Blanton explores the formal and stylistic articulations of war in English modernism, constructing a hitherto ignored lineage that leads from Eliot to Auden, and from H. D. to MacNiece. Blanton zeroes in on a negative form of intertextuality to which he refers as the poem's "shadow text." Through this shadow text, Blanton argues, contemporary history—which the high modernists supposedly ignored, just as Statehood Generation poets were later said to do—enters the poem without being replicated by it.[48] In my readings of Amichai's poetics I propose to adapt Blanton's concept of the shadow text to the formation of radical allusion typical of his poetry and, I might add, of the intertextual practices of Statehood Generation poetry and prose fiction from Amichai to Amalia Kahana-Carmon. In many cases, the crucial component of the text that an allusion evokes is omitted, relying on the reader's familiarity with that which is not quoted to do the poem's political work. This rhetorical strategy is central, I believe, to the articulation of poetic/political resistance in the early poetry of Yehuda Amichai. It is therefore in its complex verbal art and the workings of literary form that his poetry's politics speaks, rather than in slogans and direct statements.

I Want To Die in My Bed

All night Joshua's army had to climb
To make it to the killing fields on time.
There in the ground, crisscross lay the dead.
I want to die in my bed.

Like gunslits in a tank, their eyes took a narrow view.
They are always the many, and I am always the few.
They may question me. I'll have to say what I said.
But I want to die in my bed.

Stand still, O sun, on Gibeon! Your light
Will flare eternal for battle and murder by night.
I may not even see when my wife is struck dead
But I want to die in my bed.

Samson's a hero because of his long black hair.
I had to be taught to bend the bow, to dare,
They made me a hero-on-call, they sheared my head.
I want to die in my bed.

I've learned you can make a home anywhere,
Even the lion's mouth, with room to spare.
So what if I die alone. That's not what I dread.
But I want to die in my bed.

Trans. Chana Bloch and Chana Kronfeld[49]

אֲנִי רוֹצֶה לָמוּת עַל מִשָּׁתִי

כָּל הַלַּיְלָה עָלָה צָבָא מִן הַגִּלְגָּל
לְהַגִּיעַ עַד שָׂדֶה הַקֶּטֶל וְעַד בִּכְלָל.
הַמֵּתִים בָּאֲדָמָה שָׁכְבוּ בָּעֶרֶב וּבַשְּׁתִי.
אֲנִי רוֹצֶה לָמוּת עַל מִשָּׁתִי.

עֵינֵיהֶם הָיוּ צָרוֹת כְּבַטֶּנֶק הָאֶשְׁנַבִּים,
אֲנִי תָּמִיד מְעַטִּים וְהֵם רַבִּים.
אֲנִי מֻכְרָח לַעֲנוֹת. הֵם יְכוֹלִים לַחְקוֹר אוֹתִי.
אֲבָל אֲנִי רוֹצֶה לָמוּת עַל מִשָּׁתִי.

שֶׁמֶשׁ דֹּם בְּגִבְעוֹן. הוּא מוּכָן לַעֲמֹד נֶצַח.
בִּשְׁבִיל לְהָאִיר לְעוֹרְכֵי קְרָב וָרֶצַח,
אוּלַי לֹא אֶרְאֶה כְּשֶׁיַּהַרְגוּ אֶת אִשְׁתִּי,
אֲבָל אֲנִי רוֹצֶה לָמוּת עַל מִשָּׁתִי.

שִׁמְשׁוֹן, גְּבוּרָתוֹ בְּשֵׂעָר אָרֹךְ וְשָׁחוֹר,
אֶת שֶׁלִּי גָּזְזוּ כְּשֶׁעֲשׂוּנִי לְגִבּוֹר
חוֹבָה וְלִמְּדוּנִי לִדְרוֹךְ אֶת קַשְׁתִּי.
אֲנִי רוֹצֶה לָמוּת עַל מִטָּתִי.

רָאִיתִי כִּי אֶפְשָׁר לָגוּר וּלְהִסְתַּדֵּר
וְלָרַהַט גַּם לֹעַ אַרְיֵה, אִם אֵין מָקוֹם אַחֵר.
כְּבָר לֹא אִכְפַּת לִי לָמוּת בִּיחִידוּתִי,
אֲבָל אֲנִי רוֹצֶה לָמוּת עַל מִטָּתִי.

By 1958, the tightly constructed intertextual collage had already emerged as the hallmark of Amichai's most radical rhetorical practice. But intertextuality does not equal equivocation. The poem describes unambiguously the IDF's battles as leading to "killing fields" (*sde ketel*) and "murder" (*retzach*), and the speaker expresses repeatedly his refusal to die "a hero's death" in the refrain and throughout the poem in his choice of allusions—both their included and their omitted ("shadow") intertexts. The poignancy of the political critique is not achieved here by means of the propositional content of direct assertions about 1948 but rather through the choice to map the battles of 1948 onto those biblical narratives that were most frequently appropriated by the institutional discourse of the early Israeli State: the Book of Joshua as a model for the conquest of the Land; and the Samson story as a model for the new, muscular image of Jewish masculinity. Stanzas 1 and 3 allude to two parts of the story of Joshua's war on the Amorites at Gibeon (Joshua 10:9, 10:12–13); stanzas 4 and 5 allude to two different parts of the Samson story (Judges 16:17–22, Delilah and the "haircut" episode; and Judges 14:5–20, the encounter with the lion's carcass, referred to in the Hebrew as *mapelet ha-arye*, lit., the lion's defeat). Rabbinical Judaism, and the Jewish folklore and humor that it generated over the ages, unlike Zionist political discourse, did not regard either Joshua or Samson as particularly heroic figures. Thus, in turning them into the poetic subject's intertextual counter-models, Amichai lines up his critique of Joshua's and Samson's contemporary nationalist appropriations with the very rabbinical tradition that Zionism rejects, a tradition that often expresses disdain for these figures of brute force and national power.⁵⁰

In a stylistically revolutionary move, Amichai opens the poem with a graft of the then new bureaucratese of IDF Hebrew onto two verses from Joshua 10, thus linking the contemporary territorial conquest battles of the newly institutionalized Israeli army with the biblical ones:⁵¹

"וַיַּעַל יְהוֹשֻׁעַ מִן-הַגִּלְגָּל הוּא וְכָל-עַם הַמִּלְחָמָה עִמּוֹ וְכֹל גִּבּוֹרֵי הֶחָיִל"

(פרק י', פס' 7)

"וַיָּבֹא אֲלֵיהֶם יְהוֹשֻׁעַ פִּתְאֹם כָּל-הַלַּיְלָה עָלָה מִן-הַגִּלְגָּל" (פרק י', פס' 9)

Yehoshua ascended from Gilgal, he, and all the people of war with him, and all the mighty men of valor. Joshua 10:7
Yehoshua came unto them suddenly, and went up from Gilgal all night. Joshua 10:9⁵²

Through this intertextual graft, the agency of the aggressors is made entirely unambiguous. The second line embeds the biblical allusion in the then-new lingo of IDF Hebrew, and specifically in the language of battle-plan commands (*ve-ad bi-khlal*, roughly "from x to y, inclusive," is in the style of *pkudot yom*, the soldiers' daily combat orders). By the logic of the analogy with Joshua's army, the army's institutional purpose is described as getting to the killing fields (*sde ketel*), "inclusive"; in other words, the killing fields are both the geographic and the strategic goal of the campaign. The shadow of the omitted parts of the biblical text looms large here: Joshua 10 goes on to describe in emphatic detail how Joshua's army "slew them with a great slaughter at Giv'on, and chased them along the way that goes up to Bet-Horon, and smote them as far as Azeqa and Maqqeda" (Josh. 10:10–11). It is clear who is killing and expelling whom, once you read the unquoted parts of the biblical text, as Amichai's readers would have done at school in the 1950s and 60s, often with contemporary "parallels" provided by the official statist interpretations. Furthermore, the battle that for Joshua is the great miracle at Gibeon, where this prophet manqué gets to resemble Moses for a brief moment, becomes in the poem—via Amichai's radical rewriting of the biblical intertext and its contemporary political appropriation—an ethically corrupt act of enabling large-scale murder to take place. Amichai subtly changes the famous biblical quotation: *shemesh be-giv'on dom* (Stand still, O Sun, at Gibeon, in the common *KJV* translation) becomes *shemesh dom be-giv'on*; this simple inversion of word order turns the verse into a modern IDF command issued to the personified sun-as-enlisted-man to stand at attention (*dom*; note the use of the rare masculine for *shemesh*, which supports this personification); literally, the line reads: "Sun [masc. sing.], stand at attention at Gibeon."

Dom thus becomes a verb in the imperative, a military command issued to the sun, rather than an adverb describing the sun's stalled movement in the sky. Finally, by grafting the figure of Joshua onto Samson's, the heroism of both—as well as of the IDF soldiers—is called into question, though again this becomes clear only via the activation of the biblical intertext. Amichai's portmanteau *gibor chova* (lit., "compulsory hero" or "heroism-draftee") links the "mighty men of valor" (*giborey chayil*) of Joshua's shadow text with the IDF's *sherut chova* (the common term for compulsory military service), critiquing both in the process. Again, Amichai scrupulously follows the logic of the biblical text in adducing what the *refusenik* speaker learns from the Book of Judges. He refuses to accept Samson as a model of the new, muscular Jew and heroic Israeli (the 1948 commando unit *Shu'aley Shimshon* [Samson's Foxes] comes to mind, named by poet/partisan Abba Kovner in one of his battle missives).[53] Instead, the Samson analogy teaches the speaker that what emasculates the Israeli male is precisely the moment of his induction into the army, when his hair is cut off. Boldly, radically, the shadow text goes one step further to suggest that the very structure of the biblical analogy compels us to see the IDF, not the Palestinians, as taking the place of the Philistines, the cause of Samson's undoing. The army as an institution is out to get him (inverting in line 6 the nearly sacred statist slogan, *me'atim mul rabim*, "the few against the many"); it is out to get everybody—as Yossarian argues in Joseph Heller's *Catch-22*. Furthermore, the formulaic opening of David's lament for the death of Saul and Jonathan on Mount Gilboa (*le-lamed bney yehuda kashet*, 2 Samuel 1:18; "to teach the children of Judah/Yehuda to use the bow") inserts itself—via the obviously anachronistic weaponry—into the Samson allusions, adding the shadow of death in the line "I had to be taught to bend the bow."

Contrary to standard readings of this poem, I have tried to show that the poem exposes and deflates nationalistic appropriations of biblical narratives. By mobilizing the omitted but implied shadow texts, and saturating the language with cultural allusions to 1950s Israeli realia, the refrain "I want to die in my bed" comes to express not simply an individualist, liberal-humanist desire to be left alone to die in peace; but rather, as Benjamin Harshav has suggested, it consolidates itself into a speech act of resistance and refusal—albeit one that takes place within the limited agency of the interpellated national subject. At the same time, the refrain articulates a bold rejection of the national ideal of dying a hero's death, *mot giborim*. In Giorgio Agamben's terms, within the new theological status that the sovereign state grants itself over its subjects ("the state of exception"), the poem's speaker-as-subject has very little choice as to how to live his life, restricted to turning the proverbial lion's maw that is Israel into a home (stanza 5).[54] Language provides the only arena where the interpellated speaker can exercise his right of refusal: the refrain is thus a speech act expressing the wish (to be able to choose) not to die in battle but rather to die in one's own bed (a bed that—as we have just been reminded—is part of the furniture he has had to arrange within the lion's maw, since he has "no other place").[55] Note that according to the constitutive rules of the speech-act of wishing—as well as the historical conditions that govern the speaker's existence—he is by no means sure or even likely to be granted his wish; yet its very expression is a consequential act of protest. Powerless about his own life, the subject, as both Amichai's and Ravikovitch's poetry often remind us, can fantasize only about having the choice of how to die, since the choice of how to live has been irrevocably vitiated.[56] Eyal Bassan, rethinking Foucault with Agamben, has pointed out to me that the modern sovereign state assumes not only the power to inflict death on its subjects but also to regulate their lives. By returning the subject's wish to the mode of death rather than the regulation of his or her life, the protest in the speaker's refrain foreshadows the philosophical framework of this critique.[57]

In a 1987 review of Dahlia Ravikovitch's book, *Ahava amitit* (True Love), Ariel Hirschfeld commends the section of political poems in Ravikovitch's book for expressing an understanding "that a protest poem must—not 'can' or 'had better,' but must—reach its addressees . . . directly, without requiring analysis or leafing through concordances. . . . And most of all, that it must not primp and adorn itself, nor bat its eyelashes at its own peacock tail like that 'Typical NO Poem' by

Natan Zach. For what in another context would be self-adornment or wit, here would be more than a miss—it would constitute a betrayal."⁵⁸ Retheorizing political poetry through Amichai's oeuvre and with Adorno and his recent reinterpreters, I find this prescription rather limiting: thematicism as the sole criterion for the political in poetry runs the risk of implicitly accepting the very same presuppositions about the lyric as those fostered by bourgeois liberalism. This is the sense in which political poetry as verbal art—and not as mere direct thematic statement—continues to be the mark of Amichai's oeuvre till the very end, and is not restricted to his early reactions to 1948.

It was politically very unpopular of Amichai to name his post-1967 volume of poetry *Akhshav ba-ra'ash* (Now in the Earthquake), as is evidenced by some of the book's reviews.⁵⁹ The title's critical edge can again be fully appreciated only through its verbal art—its use of lexical ambiguity as well as biblical and liturgical intertextuality. Stephen Mitchell chose to translate it as "Now in the Storm," since the English "storm" can have a dual reference to natural disaster and political upheaval.⁶⁰ The modern Hebrew sense of *ra'ash* is simply "noise," thus reducing the postwar euphoria in Israel to the mere annoyance of a din. But in biblical Hebrew *ra'ash* means "upheaval," often of cosmic proportions, as in *Ve-tir'ash ha-aretz mi-mekoma* (lit., "and the earth/world was unmoored from its place," Isaiah 13:13), but also "earthquake" (e.g., in the opening verse of *Amos*, where his prophecy of doom for Israel's sins is dated to "two years before the earthquake [*shnatayim lifney ha-ra'ash*]," implying that the earthquake was the punishment for the nation's sins). This latter meaning is dominant in rabbinic and liturgical uses, and survives in the modern literary Hebrew expression for "earthquake," *ra'ash adama*. Had Amichai used the more common modern Hebrew synonym for "earthquake," *re'idat adama* (lit., "earth tremor"), the political valence might have been more obvious because in Hebrew slang one talks about a political earthquake, *re'idat adama politit*. On the other hand, the title would have lost its crucial intertextual effects, which are the allusions to Isaiah and Amos, as well as to the catalogue of deaths mentioned in the hallowed Yom Kippur *U-netane Tokef* prayer, where *mi ba-ra'ash* ("who by earthquake") appears alongside *magefa* ("plague") in the list of capital punishments awaiting those who will not "be deemed innocent in [God's] eyes" and will not be written in the Book of Life for the year to come.

In a letter addressed to Yehuda and Hana Amichai by fellow poet Dahlia Ravikovitch, dated December 2, 1967, about six months after the 1967 war, Ravikovitch expresses her admiration for Amichai's "*poema* on Jerusalem"—undoubtedly, a reference to "Jerusalem 1967," the twenty-two-part *poema* that opens *Akhshav ba-ra'ash* and provides a sustained, critical counterpoint to the nationalist celebration of the Occupation and the immediate annexation of East Jerusalem to Israel (within three hours of the end of battles). After complaining about her own inability to react poetically because she finds herself in these circumstances completely devoid of inspiration (*netulat kol hashra'a*), Ravikovitch says: "Maybe I'm a little jealous. Everybody (and I among them) sees everything, and only Yehuda manages to both see and write" (*Kulam [va-ani be-tokham] ro'im ha-kol, ve-rak Yehuda matzli'ach li-r'ot ve-likhtov*).[61] As Ranen Omer-Sherman points out, "What is perhaps most consistently apparent even in the earliest Jerusalem poems [by Amichai] is their stoic resistance to the euphoria of any form of *proprietorial* love." This, he adds, "seems especially remarkable after the Six-Day War in 1967, a conflict that unleashed an unparalleled wave of highly rhetorical and ideologically inflected verse, much of it undoubtedly triumphal or otherwise awestruck, in response to the culture's access to every quarter of the city."[62]

Poem 5 in "Jerusalem 1967" exemplifies the way Amichai uses his deep knowledge of traditional Judaism against the heightened nationalist exploitation of religion for political purposes and the increasing blurring of boundaries between "church and state" in the wake of the 1967 war, the war that saw the chief military rabbi, Shlomo Goren, blow the shofar and recite prayers moments after the Israeli soldiers conquered East Jerusalem. With the book title's allusion to the *U-netane tokef* prayer in the background, the poem starts with a description of the speaker as going against the stream of worshipers on the first Yom Kippur after the war:[63]

#5
On Yom Kippur in 1967, the Year of Forgetting, I put on
my dark holiday clothes and walked to the Old City of Jerusalem.
For a long time I stood in front of an Arab's hole-in-the-wall shop,
not far from the Damascus Gate, a shop with

buttons and zippers and spools of thread
in every color and snaps and buckles.
A rare light and many colors, like an open Ark.

I told him in my heart that my father too
had a shop like this, with thread and buttons.
I explained to him in my heart about all the decades
and the causes and the events, why I am now here
and my father's shop was burned there and he is buried here.

When I finished, it was time for the Closing of the Gates prayer.
He too lowered the shutters and locked the gate
and I returned, with all the worshipers, home.

[ה]

בְּיוֹם כִּפּוּר בִּשְׁנַת תַּשְׁכַּ״ח לָבַשְׁתִּי
בִּגְדֵי חַג כֵּהִים וְהָלַכְתִּי לָעִיר הָעַתִּיקָה בִּירוּשָׁלַיִם.
עָמַדְתִּי זְמַן רַב לִפְנֵי כּוּךְ חֲנוּתוֹ שֶׁל עֲרָבִי,
לֹא רָחוֹק מִשַּׁעַר שְׁכֶם, חֲנוּת
כַּפְתּוֹרִים וְרֻכְסָנִים וּסְלִילֵי חוּטִים
בְּכָל צֶבַע וְלַחְצָנִיּוֹת וַאֲבָזְמִים.
אוֹר יָקָר וּצְבָעִים רַבִּים, כְּמוֹ אֲרוֹן־קֹדֶשׁ פָּתוּחַ.

אָמַרְתִּי לוֹ בְּלִבִּי שֶׁגַּם לְאָבִי
הָיְתָה חֲנוּת כָּזֹאת שֶׁל חוּטִים וְכַפְתּוֹרִים.
הִסְבַּרְתִּי לוֹ בְּלִבִּי עַל כָּל עֲשָׂרוֹת הַשָּׁנִים
וְהַגּוֹרְמִים וְהַמִּקְרִים, שֶׁאֲנִי עַכְשָׁו פֹּה
וַחֲנוּת אָבִי שְׂרוּפָה שָׁם וְהוּא קָבוּר פֹּה.

כְּשֶׁסִּיַּמְתִּי הָיְתָה שְׁעַת נְעִילָה.
גַּם הוּא הוֹרִיד אֶת הַתְּרִיס וְנָעַל אֶת הַשַּׁעַר
וַאֲנִי חָזַרְתִּי עִם כָּל הַמִּתְפַּלְּלִים הַבַּיְתָה.

The scene described in the poem takes place in 1967, a year that happens to spell "forgetting" in the Hebrew calendar: *tashkach*. Amichai's
choice to vocalize the Hebrew calendar year, against the convention
to leave it as separate, unvocalized letters, clearly inscribes the sense of

"forgetting" as a mark of the times, while echoing the Hebrew name for 1948, *tashach*, the one year in Israeli history that is always vocalized in Hebrew. The poem's critical dimension can only be fully comprehended by recognizing the reference to the suffering of both the Jewish self (in the Nazi genocide) and the Palestinian Other (in the recent war), without equating the two; the poem's critique also relies on full, detailed recall of the dictates of Jewish ethics about obtaining forgiveness on the Day of Atonement and about the basic rituals and customs that pertain to this holiest of days on the Jewish calendar. Yet the only extended discussions of this poem, which are otherwise both detailed and nuanced— for example, by Glenda Abramson and Ranen Omer-Sherman—either do not read it within this ethical framework or explicitly reject the plain religious sense of the speaker's action as a performance of the *mitzvah* (commandment) to receive forgiveness from the people one has sinned against before the end of Yom Kippur.[64] The poem, I argue, presupposes such basic familiarity with the tradition on the part of the reader (a familiarity that is pretty widespread in the Jewish community worldwide, even among secular people). Thus, for example, it is common (Jewish) knowledge that one is supposed to wear white and not black—as the speaker does—on Yom Kippur. More importantly, what the speaker alone remembers—unlike the masses rushing to the synagogues—is that injustices done to one's fellow human beings cannot be atoned for by prayer and fasting on Yom Kippur until and unless one asks—and receives—forgiveness from the people one has wronged.

While the poem starts out with the speaker almost congratulating himself for being more religiously and politically correct than his fellow Jewish citizens of Jerusalem, it ends up heaping irony upon irony on the speaker's sense of self-righteousness. This ironic distance between the speaker and the implied author is entirely characteristic both of Amichai's poetry and of the Anglo-American modernist affinities of the Statehood Generation poets in general. If we reimagine the poem's dramatic situation through the point of view of the Palestinian shopkeeper, who cannot be presumed to know anything about the Jewish laws governing Yom Kippur, the speaker's act of standing silently dressed in mourning clothes all day long in front of the little shop makes no sense at all. Furthermore, although the speaker presents himself at the beginning of the poem as going "against the current" and deigning to ask forgiveness of the Palestinian, and to explain and justify his presence in Jerusalem in terms of the historical circumstances that have brought him "here," his father's shop having been burnt "there," he in fact says nothing. As both Abramson and Omer-Sherman have observed, his monologue turns out to have been entirely internal: "I said to him *in my heart*," which is idiomatic Hebrew for "I thought"; no speech act has taken place, and the speaker returns home with the rest of the worshippers, no longer a solitary agent of protest and of ethically valid religious observance. A "crucial dimension of this resolutely unsentimental poem," Omer-Sherman reminds us, is that the dialogue "proves ultimately heartbreaking because it is imagined only."[65] But it is important to note that, according to Jewish law, this silence vitiates the possibility that he be forgiven: unless he is able to ask and receive from the person he has wronged absolution of his guilt by the closure of the Holy Day, the "deadline" for being reinscribed in the Book of Life will have expired and no recourse to divine mercy will remain open. Indeed, by the end of the poem, according to the same religious law, the speaker too is implicated in the general failure to ask forgiveness for the suffering caused to the Palestinian Other. He therefore shares in the collective guilt, as concretely illustrated in his "joining the current" of synagogue-goers returning home, rather than continuing to go against it. The only radical dimension that the speaker ends up embracing—albeit in his unspoken monologue, which Amichai lets only the reader "hear"—is the silent parallel (which, of course, is not an equation) he draws between his father's store burnt by the Nazis "there" and the Occupation and destruction that his own people have recently brought to this shopkeeper's people "here."

But it is Amichai's metaphorical mapping, rather than the speaker's failed speech-act, that packs the most powerful critical punch. In the process of describing the speaker's silent apologetics, Amichai constructs a scandalously sacrilegious analogy between the Holy Ark containing the Torah in the synagogue and the Palestinian's hole-in-the-wall shop. He goes even further to metonymically imply an analogy between God and the shopkeeper:

> . . . a shop with
> buttons and zippers and spools of thread

in every color and snaps and buckles.
A rare light and many colors, **like** an open Ark.

. . .

When I finished, it was time for the Closing of the **Gates** prayer.
He too lowered the shutters and locked the **gate**.[66]

As Abramson cogently observes, "The terminology refers equally to a place of worship and the shop."[67] Thus, when the twilight Hour of Grace is over, God, like the shopkeeper, closes the gate to human petitions for forgiveness. Significantly, the Hebrew noun *Ne'ilah* (lit., "locking") and the verb *na'al* ("locked") are used in the poem not only to describe the Palestinian shuttering his shop but also to link the foreclosure of the opportunity for dialogue with the Closing of the Gates prayer (*Tefilat Ne'ilah*) at the end of Yom Kippur—effecting a radical metaphorical mapping indeed, as well as an unflinching critique of the collective ethical failure of both the speaker and his community.

Despite all this, the poem, like Amichai's later Jerusalem poems, is often just added to the celebratory nationalist canon, not attending to what the text, intertext, and figurative language say or imply. This is not to say that the biographical Yehuda Amichai was an anti- or "post-" Zionist or to call into question his love of Jerusalem, indeed his love of country; it is only to note that when Amichai's *poetry* is read closely and his verbal art attended to carefully, what becomes unavoidably clear is that, to recall Adorno and Benjamin, the "formal structures" of his poetry articulate an oppositional content that resists the celebratory version of Israeli history.[68]

The same post-1967 book, *Akhshav Ba-ra'ash* (Now in the Noise/ Earthquake), features Amichai's great epic poem, "Mas'ot Binyamin ha-acharon mi-Tudela" ("The Travels of the Last Benjamin of Tudela"), which is one of the key poems I return to from different perspectives throughout this study.[69] The poem as a whole, Amichai's longest, is perhaps his most avant-garde poetic work. It presents in jumbled snippets a simultaneous narrative of personal and communal history and— in blurred and fragmentary abstract lines—a spatial panorama of sites of memory ("*les lieux de mémoire*," in Pierre Nora's terms).[70] Yet it is one of the most sustained expressions of the politics of literary form in Amichai's oeuvre. The speaker, himself split into first, second, and third person, leaves his here (Jerusalem) and now (age forty-three) to set out on his confounding and impossible simultaneous travels through time and space. But the trip is modeled from the start on a fictional genre, the travelogue, whose history, both in the West and in Jewish literary tradition, going back at least to the Middle Ages, ties it not only to the eventual rise of realist fiction but also to its very opposite, namely the fantastic, parodic, and satirical. The most salient variation on this genre within modern Jewish literature—S. Y. Abramovitch's satirical *The Travels of Benjamin the Third* (*Mas'ot Binyamin ha-shlishi*)—is directly invoked in Amichai's title. By naming himself the last Benjamin of Tudela, he is acknowledging the other three;[71] at the same time, this act of naming adds to the systematic blurring of the historical and the fictional, as well as to the upending of the generic distinction between poetry and prose. Amichai adopts Abramovitch, the grandfather of modern Hebrew and Yiddish realist fiction, as a model for his modernist disruptions of linear order and his replacement of historical sequence with archeological simultaneity: the plot of Abramovitch's *The Travels of Benjamin the Third* depicts, after all, Benjamin and Senderl's travels as forming a completely circular motion that can never reach its goal.[72] Furthermore, when Amichai's traveler attempts to disrupt linear order and go against standard periodization, it is not the geographical Egypt, Far East, historical twentieth century, or actual Stone Age, but only their conventionalized semiotic and artistic representations in the museum to which he can have access: the Egyptian Room, the Far East wing, and so on.[73]

While the title flaunts the *poema*'s fictionality, the poem's explicit thematic materials nevertheless foreground a rhetorical impression of autobiographical and historical veracity. The rhetoric of autobiography is reinforced, as we've seen in the Introduction, through the inclusion of many concrete details from Amichai's personal biography, especially those dealing with time and place. We find out exactly how old he was while writing the poem, at what age he emigrated to Palestine, when he went to a Montessori kindergarten, where he lived, and more. But instead of providing a chronological and panoramic narrative that takes the speaker from childhood to middle age and from Würzburg to Jerusalem, the poet constructs a multilayered cross-section of tumbling images mixing then and now, there and here, autobiography and collective history.

However, while the poem's focus on personal history has been commonly acknowledged, the *poema*'s very specific engagement with the events of collective history remain for the most part outside the purview of critical discussion, and the poem as a whole has received astonishingly little scholarly attention. The few critics who do deal with the work ignore its direct references to the immediate aftermath of the 1967 war, assimilating these references to the common clichés about Amichai's universalist "antiwar" message. As a corrective, I wish to address here briefly the *poema*'s biting critique of what it presents as an unholy alliance between militarism and fundamentalism during that period, along with the threatening triangulation of religion and war with love in the speaker's personal life. This, we should note, is the period that biographically was preceded by the breakup of Amichai's marriage to Tamar (neé Horn) and the beginning of his lifelong relationship with Hana Sokolov (Amichai). Drafts of the *poema* in the archives are written on the back of Hana's seminar papers for the Hebrew University. Let me focus, however, not on the important issue of the fictional uses of autobiography, which I took up in the Introduction, but on the ethics and politics of avant-garde form: Amichai's use of the collage technique in the poem's genre, intertextuality and metaphor to express stylistically, through the workings of his verbal art, the fragmentation of the poetic subject by the forces of history, as these forces are apocalyptically experienced by him and his lover during and after the 1967 war. The poetic subject, articulated—as in S. Yizhar's novella *Ha-Shavuy*—in alternating "I's" and "you's," is neither the poet in his ivory tower, nor Benedict Anderson's privileged universal subject of the nation-state. As elsewhere in Amichai's work, it is an ordinary person whose limited agency and coherence are blown apart by the politics of state and religion.

In an interview with me,[74] Amichai associates writing "The Travels of the Last Benjamin of Tudela" directly with the 1967 war, positioning the work, to invoke Ezra Pound's definition of an epic, as "a poem including history." Amichai's account also complicates our understanding of both the work's genre and its intertextual models. Here is how he started the discussion of the poem in the interview:

> This *Poema* was written in the year following the Six-Day War, which was the most productive year of my life. I wrote my second novel then

which I consider good to this very day [*Mi yitneni malon*, published in 1971; a novel that has as yet to receive the attention it deserves, CK].[75] There was something traumatic about that year, and about having spent it in America. Trauma is an explosion [*hitpotzetzut*] which brings to the surface completely different materials.

Amichai's metaphor here may be instructive for the current critical rethinking of the historiography of Statehood Generation poetry in terms of trauma theory, especially in the recent work of Michael Gluzman.[76] Amichai's account of trauma as an explosion shifts the emphasis away from the psychoanalytic concern with the tension between repression and obsessive repetition, for example, almost as if he were foreshadowing the work of Anne-Lise François, Eyal Bassan, and others,[77] and describes the traumatic event that war is as an "opening of a secret," an explosion that makes untold fragments of consciousness and history rise to the discursive and experiential surface. The explosion and the earthquake are two of the metaphors Amichai uses repeatedly to express the ways historical crises destabilize the geological layers that make up "the archaeology of the self."

In the same interview Amichai goes on to describe the poem's dizzying composition as a correlative of the war, and provides a new variation on his recurring metaphors of dangerous movement—not earthquake or explosion but oceanic vortex:

> I don't even know how I did it, I wrote the *poema* in a couple of weeks. Though I never intended to write an autobiographical *poema*, I guess that's basically what it is, but one in which I look at the world through the lens of my life. Of course, all sorts of things entered into play, as in a whirlpool, so each strophe is like a riptide drawing all the materials around into it, and then comes another riptide, as in the ocean. The focus, in fact, is from the moment I arrived in Israel till the descent into the underworld [*ha-yerida la-she'ol*].

Till the descent into the underworld? Let me suspend for a minute the political implications of mapping the poem's present—the national euphoria in the aftermath of the 1967 war—on the descent to hell, and pose the question of genre that it gives rise to. I take Amichai's words to mean that the poem needs to be read kaleidoscopically through multiple generic models, all of which are only partially and fragmentarily adhered to: the poem is not only an autobiographical *poema*, though he suggests that this may be its main generic affiliation, but also a modernist take on the epic, and specifically on Dante's *Divine Comedy*. In fact, Amichai's poem echoes Pound's *Cantos* XIV–XVI, where Dante/Pound (or rather their fictional personae) descend to hell. Glenda Abramson links this poem, Amichai's longest, to Eliot's "Four Quartets," not to Pound's *Cantos*, but her reading too suggests that it is the modernist Anglo-American rewriting of the classical epic that is relevant here, and not just the Russian-inspired *poema*, a genre that has been very influential for modern Hebrew literature during the Haskalah (Enlightenment) and Techiya (National Revival) periods.

A modernist epic and an avant-garde *poema*; a parodic travelogue and an experimental, poetic *Bildungs* narrative; a jumbled personal autobiography and a layered palimpsest of collective history: *Travels* can be read as an anarchist collage that replaces, as Ayelet Even-Nur has suggested to me,[78] the generic and narrative *cohesion* of the individual subject and his life-story with *adhesion*, the collage model of sticking to each other without becoming whole, a collectivity of fragments adhering together in a shared space. The one aspect that critics have acknowledged, the *poema*'s upending of chronological linearity, is thus part of a large-scale rhetorical and ethical rejection of "the God of order of the Seder night" ("seder" in Hebrew means both "order" and "the Passover Seder meal").[79] The modernist collage form, with its tendency to foreground the fragments that constitute it, allows *Travels* to be both a modernist rearticulation of the epic tradition in the West and a parodic rewriting of the Hebrew travelogue tradition. Furthermore, Amichai places himself at the end of a tradition that blends the first two historical Benjamins with the third fictional one, destabilizing in the process the distinctions not only between fact and fiction but also between prose and poetry: from *Sefer Ha-Masa'ot* (The Book of Travels) by the twelfth-century Benjamin of Tudela, for whom the street where Yehuda lived at the time in Jerusalem is named (known as Mi-Tudela Street), through the nineteenth-century self-styled Benjamin the Second from Romania, and his book (1856; Hebrew 1859), *Sefer Masa'ey Yisrael* (The Book of Travels of Israel); and up to their fictional parodic and satiric rewriting in S. Y. Abramovitch's *Benjamin the Third* (Yiddish version 1878; first Hebrew version 1896). Beyond genre, the poem offers an intertextual collage of allusions too numerous to list, from Medieval Andalusian poets Yehuda Ha-Levi and Shmuel Ha-Nagid (and their very different articulations of travel poetry), to Chaim Nachman Bialik, the founder of the modern Hebrew autobiographical *poema*, to Goethe and Rilke, all of whom are figured in the text. Finally, the poem offers perhaps the most astonishing example in modern Hebrew poetry of metaphorical collage, allowing disparate domains of language and experience to be brought together while underscoring their separateness. I will return to the metaphorical collage in chapter 6.

But what, beyond the allusion to Dante and the modernist epic, to make of the last sentence in Amichai's description of the poem's transition from autobiography to the fantastic mode as the progression "from the moment I arrived in Israel till the descent into the underworld"? The *poema*'s chronological present consists of an account of the 1967 war as an apocalyptic conflation of fundamentalist religion with nationalist rhetoric and the international war machine, in the midst of which the speaker's great new love is trying to survive. This forms the thematic and rhetorical climax of the *poema* and covers some ninety lines.[80] A surrealist and grotesquely macabre catalogue mutually implicating war and religion, this is not, as critics who deal with this work would have it, just some generalized, universal antiwar poetry, but a modernist tableau that nevertheless includes a particular history. The collage puts together items from the concrete geopolitics of 1967, such as Rabbi Goren's shofar-blowing during the conquest of East Jerusalem; the mobilization of religious discourse tout court for the nationalist justification of the Occupation; and also the equally specific depiction of the role played by the superpowers in supplying—and testing out—their latest weaponry to Israel and the Arab countries, turning the local population into pawns in a dystopic chess game between Western and Eastern blocs.[81] And it is in its departure from realism and its forays into the fantastic that the poem is freer, as Tzvetan Todorov reminds us, to take on boldly this politically charged topic, drawing ancient and modern, foreign and domestic into one apocalyptic war machine:[82]

> Tanks from America, fighter planes from France, Russian
> jet-doves, armored chariots from England, Sisera's regiments
> who dried the swamps with their corpses, a flying Massada,

Beitar slowly sinking, Yodfat on wheels, . . .
Massada won't fall again, won't fall again,
won't fall again, Massada, won't. . . .

— — — — — — — — — — —

M.I.R.V., S.W.A.T., I.C.B.M., I.B.M.,
P.O.W., R.I.P., A.W.O.L.,
S.N.A.F.U., I.N.R.I., J.D.L., L.B.J.,
E.S.P., I.R.S., D.N.A., G.O.D.
Sit down. Today is the day of judgment. Today there was war.[83]

טַנְקִים מֵאַמֶרִיקָה, מְטוֹסֵי קְרָב מִצָּרְפַת, יוֹנֵי סִילוֹן
רוּסִיִּים, רֶכֶב מֵאַנְגְלִיָה בְּלִי פָּרָשָׁיו, גְּדוּדֵי סִיסְרָא
שֶׁיִּבְּשׁוּ אֶת חַבְצוֹת בִּגְיוֹתֵיהֶם, מַסָּדָה מְעוֹסֶפֶת,
בֵּיתָר צוֹנַחַת לְאַט, יוֹדְפַת עַל גַּלְגַּלִּים, . . .
. . .   שֵׁנִית מַסָּדָה לֹא תִפֹּל ,לֹא תִפֹּל,
לֹא תִפֹּל, שֵׁנִית מַסָּדָה, לֹא.   . . .

— — — — — — — — —

מַטְלַ־רִים, רַרְנַ־ט מַרְנַ־ט, מָרָמָן
וְרַבְּנָן, נוּן טֵית, נוּן מֵם, לָמֶד וָו,
חָרְמֵ־שׁ, דְצָ־ךְ, אַצָ־ג, מַוֶּר מְמַצֵּע
רַק־מַלָט, לַהַבְיוֹר, קַבִּיר, מְכְמָשׁ, תוֹב־בָא.
שֵׁב. הַיּוֹם הֲרַת עוֹלָם. הַיּוֹם הָיְתָה מִלְחָמָה.

Between the late 1960s and his death in 2000, Amichai became thoroughly appropriated both in Israel and abroad, even though he continued to express outright scorn for any institutional manipulation of
nationalist or religious sentiment. The extent of his ongoing irreverence
can be appreciated, for example, if we remember that this, after all, is
the poet who, in his personal communications, coined the expressions
sho'an miktzo'i in Hebrew, and "professional 'holocauster'" in English,
a portmanteau linking "holocaust" with "roller coaster" in sarcastic
condemnation of leaders—and writers—who have risen to prominence
by exploiting the Nazi genocide for political gain.[84] And this is also the
poet who has consistently treated the powers that be, powers that trade
in all the external trappings of religious and patriotic fervor, to large

doses of his most acerbic wit. They are, as he put it succinctly, "stupid as flags" (*tipshim kmo dgalim*)—in the words of the last line of the poem "I Guard the Children" ("Ani shomer al ha-yeladim").[85]

This poem was written in the wake of Israel's 1982 invasion of Lebanon and published in his 1985 book, *Me-adam ata ve-el adam tashuv* (*From Man Thou Art and Unto Man Shalt Thou Return*), one of his most powerful collections since *Shirim: 1948–1962*, yet a book that— like much of Amichai's later work—received mixed reviews upon its publication in Israel.[86] The poem describes a scene that is still, unfortunately, all too familiar to the Israeli reader: an aging father doing his Civil Defense (HAGA) duty as an armed guard in a schoolyard. From this patriotic and protective expression of heightened vigilance, which already contains a critique of divine providence (the old father must do it because God the Father no longer will; lines 7–8[87]), Amichai moves surprisingly, through the father's stream of consciousness, to unorthodox speculations about parent-child relations during the Shoah:

> I ask myself: During the Shoah,
> would a son still rebel against his parents, would a father beat
> his son behind the barbed wire,
> was there a mother-daughter struggle in the huts of annihilation,
> a stubborn and rebellious son in the carloads of transport,
> a generation gap on the platforms of perdition,
> Oedipus in the death chambers?[88]

אֲנִי שׁוֹאֵל אֶת עַצְמִי הַאִם בִּזְמַן הַשּׁוֹאָה
הָיָה מֶרֶד בֵּן בְּהוֹרָיו, אָב מַכֶּה
אֶת בְּנוֹ בֵּין גְּדֵרוֹת הַתַּיִל,
רִיב בֵּין אֵם לְבִתָּהּ בְּצְרִיפֵי הַכְּלָיָה,
בֵּן סוֹרֵר וּמוֹרֶה בְּקְרוֹנוֹת הַמִּשְׁלוֹחַ,
פַּעַר דּוֹרוֹת בְּרְצִיפֵי הָאֲבַדּוֹן,
אֶדִיפּוּס בְּתָאֵי הַמָּוֶת?

Though the questions remain unanswered, the mere asking breaks the most fundamental social taboos of discourse about the Shoah, at the same time that it rehumanizes and enlivens the victims. Amichai suggests that the victims' humanity is served, indeed honored, not by a sacralizing, idealizing language of heroism and martyrology but by an insistence on the details of psychological truth, unflattering as they may be.[89] And clearly, one possible answer to these not quite rhetorical questions would be no, that no such struggles took place; that the trauma of the concentration camp experience suspended all normal developmental strife in the family. But that is not the only possible answer, as Ruth Kluger has shown so brilliantly in her bold recounting of the ongoing mother-daughter conflicts even in spaces unspeakably transformed by the shadow of mass extermination and loss.[90] At any rate, it is not the answer that counts. The relevance and legitimacy of these questions themselves is what Amichai wants us to acknowledge. Furthermore, by invoking intra-Jewish violence and brutality, Amichai subtly undermines another discursive taboo about the Shoah ("Thou shalt not compare"), a taboo whose violation, as we shall see, is structurally taken to an extreme in the juxtaposition of the various sections of the poem. Both the more ordinary violence of child abuse (a father beating his son) and the unmitigated brutality of ancient Hebrew laws that decree that "stubborn and rebellious sons" be stoned to death (*ben sorer u-moreh*, Deuteronomy 21:18–21; Amichai quotes the biblical legal terminology verbatim here) are laid bare as potentially present in the Jewish family, even within the larger unspeakable institutional violence of the Nazi genocide.

As we return to the father guarding the school against terror attacks, the poem follows his stream of consciousness in a direction that upends the expected, politically manipulated analogy between the horrors of the Shoah and the very real and present danger to Jewish children in Israel, in its constant State of Emergency. In focusing on the corruption of Israel's political leaders, however, rather than on its military enemies, Amichai also gives the lie to the right wing's equation between Nazis and Palestinians.[91] If anything, in the juxtaposition between the father's two sets of associations—first the possibility of internal Jewish violence during the Shoah and then the violence in the Israeli present—it is at the Israeli government that he points an accusatory finger. In emphatic, prophetic language whose cadence, imagery, and purpose echo Ezekiel's and Jeremiah's most scathing denunciations of the leaders of Judah, the father insists that if the schoolchildren are in danger, it is only the politicians' doing.[92] The poem culminates in a devastating mock-epiphany of contemporary power politics as the real threat to the children's safety. Let me quote the last stanza in full:

> But I lift up my face and see above us,
> as in some hideous vision, wielders of power,
> uplifted by honor, vaunted and vaunting,
> clerks of war, merchants of peace,
> treasurers of fate, ministers and presidents
> flaunting their gaudy responsibilities.
> I see them pass over us
> like angels of the plague of the firstborn,
> their groin gaping and dripping
> a honeyed dreck like sweetened motor oil,
> and the soles of their feet clawing like the feet of Ashmedai,
> their heads up in the sky, stupid as flags.[93]

אֲבָל אֲנִי מֵרִים אֶת פָּנַי וְרוֹאֶה מֵעָלֵינוּ,
כְּמוֹ בְּחָזוֹן נוֹרָא, נוֹשְׂאֵי שְׂרָרָה,
מוּרְמֵי כָּבוֹד, נְשָׂאִים וּמִתְנַשְּׂאִים,
פְּקִידֵי מִלְחָמָה, סוֹחֲרֵי שָׁלוֹם
גִּזְבְּרֵי גוֹרָל שָׂרִים וּנְשִׂיאִים
מְקַשְׁטֵי אַחֲרָיוּת בְּשִׁלַל צְבָעִים.
אֲנִי רוֹאֶה אוֹתָם פּוֹסְחִים מֵעָלֵינוּ
כְּמוֹ מַלְאֲכֵי מַכַּת הַבְּכוֹרוֹת,
וּמִפְכָּעְתָּם פְּעוּרָה וְנוֹטֶפֶת
טִנֹּפֶת צוּפִים, כְּמוֹ שֶׁמֶן מְכוֹנוֹת מְמֻתָּק,
וְכַפּוֹת רַגְלֵיהֶם דּוֹרְסָנִיּוֹת כְּרַגְלֵי אַשְׁמְדַאי,
וְרָאשֵׁיהֶם בַּמָּרוֹם, טִפְּשִׁים כְּמוֹ דְּגָלִים.

The worried Jewish father, whose guard duty only intensifies his fear, is transformed in the poem's final stanza into a prophet of wrath (*nevi za'am*) who uses all the resources of biblical rhetoric to rail against power-hungry leaders who are portrayed as the demonic "angels of the plague of the firstborn" that keep hunting down our children. Unlike the God of Exodus who "passed over the houses of the children of Israel in Egypt" (Exodus 12:27) and would "not suffer the destroyer to come in unto [their] houses" as he was killing all the firstborn of Egypt (ibid., v. 23), these nefarious leaders "pass over us" (*poschim me-aleynu*) in the sense that they ignore our needs and our safety, as they kill both the enemy's and our own children, in pursuit of their own self-aggrandizement.[94] The Hebrew puns brilliantly here on *nos'ey srara / nisa'im u-mitnas'im / nesi'im ve-sarim*. In neo-midrashic fashion, Amichai's language creates an ethical connection between "wielding power" (*srara*) and acting "vaunted and vaunting" (*le-hitnase*) on the one hand, and being ministers and presidents (*sarim* and *nesi'im*), on the other, by pointing up their common etymologies (roots **n.s.a.**, "lift, vaunt" and **s.r.h.**, "rule"). In the poem's surreal, macabre ending, Amichai doesn't spare any rhetorical punches in order to expose the contrast between these leaders' oily rhetoric and the devastating consequences of their nationalist aggression. The Hebrew *tinofet tzufim* was a common slang idiom at the time for demagoguery, an idiom that functioned as a crass echo-pun by reversing another, much loftier idiom, the biblical *nofet tzufim*, which is based on the description of divine truth in Psalms 19:10–11 ("sweeter also than honey and the honeycomb," *KJV*). The slang idiom *tinofet tzufim* (which Chana Bloch and I have rendered as "honeyed dreck") thus refers sarcastically to cloying, manipulative rhetoric.

In the poem's final simile, Amichai relies on his special skill for mapping disparate visual image schemas onto one another in order to drive home most forcefully the poem's punch-line simile: "stupid as flags." Since the tops ("heads" in Hebrew) of flags literally fly *ba-marom* (on high; here translated as "in the sky"), and big-headed politicians who are full of themselves idiomatically walk with their heads held high or "in the sky," politicians and flags can be mapped onto each other. The antinationalist clincher is, of course, that quite apart from the coherence of the visual image schemas, flags here are presented as the epitome of stupidity. The poem's angry father-qua-prophet is fed up with the jingoistic rhetoric of those leaders he considers responsible for "the situation" (*ha-matzav*), but who wear their responsibilities like some gaudy decoration. Abandoning biblical rhetoric in favor of graphic contemporary slang yet again, he coins a phrase on the model of other then-common idiomatic similes for stupidity, similes whose wit depends on the very incongruity between the domain of the tenor and the domain of the vehicle (e.g., the expression *tipesh kmo lechem*, "stupid as bread," in the slang of the period). But the poem's angry, worried father doesn't simply take his frustrations out on the politicians; in the powerful final lines of the poem, he points an intertextually accusing finger at their criminally dangerous, even demonic inanity. Via the midrash, the leaders are seen to have clawing feet that trample anything that stands in their way (*kapot ragleyhem dorsaniyot ke-ragley Ashmedai*). This beastly bodily feature proves that even as they pretend to be great leaders like King Solomon, they are not even real human beings but reincarnations of Ashmedai, King of Demons. In the midrash, we are reminded, Ashmedai pretends to be King Solomon, and it is only through his clawing feet that he is recognized to be the dangerous Chief Demon that he is.[95]

III. Used Poet

"A National Poet? Me?"—This is the title of an interview Amichai gave journalist Edna Evron less than a year before his death.[96] Yet the appropriations go on. A series of literary events commemorating the tenth anniversary of his death, which featured some of Israel's central writers and literary critics, was named by the organizers "Eretz Israel, eretz Tziyon vi-rushalayim be-shirat Amichai" (Land of Israel, Land of Zion and Jerusalem in Amichai's Poetry).[97] Now, "Land of Israel" (*Eretz Israel*) in contemporary Hebrew is the coded name for the Greater Israel—the maximalist, territorial ideal of the nationalist rightwing, favored by the settler community and a term Amichai would never have used uncritically. "Land of Zion, Jerusalem," which appears in the title of the event as if it were a natural sequel to "Land of Israel," is both a quotation from the end of the national anthem "Ha-Tikva" (The Hope) and the sardonic title of Amichai's post–Yom Kippur War poem cycle *Shirey Eretz Tzyion Yerushalayim* (translated as "Songs of Zion the Beautiful").[98] What the title of the event constructs, then, is an outrageous analogy between the lingo of the settler nationalists, the Israeli national anthem, and Amichai's ironic quotation from that anthem in his post–1973 War poem cycle. The event's title, more importantly, asks us to forget not only the tone of this poem sequence as a whole but the fact that its speaker asserts directly: "I have nothing to say about the war, nothing / to add. I am ashamed" (section 4).[99]

To maintain a positive view of the war at all costs, as he adds in the last stanza of the same section, would be more than a hollow affirmation; it would be about as sensible and as valid as still believing that the sun orbits the earth and that the earth is flat or, for that matter, as still proclaiming the existence of God.[100] Amichai thus dispatches—through sarcastic affirmations-as-ultimate-negations—both military nationalism and theocentric religion:

> The sun goes around the earth, yes.
> The earth is flat as a lost drifting plank, yes.
> There's a God in Heaven. Yes.[101]

> הַשֶּׁמֶשׁ סוֹבֶבֶת סְבִיב הָאָרֶץ, כֵּן,
> הָאָרֶץ שְׁטוּחָה כְּלוּחַ אָבוּד וְצָף, כֵּן,
> יֵשׁ אֱלֹהִים בַּשָּׁמַיִם, כֵּן.

This poem sequence is also the very text where the speaker yearns for (*zokher be-ga'agu'im*) Jerusalem as a divided city (section 24), thus breaking what by the 1970s was becoming another national taboo. Self-consciously invoking the biblical metaphorical system of the Whore of Zion, Amichai describes the Greater Jerusalem as "The full-blown gaudy madam / with her gold and copper and stones / returning to a fat and legal life. // But I don't love her, / I remember at times the quiet one."[102] This is not to say that Amichai is anything but Jerusalem's greatest lover; nor is it to deny that in some of his post-1967 Jerusalem poems Amichai explicitly situates himself in the long tradition of poets who are "prisoners of passion" for the city, from Yehuda Ha-Levi on, as both Dan Miron and Sidra DeKoven Ezrahi have pointed out, though from very different perspectives. Thus, for example, Amichai celebrates Jerusalem as the enticing meeting place of all three monotheistic religions, paradoxically, and now famously, describing this landlocked mountain town as "God's Venice."[103] But even his most euphoric love poems to Jerusalem do not endorse the expansionist territorialism that his appropriations have systematically mobilized them for.

Despite the plain meaning of the text—and its decidedly more complex intertextual subversions—Amichai's poems are indeed regularly incorporated into official activities for *Yom Yerushalayim* (Jerusalem

Day), celebrating the city's reunification under Israeli rule in 1967, which is always an occasion for political speechifying and ceremonies of nationalist bravado.[104] The Hebrew novelist Meir Shalev angrily protested this appropriation in his popular newspaper column, in a piece titled "Jerusalem, Jerusalem," written in the wake of the fortieth Jerusalem Day celebrations.[105] He describes the "rising level of denial and *shmaltz*" in the official ceremonies, and adds with reference to the fortieth anniversary:

> As is the custom in our quarters, [the politicians in their speeches] are given to frequent quotations from poems. And as usual—the quoted poems were especially by U. Z. Grinberg[106] and Yehuda Amichai. . . . I protest against the outrageous and misleading quotations of Amichai in the ceremony. With Grinberg, wherever you cast a stone, some appropriate Jerusalem line or other is sure to shake out, filled with grandiose awe and horror. With Amichai you need to pick carefully. He might spoil the celebration. . . . And indeed they did not cite the lines [where] Amichai is filled with yearnings for the divided city, of all things.

After citing the same lines I quoted above from "Songs of Zion the Beautiful," Shalev says: "It's easy to recognize here Amichai's mocking disdain [*liglug*] for 'Jerusalem of Gold,'[107] but it's hard to grasp where they get the *chutzpa* to exploit him so selectively. Is it out of ignorance, which would be the best-case scenario, or is it an act of willful deception [*ma'ase remiya*], which would be the worst?"[108] That Shalev can write about these appropriating misreadings in a popular newspaper (*Yedi'ot Acharonot* is more or less Israel's equivalent of *USA Today*), and expect his readers to have no problem understanding either Amichai's sarcasm or his own, is symptomatic of one of the most important differences between the Israeli and the American reading cultures, a difference I will have occasion to return to below.

In the very same poem cycle, "Songs of Zion the Beautiful," the speaker expresses impatience with—if not sheer anger at—the national obsession with ritualized war commemorations that have been sacralized much like the traditional Jewish *Yizkor*, the personal memorial prayer for the dead. Yet it is this very section of the poem that has been incorporated into the Jewish American Reconstructionist *Machzor* (High Holidays prayer book) and inserted into the *Mussaf* prayer for

Yom Kippur in a special traditional section titled "*Eleh Ezkerah*,"[109] that here gets labeled as "Martyrology." The translation by Chana Bloch, which as we'll see is not the one included in the prayer book, reads:

> Let the memorial hill remember instead of me,
>   that's what it's here for. Let the park in-the-memory-of remember,
> let the street that's-named-for remember,
> let the famous building remember,
> let the synagogue that's named after God remember,
> let the rolling Torah scroll remember, let the prayer
> for the memory of the dead remember. Let the flags remember,
> those multicolored shrouds of history: the bodies they wrapped
> have long since turned to dust. Let the dust remember.
> Let the dung remember at the gate. Let the afterbirth remember.
> Let the beasts of the field and the birds of the heavens
> eat and remember.
> Let all of them remember so that I can rest.[110]

Trans. Chana Bloch

שֶׁהַר הַזִּכָּרוֹן יִזְכֹּר בִּמְקוֹמִי,

זֶה תַּפְקִידוֹ. שֶׁהַגַּן לְזֵכֶר יִזְכֹּר,

שֶׁהָרְחוֹב עַל שֵׁם יִזְכֹּר,

שֶׁהַבִּנְיָן הַיָּדוּעַ יִזְכֹּר,

שֶׁבֵּית הַתְּפִלָּה עַל שֵׁם אֱלֹהִים יִזְכֹּר,

שֶׁסֵּפֶר הַתּוֹרָה הַמִּתְגַּלְגֵּל יִזְכֹּר,

שֶׁהַיִּזְכֹּר יִזְכֹּר. שֶׁהַדְּגָלִים יִזְכְּרוּ,

הַתַּכְרִיכִים הַצִּבְעוֹנִיִּים שֶׁל הַהִיסְטוֹרְיָה, אֲשֶׁר

הַגּוּפִים שֶׁעָטְפוּ הָפְכוּ אָבָק. שֶׁהָאָבָק יִזְכֹּר.

שֶׁהָאַשְׁפָּה תִזְכֹּר בַּשַּׁעַר. שֶׁהַשִּׁלְיָה תִזְכֹּר.

שֶׁחַיַּת הַשָּׂדֶה וְעוֹף הַשָּׁמַיִם יֹאכְלוּ וְיִזְכְּרוּ,

שֶׁכֻּלָּם יִזְכְּרוּ. כְּדֵי שֶׁאוּכַל לָנוּחַ.

The translation used in the Reconstructionist *Machzor*, unlike the one by Chana Bloch published in *Selected Poetry* (which was readily available for over a decade before the publication of this High Holidays prayer book), completely blunts the poem's angrily ironic and critical tone. In the Reconstructionist *Machzor*, the poem-segment-turned-liturgy receives the wrong title as well as a sentimentalizing, pious rewriting. The

Machzor uses a grammatically mangled form of Amichai's book title as if it were the title for this excerpt. Amichai's book title, *Me-achorey kol ze mistater osher gadol,* which means "**Behind** All This a Great Happiness Is Hiding,"[111] is replaced with *Me-acharey (sic) kol ze,* "**After** All This," and turned into the name for the prayer, as if to indicate the aftermath of loss and grief, propping up its new function as part of the remembrance and martyrology section of the Yom Kippur liturgy. This rewriting erases the personal happiness that Amichai's book title embraces as a counterpoint to his political rage: the speaker's happiness following the birth of his new baby and the lovers' joy in each other's body (described in the first and last stanzas of "Shirey Eretz Tziyon Yerushalaylim"). All this "great happiness" is "hiding" **behind** (*me-achorey*) "all this" (*kol ze*)—a colloquial reference to the unbearable political situation (*ha-matzav*), which most of the opening poem sequence (including the excerpted segment included in the prayer book) explicitly condemns. The *Machzor*'s grammatical distortion erases the speaker's sense of shame and ignores his critique of what is taking place in Jerusalem after the Yom Kippur War and—most importantly—his irritation with the fetishized memorializations all around him, aimed to sanctify the war. Beyond replacing place with time ("behind" with "after"), the American prayer book supplants Amichai's critique of the Israeli here and now with the sweet mournfulness of a nostalgic backward gaze. Moreover, the segment is taken out of context with no apparent awareness of how ironic it is to single out—of all things—a poem that criticizes the politics of the Yom Kippur War for inclusion in the Yom Kippur liturgy; and to incorporate into the *Machzor*'s memorialization and *Yizkor* section excerpts in which the poem's speaker says he has no use for any of the national and religious forms of memorialization, including for the traditional *Yizkor* prayer itself (line 7). That the same poem, as we have seen, also denies—via sarcastic affirmation—the existence of God makes this selection almost ludicrous ("The sun goes around the earth, yes. / The earth is flat as a lost drifting plank, yes. / There's a God in Heaven. Yes.").[112] The mistranslation provided for the poem in the American prayer book (quoted below) performs an outright act of political censorship, erasing the angrily sarcastic tone and completely writing out the critique of martyrology in lines 7–9, as if the translators could count on their readers not to understand the

Hebrew. Framed, censored, and contained in this manner,[113] the poem can be safely inserted into the section of the Yom Kippur *Mussaf* prayer titled "Martyrs through the Ages." Seeing the Hebrew and the English side by side in the *Machzor* is a truly jarring experience for any knowledgeable reader of Amichai, or for that matter for anyone who knows Hebrew. This is how the editors of the Reconstructionist Prayer Book have translated this excerpt from Amichai's poem:

After All This/Martyrology

Let the Mount of Memory remember in my place
that is its purpose.
Let the garden in memoriam remember.
Let the street "in the name of" remember.
Let the building that is known remember.
Let the house of prayer in the name of God remember.
Let the rolled up Torah scroll remember.
Let the Yizkor prayer remember.
Let the banners of memorial remember.
Let the multicolored shrouds of history remember,
draped with fallen bodies that have turned to dust.
Let the heap of dung remember in the gate.
Let the remaining flesh remember.
Let beasts of the field and birds in the sky devour and remember.
Yes, let all of them remember,
So that I might rest.[114]

By contrast with this censored "translation," Bloch's version cited above retains Amichai's critical tone, for example by reproducing — in her use of hyphens in lines 2 and 3—the satirically ungrammatical and elliptical nominalized prepositional phrases of the original ("let the park in-the-memory-of remember"),[115] though it cannot quite render the dismissive/impatient quality of the insistent slang petitive *she-* in the Hebrew, whose valence is nothing like that of the well-formed and emotively neutral jussive "let." The Jewish prayer book, on the other hand, translates the line into the solemn, satire-free (and oddly Catholic!) line, "Let the garden *in memoriam* remember." Note also that Amichai's speaker crucially breaks off the iterative *she-* ("let") structure in the second half of the poem (starting with lines 7–9), to let the reader know explicitly the reason he is so fed up with sites and ceremonies of memorialization: they sanctify and thereby justify the massive death toll of the ongoing wars, obscuring the fact that underneath the nationalist cover of the flag lie nothing but the proverbial dust and ashes of war's victims. Bloch's translation captures the tone and meaning of the Hebrew with astonishing precision: "Let the flags remember, / those multicolored shrouds of history: the bodies they wrapped / have long since turned to dust." The *Machzor,* however, replicates in line 8 the parallel syntax of opening with "Let," which— with all the irony, rage, and satire written out of it—becomes a pious, prayer-like intoning anaphora of ever-present mourning: "Let the banners of memorial remember. / Let the multicolored shrouds of history remember." Inscrutably, in the *Machzor's* translation it is the shrouds that are "draped with fallen bodies that have turned to dust," rather than the other way around. Most importantly, the choice to translate the Hebrew *dgalim* ("flags"), the emblems of the nation-state as "banners," and then to cancel all the tensions engendered in the original by the enjambments, alters both the syntax and the poem's semantic import radically. It effectively writes out the poem's major political point, and neutralizes the macabre and surreal scene described in these central lines. The speaker in the Hebrew, refusing to valorize death in battle, forces us to look underground into the graves in a military cemetery. Amichai clearly refers here to the flags covering the coffins of fallen soldiers (for only soldiers are buried in Israel in coffins, which are then draped with flags).[116] But—as we find out at the end of this winding sentence—the bodies in these coffins have long since turned to dust, and the national symbols supposed to mark their heroic martyrdom are nothing but "those multicolored shrouds of history." History, if not the whole notion of historical truth, is thus a casualty of a flag-focused obsession with memorialization. The poem participates in the broader post-1973 Israeli political protest against the endless cycle of wars and memorialization (what Amichai refers to elsewhere as "the terrible *Chad Gadya* machine," invoking the violent lyrics of the cumulative song from the Passover Hagadah).[117] At least in this prayerbook representation of the organized American Jewish community, the Israeli left's political protest is replaced by the now-commonplace ritualized sacralization of Israel and its wars.[118]

In the process, this appropriation also flattens out one of the most profound aspects of Amichai's poetics: his deconstruction of the concept of memory. In a poem that metaphorically depicts the relationship between memory and forgetting as a canning or jam-making process (punning on the two meanings of "preserves"), Amichai's speaker asserts wryly: "the best way to preserve memory is to conserve it inside forgetting / so not even a single act of remembering will seep in / and disturb memory's eternal rest."[119] *Patu'ach sagur patu'ach* (Open Closed Open), Amichai's last book, ends with the sequence *"U-mi yizkor et ha-zokhrim"* (And Who Will Remember the Rememberers), as if to suggest his legacy for the reader was to be these variations on one of his most pivotal themes.[120] Many of the poems in the sequence express wistful empathy for the overwhelming pain of loss: "so much death in everything, so much packing and transport, / so much open that will never close again, so much closed / that will never open," subtly evoking the connection between wars and the refugee tragedy on both sides.[121]

But before focusing on unadorned, authentic, and personal expressions of loss in the final lines, most of the poems in this section start out with an unflinching critique of the ceremonial reifications of memory, exposing their emotionally manipulative and exploitative nationalist function. In poem #2 in the series, "How Does a Monument Come into Being?" Amichai lays bare the constructed, interpellative aspects of national fetishes in the Israeli secular cult of military relics.[122] Some background information may be in order here. One of the most vaunted *lieux de memoire*[123] of Israel's 1948 war is *Sha'ar Ha-gay* (Arabic, *Bab el Wad*) on the road to Jerusalem, where skeletons of armored vehicles that line the sides of the highway commemorate the Jewish convoys that were felled while trying to relieve the siege of Jerusalem.[124] What Amichai chooses to point up here is that the skeletons of the cars in *Sha'ar Ha-gay* are not genuine relics from the battles of 1948 but wrecks that were moved there much later, from car crashes in some other location, then painted and made to look like "the real thing." Like all sites of memory, *Sha'ar Ha-gay* has a constructed dimension, maintained by institutions of the state to elicit an emotional response from the public and channel it in a desired direction. Memorials and monuments are not simply the authentic raw traces of war, even if presented as such to the reverent visitor. In exposing the un-heroic origins of the cars at *Bab el Wad*, Amichai is also reminding us that Israel's number-one security risk is automobile accidents:[125]

#2

How does a monument come into being? A car goes up in a red blaze at Sha'ar Ha-gay. A car burnt black. The skeleton of a car.
And next to it, the skeleton of some other car, charred in a traffic accident
on some other road. The skeletons are painted with anti-rust paint, red like the red of that flame.[126]

אֵיךְ מִתְפַּתַּחַת מַצֵּבָה? מְכוֹנִית נִשְׂרֶפֶת בְּלֶהָבָה אֲדֻמָּה
בְּשַׁעַר הַגַּיְא. מְכוֹנִית שְׂרוּפָה שְׁחוֹרָה. שֶׁלֶד מְכוֹנִית.
שֶׁלֶד מְכוֹנִית אַחֶרֶת שֶׁנִּשְׂרְפָה בִּתְאוּנָה בְּמָקוֹם אַחֵר.
הַשֶּׁלֶד נִצְבַּע בְּצֶבַע נֶגֶד הַחֲלֻדָּה, צֶבַע אָדֹם
כְּאֹדֶם הַלֶּהָבָה הַהִיא.

Amichai treads gingerly here, making assertions in sentence fragments, not pronouncing judgment, refraining from assigning blame. But the very question that the poem poses: "How does a monument come into being?" (in Hebrew, literally, "how does a monument develop?") establishes the constructed economy of cultural practices of memorial-ization. The terse diction juxtaposes in an ironically ahistorical present the two burnt vehicles: the 1948 car is depicted as if it were going up in a red blaze in the poem's here and now, in the unchanging historical present that monuments erect in our cultural memory. It is as if the only thing distinguishing the car blown up at *Sha'ar Ha-gay* during the 1948 war from the car charred in a traffic accident some half-a-century later is place, not time: "on some other road" (the Hebrew literally reads: "in some other place"). Thus, the institutional manipu-lation of place (moving cars from accident site to war-memorial site) leads to a manipulation of time and memory. Ironically, while the 1948 car "**is burnt**" (*nisrefet*) in a red blaze, using an eternal memorial-ized present, the present-day auto accident is a matter of the forgotten past. Hebrew, which doesn't require agreement of tenses, can move freely from past to present in one sentence; thus, the Hebrew reads literally: "The skeleton of some other car that **was burnt** [*nisrefa*] in an accident in some other place."

As we have seen in the workings of the shadow text allusions in "I Want to Die in My Bed," it is what we are *not* told that may be of the greatest importance. For example, what branch of army or government is in charge of replenishing the skeletons of cars and painting them red? Who decides which wrecked cars among Israel's numerous automobile accidents are good candidates for the memorial? Here Amichai pointedly uses the wonderful gift that the Hebrew language grants to those who wish to shirk responsibility: the agentless verb pattern *nif'al*. Neither active nor passive, this middle-voice verb form allows for those who perform the action to remain anonymous. The literal translation reads: "The skeleton [of the car] **is painted** (*nitzba*) with anti-rust paint, red / like the red of that flame." But the speaker's voice is the one highlighting the analogy between the new red paint on the modern car-wreck and the original burnt remnants from the 1948 war, thereby attributing an additional manipulative purpose to the whole agentless operation: Charred cars are black, not red, he reminds us in his terse, elliptical syntax—*mekhonit srufa Schora* ("car burnt black"). But red works much better not only to prevent rust but also to construct the desirable memory and elicit an emotional response, invoking "that flame" of 1948, as well as the blood of the fallen soldiers.

The next poem in the sequence *And Who will Remember the Rememberers* describes how rituals of memorialization replace authentic grief, as ordinary people try to play by the rules of public mourning, though they can't quite figure out what is expected of them:

#3
What is the correct way to stand at a memorial ceremony?
Erect or stooped, pulled taut as a tent or in the slumped posture
of mourning, head bowed like the guilty or held high
in a collective protest against death. . . [127]

וְאֵיךְ עוֹמְדִים בְּטֶקֶס זִכָּרוֹן? זְקוּפִים אוֹ כְּפוּפִים

מְתוּחִים כְּאֹהֶל אוֹ בְּרִשּׁוּל שֶׁל אֵבֶל,

רֹאשׁ מֻשְׁפָּל כַּאֲשֵׁמִים אוֹ רֹאשׁ מוּרָם בְּהַפְגָּנָה נֶגֶד הַמָּוֶת...

Amichai has the impersonal, collective speakers of the poem ponder all their performative options (*omdim, zkufim, kfufim, metuchim*; the verbs are all plural in the stative present tense or the present agent-less-participial). They contemplate striking a whole catalogue of possible poses of grief, compare and contrast their potential semiotic impact, only to have them cancel each other out: the very fact that these options are being considered as alternative performances reveals that not one of them expresses real emotion. Within Amichai's poetic worldview, officially prescribed ceremony is bound to displace authentic individual feeling onto a self-conscious, hypocritical, and all-too-familiar desire not to violate some hierarchically sanctioned code of conduct. The institutional culture of mourning occludes true grief in focusing on social obedience rather than promoting spontaneous personal expression.

It is astonishing to find this poem numerous times, with no acknowledgment of its ironic or satirical edge, on official websites and publications of the Israeli Ministry of Education,[128] the Ministry of Defense,[129] the Ministry of Public Security;[130] as a part of community college curricula;[131] and as recommended and officially prescribed reading for the Memorial Day for the Fallen Soldiers (*yom ha-zikaron*), which precedes Israel's Independence Day celebrations. In many of these cases, the poem, like others that have been similarly incorporated into official state ceremonies, is framed paratextually by a worksheet for students or statements by politicians, which interpellate a reading that erases the poem's critique of the very ceremonies it is appropriated for. André Lefevere describes this form of paratextual framing as a process of rewriting, performed by what he calls the "outwork," namely the official texts surrounding the literary work (preface, postscript, blurb, curricular instructions and questions, decontextualizing official quotations, etc.). It is this outwork that allows even the most subversive of poems to be absorbed into the ideologically controlled discourse of the state, which is the modern replacement for the patronage system of old, and which functions, according to Lefevere's analysis, very much like censorship.[132]

I, along with my collaborator on the translation of Amichai's last book, the American poet Chana Bloch, heard a fine American actress read "What is the correct way to stand at a memorial ceremony?"

in our translation with full-blown pathos and without so much as a hint of irony. This is indeed a humbling experience for the translator. But more importantly, it is a reminder of the gap in culturally determined discursive practices between Amichai's American and Hebrew readerships and their respective modes of appropriation. While this poem, as we have seen, has been embraced and reframed by Israeli institutions of state, as well as in speeches by politicians of the type denounced in "I Guard the Children," I think the poem's ironic edge is at least recoverable for the common Israeli reader, who is often already cynically predisposed against official ceremonies and inclined to ironic, even sarcastic discourse. (This predisposition is what makes a piece like the one cited above by writer Meir Shalev printable in the "lowbrow" press.)

Israeli culture at large still practices sarcasm-as-norm, typical of what Benjamin Harshav has termed "Jewish discourse,"[133] although as Shalev suggests in his newspaper column, the tolerance for schmaltzy rhetoric is ever-increasing. Jewish discourse is characterized, inter alia, by a pronounced preference for ironic and sarcastic inversions over direct statement. Like many other discursive practices, it came to modern Israeli Hebrew from Yiddish, along with Yiddish's famous predilection for laughing at and with pain (the Yiddish expression *lakhn mit yashtcherkes*, "laughing with lizards," captures this well). But irony, sarcasm (referred to as *tziniyut*, lit., "cynicism" in modern colloquial Hebrew) as well as macabre humor have also become a common defense in Israeli culture against sentimentality and bombast. This has actually turned into both a major literary device and a common speech strategy for restraining and internalizing pathos. Even Israeli telenovellas, as Ma'ayan Sela has pointed out, exhibit a self-conscious irony.[134] Modern Israeli literature and popular culture equate pathos with nostalgic sentimentality and melodrama, and associate it with the ideologically rejected stereotypes of diasporic Jewish culture where, side by side with sarcasm, the heartfelt sigh and the excruciatingly detailed complaint (the *krekhtz* and the *kvetch*) were developed into an art form. But these rejected stereotypes are associated with the very same Yiddish culture that in fact has supplied Hebrew with its darkly ironic rhetorical strategies. Its rejection, as Dan Miron has shown, is a self-rejection, a rejection of the diasporic, Yiddish Other within us.[135] This is just a glance at the complexities of cultural negotiations that are in the background of the common Israeli readers' potential receptivity—institutional co-optation notwithstanding—to Amichai's antisentimental questioning of the most solemn collective ceremonies, whether national or religious, even in the face of wholesale appropriation. And yet, it is the more so-phisticated, left-wing young readers, ironically, who have tended in re-cent years to reject Amichai as part of their rejection of official cultural production—without, I believe, bothering either to read him closely or to look at his texts without the blinders of the educational and military indoctrination for which he has been recruited.

What a mainstream American reader often finds incomprehensible—as the actress declaiming "What is the correct way to stand" exempli-fies—is that it is precisely sacred, larger-than-life topics like the Shoah, the fallen soldiers, patriotism, and, yes, God and organized religion that are treated to the most irreverent ironic deflations in the poetry of Amichai, as they are in preassimilated, traditional Yiddish as well as modern Israeli discourse. Nevertheless, the two systems of appropria-tion sketched out above—by institutions of the state in Israel and of Jewish religion in the United States—are increasingly becoming inter-related, as shown by the fact that some of the same Amichai poems have been subjected to appropriations in both contexts, despite the plain meaning of the text and the differences in the culture of reader-ship. While an exploration of this issue would take me too far afield, let me just note that the increasing connection between nationalism and organized religion in Israel as well as the in United States is clearly what I have in mind here: the sacralization of the sovereign state in Israel, and the Israel-centered nationalization of Jewish ritual in the United States. Obviously, there are numerous countervoices both here and there. After all, Amichai's poetry is also being taught critically at universities, read at peace demonstrations in Israel, and embraced in feminist, gay, and progressive alternative Jewish cultural and religious organizations in the United States. However, I think it is important to underscore especially for the American reader that Amichai is not by any means the Sweet Singer of Israel (*Ne'im zmirot Yisrael*) packaged and sold in the United States.

American readers who have no Hebrew may tend to be less aware es-pecially of the ironic tone and critical edge in Amichai's use of religious

discourse, both of which would be immediately apparent to an edu-
cated Israeli audience. Thus his poems may become incorporated into
synagogue ritual and prayer, even when it is the exclusionary practice of
that very ritual and prayer that the poem is militating against. It is both
poignant and ironic that this incorporation brings Amichai's poetry full-
circle back to its origins in the synagogue of his childhood.[136] But this
incorporation is now facilitated by the opening up of some sectors of the
American Jewish community to embrace practices and discursive formations that are unorthodox in both senses of the term, while renewing
the age-old commitment to textual study.[137] However, Amichai's sardonic and critical tone, indeed his strong anticlerical politics, have often
been ignored so that his poems could be claimed as "ours." Such an appropriation depends for its success on the ever-diminishing knowledge
of Jewish textual sources by Amichai's American reading community,
because it is the ironic reversals of these intertexts that Amichai's poems
perform consistently, from his first 1955 book *Akhshav u-va-yamim
ha-acherim* (Now and in Other Days) to his last *Patu'ach sagur patu'ach*
(*Open Closed Open*), published in 1998. But in the United States, the
mere fact that the poems frequently mention God and quote the Bible
and the prayer book seems to qualify him as a synagogue poet, indeed
as a true believer.

Again, as with the nationalist appropriations of Amichai's work,
turning him into a religious poet requires a degree of defensiveness that
cannot be explained merely by ordinary readers' lack of familiarity with
the sources, or perhaps by the mainstream white American (as opposed
to British) tendency to shy away from sarcasm. However, I believe that
despite even the most undifferentiated of appropriations, Amichai's
poetry—framed, filtered, excerpted, and mediated—remains powerful
enough to have a radicalizing, even revolutionary effect. On many occasions I have witnessed the ordinary or uncritical synagogue-goer stop
and think about the true meaning of the words in the prayers, from
"El maleh rachamim" ("O God Full of Mercy") to "Avinu malkenu"
("Our Father, Our King"),[138] following an encounter with Amichai's
critique of their language and import. Prompted by a close reading of
the poems that take up these vaunted prayers, these readers are now
able to observe the careful, almost systematic dismantling of the theo-

logical and—more importantly—the theocratic framework that the prayers have come to stand for. Here I can only give a number of small examples. Poem #7 in the series of poems that constitutes Amichai's most sustained counter-theology,[139] "Gods Change, Prayers Are Here to Stay" in *Open Closed Open*, takes on one of the most sacred and most familiar of prayers, "Avinu malkenu" ("Our Father, Our King"):

"Our Father, Our King." What does a father do
when his children are orphans and he
is still alive? What will a father do
when his children have died and he becomes
a bereaved father for all eternity? Cry
and not cry, not forget and not remember.
"Our Father, Our King." What does a king do
in the republic of pain? Give them
bread and circuses like any king,
the bread of memory and the circuses of forgetting,
bread and nostalgia. Nostalgia for God-
and-a-better-world. "Our Father, Our King." [140]

אָבִינוּ מַלְכֵּנוּ. מָה עוֹשֶׂה אָב

שֶׁיְּלָדָיו הֵם יְתוֹמִים בְּעוֹדוֹ חַי ? מַה יַּעֲשֶׂה אָב

שֶׁיְּלָדָיו מֵתוּ וְהוּא יִהְיֶה אָב שַׁכּוּל לְנֶצַח נְצָחִים ?

יִבְכֶּה וְלֹא יִבְכֶּה, לֹא יִשְׁכַּח וְלֹא יִזְכֹּר.

אָבִינוּ מַלְכֵּנוּ. מָה עוֹשֶׂה מֶלֶךְ

בָּרֶפּוּבְּלִיקָה שֶׁל הַכְּאֵבִים ? יִתֵּן לָהֶם

לֶחֶם וְשַׁעֲשׁוּעִים, כְּמוֹ כָּל מֶלֶךְ,

לֶחֶם הַזִּכָּרוֹן וְשַׁעֲשׁוּעֵי הַשִּׁכְחָה.

לֶחֶם וְגַעְגּוּעִים. גַּעְגּוּעִים לֵאלֹהִים

וּלְעוֹלָם טוֹב יוֹתֵר. אָבִינוּ מַלְכֵּנוּ.

This poem poignantly unpacks two central metaphors for God in mono-theistic religion as they co-occur in one very famous Jewish prayer. The "Avinu malkenu" prayer is recycled through religious services year-round, but it is best known as the prayer said during the ten Days of Awe between Rosh Hashanah and Yom Kippur. Amichai's poem ex-poses a profound inconsistency between two foundational metaphorical systems, GOD AS KING and GOD AS FATHER,[141] and suggests how absurdly inappropriate both metaphors are for our godless world. The GOD AS FATHER metaphor, which is taken apart in the first half of the poem, entails either the image of a living father whose children are orphans (which logically undermines the assertion that there is a God);[142] or a father whose children are dead but who is himself condemned to eternal bereavement because, as a god, he cannot die (which radically reverses the metaphor in Lamentations and the midrash Lamentations Rabbah, where Israel is the widow). There is quite a bit of pathos here, though not without its own macabre twists of Jewish logic; when God is brought down to earth, he can at least be a half-sympathetic metaphor. But none of that sympathy remains in the critique of the second metaphor, GOD AS KING, which is also part of Amichai's more general struggle against all forms of authoritarianism. The question: "What does a king do / in the republic of pain" can be read as both a rhetorical and a real question. In the rhetorical reading, it comes to mean something like: "What's a king *doing* in the republic of pain?"—human pain is the great equalizer that renders the theocratic metaphor completely irrelevant. But "what does a king do / in the republic of pain?" also marks a true question about the machinations of power, to which the rest of the poem provides the bitter, sharply critical answer: conflating the proverbial God and Caesar, Amichai's brilliant wordplay links together the authorities' bread and circuses (Hebrew *lechem ve-sha'ashu'im*) with the manipulated ordinary people's hopes for religious or national redemption (*lechem ve-ga'agu'im*, literally "bread and yearnings"). The Hebrew makes it clear through the rhyming echo of the original expression's *sha'ashu'im* with its nostalgic surrogate *ga'agu'im* that the yearnings are nothing but part of the distraction (lit., the entertainment) provided by the powers that be. The poem comes very close here to reiterating Marx's definition of religion as opium for the masses, and provides an incisive analysis of how messianic hopes of any kind, including the socialist-Zionist "yearning for a better world" and its increasingly theocratic-nationalist inflections, are used to manipulate history—the selective constructions of collective memory and collective forgetting—in the human "republic of pain."

Amichai's sarcasm is at its sharpest when religion meets nationalism, but this is precisely also where the irreverence of Jewish discourse may make the poem unreadable for audiences trained on sanctifying not only God but also Zionism. Amichai starts his poetic counter-theology in *Open Closed Open* with a dismantling of theo-logic, suggesting via a neo-midrashic wordplay that Zionism is no substitute for a theology either, though Israel has come to replace God in the modern Jewish imagination. Punning on Herzl's first name, Theodor, Amichai takes a quick swipe at the subject, portraying the Father of Zionism as a child called home from the scrappy playground of young European nation-states:

> . . . Theo, Theo, come home Theo,
> don't stay there with the bad boys,
> Theo, Theo, lo! Gee.[143]

> בּוֹא הַבַּיְתָה תֵיאוֹ . . .
>
> אַל תִּשָּׁאֵר עִם יְלָדִים רָעִים,
> תֵיאוֹ תֵיאוֹ, לוֹג, יָה יָה יָה.

✳

As I will demonstrate throughout this book, the speaker in Amichai's poetry openly declares his atheism, making explicit his rejection of religious faith as well as of all other institutionally sanctioned and regulated ideologies. *Ha-ani ha-lo ma'amin sheli,* he calls it, in a resonant triple-take: "My 'I do not believe,'" "My non-credo," and "My non-believing self."[144] In numerous poems throughout his career Amichai iconoclastically upends not only complex biblical and rabbinic precepts, whose recognition would require expert scholarly deciphering, but even the most familiar of Bible stories and liturgies. But atheism for Amichai does not equal opposition to other people's personal faith. Indeed, Amichai's counter-theology differs in principal ways from the standard secular Israeli antireligious stance. It is the unholy alliance of clericalism and nationalism, rather than personal struggles of faith, that his poetry targets.[145] It is highly ironic, therefore, that his poetry has been subjected to the same clerical and nationalist manipulations that it exposes. In order to take back Amichai's words, the words I feel we need now for our ethical survival, I hope this book will open up a critical dialogue within

and between the Hebrew and the American reading communities about
Amichai as an "anti-political political poet," to quote Benjamin Harshav.[146] Reappropriating Yehuda Amichai's poetry will require reading it
through the lens of its oppositionality, a lens that his official literary reception has caused to fog up. Ironically, subversively, and yet quite literally and openly, Amichai calls this oppositionality "the language of love."

Poem #1 in the series titled "The Language of Love and Tea with
Roasted Almonds" in Amichai's last book both reflects and calls into
question the categories of gender and identity—man and woman,
the individual and the collective—as well as the authority and singularity of God. Like several of the seminal poems in his last volume,
which articulate Amichai's poetic and ethical legacy, this poem goes
beyond critique to provide a utopian—and therefore necessarily surreal—vision of an earthly divine that embodies and celebrates human
multiplicity:

> *Layla*, night, the most feminine of all things, is masculine
> in Hebrew, but it is also the name of a woman.
> Sun is masculine and sunset feminine,
> the memory of the masculine in the feminine, and the yearning
> of a woman in a man. That is to say: the two of us, that is to say: we.
> And why is *Elohim*, God, in the plural? Because All of Him
> are sitting in the shade under a canopy of vines in Akko,
> playing cards. And we sat at a table nearby and I held your hand
> and you held mine instead of cards, and we too
> were masculine and feminine, plural and singular,
> and we drank tea with roasted almonds, two tastes
> that didn't know each other and became one in our mouth.
> And over the café door, next to the sky, it said:
> "Not Responsible for Items Forgotten or Lost."[147]

לַיְלָה, הַדָּבָר הַנָּשִׁי בְּיוֹתֵר הוּא בְּלָשׁוֹן זָכָר

אֲבָל הוּא גַּם שֵׁם אִשָּׁה. יוֹם הוּא זָכָר וִימָמָה נְקֵבָה

זֵכֶר זָכָר בַּנְּקֵבָה וּכְמִיהַת אִשָּׁה בָּאִישׁ.

כְּלוֹמַר שְׁנֵינוּ, כְּלוֹמַר אֲנַחְנוּ.

וּמַדּוּעַ אֱלֹהִים הוּא בְּלָשׁוֹן רַבִּים, כִּי הוּא יוֹשְׁבִים בְּצֵל

סֻכַּת גְּפָנִים

בְּעַכּוֹ וּמְשַׂחֵק קְלָפִים וּמְשַׂחֲקִים. וַאֲנַחְנוּ יָשַׁבְנוּ
בְּשָׁלְחָן קָרוֹב וְהֶחֱזַקְתִּי אֶת יָדֵךְ וְהֶחֱזַקְתְּ אֶת יָדִי
בִּמְקוֹם קְלָפִים וְגַם אֲנַחְנוּ הָיִינוּ זָכָר וּנְקֵבָה וְרַבִּים וְיָחִיד
וְשָׁתִינוּ תֵּה עַל שְׁקֵדִים קְלוּיִּים, שְׁנֵי טְעָמִים
שֶׁלֹּא יָדְעוּ זֶה אֶת זֶה וְהָיוּ לְאֶחָד בְּפִינוּ.
וּמֵעַל לַדֶּלֶת שֶׁל בֵּית הַקָּפֶה, לְיַד הַשָּׁמַיִם הָיָה כָּתוּב
"לֹא אַחֲרָאִים לַחֲפָצִים נִשְׁכָּחִים וְלִדְבָרִים שֶׁאָבְדוּ".

Every Hebrew noun, masculine or feminine, can be construed as male or female—and is thus a potential personification. The poem starts with a challenge that is typical of Amichai's special fondness for "precision" and grammatical "dryness":[148] a meditation on the most familiar rules—and exceptions to the rule—of the Hebrew noun system. *Layla* ("night") belongs to a group of irregular nouns that are masculine, though they have the feminine ending *-ah*. By choosing a seemingly androgynous form, which contains both masculine and feminine, Amichai can suggest in a single word "the memory of the masculine in the feminine, and the yearning / of a woman in a man." Tweaking Hebrew grammar in order to advance an unstable notion of gender and sexuality and to create a new "language of love," the text's philosophical complexity and the richness of its sound pattern make poetry out of grammar. Morphological reduplication and syllabic reiteration reverberate throughout the first three lines, performing a prosodic thematization of coupling as lovemaking: *yom-yemama, zekher-zakhar, isha-ish*. In an interview with me Amichai reflected on how problematic the relation between language and gender can be, and then said: "All of us have both feminine and masculine elements in our body and soul. That's the way it is with language too."[149] In the process of forging this new language, all the old dichotomies are contested, including that between singular and plural, the human and the divine. The Hebrew *Elohim* (God) has a plural ending even though it usually takes a singular verb (but can at times take a plural adjective, as in *elohim acherim*, biblical Hebrew for "other gods").

Amichai revives the dormant (pagan) plural potential as a way of invoking in a single phrase the One and the Many, multiplying God only in order to bring Him down to earth: "And why is *Elohim*, God, in the plural? Because All of Him / are sitting in the shade under a canopy of vines in Akko, / playing cards." The literal meaning of the Hebrew—*hu yoshvim*, "He [singular] are sitting [plural]"—is blatantly ungrammatical, and reminiscent of the most radical postmodernist ruptures of the unity of the lyrical subject. For Amichai, however, it is the monotheistic god, not the poet, that is the ungrammatical, split subject. By the logic of the grammatical metaphor, *Elohim* ends up as a group of men playing cards in an outdoor café. We have come a long way from the all-powerful monotheistic God of Jewish tradition. The fact that Akko is a binational city, and the tea in question is a local Palestinian specialty, subtly suggests a metaphorical mapping of the plural—one God onto the card-playing Palestinian Israeli or Jewish Israeli men. There are, therefore, profound and unavoidably political and theological implications to the poem's meditation on the fluidity of grammatical distinctions.

Ultimately, then, the language of love makes possible the most subtle, exquisitely nuanced of political lyrics. The poem articulates an embodied politics of place and time (Akko, day and night), of the Middle Eastern place and time *as* sensual making-sense. *Layla*, the Hebrew masculine noun, is also an Arabic name of a woman, and it is a word that performs the doubleness of its identity in the morphological doubling of *la* flanking a central "y" (where the *yud* traditionally stands for God). The sensual textures of life in the binational city of Akko, its tastes and smells, are invoked but must elicit a culturally situated reading in order to make the new language of love meaningful. Here again the political edge is much more likely to be dulled for the American reader. The Israeli reader would easily see, for example, that Amichai is referring to the Arab section of the city, perhaps even recognize which outdoor café serves tea with roasted almonds (which had been soaked in rose water) under a canopy of vines. This is the setting for the coming together of self and other, as the special tastes "that didn't know each other" become one in the lovers' mouths. The combined focus on the mouth (eating the almonds/drinking the tea/kissing) is ultimately the sensual symbol for the language of love as the language of peace: a meeting of opposites that doesn't erase their separate identities (just as the roasted almonds suffuse the tea with their aroma and vice versa, but neither melts into the other). This poem, then, is the ultimate illustration of the subtle political workings of lyrical form. For while the word "Arab" or "Palestinian" is never mentioned in the text, it permeates the poem's texture from the very first word (*Layla*), pointing up that ultimately the language of love may bridge the oppositions not only of male/female, singular/plural, and divine/human but also of Arab/Jew. It is precisely this dismantling of all binary oppositions and the privileging of the space in-between them (*beynayim*) that forms the major philosophical principle of Amichai's poetic system. We are now, I think, in a better position to understand it, as well as to realize why the very existence of such a system needed to be denied in order for Amichai to be appropriated in the ways that he has been.

Two   "In the Narrow Between"
Amichai's Poetic System

A between of eyes, between waking and sleep.
A twilight betweenlight, not day and not night.
                              —Yehuda Amichai, "Beynayim"[1]

I. Reception History:
The Bias against Amichai's Poetic Philosophy

Contrary to common critical opinion, I believe that Amichai's poetry
presents a coherent poetic worldview, indeed an open-ended poetic
and philosophical system, which informs both the thematics and the
stylistics of his oeuvre. In this chapter I examine an array of systematic
correlations between his philosophy and rhetorical practices, culminating in the concept of *beynayim* or "in-between-ness" as the principle
underlying his work. I challenge accepted critical appraisals of Amichai
as a merely playful poet who writes "easy," unstructured though en-
joyable poems. These appraisals may in fact be the self-marginalizing
consequences of Amichai's poetic egalitarianism, which he describes as
his "postcynical humanism";[2] of his lifelong commitment to "write as a
person, not as a poet";[3] and of his definition of the work of the poet as
"the wisdom of camouflage / so that I won't stand out."[4] This artistic
anti-elitism, expressed as we have seen in the later poetry in the image
of a metapoetic camouflage, is rendered in his early poetry through
similes drawn from the natural world that present both the poet's
mode of writing and his mode of being-in-the-world as concretiza-
tions of the refusal to "stand out": he is like unremarkable and inconspicuous blades of grass or drops of rain, and "Not Like a Cypress"
(the title of one of his seminal early works).[5] Amichai may have been   81
too successful in conveying this anti-elitist rhetorical impression, and
the success of his rhetoric is ironically responsible for the misconceptions (prevalent especially in Israel) that he has no poetic ontology to
speak of. This, I think, may be the origin of the entrenched notion

that Amichai's poetry is mere linguistic play, and that as a poet he "lacks a worldview" or is "incapable of any metaphysical thinking," as some Hebrew critics would have it.[6] These views, I argue, mistake the rhetorical impression that Amichai's poetic persona is invested in creating for the philosophical content and aesthetic structure of the oeuvre itself.

By now, however, these misconceptions have become the norm. As a result many readers familiar with his poetry may wonder about the subtitle of my chapter: Amichai's poetic system? This lively, "easy" poet has a system? The poet for whom ideas are game pieces, and objects in the world are just "color blocks you can . . . rearrange at will, without too much concern for broadening our knowledge"[7]—are we talking about the same Amichai? Ever since the first reviews of Amichai's poetry appeared in the early 1950s, the predominant opinion in the critical literature has been, with few exceptions,[8] that his poetry is not only devoid of any philosophical systematicity but also that, as a poet, he is not given to thinking at all (*hu eyno hogeh machshavot klal*).[9]

It is important to note that this view is shared by fans and detractors alike. Indeed, sometimes Amichai's greatest admirers are in the biggest rush to accept the playful ease and readability of his poetry at face value. One can almost hear them sigh in relief: here, at long last, is a great contemporary poet who does not subject the reader to the infamous difficulty and gravitas associated with high modernism. Glenda Abramson regards Amichai as "one of [Israel's] most sensitive and perceptive literary observers," a "master poet" with "a poetic finger firmly on the twentieth-century pulse." In the conclusion to her book-length critical study of Amichai, the only English-language monograph on his work to date, she writes, "His writing presents no world-view, nor does he proceed from an identifiable system of thought."[10]

The solidification of Amichai's reception is related, I believe, to the inseparability of evaluative and descriptive criticism in the Hebrew republic of letters. The journalistic review or *retzenzya* has traditionally played an important role in canon formation within Israeli literary culture. In time, normative labels expressing the rejection of Amichai's radically innovative poetics by reviewers of the old guard have become the basis for supposedly value-free critical clichés about his work. Thus, it may be significant that the notion that Amichai's poetry presents no worldview first came into vogue in the 1950s and 60s, during the Statehood Generation poets' bitter ideological and aesthetic struggle for dominance in the literary field. Ironically, early reviewers' attacks on Amichai do not acknowledge his ambivalent position vis-à-vis his own circle of young Statehood Generation poets, an ambivalence I discuss in greater detail in chapter 6, and they treat him as a typical representative of a "valueless" new wave. The critical establishment of the time was affiliated either with 1948 Generation poets (called *dor ha-palmach*, the "Palmach Generation," or *dor ba-aretz*, "a Generation in the Land"), or with the older guard of the Russian-inspired *moderna*, take Amichai's poetic persona to be the spokesman of the individualist, "westernizing" young Israelis, who commit cultural sins against Hebraism, socialism, and Zionism by embracing Anglo-American formations of modernism. Like their alienated capitalist counterparts, they have nothing but an "empty spirit that shows off its emptiness and *lacks any worldview*."[11]

An examination of the language of the early Israeli reviews of Amichai's poetry benefits from knowing that in the context of the period, to "lack a worldview" meant something quite specific. In the critical and cultural discourse of the 1950s and 60s the phrase served as a coded reference to works that challenged—or simply ignored—any of the dominant ideological trends, be they nationalist nativism, socialist Zionism, or traditionalist Judaism. The unacknowledged conceptual slippage was ubiquitous: any *critique of ideology*, which from the first has been the basic stance of Amichai's poetics, was seen as a lack of *idealism* and, ultimately, as the absence of *ideas*. In the 1950s and 60s, Amichai was indeed one of the first to give poetic voice to what came to be described in the lingo of the younger generation at large as "adding quotation marks to Zionism" (*tziyonut be-merkha'ot*), turning "Zionism" into a synonym in the Israeli slang of the period for ideological indoctrination or any boring, preachy, and didactic verbiage. Thus, for example, in an early poem Amichai invokes the leaders' tendency to speechify, expressed in the common neologism of the time, *na'emet*, from the root *n.'a.m.*, "to lecture" or "orate," a lexical innovation that follows the grammatical pattern of disease names (something like "speechifitis").[12]

A resurgence of the attacks on Amichai in the 1970s and 80s was linked, I believe, to the rise of a new generation of postmodern Hebrew poets, some of whom wished to return to a Jewish nationalist or nativist literary philosophy. A younger generation of reviewers (among them poets who—unlike Amichai—had not managed to gain international visibility) adopted much of the early critics' stance against Amichai, accusing him, as the poet Menachem Ben did, of creating "an anti-intellectual, anti-metaphysical" "flattening of the world," or of being trapped in a "small, lackluster egotism" that leads quite easily to "contempt . . . for the whole history of Israeli heroism."[13] Ben gives expression here to the new wave of nationalist nativism and its rejection of Amichai's antiwar poetics. Even more reminiscent of the critics of the 1950s and 60s is ultranationalist critic Ortzion Bartana, who, in a long series of attacks on Amichai, claimed that "by his nature, which reflects the nature of his period, he is incapable of achieving any metaphysical thinking," and that his poetry is the central marker of the philosophical void, the "absence of ideation [*choser ha-ide'iyut*] of Israeli poetry, of Israeli culture."[14]

In the wake of the 1977 *Mahapakh* (the overturning) in the Israeli government, which routed Labor and brought the right-wing Likud Party into power for the first time, these neonationalist poets were increasingly challenged by a newly dominant group of young left-wing oppositional poets. By then, however, the official appropriation of Amichai's poetry and its incorporation into state rituals of commemoration and ideological interpellation had made him increasingly unpopular—for diametrically opposite reasons—with these younger leftist poets and intellectuals who didn't distinguish between the work and its statist co-optation. It was Dahlia Ravikovitch rather than Amichai who ended up becoming the "proleptic paragon" from among the old guard of the Statehood Generation for many of the younger poets' return to the political in the late 1970s.[15] Yitzhak Laor is one important exception. Perhaps the foremost—and most critical!—among the political poets who gained prominence during that period, Laor has nevertheless embraced Amichai as a poetic model and has resisted the nationalist appropriation of his poetry.[16] A similar resistance to the co-optation of Amichai is evinced in the poetry and poetics of Ronny Someck and the fiction of Anton Shammas.[17]

It is ironic, though not altogether surprising, that Amichai should have become at once one of the most canonical and most attacked of Israeli poets. After all, tensions between marginalization and canonization are essential to the very life of the literary field, and these tensions often center around the reception of a generational paragon. What is more remarkable, however, is that both normative reviews and purportedly descriptive scholarly accounts have persisted in maintaining that Amichai is not a "poet of thought," and that his being a *poeta ludens* somehow precludes his being a *poeta sapiens*. How could this have come about when, as Boaz Arpali points out, "almost every poem by Amichai [is a statement about the] general human condition, . . . [and] Amichai, in a certain sense, is always a philosophical poet"?[18] Moreover, how could the impression that Amichai's poetry expresses no philosophy have been preserved even in the face of his later poetry, in which he spells out the major terms of his conceptual system with increasing directness, taking care to describe the ways in which ontological and rhetorical principles match and motivate each other?

The puzzle of this persistent impression is, as I have suggested above, itself a key to Amichai's philosophical system; the popularity of the view that Amichai has no poetic worldview reveals, quite paradoxically, the workings of the rhetorical and philosophical principles whose very existence this view denies. Amichai was simply too adept at producing a new prototype of the mundane poet, "an Everyman" or "the man with the shopping bags."[19] As writer and educational philosopher Chayim Nagid shrewdly observed in 1983, at the height of the Israeli critical attacks on Amichai:

> A middle-aged Jerusalem poet puts on a mask of a middle-aged Jerusalem poet, acts [in the poems] in familiar everyday circumstances and writes poetry whose explicit poetics abolishes the divisions between the mundane and the poetic. Should we wonder, then, if a critic who has lost respect for this poetic worldview tries to correct the poet's own impressions and pass judgment on his experiences for him, according to a value system that belongs to a different world? Paradoxically, this situation isn't just part of the bullying spirit [*avirat ha-kasach*] of our society at large, but is also an immanent consequence of the new poetics, heralded by the central figure of Yehuda Amichai.[20]

In Jewish literary history, this central issue of the stature and persona of the poet and his or her relation to the reading public often differentiates poetic worldviews from each other, and marks various periods or trends.[21] Amichai's construct of the populist poet reacts against both Bialik's romanticist image of the poet as a prophet who castigates his people, and Avraham Shlonsky's early modernist persona of the poet as a linguistic wizard who charms and transforms the socialist-Zionist collective for which he is a self-appointed spokesman. As Amichai himself has described it, his poetic stance is a reaction against any form of "aristocratization of art."[22] Yet because of the minimized role of the poet qua poet in his philosophical system, and his preference for a matrilineal, nonbelligerent model of intergenerational dynamics, Amichai is not interested in taking on his literary forebears directly, as Zach took on Natan Alterman and Shlonsky, in his day, took on Bialik. To do so would require him to transform himself too dramatically and self-consciously into one of "art's generals."[23] Instead, Amichai stresses—in typically autobiographical terms—his own transitional stance between two generations.

II. "My Divided Fate"

In the 1968 lecture titled "Dorot ba-aretz," which I mentioned in the Introduction (lit., "Generations in the Land"), Amichai says:

> My divided fate [*gorali ha-mefulag*[24]] has willed it so that I should be planted between two generations, a sort of "double agent" [*meragel kaful*], for "biographically" I belong to that generation—British Army, struggle, smuggling in weapons and immigrants, Palmach, three or four wars—whereas "literarily" I belong to the generation of writers [*dor ha-kotvim*] which came later in the 1950s. I identified with the trend toward a different kind of writing: a feel for everyday language, for concrete experiences.[25]

The title of the lecture changes the singular *dor ba-aretz* (a generation in the land) used to name the group of 1948 social-realist writers in the normative literary historiography, into the plural *dorot ba-aretz* (generations in the land). This in itself suggests a historiographic multiplicity of perspectives alien to the dominant 1948 narrative. That dominant narrative was invested in its own exclusivity, constructing an equation between the elite Palmach troops of the 1948 war and a nativist notion of place, of "being-in-the-land." In changing *dor ba-aretz* into the plural, Amichai is also calling into question the singularity of generational affiliation, implying that *dor ba-aretz*, with its nation-building ethos and antimodernist poetics, does not have a monopoly on the historiographic narrative of the period. Furthermore, he positions himself humorously, but with a rather flagrant subversiveness, as a politically suspect "double-agent," situated in between—and able to spy on— two generations. Thus he is someone who can observe and comment on the official ethos of either generation but shouldn't be expected— or trusted—to express it "from within." In the speech Amichai goes on to discuss the poets of the 1950s and 60s, the ones he feels "literarily" rather than "biographically" closer to, but only insofar as their use of ordinary language and concrete experience is concerned. Clearly, as we have seen in chapter 1, he does not adhere to the Statehood Generation's normative construal as a group of "apolitical" poets. Again, the diction he uses to describe this group is telling: while they are usually referred to as *meshorerey dor ha-mdina* (Statehood Generation poets), Amichai addresses them here as *dor ha-kotvim*, literally "the generation of those who write," as opposed to *dor ha-sofrim* (the generation of writers) or *dor ha-meshorerim* (the generation of poets). This highly unusual nomenclature deflates earlier maximalist views of the poet as possessing special gifts, or even as practicing writing as a profession, and promotes an orientation toward writing as an ordinary, "physical," and concrete action—the work of writing. Thus, moving from *dor ha-meshorerim* to *dor ha-kotvim* adds a metapoetic dimension to the sociopoetic critique of historiography implied by the title. On the background of these two rearticulations of the notion of the literary generation(s), Amichai's self-depiction as a "double-agent" (*sokhen kaful*) stands out even more, especially when read in the context of subsequent nationalist appropriations of his poetry described above, and against the historical context of the delivery of this speech: on the heels of the 1967 war, and the then-new Occupation of Palestinian lands, to which Amichai was strongly opposed.[26]

What Amichai describes here simply as an accident of his "divided" or "bifurcated" "fate," or as the tensions between his "biographic" and "literary" affiliations (note that the quotation marks are his!), becomes a central ontological and rhetorical principle of his poetics: defining human existence in general, and the poet's position in particular, as forever in a state of *beynayim*, of being-in-between. At once deflating and engaging in the process of changing the model of the poet, Amichai's poetry and his explicit statements about poetics construct an alternative system whose most deceptively simple formations are a series of equivalences: between the poet and the ordinary person; between poetic language and ordinary language; and between the reading public and the poet's immediate or intimate community (family, friends, fellow soldiers, lovers). This is why, as the late Warren Bargad has observed, while "reading Amichai's poems one often has the feeling of reading a diary without days, a record of someone's personal impressions or intellectual musings, set down at random." Bargad felicitously relates this general effect to four of Amichai's central rhetorical strategies: "the quasi-autobiographical voice," "the aphoristic nature of many of his lines," "the patently casual, candid tone," and finally the creation of "sequence through seemingly disjuncted images or metaphors."[27] But the crucial terms here are "quasi-," "patently," and "seemingly": these are Amichai's rhetorical strategies aimed at creating an effect that thematizes the central principles of his poetic philosophy. Amichai's poetry reveals a conceptual interdependence between these and (many) other formations, an interdependence that is responsible for both the consistency of his system and its self-effacing rhetorical impression.[28] But it is important to recognize that this aesthetic effect is aimed at giving ethical priority to ordinary language and the struggles of ordinary human beings.

In its egalitarian commitment to the perception of the poet as Everyman, Amichai's poetry employs a general *rhetoric of autobiography*, described in my Introduction, and rearticulated here only insofar as it relates to his larger philosophical system. Amichai's proto-postmodernist, self-referential uses of autobiography blur the traditional distinctions between poetic and prosaic, fictional and nonfictional, written word and oral discourse. Many of the poems appear to be composed in this problematized, often contradictory "metagenre," using autobiography to veil and realistically motivate any philosophical generalization or metapoetic thematization. Both genre and tone suggest that the poems are nothing more than the attempts of one ordinary man to come to terms with his quotidian experiences.

The famous counter-aphorisms in Amichai's heretical poem "El maleh rachamim" (lit., "God Filled with Mercy") depict a world—and a God—that are devoid of compassion or mercy, and assert—quite misleadingly!—that the poetic subject uses "only a few of the words in the dictionary." These aphoristic reflections are presented as the personal conclusions and self-criticism of a mock-heroic speaker ("King of Salt," *melekh ha-melach,* line 8 in Hebrew; line 7 in English), a citizen-soldier who has carried corpses from the battlefield on his back (line 6 in Hebrew; line 5 in English) but could only respond to the crises of history by standing indecisively at the window (line 9 in Hebrew; line 8 in English)—seeing everything but doing nothing about it.[29]

O God Full of Mercy

If God were only not so full of mercy
There would be mercy in the world, not just in Him.
I, who used to gather flowers on the mountain
And gaze at all the valleys,
I, who carried corpses down from the hills,
Can tell you: the world is empty of mercy.

I, who was King of Salt by the sea,
Who stood undecided at my window,
Who used to count the footsteps of angels,
Whose heart lifted pain-weights
In those terrible competitions,
I, who use only a small part
Of the words in the dictionary;

I, who must solve riddles in spite of myself,
Know that if God were only not so full of mercy
There would be mercy in the world
And not just in Him.

Trans. Chana Bloch and Chana Kronfeld[30]

אֵל מָלֵא רַחֲמִים

אֵל מָלֵא רַחֲמִים,
אִלְמָלֵא הָאֵל מָלֵא רַחֲמִים
הָיוּ הָרַחֲמִים בָּעוֹלָם וְלֹא רַק בּוֹ.
אֲנִי, שֶׁקָּטַפְתִּי פְּרָחִים בָּהָר
וְהִסְתַּכַּלְתִּי אֶל כָּל הָעֲמָקִים,

אֲנִי, שֶׁהֲבֵאתִי גְּוִיּוֹת מִן הַגְּבָעוֹת,
יוֹדֵעַ לְסַפֵּר שֶׁהָעוֹלָם רֵיק מֵרַחֲמִים.

אֲנִי שֶׁהָיִיתִי מֶלֶךְ הַמֶּלַח לְיַד הַיָּם,
שֶׁעָמַדְתִּי בְּלִי הַחְלָטָה לְיַד חַלּוֹנִי,
שֶׁסָּפַרְתִּי צַעֲדֵי מַלְאָכִים,
שֶׁלִּבִּי הֵרִים מִשְׁקָלוֹת כְּאֵב
בַּתַּחֲרֻיּוֹת הַנּוֹרָאוֹת.
אֲנִי, שֶׁמִּשְׁתַּמֵּשׁ רַק בְּחֵלֶק קָטָן
מִן הַמִּלִּים שֶׁבַּמִּלּוֹן.

אֲנִי, שֶׁמֻּכְרָח לִפְתּוֹר חִידוֹת בְּעַל כָּרְחִי
יוֹדֵעַ כִּי אִלְמָלֵא הָאֵל מָלֵא רַחֲמִים
הָיוּ הָרַחֲמִים בָּעוֹלָם
וְלֹא רַק בּוֹ.

Writing in 1998, the poet Mordekhai Geldman states: "It seems that the first three lines of this poem have become in recent years Hebrew poetry's most quoted lines," often used by bereaved families to voice bitter protest and a refusal to accept their loved ones' death as an expression of divine justice. In this context, the lines suggest that "there is no God and [thus] no merciful God, and no mercy in the world, for the dead are lying here before us."[31] This common citational practice is evidence that the crushing force of Amichai's lines, with their untranslatable pun, remains accessible to common speakers of Hebrew. Indeed, the iconoclastic counter-theological positions in the opening lines of the poem get their punch from a pseudo-midrashic wordplay whose intertext is commonly known to Jewish readers. There is therefore no elitist effect in the speaker's exegetical punning. Rather, the lines depend on a sense of communal familiarity and a culturally shared recourse to bitter sarcasm in the face of death. The speaker starts by quoting what midrash scholars call the object text, in this case the hallowed lines of the prayer "El maleh rachamim," popularly associated with the Jewish funeral service—and only then with the more abstract doctrine of *tziduk ha-din*, the justification of divine justice. Amichai's sarcastic, disillusioned speaker then proceeds to empty the prayer of its faith-affirming meaning: first, by using paronomasia to reduce the belief that God is filled with (*el maleh*) mercy to the counterfactual Talmudic logical conditional (*ilmale*, "had it not been for," or "if x had not been the case");[32] and second, by literalizing the sense of "filled with"—describing God as a selfish child who takes all the candy of mercy to himself, filling his mouth with it, and leaving nothing to others. While arguing with divine justice is definitely a common topos in Jewish traditional discourse, it's important to note that Amichai here is wrestling with a God who is merely a literary character, not an object of faith; Amichai's credo is always a non-credo (*ha-ani ha-lo ma'amin sheli*; see discussion below). As a literary character, Amichai's God has compassion and empathy only for himself; he literally stuffs himself narcissistically with it. But it is the speaker's experience-based raging at the heavens, not some theosophical contemplation, that is foregrounded here. Yet this speaker too is subjected to the same biting irony, an effect achieved through a similar type of wordplay (*melekh ha-melach*, King of Salt) and criticized for his ineffectuality by an always distanced "implied author." The philosopher-poet in search of "what will suffice," in Wallace Stevens's terms—whether post-theological humanism or a post-Romantic poetics—is never allowed in Amichai's poetry (unlike Stevens') to be placed front and center.

While many poems deviate from this quasi-autobiographical mode, there are nevertheless good reasons why "El maleh rachamim" and poems like it have become the prototypes for Amichai's treatment of philosophical and rhetorical issues, camouflaged as autobiographical recollections. Furthermore, when his poems are explicitly nonautobiographical, their sustained meditative feel is often veiled through other means, especially those associated with the concept of easy, simple "play."[33] "I write as a person, not as a poet," Amichai told me in a 1986 interview, "that's what the whole thing is about."[34] This deflation of the poet's traditional self-conception in the West, and the concomitant rejection of poetry as either a profession or a calling, is matched by a corresponding valorization of the ordinary human voice and of traditionally unpoetic occupations: "Writing poetry is the most amateurish of all arts. And . . . I mean this as praise," Amichai told his interviewers on several occasions.[35] As early as 1978 he described writing as "the product of an wondrous laziness."[36] As a corollary, direct metapoetic messages are extremely rare in Amichai's poetry. When they do appear, they are more likely to be voiced in those poems whose speakers are enlisted men, lovers, children, archaeologists, geologists, or gardeners, rather than the "professionally" lyrical "I." On those few occasions when Amichai does dedicate poems to his poetic precursors, as in "Yehuda Ha-levi," "Ibn Gabirol," "Leah Goldberg meta" (Leah Goldberg died), "Moto shel Celan" ("The Death of Celan"), or "Paul Celan likrat ha-sof" ("Paul Celan Toward the End"),[37] the concrete poet's life or death, and the lyrical I's ordinary human response to it, occupy center stage rather than serving as some explicitly metapoetic meditation in the abstract on the position of the poet. As Hillel Barzel has pointed out, while Amichai's poetry cannot focus directly on poetry as an object of outright contemplation, "for this might magnify the topic under discussion and restore to it the metaphysical aura," no such "danger" exists if the poem focuses on a particular poet, "identified by name, to whom the words are addressed naturally," since he or she is "an admired, close or deceased poet, who deserves a eulogy like any other friend."[38] For Barzel, Amichai's revolutionary perception of the poet derives from "a rejection of the infinite as a source of poetry," a reversal that puts "the finite before the infinite" (*hipukh ha-makdim et ha-sof la-eynsof*), and the human before the divine.[39] I believe Amichai goes even beyond this simple existentialist posture, so trendy in the literature of his generation (especially, however, in prose fiction; see, for example, A. B. Yehoshua's early short stories). Within Amichai's model of the poet, this step beyond existentialism is expressed in the deliberate and systematic tensions between the poems' explicit "deflation" of the poet and their implicit insistence on the poet's indispensability (albeit in new, egalitarian, antiprophetic and quotidian terms).[40]

Amichai's ambivalent "self-marginalization" of his role as a poet is consistently evident not only in the tone and thematics of his poetry but also in the discursive choices that—in his public persona—he has repeatedly made over the years. Although he was a founding member of the modernist group whose journals, *Likrat* and later *Akhshav*, first published the works of the Israeli neoimagists in the 1950s and 60s, Amichai maintained, quite self-consciously, a marginal role in the group's explicit poetics and politics. Unlike Zach and the Anglo-

American paragons who influenced *Likrat* (Eliot and Pound, especially), Amichai has never written an artistic manifesto or credo. His only credo, as he would often repeat in interviews, as well as in a poem of the same title, is *ha-ani ha-lo ma'amin sheli* ("my non-credo"), which is a brilliantly simple syntactic ambiguity that rejects religious faith and aesthetic positivism in a single move: "my [theologically] non-believing self," and "my artistic 'I don't believe'" or "anti-manifesto."[41] Ironically, Amichai replicates in this anti-credo the manifesto of the *Likrat* group, which also defines itself by an anti-credo:

באנו ואמרנו רק: ל ק ר א ת. לקראת – בלי קוו... לקראת – בלי כרזות,
בלי מניפסטים.

We came and announced just: T o w a r d s. [*Likrat*]. Towards—without a line. . . . Towards—without placards, without manifestos.[42]

In Amichai's oeuvre, the prototypically modernist genre of the manifesto is replaced by the pre- and postmodernist genre of the "diary,"[43] and the metapoetic essay is exchanged for the oral interview, public lecture, or poetry reading. Most importantly, the self-conscious dedication of poems to the theme of poetry and poetic technique, so common among the high modernists and their Israeli belated representatives, is almost entirely absent; in its stead Amichai's oeuvre presents poems on the nature of ordinary language, especially the kinds of language that are traditionally considered unpoetic. Grammatical patterns,[44] idioms, and fixed expressions; familiar quotations; and word etymologies not only show up in new ways that make them perceptible in the poems' rhetorical makeup but also, quite often, become the very focus of the speaker's (philosophically unpretentious and ever so informal) meditations. Poems are frequently *about* grammar—the Hebrew verb patterns, morphology, and gender system, which are subjects Amichai taught in school for many years. The combination of precision and play offered by Hebrew grammar was for him one of the greatest aesthetic attributes (teasing out the connection between *diyuk*, "precision"; *dikduk*, "grammar"; and, in his final book *Open Closed Open*, also their playful, phonologically voiced counterpart, *digdug*, "tickling"). It is from this metalinguistic meditative play that the veiled metapoetic discussion emerges for Amichai, rather than

from typically modernist "poetry for poets," which makes poetics
and the poet's role central thematic concerns. For the poet, as for the
reader, poetry should be—or rather should appear—easy. It is ordinary
language—and the labor of ordinary people—that is hard, complex,
and more creative than any poetic work can ever hope to be.[45]

But clearly, this is not the whole story. In an interview with me,[46]
Amichai compares an effective poem to a well-made car: the complex
machinery is all under the hood. Thus, he explains, those who understand auto mechanics can analyze and admire its intricate engineering,
but what matters to all readers/drivers is that it run well. And what
Amichai's poems have under the hood is quite intricate indeed. After
all, this "easy" poet has also produced some extraordinarily challenging works, like the surrealist *poema* "Mas'ot Binyamin ha-acharon mi-
Tudela" ("The Travels of the Last Benjamin of Tudela"), the Elegies
in the early poetry, or the "Conferences, Conferences" cycle in *Open
Closed Open,* to name just a few salient examples.[47] And, as far as the
thematization of poetry is concerned, the very reduction of poetic language to nonpoetic and ordinary usage allows poems to be implicitly
metapoetic even while discussing—or employing!—colloquial, legal, scientific, commercial, military, or religious discourse. When the metapoetic resides in nonpoetic uses of language, it can also model a lyric that
is the very opposite of an elitist, self-referential conversation-stopper.
Whereas Amichai's construct of "the poet as Everyman"[48] foregrounds
the accessibility and directness of his poetry and the ordinariness of his
language, other aspects of his rhetorical and philosophical system, such
as his conception of time, order, and tradition, often mandate allusive-
ness, strong metaphoricity, and radical intertextuality. The translator as
a figure for the poet mediates, as I argue in chapter 4, between these
two models.

Throughout this book I am interrogating different aspects of Amichai's poetry and poetics in an attempt to understand how it can be
both things at once: easy and complex, literal and figurative, colloquial
and allusive. How, to return to my initial query, can a poet who consistently demystifies the poetic process and whose persona declares, as
we have seen, that he uses "only a small part of the words in the dictionary" get away with placing that same poetic process at the center
of complex intertextual collages and extravagant, multilayered figura-

tive junctures? Amichai's work develops numerous strategies for doing exactly that: abstaining from the exclusivist, self-conscious "poetry for poets," and at the same time—indirectly, surreptitiously—making poetry the covert subject of the poem. While a fuller exploration of these strategies will take up the bulk of the following chapters, a closer look at a few poems that articulate and thematize the coexistence of these dualities may help provide a preliminary account of the most central principles of Amichai's philosophical and rhetorical system in action.

"Lo ka-brosh" ("Not Like a Cypress")[49] is a seminal early poem that has come to represent for many readers the antiheroic and unassuming position so typical of Amichai's poetic persona:

Not Like A Cypress

Not like a cypress,
not all at once, not all of me,
but like the grass, in thousands of cautious green exits,
to be hiding like many children
while one of them seeks.

And not like the single man,
like Saul, whom the multitude found
and made king.
But like the rain in many places
from many clouds, to be absorbed, to be drunk
by many mouths, to be breathed in
like the air all year long and scattered like blossoming in springtime.

Not the sharp ring that wakes up
the doctor on call,
but with tapping, on many small windows
at side entrances, with many heartbeats.

And afterward the quiet exit, like smoke
without shofar-blasts, a statesman resigning,
children tired from play,
a stone as it almost stops rolling
down the steep hill, in the place
where the plain of great renunciation begins,
from which, like prayers that are answered,
dust rises in many myriads of grains.[50]

לֹא כַּבְּרוֹשׁ

לֹא כַּבְּרוֹשׁ,
לֹא בְּבַת אֶחָת, לֹא כֻּלִּי,
אֶלָּא כַּדֶּשֶׁא, בְּאַלְפֵי יְצִיאוֹת זְהִירוֹת־יְרֻקּוֹת,
לִהְיוֹת מֻסְתָּר כְּהַרְבֵּה יְלָדִים בְּמִשְׂחָק
וְאֶחָד מְחַפֵּשׂ.

וְלֹא כַּגֶּבֶר הַיָּחִיד,
כְּבֶן־קַיִשׁ, שֶׁמְּצָאוּהוּ רַבִּים
וְעָשׂוּ אוֹתוֹ לְמֶלֶךְ.
אֶלָּא כַּגֶּשֶׁם בְּהַרְבֵּה מְקוֹמוֹת
מֵעֲנָנִים רַבִּים, לְהִתְחַלְחֵל, לִהְיוֹת שָׁתוּי
פִּיּוֹת רַבִּים, לִהְיוֹת נָשׁוּם
כָּאֲוִיר בַּשָּׁנָה וּמְפֻזָּר כִּפְרִיחָה בָּאָבִיב.

לֹא הַצִּלְצוּל הַחַד, הַמְעוֹרֵר
בְּשַׁעַר הָרוֹפֵא הַתּוֹרָן,
אֶלָּא בִּדְפִיקוֹת, בְּהַרְבֵּה אֶשְׁנַבִּים
בִּכְנִיסוֹת צְדָדִיוֹת, בְּהַרְבֵּה דְפִיקוֹת לֵב.

וְאַחַר־כָּךְ הַיְצִיאָה הַשְּׁקֵטָה, כְּעָשָׁן
בְּלִי תְּרוּעָה, שַׂר מִתְפַּטֵּר,
יְלָדִים עֲיֵפִים מִמִּשְׂחָק,
אֶבֶן בַּגִּלְגּוּלִים הָאַחֲרוֹנִים
לְאַחַר הַמּוֹרָד הַתָּלוּל, בַּמָּקוֹם שֶׁמַּתְחִיל
מִישׁוֹר הַוִּתּוּר הַגָּדוֹל, אֲשֶׁר מִמֶּנּוּ,
כַּתְּפִלּוֹת הַמִּתְקַבְּלוֹת,
עוֹלֶה אָבָק בְּהַרְבֵּה רִבּוֹא גַּרְגִּרִים.

Whether the poem is taken to present a critique of accepted norms or a series of personal wishes, whether it expresses the poet's perception of his art or remains completely without a concrete referent,[51] "Lo ka-brosh" is a dazzling example of Amichai's rhetorical-philosophical sleight of hand. It is a sustained meditative poem about the need to be both "diffuse and ubiquitous,"[52] featuring a subject who is (semantically and syntactically) at once absent and perfectly clear, and a speaker who makes his wishes appear quite personal even though he almost never uses the first-person point of view.[53]

Through what Arpali describes as an open-ended catalogue technique, the poem presents, in apparent free-association, a series of negated and affirmed similes, analogies and metaphors—figurative vehicles whose tenors (which are also the subjects and predicates of the poem's elliptical sentences) are never explicitly stated. Most importantly for our purpose, this rhetorical strategy allows Amichai to describe "the manner in which he would like to be accepted as poet and person in the world"[54] without ever mentioning poetry or the poet. The clusters of similes (stanzas 1 and 2) and predications (stanzas 3 and 4) appear to lack any linear or narrative unity.[55] But, in fact, the sequence is held together loosely by the form of a pseudo-argument, an enthymeme or rhetorical syllogism in the style of the Metaphysical poets:

Not as a but as b (stanza 1),
and not as c but as d (stanza 2),
not e but f (stanza 3),
and then g, h, i, j (stanza 4).

The concluding stanza is thus the only component that does not have an antithetical structure. Note that this modal, petitive series of statements expresses propositional attitudes, ways of being the speaker wishes to attain rather than a stative narrative that has already been achieved.

Amichai has often been criticized for what has been described as the loose structure of his poems, a looseness that would allow, as Nissim Kalderon has argued, an editor to shift lines and stanzas around without changing the poem's meaning.[56] This, I believe, is merely the rhetorical impression many poems are meant to create. More specifically, in this poem, the sense of a casual composition serves as a structural correlative for the very inconspicuousness that the lyrical "I" seeks out as a mode of existence. Because the text flaunts its unstructured sequence, it is harder to notice—as it is in many other Amichai poems—how tight and symmetrical the "spatial form"[57] tends to be. This poem and others—especially those that employ four stanzas and sonnet-like forms—display exactly the same types of systematic relations of equivalence among their four strophic units that Roman Jakobson has identified in his influential analysis of the various structural configurations of lines in Shakespeare's Sonnet 129:[58] (1) alternation (abab), (2) framing (abba), (3) neighborhood (aabb), and, in addition—the relationship that Jakobson conceived of as peculiar to the Shakespearean sonnet—(4) contrast between terminal and nonterminal strophes (aaab). It's interesting that all four configurations, including the ones supposedly distinctive of Shakespeare, are typical compositional patterns in Amichai's poetry, both early and late. This is hardly the mark of loose, interchangeable poetic structure.

As my outline of the rhetorical argument that constitutes "Lo kabrosh" suggests, the last ("Shakespearean") structural pattern (aaab) marks the most important turn in the poem. Here the speaker finally emerges from the cloak of antithesis and litotes—the description of his wishes by the negation of their opposites—and allows the heterogeneous catalogue to come to rest in the extended metaphor of *mishor ha-vitur ha-gadol* ("the plain of great renunciation").[59] The catalogue stops short at the end of the last strophe just like the stone, "as it almost stops rolling" at the bottom of the hill. Thus, through the very tension between the poem's temporal and spatial structure, Amichai's poem both embodies and describes the role of the poet, without mentioning him even once.

The structural tension between the poem's vertical and horizontal composition is paralleled by a thematic oscillation between deflation and valorization of the poet's ontological status and social role. The speaker's goal is to avoid being prominent and conspicuous like the tall, pointed cypress, jutting up "all at once," all in one spot. The cypress functions here as a Mediterranean substitute for the Western cliché of a poet's ivory tower. That's not the way to be in the world, Amichai seems to be saying, as poets or as human beings! Furthermore, the cypress is a standard textbook example of fruitless trees, a category named literally in Hebrew as "useless trees" (*atzey srak*), and subject to different rabbinic laws (*halakhot*) than "food trees" (*atzey ma'akhal*). Note how Amichai's stylistic practice here performs and embodies his refusal to stand out as a poet: his language avoids any explicit reference to poetry or the poet as the subject of the poem. Never saying "I," the speaker nevertheless expresses his wish to leave a mark on the world. But his wish is not simply to be inconspicuous, as the title suggests, just as the persona of the great Hebrew acmeist poet Rachel does not simply endorse the ant's point of view of poetry when she declares, *Rak al atzmi le-saper yada'ti / tzar olami ke-olam nemala* ("Only of myself do I know how to tell / Narrow is my world like the world of an ant").[60] On the one hand, the speaker wants to remain unnoticed, hidden, almost passive. On the other, he wishes to make his presence all-encompassing, comingling with and reaching out to as many people as possible. Desired inconspicuousness and secrecy in the *mode* of existence are paralleled, antithetically, by a desired comprehensiveness and communality in the *scope* of existence. To be needed but not to stand out, given the socialist ethos of Amichai's politics in the 1950s: this is not such a surprising or paradoxical wish, nor would it have been for many of his readers who shared that utilitarian and egalitarian view of art, even—or especially—of avant-garde art. Only when taken together do these political-thematic features motivate the tensions between pervasive symmetry and overt looseness in the composition of the text, and between elliptical, concealing syntax and detailed, innovative figurative language. Thus, the course of the poem may be the occasion for the fulfillment or frustration of the very wishes that are its topic.

In the first set of images, the lyrical "I" describes himself not as a salient, singular vertical presence but as hidden, multiple horizontal emergences. The progression of the poem and its catalogues of indirect descriptions are thematized almost geometrically, as in an abstract expressionist painting, in these opening similes.[61] We do not find out about the poet's self-perception through one neatly defined model (metapoetically represented by the cypress), but rather through a series of numerous half-articulated and seemingly unconnected images (symbolized by the blades of grass). "Not Like a Cypress" names therefore not only the poet's desired ontology but also a formal strategy for the poem's composition. Only by implication can we then infer that, like blades of grass, drops of rain, air breathed by people over a year and blossoms scattered in springtime does the poet's work aim wide rather than high, wishing to be absorbed by all, like simple and necessary nourishment. Note that the rain functions here as a veiled symbol of the poet's populist impact, not in accordance with the rain's conventional lyrical valence in the West, but rather by being true to the realia of a Middle Eastern climate and the culture that sprang up around it: the rain is what everyone prays for after the long, parched summers (e.g., *tfilat ha-geshem*). The image of the many mouths raised to drink the raindrops revives the idiomatic Hebrew expression *shotim dvarav ba-tzama* that depicts an attentive audience as drinking eagerly (lit., "thirstily") the words of a speaker—or writer. Amichai's aesthetic—as that of the poem's own structure and figurative language—is thus modeled after the disorganized and scattered (*mefuzar*) blossoms of the brief Israeli spring (*ki-fricha ba-aviv*), rather than on any classic ideals of eternal, transcendent beauty; a modernist chaotic and fragmentary model for poetry, masquerading as a romantic nature scene.

Alternating between the natural and the social realm, Amichai's similes of child's play and kingship are picked up again in the metaphors of a medical emergency in the third stanza. Once more, the poet's work (to risk again inferring the same tenor for the entire catalogue of vehicles in a poem where no tenor is ever mentioned) is deflated and stripped of all heroism or glamour; yet for that very reason, the poet is also integrated into life and community. Rather than fashioning himself after the first Israelite king, the chosen one, who—as we recall—was head and shoulders above his people (like a cypress), the poet-speaker likens himself to children in a game of hide-and-seek.[62] It is, however, the children at play who enjoy and always ultimately find what they are seeking. Saul, by contrast, went looking for his father's asses, and before he knew it, he was uprooted from both family and community by the unwanted, isolating role of king imposed upon him.[63] Similarly, in an antipoetic comparison between two blatantly antipoetic sounds, the poet's position and the work of writing are not like a single sharp ring at the door of the doctor-on-call, but like the tedious process of securing medical care from a faceless institution by repetitive knocking on many bureaucratic windows and doors. At the same time that the poetic process is deflated through the bureaucratic imagery, the context of the medical emergency serves to do just the opposite—to imbue the poet's position with the urgency of a life-and-death situation. Thus, the poet's social mode of existence touches human lives *be-harbe dfikot lev*, which can be taken here both idiomatically to mean "with a lot of anxiety," "with trepidation," and literally—"with many heartbeats," or "the heartbeats of many [people]." As Nili Scharf Gold points out, this affirmation of an antiheroic mode of existence "is articulated principally through a rejection of traits that are stereotypically considered 'masculine' in favor of those that are conventionally perceived as 'feminine.'"[64]

Lacking the antithetical structure of the first three stanzas—"not [as] *a* but [as] *b*"—the fourth stanza seems at first to present a complete collapse of all linear order. Within the inverse logical relation between "the poem's theme and its mode of presentation,"[65] it is quite consistent that the poem's theme, which so far had to be reconstructed exclusively by the reader, will be expressed more directly at the very point where the poem's order seems to collapse into an open catalogue of freely associated items (the quiet exit, smoke without a blaring sound [*tru'ah*], a government minister resigning,[66] children tired of their play). At this very moment, in the middle of the last stanza, appears the philosophically most explicit and figuratively most developed image: *ba-makom she-matchil / mishor ha-vitur ha-gadol, asher mi-menu, / ka-tfilot ha-mitkablot, / oleh avak be-harbe ribo gargerim* ("in the place / where the plain of great renunciation begins, / from which, like prayers that are answered, / dust rises in many myriads of grains"). Keynar's interpretation, stressing the *biographical* sense of an end to the poet's life, also sees "the plain of great renunciation" as a frustration of the poet's wishes. His prayers are just like dust; his wish "to be absorbed by many" is ironically and cruelly frustrated in the image of "the many myriads of grains" of fruitless dust.[67] In a very different vein, Tzukerman-Teres identifies the resignation with giving up both extremes, abrogating all poetic wishes, and offering oneself up to nature.[68] Yaniv points out the ways that this stanza reinterprets the poet's creative wishes from earlier sections of the poem as indicators of his imminent death: the "cautious green exits" become a "quiet exit," "the single man" becomes "the statesman resigning," and so forth. Like the other critics, Yaniv also argues that the fulfillment of the poet's wish is already within "the plain of great renunciation" and that "it too is nothing but dust." "The movement in the last stanza," Yaniv concludes, "of the rising smoke, the descending stone and again of the rising dust matches the ups and downs of human life, and ultimately forms a cycle with no way out."[69]

These readings fail to grasp the radicalism of Amichai's critique of accepted norms—aesthetic and other—and fall back on the monologic autobiographical model, in which resignation and dust represent personal failure, meaninglessness, and death. Note, however, that the dust is rising up—not falling; and that it rises like "prayers that are answered," not rejected! (and not the reverse, as Keynar suggests: prayers that are rising like dust). Note also that if the phrase is parsed not as "the plain of great renunciation" but as "the great plain of renunciation" it marks an achievement rather than a failure. Finally, the poem ends with richly alliterative, biblical diction and intertextual resonances in the phrase *harbe ribo gargerim* ("many myriads of grains"), which is not only closer to poetic diction and traditional euphony than anything else in the poem but also echoes two contradictory—yet traditionally linked—biblical themes: God's promise to make Abraham's offspring as numerous and uncountable as grains of sand, and the specific use of *harbe ribo* ("many myriads") in the threat of Nineveh's destruction in the last verse of the Book of Jonah.[70] The special force of this final sustained image derives, I believe, precisely from the contradictory, and therefore profoundly unsettling, import of its components. Within a metapoetic perspective, the poem's ending both describes and constitutes the—always modified, self-ironic, and not very substantial—*fulfillment* of the poet's wishes. (Interestingly, the readings I cite above all hasten to abandon any metapoetic perspective once biographical death is implied in this final image.) To compare the dust rising from the plain to the answered (lit., "accepted") prayers is only to emphasize the gap between the two: the poet's aesthetics of dust does not rise up into any poetic heaven. But even this poorhouse apotheosis—by simply undoing any delusions of grandeur and permanence—paradoxically overcomes the finiteness of the death it connotes. It points to a new beginning; in the locative phrase *ba-makom she-matchil / mishor ha-vitur ha-gadol* ("in the place / Where the plain of great renunciation begins"), the word "begins" significantly *ends* a line in both the Hebrew and the English. It toys with our biographical expectations for an end-of-the-road despair, but suggests instead that a new beginning comes with the abdication of all transcendental poetic and religious expectations, with a resignation even from the struggle against what the poet cannot or does not want to be: logically, the end of the antithetical argument, and geometrically, the replacement of the vertical salience of the cypress with the flatness of the horizontal plain.[71] Giving up (*vitur*) gives rise to a new beginning that marks the poet's initiation into a world he has given up fighting for, rather than a world he sets out to conquer. Renunciation as an apotheosis manqué is not a Zen principle for Amichai but the logical consequence of his ideology critique, his rejection of manufactured hope as a manipulative tool that institutions of state and religion use to make individuals sacrifice themselves for some "better future." And this critique, I argue, permeates his entire oeuvre.[72]

Amichai's 1989 book *Gam ha-egrof haya pa'am yad ptucha ve-etzba'ot* (*The Fist, Too, Was Once the Palm of an Open Hand, and Fingers*),[73] which is in many ways an entire volume of covert *ars-poetica*, provides counterpart poems to many early seminal works, including "Lo ka-brosh." The poem titled "Ma lamadeti ba-milchamot" ("What Have I Learned in the Wars") in this volume accounts for the poet's commitment to "dim the splendor" of his poetic vision (*zohar ha-chizayon*) and to veil his artistry as measures that are necessary for poetic survival. In the second half of the poem, the speaker, having learned in the wars *li-tz'ok 'ima', bli she-hi shoma'at / ve-li-tz'ok 'elohim', bli le-ha'amin bo* ("to cry out 'mommy' without her hearing / and to cry out 'God' without believing in him"),[74] relates the poet's desire to remain inconspicuous to the veteran's *chokhmat ha-hasva'a*—his "wisdom," but also his "philosophy," "art," and "craft"—"of camouflage":[75]

From: What Have I Learned in the Wars[76]

But above all I have learned the wisdom of camouflage
so I won't stand out, so that they[77] won't recognize me,
so they won't be able to tell me from my surroundings
not even from my love,
so they may think I am a bush or a sheep,
I am a tree, or the shadow of a tree
I am a doubt, the shadow of a doubt,
a hedge,[78] a dead stone
a house, the corner of a house.

If I were a prophet I'd dim the splendor of vision
and darken[79] my faith with black paper
and cover the Divine Chariots with nets.

And when the time comes I'll wear the camouflage clothes of my end:
White of clouds and lots of sky blue
and stars that have no end.

אַךְ מֵעַל לַכֹּל לָמַדְתִּי חָכְמַת הַהַסְוָאָה,

שֶׁלֹּא אֶבְלֹט, שֶׁלֹּא יַכִּירוּ אוֹתִי,

שֶׁלֹּא יַבְחִינוּ בֵּינִי וּבֵין מַה שֶּׁסָּבִיב לִי

אֲפִלּוּ בֵּינִי וּבֵין אַהֲבָתִי,

שֶׁיַּחְשְׁבוּ שֶׁאֲנִי שִׂיחַ אוֹ כֶּבֶשׂ,

שֶׁאֲנִי עֵץ, שֶׁאֲנִי צֵל שֶׁל עֵץ

שֶׁאֲנִי סָפֵק, צֵל שֶׁל סָפֵק,

שֶׁאֲנִי גֶּדֶר חַיָּה, אֶבֶן מֵתָה

בַּיִת, פִּנַּת בַּיִת.

אִלּוּ הָיִיתִי נָבִיא הָיִיתִי מְעַמְעֵם אֶת זֹהַר הַחִזָּיוֹן

וּמַאֲפִיל עַל אֱמוּנָתִי בִּנְיָיר שָׁחֹר

וּמְכַסֶּה אֶת מַעֲשֵׂי הַמֶּרְכָּבָה בִּרְשָׁתוֹת.

וּבְבוֹא הָעֵת אֶלְבַּשׁ אֶת בִּגְדֵי הַהַסְוָאָה שֶׁל סוֹפִי:

לָבָן שֶׁל עֲנָנִים וְהַרְבֵּה תְּכֵלֶת שָׁמַיִם

וְכוֹכָבִים שֶׁאֵין לָהֶם סוֹף.

In order to avoid becoming a target, the veteran soldier-poet has learned to take on the appearance of his surroundings, not in a pantheistic or socialist-Zionist union with the land, as in the works of Shaul Tchernichovsky or Avraham Shlonsky, respectively, but in a gesture of poetic and existential self-defense.[80] Veiling the poet's intricate artistry under the camouflage net of artlessness is as necessary as covering the windows with black paper during an air raid, or dimming the brilliance of prophetic vision during the precarious moments of divine revelation. The evocatively dense compound *ma'asey merkava* (which I translate above as "the Divine Chariots"; an untranslatable expression, rendered by the Harshavs somewhat reductively as "magic") is also an idiom suggesting the speaker's awe at some artistic complexity. This translational impasse affords us a glimpse of the allusive depths,

indeed the plenitude, beneath the poet's (literally) self-effacing rhetoric ("A tree, or the shadow of a tree, / . . . a doubt, the shadow of
a doubt"). Amichai's self-imposed minimalism, his project of "dimming the splendor," which tradition associates with poetic/prophetic
vision, is articulated in terms that are anything but minimalist: they
go to the heart of the complex and often arcane intertextual web that
constitutes the rabbinical genre of *merkava* literature, a genre whose
originary moment and locus classicus is Ezekiel's uninhibited, fantasti-
cal depiction of "the lineaments of the divine chariot-throne and its
angelic bearers," in Joel Rosenberg's vivid terms.[81] Idiomatically in Hebrew, the expression *ma'aseh merkava* invokes, as I have suggested,
the secrets of both divine and artistic wisdom and craft. Yet at the
same time it can be taken literally here as an implicit elaboration of the
image of war, which—given the role of mock-teacher throughout—
deflates and demystifies the traditional discourse of poetic and divine
wisdom, while pointing up the sacrilegious use of the sacred in the
discourse of modern Israeli warfare. The concrete experiences of war
are described in the poem's title and in the first half of the poem—not
without irony—as a hands-on tutorial in the art, theory, or wisdom of
camouflage.[82] The mock-divine chariots (*merkavot*) of our time may
simply be tanks hidden under camouflage nets: *Merkava* is actually a
brand-name of an Israeli-made tank, an example of military newspeak,
with its implicit attribution of both imperial and divine powers to the
weaponry of the Israeli Defense Forces (IDF). From his typically unaf-
filiated or in-between position, which endorses neither the religious
nor the martial, Amichai's poetic persona allows the two sets of meanings of *merkava* to negate each other, leaving him with nothing but
the holes in his camouflage net.

As Shaul Setter has pointed out to me, the second half of this stanza,
which on its own is very unclear, becomes much more lucid when read
as a commentary on, if not a coded rejection of, Natan Zach's famous
1960 poem from *Shirim shonim* (Various Poems), "Ha-tzayar metzayer"
(The Painter Paints):[83]

אַךְ הַמְשׁוֹרֵר אֵינוֹ שָׁר,

הוּא הָר בְּצִדֵּי הַדֶּרֶךְ,

אוֹ עֵץ, אוֹ רֵיחַ,

אוֹ עֵץ, אוֹ רֵיחַ,

מַשֶּׁהוּ בּוֹרֵחַ,

[...]

מַשֶּׁהוּ שֶׁמַּשְׁאִיר

מַשֶּׁהוּ.

The painter paints [*ha-tzayar metzayer*], the storyteller tells [*ha-sofer mesaper*, also, the fiction-writer writes], the sculptor sculpts [*ha-pasal mefasel*] / but the poet [*meshorer*, also "singer"] doesn't sing [*shar*] / he's a mountain [*har*] on the roadside [*tzidey ha-derekh*] / Or a tree [*etz*], or a smell [*re'ach*] / something fleeting [*bore'ach*; also "escaping"] . . . / something that leaves something [behind] [*mashehu she-mash'ir mashehu*]. (literal translation and emphases of sound patterns mine, CK)

Zach's poem flaunts its metapoetic declaration by explicitly struggling to define the position of the poet. The speaker points out from the start, through Zach's typical linguistic play and pseudo-tautological rhetoric and soundplay, poetry's anomaly among the arts: unlike the painter who paints, the poet (*meshorer*) does not sing (*shar*); in Hebrew, the noun *shira* signifies both poetry and song, as well as the act of singing. In modern Hebrew, however, the verb *la-shir* is restricted to singing and does not denote writing poetry. Zach thus finds the uniqueness of poetry precisely in its being cut off from the quotidian and folkish act of singing; he embraces that which the romantics have mourned—the lyric's loss of its musical, oral origins. In this epoch-making poem, which served as a model for the official poetics of the Statehood Generation, Zach describes poetry as anything but the popular, ordinary-language activity of song making. Instead, Zach underscores poetry's *Sachlichkeit*, an essence whose ontological status—however polyvalent (see the series of disjunctions: "or . . . or"), unstable ("something fleeting"), and marginal to the social world ("on the side of the road")—remains distinctive and leaves its mark on the world of phenomena. Poetry's difficulty and even unintelligibility may indeed be for Zach part of its unique essence. Both poetry and the poet are ultimately at one and the same time the most concrete (a mountain, a tree) and the most abstract, the most referentially opaque (the double use of the indexical *mashehu*) and the most enduring artistic formations: "Something that leaves something behind" (the Hebrew has the sense of leaving a trace or a mark, not of abandoning).

Almost thirty years later, Amichai, who was finally writing the closest thing to a metapoetic book, *The Fist, Too, Was Once the Palm of an Open Hand, and Fingers,* defines his own "wisdom of camouflage" in contradistinction to Zach's neoimagist, elitist, Pound-like poetics. Through a series of intertextual practices that mimic parodically Zach's disjunctive syntax as well as his catalogues of objects (most directly, the quotation of "tree" [*etz*]), Amichai rejects, in the poem "What Have I Learned in the Wars," both high modernist and romantic notions of the uniqueness of poetry and the poet. He suggests instead that it is of vital importance for the poet to avoid any explicit, thematic, metapoetic exposure. In contrast to Zach's ontological investment in exploring the unique essence of the poetic, Amichai's poem articulates an equally intense investment in the egalitarian, social relationality of the poet's image ("so they may think I am . . ."): poetic language must never appear to be superior to ordinary language, nor is the poet to be seen as having access to any special vision. Note that Amichai does not say anywhere in this poem that there "really" is no difference between poetic and ordinary language, or between the poet and Everyman; the crucial point is to create the *rhetorical impression* that poetic discourse is seamlessly integrated into the "sociolects" of ordinary language use, and that the poet is similarly assimilated into the culture of everyday life. But here, in addition to the egalitarian opposition to "the art of generals" that we have observed in Amichai's early poetry, he provides another dimension, one that may also be his way of responding to his own institutional reception in Israel and the United States: he expresses in this poem with great urgency the need to protect the poet's artistry and vision from the same appropriations by powerful institutions of war and religion (two of the implications of *merkava*), which can use it—and have used it—to manipulate the masses and co-opt the poet's vision, while ignoring the "precision" (*diyuk*) of the grammar (*dikduk*) so crucial to his poetics. It is therefore highly ironic and perhaps not entirely coincidental that the realms that serve as the speaker's

mock-tutors in the poem, the military/national and the biblical/
religious, are—as I have argued in chapter 1—the areas where Amichai's
poetry has seen its most consistent institutional appropriations. This
and other veiled metapoetic poems in his later oeuvre should, I believe,
be read in part as responses to his changed status from the "dangerous" poet of the 1950s and 60s to that of the Israeli and Jewish American "establishment" poet par excellence, a status he personally scorned
and often made fun of in conversation with his friends.

III. In-Between

The metapoetic, for Amichai, even when it is the implicit subject of
the poem—as is the case in "What Have I Learned in the Wars"—
must therefore always be embedded in mundane realia and ordinary
use of language. Flaunting the poet's artistry is nothing short of existentially and politically dangerous: it is like forgetting to black-out
the windows before an air raid or getting too close to divine revelation. The poet's retreat into the shadow of a tree and the shadow of
a doubt is not only a commentary on his self-decreed marginality.
These actions also define a more general principle of Amichai's rhetorical ontology: the principle of existing in between categories. At
this point the camouflaged artist—soldier, lover, or Everyman: the
recurring personae in his poetry—merge and, in effect, systematically
challenge the common tendency to reduce rhetorical and philosophical distinctions to neatly discrete binary oppositions. Rather, Amichai's poetry defines its place in between these oppositions, in the
"narrow between" (*ba-beynayim ha-tzarim*) that both bridges and
penetrates all bipolarities.[84]

> *From: Between*
>
> Where will we be when these flowers turn into fruit
> in the narrow between, when the flower is no longer a flower
> and the fruit not yet a fruit. And what a wonderful between we made
> for each other between body and body.
> A between of eyes, between waking and sleep.
> A twilight betweenlight, not day and not night.

אֵיפֹה נִהְיֶה כְּשֶׁהַפְּרָחִים הָאֵלֶּה יַהַפְכוּ פֵּרוֹת
בַּבֵּינַיִם הַצָּרִים, כְּשֶׁפֶּרַח שׁוּב לֹא פֶּרַח
וְהַפְּרִי טֶרֶם פְּרִי. וְאֵיזֶה בֵּינַיִם נִפְלָאִים עָשִׂינוּ
זֶה לָזֶה בֵּין גּוּף לְגוּף. בֵּינַיִם עֵינַיִם בֵּין עֵרוּת לְשֵׁנָה.
בֵּינַיִם עַרְבַּיִם, לֹא יוֹם, לֹא לַיְלָה.

The "wonderful between," which the lovers made "for each other between body and body," is the spatial corollary of the temporal "narrow
between" evinced in nature, when change from one botanical or diur-
nal state to another (flower to fruit, day to night) is not dreaded as a
loss of self but valued for the magic of transformation and intimacy it
affords. This embodied valorization of the liminal, and its expression in
the concept of *beynayim*, is central to Amichai's poetic philosophy. The
makeshift space of *beynayim* (also described in the earlier poetry tem-
porally as *be-terem*, "before")[85] is used here, as elsewhere in Amichai's
poetry, both in its *dual* grammatical form (*-ayim*) and in its biblical
semantic sense of a "duel" (*milchemet beynayim*) or a "duelist" (Goliath, we recall, is referred to as *ish beynayim*, a warrior dueling before
the camps, in 1 Samuel 17:4). This *beynayim* state marks for Amichai
throughout his poetry the threat war presents for love and the lovers:
the unequal power relation between the beloved or the couple on one
end, and the forces of history and institutional order on the other (see
chapter 5). In a famous early poem, "Shneynu be-yachad ve-khol echad
le-chud" ("The Two of Us Together and Each of Us Alone"), Amichai first develops the concept of *ahavat-beynayim*, a highly ambiguous, simultaneous description of love's transience, and of the lovers as
a threatened intersubjective entity. They are depicted as duelists performing their love before and in between the warring armies, as the
playthings of unnamed powers who use them to provide the masses
with "bread and circuses."[86] Thus, in trying to stop the armies and
"make love, not war," they also paradoxically become, like David and
Goliath, token opponents who do battle with each other for the diversion and distraction of the masses. This interpenetration of love and
war, foregrounded in the ambiguous concept of *beynayim*, is typical of
all actively opposed categories in Amichai's oeuvre, as well as of their
linguistic and rhetorical corollaries. The need for opposite concepts

to switch places, to be camouflaged as each other, or ultimately to be revealed as the same, is the philosophical and rhetorical principle that underlies the function of *beynayim*. Thematically, it accounts for concerns as diverse as the indistinguishability of memory and forgetting, self and other, hope and danger, male and female, Jew and Arab, sacred and profane, God and human being, and, ultimately, life and death.[87] Rhetorically, this principle of an in-between existence motivates the interpenetrations of opposing genres (sonnet[88] and ode, elegy and joke), of literal and figurative, and of poetry and non-poetry. It is no accident, then, that Amichai's 1982 book is titled *The Hour of Grace* (*she'at ha-chesed*), rabbinical Hebrew's name for what Chana Bloch has so ingeniously translated as "twilight betweenlight" (*beynayim arbayim*), the hours at the end of day and before nightfall. According to Jewish tradition, heaven's gates are most wide open and most receptive to human prayers at twilight, yet this is also an hour when life comes precipitously close to death. The in-between state is thus both precious and dangerous.

Amichai's later poetry provides some of the most crystallized statements (which are, of course, always non-statements) of this principle, as in the poems "Atzvut ve-simcha" (Sadness and Joy), "Ha-nefesh" (The Soul), and "Eyze min adam" (What Kind of Man).[89] In the special botanical imagery that his most metapoetic book, *Gam ha-egrof*, perfects,[90] the coexistence of *ahava u-vilti-ahava, shney tzva'im / be-vered echad* ("love and unlove, two colors / in one rose") is not some wild mutation but *zan nifla / heseg li-megadel ha-vradim, she-shmo nish'ar ba-vered* ("a wonderful species / an accomplishment for the rose grower, whose name remains in the rose").[91] The poet as gardener is a creator of hybrid identities; he gives way to the familiar trope of the poet as traveler who passes *in between* the blessing and the curse, justice and injustice.[92] Finally, it is the very proximity of death that gives the speaker the freedom to abolish the opposition between the human and the divine, claiming for himself both the apotheosis of the human and the deflation of the divine: *ani adam / ani adam-elohim, ani elohim-adam / she-yamav sfurim. Haleluya* ("I am a human being, / a man-god, a god-man / whose days are numbered. Hallelujah").[93]

But how does Amichai's union of opposites differ from other dialectical systems? Sidra DeKoven Ezrahi cogently describes his philosophy as "dialogical" and "post-dialectical."[94] Amichai himself links his post-dialectical and antimonological poetic worldview to his disillusionment at a young age with both Marxism-Leninism and Orthodox Judaism. "Both," he told me in an interview, "have a total, linear conception of the human being" (*tfisa line'arit totalit shel ha-adam*).[95] An additional dimension may lie in the least understood aspect of Amichai's poetic worldview, and perhaps its most revolutionary one: "the rage for chaos," to use Morse Peckham's controversial term. "There must be . . . some human activity which serves to break up orientations, to weaken and frustrate the tyrannous drive to order. . . . This activity, I believe, is the activity of artistic perception."[96] To be sure, Amichai doesn't subscribe to Peckham's peculiar mixture of early postmodernism and psychobiology, but he does maintain—on all levels of his poetics, as we have seen—an active or passive resistance to *elohey ha-seder,* "the gods of order" (and of the Passover seder ritual).[97] Let me once more illustrate this point briefly with a poem from *Gam ha-egrof:*

The Sea and the Shore

The sea and the shore always next to each other. Both
wanting to learn to speak, to learn to say
just one word. The sea wants to say "shore,"
and the shore wants to say "sea." They have been getting closer,
for millions of years, to speaking, to saying
that one word. When the sea says "shore,"
and when the shore says "sea,"
salvation will come to the world,
the world will return to chaos.

Trans. Chana Kronfeld[98]

הַיָּם וְהַחוֹף

הַיָּם וְהַחוֹף זֶה לְיַד זֶה תָּמִיד. שְׁנֵיהֶם
רוֹצִים לִלְמֹד לְדַבֵּר, לִלְמֹד לוֹמַר
רַק מִלָּה אַחַת. הַיָּם רוֹצֶה לוֹמַר ״חוֹף״,
וְהַחוֹף רוֹצֶה לוֹמַר ״יָם״. הֵם מִתְקָרְבִים,
שְׁנוֹת מִילְיוֹנִים, אֶל הַדִּבּוּר, אֶל אֲמִירַת
הַמִּלָּה הָאַחַת. כְּשֶׁהַיָּם יֹאמַר ״חוֹף״,

וּכְשֶׁהַחוֹף יֹאמַר "יָם",
תָּבוֹא גְּאֻלָה לָעוֹלָם,
יַחֲזֹר הָעוֹלָם לַתֹּהוּ.

This parabolic poem defines its own code, which in retrospect makes sense of a consistent trend in Amichai's poetic worldview. Salvation is described as a release from the bonds of any superimposed, textual, or institutionalized (theological, political, aesthetic) order, exemplified by binary oppositions. The biblical story of creation—and the religious institutions based on a system of separations and classifications that developed from it—set up, through the powers of *dibur* or *amira* (speech), an artificial border between the fluid and contradictory categories of existence, as a form of control over elemental, chaotic forces (such as the sea and the shore). It is this enforced order, this commitment to separateness, that is for Amichai the source of all evil: it breeds conflict and disrupts love—that energy that empowers the self to blur boundaries with the other, and to cross all lines of separation. Running against the imposed order, confusing the periods, or mixing up the Bible[99] are therefore necessary measures for staying alive as lover, as critical subject, and as poet. The de-creation of categorical borders is also to be achieved *ba-amira* (by speech), as in the original biblical account of creation; but, significantly, it is to be attained not through divine speech but rather through the dialogic, immanent ability of premonotheistic, personified primordial forces to name each other. Evolution is thus redefined as the gradual acquisition of the language of the other, and is enabled by a devolution away from any "linear, total" order:[100] the sea gradually learning over millions of years to say "shore," the shore to say "sea." Ultimately, equating *ge'ula*, "salvation," with its apocalyptic opposite, *tohu*, "chaos," is itself a utopian manifestation of Amichai's unique version of *rhetorical anarchism*.

If there is one work within Amichai's corpus that combines and embodies all the rhetorical and philosophical aspects of this complex yet open system it is, without a doubt, "Mas'ot Binyamin ha-acharon mi-Tudela" ("The Travels of the Last Benjamin of Tudela"). This is one of the key poems I revisit periodically in this study from a variety of angles:[101] In the Introduction I discuss it in the context of Amichai's

"archaeology of the self" and of his rhetoric of autobiography.[102] Here
I will use small sections of this long *poema* to illustrate some ways in
which the various components of Amichai's rhetorical and philosophical system come together:

Sometimes I want to go back
to everything I had, as in a museum,
when you go back not in the order
of the eras, but in the opposite direction, against the arrow,
to look for the woman you loved.
Where is she? The Egyptian Room,
the Far East, the Twentieth Century, Cave Art,
everything jumbled together, and the worried
guards calling after you:
You can't go against the eras! Stop!
The exit's over here! You won't learn from this,
you know you won't. You're searching, you're forgetting.[103]

לִפְעָמִים אֲנִי רוֹצֶה לַחֲזֹר
אֶל כָּל מַה שֶּׁהָיָה לִי, כְּמוֹ בְּמוּזֵיאוֹן,
כְּשֶׁאַתָּה חוֹזֵר לֹא לְפִי סֵדֶר
הַתְּקוּפוֹת, בְּכִוּוּן הָפוּךְ, לֹא לְפִי הַחֵץ,
כְּדֵי לְחַפֵּשׂ אֶת הָאִשָּׁה הָאֲהוּבָה.
אֵיפֹה הִיא? הַחֶדֶר הַמִּצְרִי,
הַמִּזְרָח הָרָחוֹק, הַמֵּאָה הָעֶשְׂרִים, אָמְנוּת
הַמְּעָרוֹת, הַכֹּל בְּעִרְבּוּבְיָה, וְהַשּׁוֹמְרִים
הַמֻּדְאָגִים קוֹרְאִים אַחֲרֶיךָ:
זֶה בִּגְוּד לַתְּקוּפוֹת! לֹא לְשָׁם!
כָּאן הַיְצִיאָה. אַתָּה לֹא תִלְמַד מִזֶּה,
אַתָּה יוֹדֵעַ שֶׁלֹּא. אַתָּה מְחַפֵּשׂ, אַתָּה שׁוֹכֵחַ.

This programmatic, metapoetic statement is cast in an indirect and figurative rhetoric of autobiography, yet it embodies one of the major principles articulated in this central work and in Amichai's entire poetry: the
poem as an achronological, simultaneous, discontinuous, and disruptive reconstruction of the various layers of the speaker's experience of
personal and collective history. Although his quest always has a specific

goal, such as to find the lost beloved woman or the (permanently lost) God of his childhood, these disruptions of personal and communal chronology cannot bring the speaker back to "everything [he] had." Still, by retrieving arbitrary (or seemingly arbitrary) images from his personal and historical museum, and engaging them in interdependent and interpenetrating juxtapositions, the speaker can at least protest actively against the deadening effects of religious, social, and aesthetic order. As Amichai's traveler attempts to effect simultaneity or return linear order to chaos, he is aware that he is moving across aesthetic dimensions rather than their geographic and historical referents. The attempt to recover personal loss involves daring to confront disorder, "everything jumbled together." The "as if" simile takes over, as the speaker gets caught up not so much in the recovery of a lost love but in the violation of the guards' admonition: "You can't go against the eras! Stop!" However, as I indicated earlier, instead of the temporal chronology of historical periods and events and the actual geographical routes, it is the organizational principles of the museum and its proper order (the arrow) that he wishes to disrupt: the Egyptian Room, the Far East wing in the museum, and not their real-world historical and geographical counterparts.

The ways in which the poetic "I" conceives of himself form crucial rhetorical and philosophical links in Amichai's system. The poet's persona, always self-described as a transitional figure, embodies the same existence in-between categories, the *beynayim* state, which his philosophy and rhetoric expound. When the lyrical "I" looks inside his "self," he encounters the simultaneous layering of opposing personal and collective forces. The volatility and precariousness of this layered self can only be mitigated by a brutally honest recognition of how fragmentary these layers of the poetic persona are.[104] Still, as in "Lo kabrosh," this recognition itself is redemptive and deeply liberating. For paradoxically, only when the process of resignation has begun—and the speaker renounces any inalienable possession of that which is "his," any uniqueness for his conceptions of self and of poetry, home and territory, personal and national history—can the cosmic reaches of his world become embodied within him. Only then can he describe his being-in-the-world as a symbiotic ethnocosmic circulation, the blood flowing from the heart of stars, through the great artery of the Milky

Way, through his and Jerusalem's body cosmic to the hot, dry Middle
Eastern *hamsin* in the heavens:[105]

> I'm sitting here now with my father's eyes
> and with my mother's graying hair on my head, in a house
> that belonged to an Arab, who bought it
> from an Englishman, who took it from a German,
> who hewed it out of the stones of Jerusalem, which is my city;
> I look at the world of the god of others
> who received it from others. I've been patched together
> from many things, I've been gathered in different times,
> I've been assembled from spare parts,[106] from disintegrating
> materials, from decomposing words. And already now,
> in the middle of my life, I'm beginning to return them, gradually,
> because I want to be a good and orderly person
> at the border, when they ask me: "Do you have anything to declare?"
> So that there won't be too much pressure at the end,
> so that I won't arrive sweating and breathless and confused.
> So that I won't have anything left to declare.
> The red stars are my heart, the distant Milky Way
> is the blood in it, in me. The hot
> *hamsin* breathes in huge lungs,
> my life is close to a huge heart, always inside.

אֲנִי יוֹשֵׁב עַכְשָׁו כָּאן עִם הָעֵינַיִם שֶׁל אָבִי
וְעִם הַשֵּׂעָר הַמַּאֲפִיר שֶׁל אִמִּי עַל רֹאשִׁי, בְּבַיִת
שֶׁהָיָה שֶׁל עֲרָבִי שֶׁקָּנָה אוֹתוֹ
מֵאַנְגְּלִי שֶׁלָּקַח אוֹתוֹ מִגֶּרְמָנִי,
שֶׁחָצֵב אוֹתוֹ מִסַּלְעֵי יְרוּשָׁלַיִם שֶׁהִיא עִירִי;
אֲנִי מַבִּיט אֶל עוֹלָמוֹ שֶׁל אֱלֹהִים שֶׁל אֲחֵרִים
שֶׁקִּבְּלוּ אוֹתוֹ מֵאֲחֵרִים. צֹרַפְתִּי
מִדְּבָרִים רַבִּים, נֶאֱרַרְתִּי בִּזְמַנִּים שׁוֹנִים,
הֻרְכַּבְתִּי מֵחֶלְקֵי־חָלוּף, מֵחֲמָרִים
מִתְבַּלִּים, מִמִּלִּים מִתְפַּלּוֹת. וּכְבָר עַכְשָׁו,
בְּאֶמְצַע חַיַּי, אֲנִי מַתְחִיל לְהַחֲזִיר אוֹתָם לְאַט, לְאַט,
כִּי אֲנִי רוֹצֶה לִהְיוֹת אָדָם טוֹב וּמְסֻדָּר
בַּגְּבוּל, כְּשֶׁיִּשְׁאֲלוּ אוֹתִי: "יֵשׁ לְךָ עַל מַה לְהַצְהִיר?"
כְּדֵי שֶׁלֹּא יִהְיֶה לַחַץ גָּדוֹל מִדַּי בַּסּוֹף,

שֶׁלֹּא אַגִּיעַ מֵזִיעַ וּקְצַר־נְשִׁימָה וּמְבֻלְבָּל.
שֶׁלֹּא יִשָּׁאֵר לִי עַל מַה לְהַצְהִיר.
הַכּוֹכָבִים הָאֲדֻמִּים הֵם לִבִּי, שְׁבִיל הֶחָלָב
הָרָחוֹק הוּא הַדָּם שֶׁבּוֹ, שֶׁבִּי. הַשָּׁרָב
הֶחָם הוּא בְּתוֹךְ רֵיאוֹת גְּדוֹלוֹת,
חַיַּי הֵם בְּקִרְבַת לֵב גָּדוֹל, תָּמִיד בִּפְנִים.

Three   **"I Want to Mix Up the Bible"**

Intertextuality, Agency, and the Poetics
of Radical Allusion

> Broken fragments of the Golden Calf
> and broken Tablets of the Law
> jumbled together in one great heap.
>
>   —Yehuda Amichai[1]

I. Theorizing, Not Theories

Amichai's poetic signature—those aspects of his writing style that allow
a reader to immediately recognize a poem as his—consists at least in
part of his famous iconoclastic allusions to sacred texts. My aim in
this chapter is not simply to characterize his intertextual practices, but
rather to tease out from that characterization the implicit theory of
intertextuality embedded within his oeuvre—a theory that, I believe,
can provide a corrective to the dominant models in the field. I will proceed from describing to theorizing and from poetry to poetics, using
Amichai's work as my anchor for both. That the intertextual practice
and theory remain inseparable, despite this methodological move, is
precisely the point I wish to make.

In the first section of this chapter I describe some of Amichai's distinctive uses of intertextuality, especially his famous radical biblical allusions and their equally famous bilateral effect: the deflation of the
sacred and the sacralization of the mundane. At the same time I call
into question—as Sidra DeKoven Ezrahi has done as well—their very
separateness.[2] Focusing on close readings of several of his seminal
poems, I describe the tensions between—and the ultimate reconciliation of—Amichai's layered and complex intertextual practices with his
commitment to an egalitarian poetics and the rhetorically accessible
poem. It has long been a critical commonplace that Amichai's poetry
is characterized by a reversal of traditional biblical narratives and an
inversion of normative rabbinic and liturgical texts. What is less frequently acknowledged, however, is his refusal to privilege his omni-

present radical engagement with traditional forms of Jewish textual exegesis over culturally less privileged citational practices that "recycle" (his term!)[3] snippets of ordinary conversation, popular song, children's language, or military slang. Following DeKoven Ezrahi, I believe that this refusal is itself an important aspect of Amichai's resistance to a dichotomous separation of the sacred and the quotidian.

The close readings I provide in section I of this chapter are meant to help us understand how this intertextual egalitarianism maintains the accessible, transparent quality of Amichai's poetry even while it engages in an involved dialogue with numerous precursor texts—from the Hebrew Bible, midrash, rabbinic literature, and liturgy, through classics of the Western canon and Christian models of text-based meditation, to the genres and forms of classical Arabic poetry. I outline some of the ways in which Amichai's poetic worldview, discussed in detail in chapter 2, is implicated in his lifelong struggle against—and love affair with—diverse textual traditions. Methodologically, and in a gesture of homage to Amichai's critique of "order" (*seder*, with all its implications of the Passover ritual and the linear narrative of national redemption, as we've seen in previous chapters), I choose to avoid a typology listing his various intertextual practices. Instead, I try to provide here a number of (only partially consistent) takes that emerge from or are suggested by discussions of poems by Amichai. These poems are written in diverse styles and during different periods, and engage a range—but not necessarily a representative cross-section—of his intertextual practices. In the process, I hope to introduce the American reader, among others, to a reading and writing community that sees textual allusions and textual commentary as still integrated, to some extent at least, into the culture of everyday life.

These readings set the stage for section II of this chapter, where I explore the ways in which Amichai's poetry compels a retheorizing of intertextuality through its insistent focus on agency. At the center of Amichai's project is not the poet as such but the pressured, confined human subject, caught between the "grindstones of history,"[4] for whom the radical revisions of textual authority are at times the only available forms of resistance. Engaging critically with contemporary theories of influence and intertextuality, I discuss Amichai's reinscription of a historically inflected human agent into the process of rewriting texts of religious and cultural authority. An account of this agency is central, I believe, following Amichai, to an adequate theorizing of the processes of recycling and recasting precursor texts. I hope to challenge through Amichai's work both the patriarchal, authoritarian models of influence—from traditional "source criticism" to Bloom's "anxiety of influence"—and the agentless poststructuralist views of intertextuality as a "tissue of citations," which is "anonymous, untraceable, yet *already read*," in Roland Barthes's terms.[5]

II. "Words Accompany My Life": Everyday Speech as Intertextual Model

Let me start with the puzzle of Amichai's accessibility. In the hands of another poet, this poetry's steady diet of allusions, parodic midrashim, pseudo-commentary, textual meditations, and other modes of intertextuality would result in a dauntingly difficult body of work. Yet Amichai continues to be a phenomenally readable poet, accepted and admired—or derided and rejected—as the crafter of the "easy poem."[6] Because Amichai's layered intertextuality does not present itself as a necessary precondition for an understanding of his poetry, the opinion still persists that there is nothing much for scholars to do with his corpus. Indeed, the number of scholarly books devoted to his oeuvre is appallingly small, especially given his central status in the Israeli and international canon. As I argue in chapter 2, Amichai's own poetics of simplicity and the "wisdom of camouflage" with which he veils his complex artistry have a lot to do with the persistence of this opinion.

I find Amichai's combination of canonical centrality and scholarly marginality particularly instructive: it challenges some tenets common in contemporary theories of literary historiography and exposes the Anglocentric focus of those theories themselves. Michael Bérubé, for example, equates a writer's canonicity with his or her stature within academic critical discourse.[7] While this correlation may indeed be crucial for the reception of contemporary American writers, it is much more problematic when applied to Hebrew literary culture. For one, the popular tradition of the *retzenzya*—the polemical journalistic review—and the role of the literati as public intellectuals have always been more powerful canon-makers in modern Jewish literature than any academic literary institutions could ever hope to be.[8] Furthermore, in Israeli culture—where the intersection of Middle Eastern and Eastern European norms has resulted in an enhanced valorization and popularization of poetry—even experimental and highly allusive poems serve as lyrics for popular musical adaptations. Popular culture may therefore play a greater role than academic discourse in establishing an Israeli poet's canonicity.

The following episode might bring home this crucial cultural difference in the reception and status of poetry: many years ago, while having my car fixed in a poor south Tel Aviv neighborhood, I suddenly noticed that the song the *garagenik* (mechanic) was singing, stretched out on his back underneath my car, was in fact an Amichai poem. It had been set to music and—in Shlomo Artzi's pop/rock rendition—gained instant popularity. It didn't matter that the "lyrics" of this poem-turned-song were quite a mouthful. In fact, the poem ("Through Two Points Only One Straight Line Can Pass")[9] develops a sustained and complex allusion to John Donne on the one hand and Ecclesiastes on the other by way of quoting a theorem in geometry. The poem constructs, in truly English metaphysical fashion, a correlation between the geometric theorem and the lovers' struggle for intimacy in a world of contradictory, feuding forces.[10] The point of my story is *not* that neither the mechanic nor indeed Shlomo Artzi, the singer-songwriter, could be expected to fully "do justice to" the poem's intertextual intersections of Hebraic and Western allusions. Rather, it is that the semantic complexity or interpretive difficulty of this poem, or indeed its affiliation with the trends and genres of highly canonical poetry past and present, were not experienced—at least at the time—as a problem for their popular consumers or performers.[11] It occurred to me as I was standing there listening to the song that this is precisely what Amichai's poetry is after: closing the divide between high and low culture, canonicity and popularity, difficulty and simplicity. For in lying underneath my car, the mechanic was also unwittingly enacting a famous metaphor from Amichai's early poetry, thus physically engaging the intertextual slippage between the sacred and the profane that has become so emblematic of this poet. The metaphor I am referring to depicts God as the universal *garagenik* (in a poem I discuss further in chapter 4):

> Underneath the world, God lies stretched on his back,
> always repairing,[12] always things get out of whack.[13]

אֱלֹהִים שׁוֹכֵב עַל גַּבּוֹ מִתַּחַת לַתֵּבֵל,

תָּמִיד עָסוּק בְּתִקּוּן, תָּמִיד מַשֶּׁהוּ מִתְקַלְקֵל.

Seeing God as a mechanic and the mechanic as God is no mere iconoclasm or heresy, though these were important goals in themselves for Amichai in the context of the 1950s. In this famous early poem, "Ve-hi tehilatekha" ("And That Is Your Glory"), as in other poems, the figures of speech are always the figures of *someone's* speech, the "small outcry" (line 1 of the poem) of a human agent who has "been through low and through high" (line 2) and is trying to find a language to deal with a world in which "God is hiding, and man cries Where have you gone" (line 4):

> I've yoked together my large silence and my small outcry
> like an ox and an ass. I've been through low and through high.
> I've been in Jerusalem, in Rome. And perhaps in Mecca anon.
> But now God is hiding, and man cries Where have you gone.
> And that is your glory.[14]

בְּשְׁתִיקָתִי הַגְּדוֹלָה וּבְצַעֲקָתִי הַקְּטַנָּה אֲנִי חוֹרֵשׁ

כִּלְאַיִם. הָיִיתִי בַּמַּיִם וְהָיִיתִי בָּאֵשׁ.

הָיִיתִי בִּירוּשָׁלַיִם וּבְרוֹמָא. אוּלַי אֶהְיֶה בְּמֶכָּה.

אַךְ הַפַּעַם אֱלֹהִים מִתְחַבֵּא וְאָדָם צוֹעֵק אַיֶּכָּה.

וְהִיא תְּהִלָּתֶךָ.

The Hebrew translated by Mitchell as "I've been through low and through high" rewrites the famous "U-netane Tokef" prayer recited on Yom Kippur, which reads literally: "who by fire and who by water." This allusion is then grafted onto a reversal of the Garden of Eden story (Genesis 3:9), whose language is cited verbatim in Amichai's Hebrew (literally, "but this time God hides himself and the human cries out where art thou [*ayekah*]"). This small part of the poem's extensive and multilayered intertextual collage thus boldly portrays God as the sinner who is hiding from the human beings he has put through so much unjust suffering. The insistence on human agency, as well as the anthropomorphism that cuts God down to human size, result in an investment in the quotidian details of human and divine labor and, concomitantly, in the circulation of poetry beyond the confines of high culture and without privileging one formation of cultural exchange over another.

The intertextual work that a poem must perform is engaged in Amichai's later poetry through a meditation in which ordinary conversation rather than some quotation of a canonical, sacred text serves as the exemplum.[15] The poem "Hadera," for example, published in his 1989 metapoetic book *Even the Fist Once Was an Open Hand and Fingers*, starts out with a self-quotation from an ordinary phone conversation Amichai and I had a few years earlier:[16]

Hadera

"I never was in Hadera" is like
A verdict killing by sorrow and establishing a fact, like death.
"I just passed through and didn't stay."

The Street of the Heroes I understand,
I understand heroes and their death.
The water tower I understand,
But I never stayed in Hadera.

The roads of my life I thought were roads
Were only light bridges
Above places where I never was.

In the old house the tiles still perform
The tapping of a dance that was.
Hosts forgot whom they invited
Guests didn't know they were invited
And didn't come and those who could have met didn't meet.

People had hopes like eucalyptuses,
They were brought from far away and remained.
And in the abandoned orchard, citrus trees beg
For a fence around them as a soul
Begs for a body again. The pumping shed is ruined,
An old engine rusting outside like an old man at the end of his days

Sitting in the door of his house, full of years,
At his side the remnants of a spring, throbbing weakly
In the scum of a shallow swamp, as a memory.

What determined my life and what didn't
Oh summer 1942, oh Hadera
Where I only passed by and didn't stay.
Had I stayed my life would be different.

חֲדֵרָה

"מֵעוֹלָם לֹא הָיִיתִי בַּחֲדֵרָה" זֶה כְּמוֹ
פְּסַק דִּין מֵמִית מְצֻעָר וְקוֹבֵעַ עֻבְדָּה, כְּמוֹ מָוֶת.
"רַק עָבַרְתִּי דַּרְכָּהּ וְלֹא שֶׁהִיתִי בָּהּ".

אֶת רְחוֹב הַגִּבּוֹרִים אֲנִי מֵבִין,
אֲנִי מֵבִין גִּבּוֹרִים וְאֶת מוֹתָם.
אֶת מִגְדַּל הַמַּיִם אֲנִי מֵבִין,
אֲבָל מֵעוֹלָם לֹא שֶׁהִיתִי בַּחֲדֵרָה.

דַּרְכֵי חַיַּי שֶׁחָשַׁבְתִּי אוֹתָן דְּרָכִים
הָיוּ רַק גְּשָׁרִים קַלִּים
מֵעַל לַמְּקוֹמוֹת שֶׁבָּהֶם לֹא הָיִיתִי.

בַּבָּתִּים הַיְשָׁנִים עֲדַיִן מַשְׁמִיעוֹת הַמַּרְצָפוֹת
קוֹל תִּקְתּוּק שֶׁל רִקּוּד שֶׁהָיָה.
מְאָרְחִים שָׁכְחוּ אֶת מִי הִזְמִינוּ
אוֹרְחִים לֹא יָדְעוּ שֶׁהֻזְמְנוּ
וְלֹא בָּאוּ וְאֵלֶּה שֶׁיָּכְלוּ לְהִפָּגֵשׁ לֹא נִפְגָּשׁוּ.

לָאֲנָשִׁים הָיוּ תִּקְווֹת כְּמוֹ לָאֵיקָלִיפְטוּסִים
שֶׁהוּבְאוּ, כְּמוֹהֶם, מֵרָחוֹק וְנִשְׁאָרוּ.
וּבְפַרְדֵּס הֶעָזוּב מְבַקְּשִׁים עֲצֵי הֶהָדָר
שׁוּב גָּדֵר סְבִיבָם כְּמוֹ שֶׁנָּשְׁשָׁמָה
מְבַקֶּשֶׁת שׁוּב גּוּף. בֵּית הַמַּשְׁאָבָה חָרֵב,
מָנוֹעַ יָשָׁן מַחֲלִיד בַּחוּץ כְּמוֹ זָקֵן בְּעֶרֶב יָמָיו
שֶׁיּוֹשֵׁב לִפְנֵי פֶּתַח בֵּיתוֹ שֶׁבַע יָמִים
וּלְיָדוֹ שְׂרִיד מַעְיָן, מְפַכֶּה חַלָּשׁ
בִּירֹקֶת שֶׁל בִּצָּה רְדוּדָה לְזִכָּרוֹן.

מַה קָבַע אֶת חַיַּי וּמַה לֹּא קָבַע.

הוֹ, קֵיץ 1942, הוֹ חֲדֵרָה

שֶׁרַק עָבַרְתִּי בָּהּ וְלֹא שָׁהִיתִי בָּהּ.

וְאִלּוּ שָׁהִיתִי הָיוּ חַיַּי אֲחֵרִים.

At the time, of course, I had no way of knowing that the innocuous phone call in which I gave Amichai directions on how to come with his family to my in-laws' house in Hadera for a weekend visit ("near the water tower you make a left turn on Heroes Street") would end up as the textual exemplum for exegetical meditation in a poem. I cannot recall whether the lines in quotation marks at the beginning of the poem are the exact words Yehuda used on the phone, but I know he said something about not knowing the way because he'd passed through Hadera only once before many years earlier but never really stayed there. I think it's safe to assume, however, that he did not use the literary *me'olam* (but rather the more colloquial *af pa'am*) for "never"; that he did not use the highly formal *ba-chaderà* (like everyone else, he probably used the colloquial pronunciation *be-chaderà* for "in Hadera");[17] and that in all likelihood he did not use the literary verb *shahiti* (lit., "lingered") with the high-falutin' inflected prepositional *ba* ("in it"; lit., "in her"). But, of course, these stylizations are needed if a quotation from a phone call is to get the reader thinking in terms of the philosophical discourse of life and death, love and war, place as the site of stasis or motion[18]— all the while preserving the impression of quoted conversational discourse (as contrasted with biblical or literary allusion, for example). In fact, however, a highly canonical intertextual dialogue is "camouflaged" here as an ordinary phone call—a dialogue that many other poems by Amichai conduct more directly—with the great medieval Hebrew poet Shmuel HaNagid.

In an article titled "'Kemo be-shir shel Shmuel Ha-Nagid': beyn Shmuel ha-Nagid li-Yehuda Amichai" ("As in a Poem by Shmuel Ha-Nagid": Between Shmuel Ha-Nagid and Yehuda Amichai), Tova Rosen describes the discourse structure unique to Ha-Nagid, where the starting point for a meditation is found in the speaker's self-quotation, and in "the articulation in the first person of a personal experience (biographic or pseudo-biographic)."[19] The stylistic elevation of self-quotation in the first stanza of "Hadera" is therefore not merely a way to make mundane linguistic materials worthy of poetry but the first step in a carefully constructed meditative discourse modeled, as Rosen astutely observes, on Ha-Nagid's self-quoting personal meditations. Thus, the conversational allusion embeds in its positioning as the opening exemplum of the poem's meditation a canonical and highly literate intertextual dialogue. The stylization of the quoted phone conversation produces an implicit but undeniable sexual metaphor, which maps traveling through the city-as-woman onto lovemaking. In an interview with me,[20] Amichai described Ha-Nagid as his most beloved medieval Hebrew poet, because of the bluntness and directness with which he uses the "real things around" him as a source for exegetical meditation. Amichai derives from Ha-Nagid a model for poetry as meditation on the quotidian. As he told me in the same interview, "The poem turns around the real world the way the Oral Torah [rabbinic exegesis] turns around the verse."

Thus, for example, when *be-chadèra* becomes *ba-chadèrà*, the accompanying change in register from colloquial to literary Hebrew enables a pseudo-etymological midrash on *chadirà* ("penetration," same stress pattern; root *ch.d.r.*) and an erotic reading of *darka* ("through it/her"; lit., "her way" or "road"; the femininity of place terms in Hebrew is, of course, very useful here in establishing the metonymic identification of Hadera with the desired woman who was in it in 1942; see below). This stylized part of the self-quotation in turn enables the self-exegetical speaker to meditate on the question of how one's way or route in life (*derekh chayim*) is often determined by momentary and seemingly trivial decisions.[21] The biographical background, on which Amichai has since expanded in several conversations with me, clarifies the connection between a literal passing through Hadera, the linking of love and war in the poem, and a metaphorical meditation on the ways of life. In the summer of 1942, Yehuda Amichai passed through Hadera en route to enlisting in the Jewish Brigade of the British army. He had there, as he told me, a meaningful but brief encounter with a woman. Had he "stayed in" Hadera and not just "passed through it/her"—his life would have been different. My point, however, is that the pseudo-quotation or internal translation from colloquial to literary Hebrew—and the sexual encounter it invokes—are, for Amichai, as poetically worthy of contemplation as the more veiled intertextual model of Ha-Nagid's meditative poetry. Common personal conversation, even a phone call asking for directions, is every bit as important a source of intertextual engagement and philosophical reflection as any canonical cultural text.[22]

The poem "Menuchat kayitz u-milim" ("Summer Rest and Words")[23] is another example from the late poetry of the anti-elitist impact of Amichai's reinscription of personal agency into intertextual practice; it is also a carefully wrought thematization of this practice, a metapoetics of intertextuality that—like the other metapoetic poems in his later work—carefully veils its own radical artfulness:

Summer Rest and Words

The sprinklers calm summer's wrath.
The sound of the sprinkler twirling
And the swish of the water on leaves and grass
Are enough for me. My wrath
Spent and calm and my melancholy full and quiet.
The newspaper drops from my hand and turns back into
Passing times and paper wings.
I shut my eyes,
And return to the words of the rabbi in my childhood
On the bimah of the synagogue: "And give eternal salvation
To those who go off to their world." He changed
The words of the prayer a little, he did not
Sing and did not trill and did not sob
And did not flatter his God like a cantor
But said his words with quiet confidence, demanded of God
In a calm voice that accompanied me all my life.

What did he mean by these words,
Is there salvation only for those who go to their rest?
And what about our world and what about mine?
Is rest salvation or is there any other?
And why did he add eternity to salvation?
Words accompany me. Words accompany my life
Like a melody. Words accompany my life
As at the bottom of a movie screen, subtitles
Translating their language into mine.

I remember, in my youth the translation sometimes
Lagged behind the words, or came before them,

The face on the screen was sad, even crying,
And words below were joyful, or things lit up
And laughed and the words spelled great sadness.
Words accompany my life.
But the words I say myself
Are now like stones I fling
Into a well in the field, to test
If it is full or empty,
And its depth.

מְנוּחַת קַיִץ וּמִלִּים

הַמַּמְטֵרוֹת מַרְגִּיעוֹת אֶת זַעַם הַקַּיִץ.
דַּי לִי בְּקוֹל הַמַּמְטֵרָה הַמִּסְתּוֹבֶבֶת
וּבְרַחַשׁ הַמַּיִם עַל עָלִים וְעֵשֶׂב
וַעֲמִי רָוֶה וְרָגוּעַ וְעַצְבוּתִי מְלֵאָה וּשְׁקֵטָה.
אָז הֶעָתוֹן צוֹנֵחַ מִיָּדִי וְהוֹפֵךְ לִהְיוֹת שׁוּב
עֵתִּים חוֹלְפוֹת וּנְיָר כְּנָפַיִם,
אָז אֲנִי עוֹצֵם אֶת עֵינַי,
אָז אֲנִי חוֹזֵר אֶל הַמִּלִּים שֶׁל רַב יַלְדוּתִי
מֵעַל בִּימַת בֵּית הַכְּנֶסֶת "וְתֵן יְשׁוּעַת נֶצַח
לַהוֹלְכִים אֶל עוֹלָמָם". הוּא שָׁנָה קְצָת
אֶת הַמִּלִּים מִן הַתְּפִלָּה, הוּא לֹא
זִמֵּר וְלֹא סִלְסֵל בִּגְרוֹנוֹ וְלֹא הִתְיַפַּח
וְלֹא הִתְחַנֵּף לֵאלֹהָיו כְּדֶרֶךְ הַחַזָּנִים
אֶלָּא אָמַר אֶת דְּבָרוֹ בְּשֶׁקֶט וּבִטְחָה, דָּרַשׁ מֵאֱלֹהָיו
בְּקוֹל רָגוּעַ אֲשֶׁר לִוָּה אוֹתִי בְּכָל חַיָּי.

אֲנִי שׁוֹאֵל אֶת עַצְמִי לְמַה הִתְכַּוֵּן בַּמִּלִּים הָאֵלֶּה,
הַאִם יְשׁוּעָה רַק לַהוֹלְכִים אֶל עוֹלָמָם?
וּמָה עִם עוֹלָמֵנוּ וּמָה עִם עוֹלָמִי?
הַאִם מְנוּחָה הִיא יְשׁוּעָה וְאוּלַי יֵשׁ אַחֶרֶת?
וּלְשֵׁם מַה הוֹסִיף נֶצַח לִישׁוּעָה?

מִלִּים מְלַוּוֹת אוֹתִי. מִלִּים מְלַוּוֹת אֶת חַיַּי
כְּמוֹ מַנְגִּינָה. מִלִּים מְלַוּוֹת אֶת חַיַּי
כְּמוֹ הַמִּלִּים עַל מָסַךְ הַקּוֹלְנוֹעַ לְמַטָּה, בַּשּׁוּלַיִם
שֶׁמְּתַרְגְּמוֹת אֶת שְׂפָתָם לִשְׂפָתִי.

אֲנִי זוֹכֵר שֶׁבִּנְעוּרַי הַתַּרְגּוּם לִפְעָמִים
פִּגֵּר אַחַר הַנֶּאֱמָר אוֹ הִקְדִּים אוֹתוֹ,
הַפָּנִים עַל הַמָּסָךְ הָיוּ עֲצוּבִים וַאֲפִלּוּ בּוֹכִים
וְהַמִּלִּים לְמַטָּה אָמְרוּ שִׂמְחָה, אוֹ שֶׁפְּנֵי הַמְדַבְּרִים
אֹרוּ וְצָחֲקוּ וְהַמִּלִּים אָמְרוּ עַצְבוּת גְּדוֹלָה.
מִלִּים מְלַוּוֹת אֶת חַיַּי.
אֲבָל הַמִּלִּים שֶׁאֲנִי עַצְמִי אוֹמֵר
הֵן עַכְשָׁיו, כְּמוֹ אֲבָנִים שֶׁאֲנִי זוֹרֵק
לְתוֹךְ בְּאֵר בַּשָּׂדֶה לִבְדֹּק
הַאִם הִיא מְלֵאָה אוֹ רֵיקָה,
וּמָה עָמְקָהּ.

Radical reversals of liturgical texts are subversively presented here as pseudo-tradition and a sleepy nostalgic return to "the words of the rabbi in my childhood," a rabbi who liked to change the text of the prayer just a little bit, and who modeled for the speaker both an aesthetics and a theology of change through valorized simplicity. His calm voice and unadorned style, as well as his practice of changing ever so slightly the words of the prayer, have accompanied the speaker throughout his life.[24] Amichai links in this fashion his own radical rewriting of the sacred to an established rabbinical tradition, and a homespun, mild-mannered version of it to boot. All this is, of course, a nonthreatening way of presenting—and justifying—his own poetics of intertextuality as only a "slight" rewriting of the sacred, canonical texts. This thematization veils the radicalism of his practice, at the same time that it opens the door to his uncritical reception, especially—as we have already seen—in the United States, as a poet of nostalgic *Yiddishkayt*. Thus, this part of the poem reduces the intertextual heritage with which the speaker struggles to a handful of words that follow him around throughout his life, or to verbal free-associations that pass through his mind as he dozes off on a hot summer day. As it turns out, however, the poem engages in a series of deliberate and powerful deflations that mimic the secularization of the sacred in Amichai's earlier allusive poetry.

The sleepy surface of this text is increasingly disturbed toward the end of the poem, as a rupture is revealed within the intertextual baggage of the culture. The sacred intertexts are now seen as anachronistically inap-

propriate to the speaker's personal modern condition: they are an inade-
quate translation from the past to the present, from "their language into
mine." But the speaker's tone remains accepting, as he deliberately trivi-
alizes the inadequacy of traditional authoritative texts through a simile
that is itself drawn from a memory of ordinary, communal experiences
and not from the stock of literary or sacred rhetorical figures. The traditional words that accompany the speaker's life keep lagging behind—
or anticipating—their referents, just like the handwritten subtitles in
old movies in the Israel of the 1940s and 50s. This metaphorical image
may require a few notes of clarification for the contemporary American
reader: Amichai is referring here to the scrolling handwritten subtitles
in old movie theaters in Israel that would be operated by hand by a
projectionist, who could never crank the machine at the right speed for
the text to coincide with the picture. The intertextual heritage that accompanies the speaker is thus as hopelessly out of sync with the expressive needs of his reality as that primitive subtitles machine was with the
cinematic representation of emotions—the sad or happy human faces on
the screen. Yet the speaker forgives or excuses this as a "technical problem," the malfunctioning of an old subtitles projector, most likely of the
kind that had the translation "from their language to mine" on the side,
"ba-shula'yim," "in the margins," as the original Hebrew has it.[25]

Only after the speaker has asserted a new, critical agency over the
mistranslations and misquotations that he has inherited can the words
become more than soporific nostalgia for Old World Jewish traditions—
more than background music or mere verbal accompaniment. In the
final lines of the poem the words become, instead, personal touch-
stones—projectiles that actively, aggressively test the waters, question the
plenitude or depth of tradition, and proclaim the human agents' right to
assess for themselves whether there is anything in it for them, any water
left in the well to quench their thirst. And it is in the end, defiantly, into
the well of traditional sources, the well from which he has been drinking
all his life, that the speaker now throws the stones of his words: "Words
accompany my life. / But the words I say myself / Are now like stones
I fling / Into a well in the field, to test / If it is full or empty, / And its
depth." For the Hebrew reader, this is a flagrant reversal of the proverbial injunction *bor she-shatita mi-meno al tizrok bo even* (Don't throw a
stone into a well you've been drinking from).[26] It is almost as if in late

poems such as "Summer Rest and Words," in the space between summer siesta (*menuchat kayitz*) and final rest (*menuchat olamim* or *menuchat ha-ketz*), Amichai feels compelled, his Everyman persona notwithstanding, to provide an accounting of his intertextual practices and claim them as his own (the first six lines are a collage of internal allusions to earlier poems by Amichai)—and in the process to take personal responsibility for their success or failure, resonance or emptiness.

While such meta-intertextuality seems especially prominent in the later poetry, Amichai already established intertextuality in general, and the intertextual collage in particular, as the center of his poetic practice even in the early poems. This intertextual arena is where Amichai's poetic agent conducts his often grotesque and quixotic but always valorized struggles with authority. Thus, in the early poem "Jacob and the Angel" ("Ya'akov ve-ha-mal'akh"),[27] this leveling out of textual authority results in the simultaneous elevation of the mundane and naturalization of the divine, replacing their opposition with a continuum. The tone is at once playful and dead-serious: Amichai sanctifies the mundane sexual encounter between a man and a woman at the same time that he deflates the nation-forming biblical narrative of Jacob's struggle with the angel through which Jacob becomes Israel, the father of the nation. In the process, he exposes the degree to which the vocabulary of war-making has invaded the Israeli vocabulary of lovemaking, turning love and war into oxymoronic synonyms. But, as we shall see, the poem is no less about the need to grant the same aesthetic weight that is traditionally reserved in Jewish literature for biblical and rabbinic intertextuality also to ordinary language allusions—to pop songs, slang idioms, and the discourse of children's play.

Jacob and the Angel

Just before dawn she sighed and held him
that way, and defeated him.
And he held her that way, and defeated her,
and both of them knew that a hold
brings death.
They agreed to do without names.

But in the first light
he saw her body,

which remained white in the places
the swimsuit had covered, yesterday.

Then someone called her suddenly from above,
twice.
The way you call a little girl from playing
in the yard.
And he knew her name; and let her go.

יַעֲקֹב וְהַמַּלְאָךְ

לִפְנוֹת בֹּקֶר נֶאֶנְחָה וְתָפְסָה
אוֹתוֹ כָּךְ, וְנִצְּחָה אוֹתוֹ.
וְתָפַס אוֹתָהּ כָּךְ, וְנִצַּח אוֹתָהּ,
הֵם יָדְעוּ שְׁנֵיהֶם תָּפֵס
מֵבִיא מָוֶת.
וּתִּתְרוּ זֶה לָזֶה עַל אֲמִירַת הַשֵּׁם.

אֲבָל בָּאוֹר הָרִאשׁוֹן שֶׁל שַׁחַר
רָאָה אֶת גּוּפָהּ,
שֶׁנִּשְׁאָר לָבָן,
בַּמְּקוֹמוֹת שֶׁבֶּגֶד הַיָּם
אֶתְמוֹל כִּסָּה.

אַחַר כָּךְ קָרְאוּ לָהּ פִּתְאֹם מִלְמַעְלָה,
פַּעֲמַיִם.
כְּמוֹ שֶׁקּוֹרְאִים לְיַלְדָּה מִמִּשְׂחָקָהּ
בֶּחָצֵר.
וְיָדַע אֶת שְׁמָהּ וְנָתַן לָהּ לָלֶכֶת.

This poem constructs three simultaneous internal frames of reference[28] to form a tightly woven, kaleidoscopic intertextual collage, typical of Amichai's early poetry. (In his later poetry, these frames of reference often occur one *after* the other rather than layered one "on top of" the other.) Each frame introduces its own stylistic register and its own set of intertextual functions. The first frame narrates an erotic encounter between a man and a woman. Here belong, for example, the connotative uses of *yada* ("know") in the biblical sexual sense (lines 4 and 15), as well as the erotic sense of "death" in European poetry, as a periphrasis for orgasm (line 5). On this level, Amichai intertextually invokes and up-ends not some specific source-text but the stylistic conventions of love poetry in the West more generally. He attributes the same transcenden-tal valence to a one-night stand that traditional European love poetry reserves for the eternal and spiritual aspects of love. Genre conventions, Amichai's poetry reminds us, are as important an intertextual modal-ity as allusion, parody, or translation, yet they are often overlooked in theorizing intertextuality.

The second frame of reference constructs a scene of children at play and serves as a metonymy for the first literal frame (a girl for the woman, a boy for the man). This frame incorporates—quite unusually for such an early poem—the stylistic register of children's Hebrew, for example, the verb *le-natze'azh* ("to win," translated by Mitchell as "to defeat"), which in children's slang refers not only to getting the upper hand in a scuffle or a game but, specifically, to forcing the other kid "to the mat," making him or her give up or "say uncle." The language of war is thus invoked only to be rewritten as the mo-tions of the bodies in lovemaking and play. The sexual athletics of the couple's erotic encounter are read within this frame of reference as children's physical play: a naïve, if aggressive and warlike, struggle that in spite of its naïveté—or because of it—can mimic the symbolic, transcendental encounter between life and death, the human and the divine. The metonymic relation of this frame to that of the lovers is laid bare at the end of the poem, when the woman-as-child is called "suddenly from above" (from upstairs) (*mi-lema'la*), a typical Israeli scene of a parent standing on the balcony, calling the child to come up home at the end of an afternoon of play. In a world dominated by warring states and religions, sexual intimacy is thus reclaimed as a ci-pher for innocence, not sin, and the mother replaces God as a source of divine summons.

Amichai introduces the third frame of reference in the title, but the poem itself contains few other explicit allusions to the biblical narra-tive.[29] In fact, if we were to read the poem without the title, it would probably not occur to us that this is a rewriting of Jacob's struggle with the angel. All the local biblical and religious allusions in this poem, such as the play on *ha-shem* ("the name," also a common peri-phrastic euphemism for "God"), depend almost exclusively on the title for their intertextual dialogue with the biblical story of Jacob's fateful encounter with the angel in Genesis 32. Notably, however, there is no trace of primarily biblical *diction* or *syntax* in the poem, even though some polysemies do contain optional biblical or religious senses. The title maps onto the frames of sexual and children's play the outlines of the narrative of Genesis 32 in a way that creates a radical, bilateral biblical allusion, a practice that is to become central to Amichai's poetry in all its phases. In this form of allusion, the Bible provides a novel and unexpected reading for the profane contemporary context described in the poem, while at the same time the modern secular poem also enacts a radical, iconoclastic rereading of the biblical text and its rabbinical exegetical tradition.

Quite typically of Amichai's poetry—early as well as late—these three frames of reference are linked through ordinary language rather than by traditionally poetic means. Within the erotic script, applying the grammatically masculine attribute "angel" (*mal'akh*) to a flesh-and-blood woman is anchored in the conventional metaphor of colloquial idiom, where it is often used of a woman (in the sense of "a wonderful person" or "a pretty woman"). Within the children's-play script, "angel" in Hebrew slang—as in English—often refers to a male or female child ("a beautiful, peaceful, and pure creature"). Amichai can thus introduce into the poem the weighty intertextual baggage of the biblical story of Jacob's struggle with the angel, with all its national and metaphysical implications, in order to assign a transcendent valence to a one-time erotic encounter, and recast the divine messenger as a woman.[30] He domesticates and thoroughly demystifies these biblical materials and their exegetical history through the second, metonymic frame of children at play. In the process, as he is famously known to do, he also effects the sanctification and elevation of both erotic and childlike forms of intimacy, and the deflation of both the encounter with the divine and the narrative of the birth of the nation (Jacob-Israel).

Clearly, however, there is a hierarchy among the three frames of reference: the poem reads primarily as an account of lovemaking (the metaphor's "tenor," or its "target domain" in Lakoff's terms),[31] which is seen through the prism of two metaphorical intertextual mappings (the metaphor's "vehicles" or "source domains"): first, as the title suggests, through Jacob's encounter with the angel, and second through the domestic scene of children wrestling at play. This hierarchy inverts, of course, the terms of both Jewish and Christian traditions of eroticizing the encounter with the sacred and the conventions of portraying angels and cherubs as childlike. Here, by contrast, the erotic encounter is the metaphor's tenor (or target domain), and the struggle with the divine is its vehicle (or source domain). The poem finds the sacred in a single night of lovemaking where two human beings struggle to let go of immanent and permanent claims on knowing (the name of) the other, and celebrate their short-lived intimacy as a manifestation of all that is ineffable and pure.

Within the specific conditions of Hebrew poetry at the end of the 1950s, the poem achieves an additional stylistic innovation: it grants legitimacy to the literary use of relatively new and "unpoetic" registers of modern Hebrew, such as slang, children's language, and the new register of military Hebrew. But these stylistic moves are also fraught politically. Thus, for example, the then new noun *tefes* ("a hold," from the common verbal root *t.f.s.*, "to grab," "hold on to," "catch"), in line 4, can refer to the catch that holds the clip of cartridges in a rifle, marking one of the first occurrences of military Hebrew in Israeli poetry. Modern poetry in the Holy Tongue had resisted these "low" registers for a long time, so Amichai's poem was read as sacrilegious not only thematically but also linguistically. Indeed, its stylistics thematizes the inseparability of love and war in Israeli life and in modern Israeli Hebrew—a central concern for Amichai's poetic worldview. The *tefes* in its military sense is literally a "hold / [that] brings death" (lines 4–5). Similarly, at the end of the poem, the contemporary reader would recognize, perhaps even start to hum, another military reference associated with war, love, and death, an allusion to the lyrics of a popular song of the 1956 Sinai campaign era, "Hu lo yada et shma" (He Did Not Know Her Name).[32] This "lowbrow" allusion restrains the metaphysical pathos of the search for meaning in a name that no longer refers to God (*ha-shem*) but is instead a coded reference to anonymous sex; and conversely, the allusion to the song makes the ordinary uses of language just as meaningful as the sacred ones, while it simultaneously deflates the sentimental heroism of the military love song. Finally, uttering the name (the literal translation of the end of line 6, *amirat ha-shem*), could also be a metapoetic reference to Amichai's intertextual practice in this very poem: naming the biblical intertext only in the name of the poem.[33]

But as befits the bilateral structure of radical allusion in Amichai, the poem "Jacob and the Angel" also modifies our understanding of the biblical narrative itself: it highlights an obscure but implicitly crucial aspect of the struggle between Jacob and the angel. Amichai's metaphoric title for a night-long love encounter guides us to look anew at the details of the biblical story of Jacob and the angel. We discover in Genesis 32, through the prism of the modern poem's carnal narrative, an intriguing (homo)erotic moment in the encounter between God and man; or between Man (*ish*; the biblical text, unlike later traditions, has no mention of an angel but instead describes the mysterious messenger as a human male!) and man (Jacob). And this encounter, as we know, left Jacob/Israel injured in a very sensitive spot.[34] Ironically, it is the blatant heteroeroticism of the poem's encounter that releases—through its radical, bilateral intertextuality—the homoerotic potential in the biblical narrative.

As a final example that sets the stage for retheorizing intertextuality via Amichai's poetry, I would like to take a closer look at the title poem of my book, and to begin with the particular intertextual formation presented in the poem's title: "Be-khol chumrat ha-rachamim," which Chana Bloch and I have rendered as "To the Full Severity of Compassion."[35] This title is a deliberate catachresis, a (mis)use of an idiom whose meaning depends on the echo of the mangled fixed expression that nevertheless still reverberates in the background. The Hebrew expression echoed here, *be-khol chumrat ha-din*, literally translates as "in the full severity of judgment." It is legalese for "judged severely," or "according to the strict letter of the law," and is more or less the equivalent of "to the full extent of the law" in English; it is the ultimate expression of the principle of *midat ha-din*, the measure of (severe) judgment or law in Jewish jurisprudence. But, Amichai's catachresis reminds us, Jewish ethics is equally committed to the opposite principle, *midat ha-rachamim*, the measure of mercy, empathy, and compassion. Amichai doesn't only undo this dichotomy by blending both measures,

but demands of us to exercise compassion with the same rigor and ex-
acting severity (*chumra*) with which we judge and condemn:

To the Full Severity of Compassion

Count them.
Yes, you can count them. They
are not like the sand upon the sea shore. They
are not like the stars of the heaven for multitude.
They're like lonely people.
On the corner and in the street.

Count them. See them
seeing the sky through ruined houses.
Find a way out of the stones and come back. What
will you come back to? But count them, for they
do their time in dreams
and they walk around outside and their hopes, unbandaged,
are gaping, and they will die of them.

Count them.
Too soon have they learned to read the terrible
handwriting on the wall. To read and write upon
other walls. And the feast goes on in silence.

Count them. Be present for they
have already used up all the blood and there's still not enough,
as in a dangerous operation, when one is exhausted
and beaten down like ten thousand. For who's judge and what's
    judgment
unless it be to the full extent of Night
and the full severity of compassion.

                      Trans. Chana Bloch and Chana Kronfeld[36]

בְּכָל חָמְרַת הָרַחֲמִים

מְנֵה אוֹתָם.
אַתָּה יָכוֹל לִמְנוֹת אוֹתָם. הֵם
אֵינָם כַּחוֹל, אֲשֶׁר עַל שְׂפַת הַיָּם. הֵם
אֵינָם כַּכּוֹכָבִים לָרֹב. הֵם כָּאֲנָשִׁים בּוֹדְדִים.
בַּפִּנָּה וּבָרְחוֹב.

מְנֵה אוֹתָם. רְאֵה אוֹתָם
רוֹאִים אֶת הַשָּׁמַיִם דֶּרֶךְ בָּתִּים הֲרוּסִים.
צֵא מִן הָאֲבָנִים וַחֲזֹר. לְאָן
תַּחֲזֹר? אֲבָל מְנֵה אוֹתָם, כִּי הֵם
מַרְצִים אֶת יְמֵיהֶם בַּחֲלוֹמוֹת
וְהֵם מְהַלְּכִים בַּחוּץ, וְתִקְווֹתֵיהֶם שֶׁלֹּא נֶחְבָּשׁ
הֵן פְּעוּרוֹת, וּבָהֶן יָמוּתוּ.

מְנֵה אוֹתָם.
מִקֶּדֶם מְדַּי לָמְדוּ לִקְרֹא אֶת הַכְּתָב
הַוּוֹרָא עַל הַקִּיר. לִקְרֹא וְלִכְתֹּב עַל
קִירוֹת אֲחֵרִים. וְהַמִּשְׁתֶּה נִמְשַׁךְ בִּדְמָמָה.

מְנֵה אוֹתָם. הֱיֵה נוֹכֵחַ, כִּי הֵם
כְּבָר הִשְׁתַּמְּשׁוּ בְּכָל הַדָּם וַעֲדַיִן חָסֵר,
כְּמוֹ בְּנִתּוּחַ מְסֻכָּן, כְּשֶׁאֶחָד הוּא עָיֵף
וּמֻכֶּה כְּרְכָבָה. כִּי מִי דָן וּמַה דִּין
אֶלָּא בִּמְלֹא מוּבַן הַלַּיְלָה
וּבְכָל חֶמְרַת הָרַחֲמִים.

In a typical move, the speaker of Amichai's poem issues a series of instructions to an unidentified addressee, who may be either the reader
or a rhetorical objectification of the poetic persona himself. But despite
the speech rhythms of the poem's syntax, the diction has just enough
formality—especially for a poet who insists that he uses "only a small
part of the words in the dictionary"[37]—to alert a Hebrew reader not
to take the speaker's address literally. The command *mene* ("enumer-
ate," "count") is much more formal than the more colloquial term for
"count," *sefor,* and so is the use of the imperative rather than the future
for commands. And indeed, *mene* turns out to be the main trigger of an
intertextual mapping onto the poem's contemporary setting not only
of one specific biblical passage but also of the recurring biblical narrative type-scene of the divine promise to make the children of Israel as
countless (*lo yimanu*) as the sand on the seashore and as numerous as
the stars in the sky (lines 3–4).[38]

Note that this allusive formation is somewhat different from that of "Jacob and the Angel." Here the key words of the biblical promise itself are evoked in the body of the text only to be rejected outright: "They / are not like the sand upon the sea shore." The familiarity and generality of the biblical uses of *mene* (as well as their later rabbinic and liturgical reworkings) make the speaker's series of commands and assertions readily interpretable for the Hebrew reader. The allusion isn't any less accessible because the poem explicitly negates both the message and the tone of the major biblical topos evoked here, as well as its most famous manifestation—God's promise to Abraham and his descendants to make them countless (Genesis 15:5, 22:17). Less obviously (because the evoked text is less well-known), the speaker's command also negates the implied biblical injunction against counting people. It evokes the story of David's temptation by Satan to count his people, and the terrible devastation that befell the nation as a collective punishment for his attempt to do so (1 Chronicles 21).[39] The two evoked texts, the promise and the punishment, are in direct conflict, but they are both activated through the same familiar and resonant command, *mene*.

With the transition from affirmative instruction ("count them!") to description by negation ("They / are not like the sand") in lines 3–4, it is no longer God's injunction that is being upended but his *figurative language*. Using his favorite rhetorical pseudo-argument, the enthymeme, Amichai exposes the falsehood of the two stock similes of the biblical narrative of promise when he takes them literally: the fact that these people are few enough to be counted "proves" that "like sand" is not a valid analogy. The speaker's unadorned use of syntactic repetition ("they are not like *x*, they are not like *y*, they're like *z*") emphasizes his obsession with literal fact and logical argument in his rejection of the seductive figurative comparison and hyperbole embedded in the biblical similes of sand and stars. These *are* lonely or precious few people (*bodedim* can mean both). The final line of the first stanza sparely but insistently establishes the replacement of the figurative by the literal, of hyperbolic promise by a clipped affirmation of homelessness and loss.

In this initial activation of allusive material, Amichai's poem already reveals his signature modernist intertextual practice of rejecting the dichotomy between the sacred and the profane through two major modalities: (1) the iconoclastic deflation of the traditional and sacred source, namely, of the *values* associated with the biblical text and its exegetical tradition; and, simultaneously, (2) the elevation and trans-valuation of mundane human existence, which comprises the scene of Amichai's modern rewriting. However, the two polarities are not sim-ply flipped to create another (equally reductive) binary opposition. It is the very *logic* of such oppositional thinking that is being undone here. Amichai's speaker urges his addressee to renounce biblical promises of plenitude—and the national notions of chosenness associated with them—in favor of rigorous compassion for the lonely and few survi-vors who ironically can see more clearly the truth about the heavens and their promise thanks to the roofless ruins of their houses (line 7). Compassion for these disenfranchised people is an early expression of what Amichai refers to repeatedly later on in his career as his "postcyni-cal humanism," refusing the categories of "us" and "them." He focuses instead on these countable people's dependence on impossible dreams and empty promises, a dependence that leaves them open to exploita-tion and victimization. Their hopes are like gaping untended wounds that will eventually kill them (line 12). These people, Amichai says, are the ones who are entitled—after all the waiting and hoping—to the full severity of our compassion. This oxymoronic *inclusio* starts and ends the poem with an allusion based on the echo effect of the deliberate catachresis discussed above: the replacement of a key word in the col-location *be-khol chumrat ha-din* (idiomatically, "to the full severity/extent of the law") with its ethical opposite. Note that the full force of this critique can be appreciated only against the background of the centrality of the "Measure of Law" (*midat ha-din*) and the "Measure of Compassion" (*midat ha-rachamim*) as leading oppositional princi-ples that constitute traditional Jewish ethics. The oxymoronic "sever-ity of compassion" (so resonant in Hebrew: ***chumrat ha-rachamim***) conflates *chumra* ("severity," "rigor") with *rachamim* ("compassion," "pity," "mercy," "empathy"), first prosodically—since the two terms share (through metathesis) the same consonantal root letters in a differ-ent order (*ch.m.r.—r.ch.m.*)—and second, thematically, when Amichai redefines true mercy and compassion as a counter-theological absolute refusal to give false hope, hence as "rigor" or "severity." This, then, is the full reversal of the biblical covenantal, national promise, a prom-ise that according to Amichai is full of (dangerous, misleading) hope but empty of mercy and compassion. This has its parallel in Amichai's critique of the manipulative, institutional exploitation of human hopes and dreams (discussed in chapter 2). These dreams are used to imprison the people who are waiting for them to come true and thus "do their time" in them; their hopes for a better future are open, unbandaged, and lethal wounds.

The ease with which even the secular, ordinary Hebrew reader can be drawn into full dialogue with traditional Jewish texts and their modern rewritings in this short segment of the poem enables the anti-elitist stance of Amichai's style and thematics. Like the very identification of the biblical allusion *mene*, the intertextual import is laid bare on the poem's surface as the speaker directly sides with the *lonely* or *precious few* rather than the *chosen* people. Amichai thematizes this identification by using anti-elitist allusions, namely biblical terms that every native speaker of the language can identify and activate because they are part of his or her most elementary education (at least within the reading community for which this early poem was originally written). With accessibility as the primary aesthetic goal, and a critique of the Eliot-Pound model of elitist allusion perhaps as an implicit poetic target as well, Amichai can then allow the allusion hunters among his more learned readers the "treat" of subtle and intricate intertextualities. But he does that only after he has supplied the entire poem with an allusively naïve surface, because—as he told me in an interview— "the first reading must be accessible to everyone": the gesture toward the readers is also an homage to them.[40]

Still then on this first level of the readily accessible allusive gesture, the second half of the poem appears to foreground—through the very same word *mene*—a third biblical text, which is so well known it has become a cliché, not only in Hebrew but also in many other languages, including English. This, of course, is the reference to the "writing on the wall" (*mene mene tekel u-farsin*, lit., "count, count, weigh, and cut"), which—like the *mene* of the promise—is not meant to be elucidated by scholars. It is right there in the explicit language of the third stanza, as are the reversals of its original biblical meaning. But this overt simplicity is more a matter of a rhetorical impression than the actual conditions of possibility for the intertextual process to take place. For a readerly exegetical knowledge of the Book of Daniel—even in its broadest strokes—nevertheless depends on an active construal of the irony, metaphor, and wordplay within this difficult biblical text itself, and in fact requires a rather precise knowledge of the (hermetic, Aramaic) biblical text's exegetical history and its own metatextual themes and puns. Daniel 5 describes how Belshazzar, the last king of Babylon, and his lords could not read the writing that appeared on the wall during their feast. *Mene mene tekel u-farsin,* the words that foretold their doom, were unreadable to them—because they didn't understand the Jewish God's Aramaic? Because even in Aramaic this is at best a coded series of metaphors? Daniel's decoding of the writing on the wall is usually read as saying: "God has numbered [root *m.n.h.*] the days of your kingdom, has weighed [your actions] [Aramaic root *t.k.l.*; equivalent of Hebrew *sh.k.l.*] in the balance, and decided to cut off [root *p.r.s.*] your kingdom from you and give it to Persia [also root *p.r.s.*] (Daniel 5:25–28; the pun is part of Daniel's subversive act of translation-cum-interpretation). Hence, people who fail to see the warning signs of disaster are, according to what has become a cliché, those who cannot read the writing on the wall.[41] The Hebrew sense of the expression based on the Daniel narrative is, however, slightly different from the English: it is used to condemn an escapist carpe diem mindset in the face of impending disaster ("let us eat and drink, for tomorrow we die"), a mindset that is all too familiar to Israelis.

As in the first half of the poem, Amichai's speaker negates here precisely what the Bible—and the modern Hebrew idiom—assert (just as "count them" affirms what the Bible negates and the tradition prohibits). Knowing the destructiveness of divine intentions, being able to read the writing on the wall, is not much help at all: "Too soon have they learned to read the terrible / handwriting on the wall." This lesson has become part of basic education, as elementary as learning how "to read and write" (line 16). The disaster has "always-already" happened. Aware of their own impending destruction and that of others, the few surviving human beings can only continue this mock-feast-turned-Last-Supper in stillness (line 16). The Hebrew *bi-dmama* implies absence of sound and of motion, total inertia, at the same time that it echoes phonetically the blood (*dam*) of the extended figurative network of wounds, surgery, and blood donors developed in the second and fourth stanzas as metonymic stand-ins for the never-ending "need" for war: "And the feast goes on in silence. // Count them. Be present for they / have already used up all the blood and there's still not enough, / as in a dangerous operation, when one is exhausted / and beaten down like ten thousand" (lines 17–21). The prophecy of doom and defeat for the biblical conqueror of Israel is boldly applied to the post-1948 Israeli context of the poem's composition, implicitly reversing friend and foe and launching a critical political reading, enabled by the intertextual collage that grafts biblical promise onto biblical threat.

Thus, once the poem has been read in its sequence (Amichai's gesture of an accessible "first reading"), the more subtle intertextualities and their political implications can no longer be ignored. The repeated echoing of *mene* comes to function as the junction point in an allusive collage—here, a complex allusion that sutures together several biblical texts or blocks of texts. As such, it allows the reader not only to engage intertextually with one particular biblical passage but also to note the interaction between and among the various occurrences of *mene* in the Bible. Amichai's collage poignantly conflates the promise of the Pentateuch with the epitome of prophetic threat or curse in Daniel, allowing us increasingly to perceive the promise *as* jeopardy and affliction. His diction also refuses to restrict the biblical text and its modern rewritings to an exclusively Jewish narrative but, as we have seen in chapter 1, focuses on the victims of power—both Jews and Palestinians—as emblems of the need for existential compassion for the "other." The destruction of Belshazzar's empire becomes a metaphor for the human apocalypse caused by ruling authorities, and compels even the Jewish reader to interpret the Judaic idea of divine promise in less parochial terms.

Again, the radical political potential of such poems as this has rarely been observed. Note that it is crucial for Amichai's poetic egalitarianism to refuse to pinpoint any national or religious identity for those lonely/precious few people, who, in line 7, are "seeing the sky through ruined houses." The subjectivity that informs this poem, and Amichai's poetry as a whole, is always situated in the ruins of history. It is, as suggested earlier, a poetry that gives voice to what Walter Benjamin has described as the history of the vanquished[42] rather than to the universal (normatively male) national subject, as recent postcolonial Israeli critics have claimed with regard to Statehood Generation poetry. The addressee of the poem is commanded not to turn a blind eye to the displaced people's desperate gaze at the heavens but rather to "see them seeing" the lie of divine promise through the lens of its victims. As in poems such as "An Elegy on an Abandoned Village" ("Elegya al kfar natush"),[43] only by looking directly at the "half ruined" (*rak be-charev le-mechetza*) can we understand human vulnerability to political and religious false promises. The slogan "hope for a better future" is nothing more than another blood-drive organized by the superorganisms of religion or state, which are always willing to accept any eligible donor, whether Arab or Jew: as in a dangerous surgery, when "they / have already used up all the blood and there's still not enough" (line 20). The reversal of the biblical promise is thus also a refusal to make only the suffering of "the chosen people," and their ruined houses during the Nazi genocide and throughout a history of persecution, the subject of the poem. As I argued above, it is impossible in an Israeli poem written in the post-1948 decade *not* to see the ruined houses and "the few people" who remained in them *also* as referring to the displaced Palestinians. Amichai's refusal to distinguish between "us" and "them" underlies his critique of the biblical promise from his earliest poetry to the latest, as well as the position of "ideology critique" (to use Marxist terminology), a position that his poetry assumes throughout. This ideology critique is also the basis for his rereading of the biblical Binding of Isaac (Genesis 22), reminding us that it is the ram—the native, forgotten "son," "with his human eyes and curly hair"—who gets sacrificed, not the pampered, Westernized Isaac.[44]

We have come full circle from a simple, explicit challenge to the validity of the biblical promise to its rearticulation as curse and punishment, a writing on the wall, a warning that will not prevent disaster. Readers of this unorthodox version of the biblical promise who are more closely familiar with biblical scholarship will note that the conflation of promise and punishment, blessing and curse, is already present in the Bible.[45] The complex allusive collage marked by *mene* thus triggers—quite typically!—also an interaction between the *missing* parts of the famous evoked texts, what I've referred to above, following C. D. Blanton, as the "shadow text." This unpredictable element of the allusive interaction can be discerned in the precise choice of language in Amichai's initial reference to the biblical promise. In these exact words (*Ka-chol asher al sfat ha-yam . . . Ka-kokhavim la-rov;* lit., "like sand

which is upon the seashore . . . like the stars [in their] multitude"),
the promise appears only *once* in the Bible: It is used exclusively in
the coda to the highly symbolic narrative of the Binding of Isaac (the
akeda), which has famously become a major topos for Jewish martyrology, for the Shoah, and more recently for the Israeli fallen soldiers.
Amichai—like other poets of his and later generations—consistently
critiques the nationalist and parochial appropriations of the *akeda*. It is
significant, then, that the first time God's promise combines the similes
of sand on the seashore and stars in the sky, and the only time in which
the verse appears verbatim as in the poem, is in Genesis 22:17, a few
narrative moments after the disaster of the Sacrifice of Isaac was nar-
rowly averted, though it is nevertheless (mis)remembered consistently
in the postbiblical tradition as a sacrifice that did occur.[46]

One of the more surprising discoveries that a reader who goes back
to the Bible with Amichai's use of radical allusion and allusive collage
in mind is that, beyond the promise of Genesis, in all the historical
books of the Bible, the similes of sand and stars are used exclusively in
dangerous, militant descriptions, and most often occur in the portrayal
of the "local" enemy. When Joshua fights the Canaanites (Joshua 11:4),
it is they who are like the sand on the seashore; when Gideon fights the
Midianites, their camels and their army are like sand on the seashore
(Judges 7:12). The only time in which the metaphor is applied to an
Israelite (2 Samuel 17:11), it is still ironically the enemy: Absalom's army
is misleadingly described by Hushai, David's spy and adviser of this
would-be usurper of David's reign, as "sand on the seashore." Thus,
as in many of Amichai's radical reversals of biblically based sacred concepts, his anachronistic rereading turns out to reveal a similarly radical moment within the biblical text itself: not only the proximity of
promise and jeopardy, but also the biblical use of the same similes to
describe both "the chosen people" and "the enemy."

III. Theorizing Intertextuality from Amichai's Poetry[47]

I believe that, whether we are aware of it or not, we always theorize
from the literary works and cultural contexts that we study, and that is
as it should be! However, until the very recent past, theories have been

formed around an unacknowledged, unmarked (often canonical, white, male, heterosexual, and decidedly Western) normative set of paradigm examples, which are then taken as universals. In making explicit my own theorizing from the poets I read and the cultures I study, whether in their majoritarian or minoritarian formations, I try to follow Barbara Christian's injunction in "The Race for Theory" to theorize from— rather than into—the works we deem important.[48] The poetics implicit in Yehuda Amichai's oeuvre embodies as one of its central components a complex and consistent, though open-ended, view of intertextuality. This view, as I will try to show, is rooted in a critical concept of agency. Amichai's account of the resistant intertextual agent and his or her struggle with textual authorities is in dialogue with a larger Hebraic tradition of critical, even iconoclastic recycling of the foundational and most authoritative texts of the culture, although he takes this tradition quite a few heretical steps further.

Amichai's implicit theory of intertextual agency provides an important corrective to what has until recently been viewed as an irreconcilable binary opposition between models of influence and models of intertextuality. Some background may be helpful here. Authorial agency was typically associated with some version of an influence model: either traditional source criticism or a Bloomian theory of the anxiety of influence.[49] Models of intertextuality, on the other hand, located agency within the texts themselves, which were then viewed as an anonymous "tissue of citations."[50] The two models have always been construed as incompatible. For the first, no agency other than authorial was considered possible: while source criticism privileged the authority of the precursor poet, Bloomian views placed agency with the belated "ephebe." Both traditional source criticism and the Bloomian approach upheld a hierarchical, canon-oriented view of literary dynamics, and focused on the author and his (and for Bloom it could only be his) authority over "tradition and the individual talent." I will be referring to both approaches, therefore, as the influence model. The second model, which I will refer to as the intertextuality model, was hailed in the 1960s as the great equalizer, but in fact resulted in a depersonalization and erasure of the agency of the human beings involved in the production and reception of these texts. This is not to deny that poststructuralist intertextuality allowed for an egalitarian and inclusive view of the reworked and recycled nature of all texts, only to call into question one of its unfortunate side effects.

In recent decades, following the historicist/political turn in literary studies, we have seen the beginning of attempts at integrating and bridging those models: on the one hand, post-Bloomian rewritings of influence theories that do not involve a return to pretheoretical source-criticism; and on the other hand, post-Kristevan rewritings of theories of intertextuality that recognize a historically inflected poetic agency without replicating an authoritarian hierarchy of strong versus weak, early versus late. By retheorizing these aspects of the literary field through Amichai's oeuvre, I aim to contribute to this project of bridging influence and intertextuality, and to work toward extricating our discussion from the confines of the dichotomy between the two. It's high time, as Amichai shows us, that we stopped telling only the stories of some literary giants or others in their struggle against the literary giants who preceded them (stories that tend to be fairytales anyway). Instead of devoting our efforts to comparative domination (whose *agon* is bigger), we can learn a lot from Amichai's focus on the intertextual discursive practices that serve ordinary human beings—and poets among them—in the culture of everyday life, a culture that encompasses literary production and circulation as well. It may be wise to let go of the repetitive attempts to adapt Bloom's model to the needs of a more open and less aggression-dominated canon, not in the least because Bloom is utterly uninterested in the intertextual details of any literary text. After all, analyzing specific linguistic echoes suits, in Bloom's view, only "those carrion-eaters of scholarship, the source hunters." He goes on to state flatly that "[p]oetic influence, in the sense I give to it, has almost nothing to do with the verbal resemblances between one poet and another."[51] Interestingly, Bloom shares this view with the poststructuralists, whose theory of intertextuality—at least in its original form—leaves no room for analysis of any allusions, parodies, and other intertextual practices.[52]

Similarly, it is important to develop an egalitarian, nonexclusionary way to speak theoretically—as Amichai does poetically—about the ways people rewrite and "recycle" (his term!) both canonical and noncanonical texts; and to do so without erasing the rewriters, their historical contexts, and the poetic, political, and social functions their intertextual practices fulfill in the conflicted and yet continuous circulation of cultural life. For that purpose, I propose below to follow Amichai in zeroing in on the limited and threatened agency of the poetic subjects in their historical context; and to tease out the ways they are constituted by the hegemonic discursive system, without neglecting their ability both to struggle with that system and to construct complex kinship relations with other poetic subjects through an intersubjective, intertextual dialogue. Amichai thus helps us return the poststructuralist notion of intertextuality to its pre-Kristevan Russian sources. As is well known, Julia Kristeva was the one who coined the term "intertextuality" in 1966. Less well known, however, is the fact that Kristeva's coinage was her cultural translation (from east to west) of the Bakhtinian notion of dialogic intersubjectivity:

> In Bakhtin's work . . . *dialogue* and *ambivalence* are not clearly distinguished. Yet, what appears as a lack of rigor is in fact an insight first introduced into literary theory by Bakhtin: any text is constructed as a mosaic of quotations, any text is an absorption and transformation of another. The notion of *intertextuality* replaces that of intersubjectivity.[53]

By introducing her own notion of intertextuality (without acknowledging her own role in that substitution; note the agentless sentence: "intertextuality replaces . . . intersubjectivity"),[54] Kristeva performs here "a radical deconstruction of subjectivity," as Lars Eckstein has argued.[55] Both Bloom and Kristeva, in spite of the vast differences between them, in fact erase the specific meaning of any intertextual practice, albeit for diametrically opposite reasons. Situating these seemingly dichotomous views historically and ideologically may help us both to point up their conceptual limitations and to use Amichai's poetry to propose a more integrative alternative.

Amichai's trenchant critique of textual authority, which is inseparable from the antiauthoritarian worldview that permeates his entire poetics, is anchored in the rebellious agency of an Everyman who is compelled to dismantle the oppressive clichés of the culture in order not to lose his or her humanity or even simply in order to survive. Amichai's refusal to accept the Oedipal model of literary parricide on the one hand, and of impersonal, agentless intertextuality on the other, points us in the direction of a third option: a critical intertextual agency (which, as in Bakhtin, is not only the author's!)[56] that is limited, censored, and constrained, yet claims the right to embrace both change and continuity.

Influence

The influence model, at least in its Western articulations, has had a lasting evaluative and "honorific force," to quote Clayton and Rothstein,[57] a force that has been hard to shake since it first gained prominence in the mid-eighteenth century, with the consolidation of (personal) originality and (national) genius as explicit aesthetic criteria. Marko Juvan, in his historically illuminating study, reminds us that the term "influence" was "coined from the Latin word *influere*, 'flow into something'" and, "[c]oming from a celestial metaphor, it denoted a secret creative or ethical energy that flows from higher, more powerful agencies (the stars, gods, muses and saints) into the spirituality of mortals, of weaker beings, and changes their behavior or ways of expressing themselves."[58] The concept has retained its one-directional, hierarchical import in accounts of influence in literature and the arts. Susan Stanford Friedman goes one step further to assert that "influence is implicated in the rationalizing ideology of the conqueror, the colonizer, who envisions his influence as a hegemonic penetration of the conquered, the colonized."[59] The influenced subject has no choice but to be penetrated and conquered by the influencing source, whether that source represents the dominant cultural forces of the present or the textual (and often also the religious and national) authorities of the past. What the influence model conceals behind its imperialist rationalization is the fact that it is based on a logical/linguistic fallacy in the conceptualization of the relationship between influencer and influenced. Michael Baxandall was the first, to the best of my knowledge, to point out this fallacy as early as 1985, but because his field was art criticism, few literary scholars have benefited from his insights.[60] The idea of influence, Baxandall argues, involves a

> wrong-headed grammatical prejudice about who is the agent and who the patient; it seems to reverse the active/passive relation. . . . If one says that X influenced Y it seems that one is saying that X did something to Y rather than that Y did something to X.[61]

Thus, if we say, as several critics have, that Rilke and Auden have greatly influenced Yehuda Amichai, we are attributing agency only to the dead poets he read as a young man and not to Amichai himself, even though he is the one who oftentimes makes active, and even parodic, critical use of their work.[62] Furthermore, while Auden was certainly still very much alive during the 1940s when Amichai was beginning to write, he wouldn't even have been aware of Amichai's existence at that point, hence could exercise no agency in influencing him.[63] And clearly it doesn't make any sense to attribute influential agency to Rilke, who died when Amichai was two years old. So perhaps we should argue, instead, that Auden's and Rilke's *texts* influenced Amichai. But that, as we shall see, is precisely the problematic moment in models of inter-textuality: they attribute agency to the texts rather than to the human beings who produce and receive them and to the social institutions that make use of them.

Whenever he was asked about his "influences," Amichai would an-swer with a story: While he was serving in the Jewish Brigade of the British army during World War II in the Egyptian desert near Cairo, a military mobile-library truck got stuck in the dunes, and a bunch of books came tumbling out the back. Yehuda happened to be riding in the jeep behind the truck and *ati aleyhem ke-motze shalal rav* ("I swooped upon them as one that finds great spoils").[64] Lo and behold, one of the books he "borrowed" in this manner from the British li-brary just happened to be the epoch-making *Faber Book of Modern Verse* (1936), an anthology that played a major role in solidifying the canonization of Anglo-American modernism, later to be known as high modernism, even though the anthology also included poets like Auden, whose stand toward modernism was critical or at least ambiva-lent. How does this narrative of Amichai's first encounter with Auden's poetry, as well as with the poetry of Hopkins, Eliot, Pound, and Dylan Thomas, modify the dichotomous view of influence and intertextual-ity? There's no reason to doubt the veracity of Amichai's account, but its details and rhetorical moves, especially his use of the same type of intertextual midrash that is often found in his poetry, establish this narrative as a meaningful foundational story.[65]

The antihero of Amichai's narrative is a figure that recurs in his early work: the soldier-poet as a mock-prophet in the desert of army life.[66]

On the face of it, this narrative corroborates the colonial model of influence condemned by Stanford Friedman: The influence of Anglo-American modernism, which the future poet would be nurtured by, flows from the British occupiers' dysfunctional vehicle—and in the colonial language!—in the midst of the Middle Eastern desert, as if it were manna from heaven or water from the rock. But Amichai's diction emphasizes, at least in this version of the story, the active agency of the influenced subject. The idiomatic biblical simile, *ke-motze shalal rav*, is a common expression in modern Hebrew, meaning something like "as someone who comes across a great find." But it is also a *hapax legomenon* (an expression that occurs only once in the Bible), appearing in Psalms 119:162 as a metaphor for human pleasure in divine utterance, a pleasure that is emphatically textual: *sas anokhi al imratekha ke-motze shalal rav*, literally: "I leap with joy upon your words as one that findeth great spoils." The speaker in Psalms models the excitement with which he anticipates receiving God's words on the joy of a fighter who comes upon the spoils of war, a simile that gets literalized in the biographic context of Amichai's soldier narrative. Moreover, as is often the case in Amichai's poetry as well, the expression he uses to describe his first chance encounter with Anglo-American modernism includes another biblical allusion, also a *hapax*, whose context is diametrically opposed to the one in Psalms. When Samuel condemns Saul for allowing his army to "fly upon the spoils" and do "evil in the sight of the Lord" (1 Samuel 15:19), he compares Saul implicitly to a vulture swooping (*at*) upon dead carcasses. Amichai's narrative conjoins, therefore, in portmanteau fashion, two different allusions with opposing intertextual implications (much as his speaker did with *mene* in "To the Full Severity of Compassion"). On the one hand, the books of the British library are implicitly compared to divine utterance; on the other hand, the internal logic of the allusion to 1 Samuel, and the literalization of the simile from Psalms in Amichai's military context— a Jewish soldier in the army of the British Occupation during World War II—locate any active intertextual agency unequivocally—but not univocally!—within Amichai himself. He is not conquered by the hegemonic texts that come into his possession but chooses to appropriate them, to "plunder" them. Furthermore, Amichai's narrative attributes agency not to the textual authority of the high-modernist canonical poets, but to his own active, joyful (*sas*) and even aggressive (*at*) appropriation of them, using them to enrich his own poetic subjectivity and intertextual echo chamber.

Inverting or correcting the direction of agency in the conception of influence is, in fact, at the core of an influential modernist theory of literary history, proposed by the initiator of the famous Faber anthology, T. S. Eliot himself.[67] His "Tradition and the Individual Talent" is, of course, a salient example, where the contemporary poet, who in "The Waste Land" is shoring classical and modern textual fragments against his ruins, also has the power to rearrange literary history into a different order by the mere act of inserting himself into it:

> [W]hat happens when a new work of art is created is something that happens simultaneously to all the works of art which preceded it. The existing monuments form an ideal order among themselves, which is modified by the introduction of the new (the really new) work of art among them. The existing order is complete before the new work arrives; for order to persist after the supervention of novelty, the whole existing order must be, if ever so slightly, altered; and so the relations, proportions, values of each work of art toward the whole are readjusted.[68]

Amichai's articulation of the same position—typically expressed not in programmatic manifestos but through a poetic engagement with subject matter that on the surface is not metapoetic at all—radically inverts the direction of influence as well. But unlike Eliot—or Natan Zach, the leader of the impersonal modernist trend within Hebrew Statehood Generation poetry—Amichai's view of influence is centered on a critical agency that is open to, even required by, every individual. In poem after poem, Amichai's speaker boldly asserts every person's ability—indeed his or her duty—to effect a change in the sacred texts of old. And it is the agency of ordinary human beings, not of "strong poets," that Amichai celebrates—precisely because of its ordinariness.

"Every day of our life together / Ecclesiastes erases a verse of his book" (*be-khol yom shel chayeynu yachdav / kohelet mochek shura mi-sifro*), he writes in his 1955 "Six Poems for Tamar."[69] With the exuberance of young love, the speaker goes beyond proclaiming that the lovers' happiness disproves the nihilistic maxims of the Book of Ecclesiastes. Here the translation masks the double agency, so to speak, of the intertextual process.[70] Amichai's dissident intertextual agent paradoxically revives the agency of the long-dead biblical poet, as if he were an individual subject, even as he rejects his authority. The transition from text to poet is enabled in Hebrew by the fact that "Kohelet" is both the name of the book and the proper name of its fictional narrator, "Kohelet ben-David, King in Jerusalem,"[71] traditionally considered a pen name for King Solomon in his later years. "Ecclesiastes," on the other hand, is just the name of the book, Greek for "member of an assembly," and comically translated in the King James Version as "The Preacher," making the book sound like a medieval morality play. (Not really a proper name, "Ecclesiastes" is the Septuagint rendering of the Hebrew name Kohelet, from the root *k.h.l.*, "community.") But in Amichai's Hebrew, Kohelet becomes a vivid character again, a disillusioned old man who is nevertheless an agent capable of change and of being influenced by the "belated" lovers, even as he is compelled by their simple daily happiness to "de-write" his canonized text and to undo his own depressive intertextual authority over future poets and lovers. What we don't find in Amichai—even when he explicitly rejects the most canonical intertextual models—is a Bloomian parricide of a poetic forefather. Whereas Bloom's Oedipal model implicitly accepts the precursor's authority in asserting the need to kill him off, Amichai rejects any such sense of authority and revives the precursor by acknowledging both his agency and his need to respond to the belated generations' challenge, albeit by de-creating his work.[72]

Rereading Bloom's "anxiety of influence" through Amichai, it becomes clear that in many ways Bloom is but a "belated" anxious epigone of Eliot. Bloom restores agency to the poet who actually does something with the textual tradition. But, despite providing a detailed (and quite idiosyncratic) taxonomy of the "ephebe's" various possible relations to his precursor "strong" poet, Bloom remains very much within an authoritarian, masculinist, and fundamentally militant model of literary lineage. Furthermore, contrary to his claims to complete historiographic revisionism, Bloom actually preserves the authoritarian view of literary lineage that has characterized pre-theoretical source critics, those same "carrion eaters" whom he so despises. This is the case even if the directionality of authority is reversed in his model by his attempt to make room for the various possible ways in which the belated ephebes can kill off their strong precursors. Michael Gluzman has shed light on the masculinist, militant aspects of this view, and its resulting bizarre historiographic genealogy: a literary family without mothers and sisters, a monarchy without queens, princesses, or even la-dies-in-attendance.[73] Here Gluzman critiques not only Bloom's anxiety of influence but also the androcentric aspects of the Russian Formal-ists' view in Shklovsky's famous articulation. According to this account, rebellion against the father, which is necessary for literary dynamics, is made possible by an identification with the literary uncle.[74] Although I am in complete agreement with Gluzman's critical project, I think it is important to distinguish between the Formalists' sociopolitical agenda—as it is expressed, for example, in their critique of literary historiography as a "history of generals"—and the pseudo-kabbalistic bourgeois individualism of Harold Bloom. Furthermore, for the For-malists, as for Bakhtin, agency is located in the language as a social institution comprising the speech community, not in an objectified agentless text or in the personal authority of one powerful speaker.[75]

Even though Yehuda Amichai accepted Eliot's reversal of agency in literary influence from the precursor to the belated poet, he would never have referred to canonical works of the past as the "existing monuments" forming "an ideal order." Moreover, Amichai refused to describe his relation to the poets that preceded him in terms of a lit-erary patrilineage based on a generational struggle. Time and again Amichai reiterated, in interviews as well as in a number of poems, his indebtedness to the women poets who came before him, especially the German expressionist poet Else Lasker-Schüler and the Hebrew poet of the *moderna,* Leah Goldberg.[76] Indeed, Amichai is the only leading male Hebrew poet to present his own poetic lineage, at least in part, as a matrilineage.[77] He even departed from his consistent avoidance of critical writing when he composed introductions to his Hebrew trans-lation of Lasker-Schüler's book of poems and to her selected poems in English, as well as to an English translation of Leah Goldberg's poetry.[78] Amichai, who knew Lasker-Schüler as a Jerusalem eccentric in his teenage years, describes her in his introductions to the Hebrew and English translations as "one of the great poets of the [twentieth] century." In the English translation's foreword he adds: "Her image

has often revisited me, as have her poems."[79] Her importance as a
model for Amichai's poetry was recognized in the earliest reviews of
his work but, until recently, has remained largely overlooked in the
academic research.[80]

Nor has Amichai's affiliation with Goldberg been sufficiently explored, even though we now know that it had a deep foundation both
biographically and poetically. In the Goldberg Archives in Tel Aviv,
Giddon Ticotsky recently discovered a letter and three poems that
Amichai sent to Leah Goldberg on March 22, 1949, a fact I have related briefly in the Introduction. Amichai tells her in the letter that
he has "been writing poems more or less continuously for about four
years" and that until then he "didn't want to reveal [him]self as a versi-
fier" to his army-buddies; but once "the time was right to present [the
poems] for a more general and more expert critique," he chose to turn
to Goldberg. "How did I come to you?" Amichai asks, and he supplies
the answer: "Simply because your poems speak to me. When I left my
life [*be-ozvi et chayay*] in order to go down to the Negev, a very dear
person gave me [your] little book *From My Old Home.* Very often, in
the lull between battles, or in the gloomy wasteland of the Negev, I'd
read in it, and all was good [*ve-tov li*]."[81] In his 1976 introduction to
Robert Friend's small selection of Goldberg's poetry in English, Amichai describes her poems' importance for him during the 1948 war:
"Her poetry meant much to me [during that period]. I have a vivid
remembrance of myself as a young commando in the 1948 war carry-
ing one of her little books, much tattered, in my knapsack. But her
poems are far from nationalistic in the narrow sense of the word."[82]
The reader familiar with Amichai's poetry knows well the image of the
pocket-size book, the format that Amichai adopted for all of his own
Hebrew books of poetry. Equally familiar is the image of the "tattered
knapsack," which in Amichai's first sonnet from the cycle "Ahavnu
kan" (We Loved Here) contains not the poet's "spiritual provisions"
(*geistige Speise* in his native German), such as a book of poems by a
poetic mother, but rather the soldier's literal provisions given to him
by a literal mother: the soldier's "remnants of his mother's hardening
cake."[83] And indeed in 1958, when Amichai's second book of poetry
Be-merchak shtey tikvot (*Two Hopes Away*) appears, it's clear from the
emotional diction of Amichai's handwritten dedication to Goldberg

that in the nine years since his first letter to her, a close and loving connection developed between the young poet and his literary mother.[84]
Earlier in the 1950s Goldberg also became Amichai's professor at the
Hebrew University, where she held the Chair in Comparative Literature. And when his first book of poems (1955) was severely attacked
by the old guard, many of whom were members of her own literary
generation, she published a staunch defense of the work.[85] As Ticotsky
suggests, she may have also facilitated some of his poems' initial publication in the literary supplement of *Al Ha-Mishmar* as early as 1949.
Dan Miron relates Amichai's refusal to accept the Oedipal model of
generational rebellion to the fact that the *biographical* Amichai had
"a good father,"[86] and indeed, as I suggest in the Introduction, the
tenderness of paternal love modeled for Amichai also a poetics of alternative masculinity. But it seems to me important to acknowledge
that the *poetic* Amichai also had "a good mother." Moreover, the historiographic discourse that is most relevant for Amichai's "genealogy"
as a poet involves a "feminine" modeling of literary generations as a
continuous rather than a combative chain of transmission, though one
that is not unidirectional or linear.

A "feminine-modeled" intergenerational continuity (where "feminine" is not to be construed biologically, and can therefore easily be
associated with the figures of the father or the childhood rabbi in his
poetry!) does not imply for Amichai either a conservative acceptance of
the cultural past or a relinquishing of the poetic subject's right to resist
an oppressive authority. Beyond the biographical connection and poetic
affiliation he maintained with precursor women poets, Amichai often
uses the figures of women in his poetry as representative of a *politically
resistant intertextuality*, in Nancy K. Miller's terms.[87] But as far as Amichai is concerned, this resistance is always directed against ideological
systems and their institutional powers, and not simply against the individual "strong poets" of the past. In this sense, Amichai's conception
of poetic agency shares a basic affinity with Pierre Bourdieu's model of
action within the literary field, a model that underscores the fact that
the intergenerational conflict between poets doesn't take place simply
between two individuals but bears the mark of the larger conflict between what Bourdieu terms "orthodoxy" and "heresy" as conditions
of change in the cultural field.[88]

Amichai often uses female characters—the mother or the beloved woman in the early poetry, the women behind the partition in the Orthodox synagogue, or the female simultaneous interpreters in their cubicles in the later poetry—to thematize the limited and threatened agency of a poetic subject who struggles with oppressive institutional authority and tries to rewrite its constitutive texts.[89] From their de-centered position, the female characters—like matrilineal affiliation in general—challenge established intertextual authority by dismantling its hegemonic discourse. In this respect, Amichai's women, and the theory of agency embedded in their figuration, foreshadow another aspect of Pierre Bourdieu's theory, namely his critique of the deterministic aspects of Althusser's notion of interpellation:

> I wanted, so to speak, to reintroduce agents that Lévi-Strauss and the structuralists, among them Althusser, tended to abolish, making them into simple epiphenomena of structure. And I mean agents, not subjects. Action is not the mere carrying out of a rule, or obedience to a rule. Social agents . . . are not automata regulated like clocks, in accordance with laws they do not understand.[90]

Thus, for example, in the poem "To the Mother" ("La-em"), what the speaker inherits from his mother is also what Amichai as poet receives and further transmits from the tradition of women's poetry: the right to domesticate and translate into the first-person singular both historical and theological discourse norms, and to turn precisely that domestic and personal voice into a powerful tool capable of unsettling even the most impenetrable formations of universal and impersonal authority. The opening simile of this poem from the late 1950s presents the mother's body as the dialogical site of cross-cultural intertextual critique:[91]

Like an old windmill
Always two arms raised to yell at the heavens
And two lowered to make sandwiches.

Her eyes clean and polished
Like Passover eve.

At night she lines up all the letters
And the photographs in a row,

To measure with them
The length of God's finger.

Trans. Chana Kronfeld

כְּמוֹ טַחֲנַת־רוּחַ יְשָׁנָה,
תָּמִיד שְׁתֵּי יָדַיִם מוּרָמוֹת לִצְעוֹק אֶל רָקִיעַ
וּשְׁתַּיִם מוּרָדוֹת לְהָכִין פְּרוּסוֹת.

עֵינֶיהָ נְקִיּוֹת וּמְצֻחְצָחוֹת
כְּמוֹ עֶרֶב פֶּסַח.

בַּלַּיְלָה תָּשִׂים אֶת כָּל הַמִּכְתָּבִים
וְהַצִּלּוּמִים זֶה לְיַד זֶה,

כְּדֵי לִמְדוֹד בָּהֶם
אֹרֶךְ אֶצְבַּע הָאֱלֹהִים.

The image of the mother as a windmill clearly evokes what for Jerusa-lemites like Amichai is a thoroughly domestic association: the famous windmill at Yemin Moshe, where ironically Amichai and his family would build their home years later. However, the same image also turns the mother simultaneously into an agent of protest against the heavens and of quotidian caregiving to her family. In the background is the Yiddish complaint, which was adopted as a calque, a loan translation in colloquial modern Hebrew, *a mame darf hobn fir hent* (Yiddish) or *ima tzrikha arba yadayim* (Hebrew) ("A mother needs to have four hands/arms")—or its first-person negative variant, *kh'hob dokh nit keyn fir hent* (Yiddish) or *harey eyn li arba yadayim* (Hebrew) ("I don't have four hands, do I?"). But Amichai engages this Jewish ordinary-language allusion also in a complex visual and linguistic intertextual play, which thoroughly rewrites the clichés around Don Quixote's status as a cornerstone of the patrilineal Western canon. Instead of describing the existential human struggle as tilting at windmills (which in Hebrew is literally waging war against them, *le-hilachem be-tachanot ru'ach*), Amichai replaces the quixotic, grotesque masculine knight with the feisty and combative windmill of a mother (*tachanat ru'ach* is gendered feminine in Hebrew). The mother does not give up her right to raise a voice—

and a hand—against the heavens (*raki'a*, gendered masculine), even as she continues to care for her family. The windmill, and the mother along with it/her, turn from object to subject, from attacked to attacker, and become the focus of redoubled agency—two and two—of protest and caregiving. In the process, Amichai also radically humanizes the saliently theological emblem of *yad* (hand, arm), a lexicalized metaphor as well as a synecdoche in biblical and rabbinic Hebrew for divine power, providence, or inspiration.[92]

The mother, like Amichai's critically engaged human agent, occupies the privileged yet precarious crossings of cultural categories, between the sacred and the secular, the Judaic and the Western. By placing her between heaven and earth, and between the ironic pathos of Jewish slang and the parodic bathos of Cervantes, Amichai both undercuts and redoubles her empowerment. While God's power in the Bible is always described as a singular *yad* (hand or arm), Amichai's version of the proverbial Jewish mother is a mock-heroic yet powerful four-armed heroine. And in Cervantes, of course, it is the windmills who in the most direct sense win.[93]

In the third stanza of the poem, the mother's hands create her own unique ethical criterion, as she arranges "all the letters / and the photographs in a row, // to measure with them / the length of God's finger." The larger context of the series of poems from which this section is taken, as well as the somewhat later (untranslated) poem "Diney ne-fashot va-efer" (Capital Punishment Laws and Ashes) where a similar image is repeated,[94] suggest that these might be letters and pictures of loved ones who died, perhaps "in the war . . . / in one of the wars," in the words of the last stanza of poem C of "To the Mother."[95] In her silent act of protest, the mother uses traces of visual and textual memory—photos and letters—as a homemade yardstick to measure the length of God's finger. The biblically and rabbinically privileged notion of *etzba elohim* (lit., "God's finger"; idiomatically, miraculous divine intervention or providence; see, for example Exodus 8:15) is itself a metonymic entailment, in Lakoff's terms, of the Judaic concept of *yad elohim* (God's hand) and of the more general Western concept of the hand of fate (*yad ha-goral*).[96] In the course of this maternal anatomy of the divine, *etzba ha-elohim* becomes merely a literalized single finger of divine power, as opposed to the mother's four hands or arms (and adding the definite article to the idiom reinforces its literalization). In the process of personally assessing God's achievements in the world, the mother—and Amichai with her—call into question both the Judaic notion of justified fate (*tziduk ha-din*),[97] which is associated with *etzba elohim*, and the Western visual emblematics of a life-giving, healing divine finger, from Michelangelo to E.T. As in many other poems, the mother appropriates the clichés that are used by the apparatus of national and religious authority to justify "dying for a sacred cause," only to expose their hypocrisy: when lined up against the row of pictures and letters representing a single family's loss, God's finger simply does not measure up.

A Jewish mother who measures the length of God's finger is not exactly the paradigmatic example of intertextuality in current critical theory. I would like to suggest that it may be a mistake to ignore such examples and the type of personal intertextual engagement that they model. The mother could also serve as a counterpoint to the exclusion of women from models of literary influence and from theories of critical agency in general. Whereas for Amichai women poets undoubtedly function as strong poets, and female figures are the paradigmatic example he often uses for the construction of a poetic and critical subject, Harold Bloom's entire approach presupposes that women simply cannot fulfill these functions.[98]

Many feminist theorists have protested the exclusionary practices of the strong poet model, a model that leaves women poets permanently outside the canon. But instead of questioning the very premises of the approach, critics such as Sandra Gilbert and Susan Gubar have simply struggled for inclusion,[99] while others, especially within French feminist criticism, have argued for the creation of a parallel but separate feminine literary lineage.[100]

Quite apart from the issues of gender, the very metaphors used in discussions of influence in the West often criminalize or pathologize it as an unhealthy economy of textual exchange (in the case of traditional source criticism), and as a dysfunctional family romance (in later Formalist and Bloomian versions): the belated poet is a debtor, pickpocket, or thief in the former;[101] a usurper, rebellious son, or parricidal murderer in the latter. The idea that agency is always private and conflictual may, however, be limited to a strictly Western construction of textual transmission. Joseph Brodsky, the famous Russian poet and Amichai's good friend, has shrewdly protested that such accounts of influence have no concept of the continuity and collectivity of culture. As Leon Burnett has pointed out, influence for Brodsky is not a source of anxiety, and acknowledging it is not "a faint-hearted surrender to precursors who have come to assume the disproportionate and terrifying guise of giants, but a recognition of kinship, affinity and literary evolution."[102] In an article that was translated into English only in 1999, Brodsky exclaims:

> There is nothing more pleasant physically (even physiologically) than repeating someone else's lines—whether to oneself or out loud. Fear of influence, fear of dependence, is the fear—the affliction—of a savage, but not of culture, which is all continuity, all echo.

He concludes by adding parenthetically: "(I wish someone would inform Mr. Harold Bloom)."[103] It bears emphasis that this view of transmission and circulation has been the normative position not only for Russian poetic culture but more generally for non-Western or other nonmajoritarian models of influence, from Hebrew and Arabic to Chinese and Japanese, and from folk literature to jazz,[104] where the recycling of (inter)textual treasures has been and continues to be a source of collective and personal pleasure both in the culture of everyday life and in artistic production.

But repeating someone else's lines, enjoying the oral physicality of communal textual transmission, also leaves open the possibility of change, as Amichai's poetics reminds us. Moreover, in the Jewish textual tradition, and the theories of allusion produced by it—from medieval rhetoric to the contemporary accounts of intertextuality by Daniel Boyarin and Ziva Ben-Porat—the norms, as well as the source of aesthetic pleasure, have always resided in the radical rewriting of the authoritative "sources."[105] In fact, I argue that Judith Butler's analysis of the resistance to interpellation, an analysis that is entirely structured on the tension between iterability and change, is, not coincidentally, modeled on precisely this type of an intertextual tradition. The language of canonical cultural authority indeed brings to bear its full institutional power in order to constitute, define, and confine the poetic subject. On the face of it, this view is entirely consistent with Althusser's analysis of the workings of interpellation in every hegemonic apparatus.[106] But, as Butler sharply points out, in the response to such linguistic performative force, the subject may leave herself the possibility—limited as it may be—to reappropriate the texts of authority, to have a claim on them, and to repeat them *differently*. This "gap between redundancy and repetition," argues Butler in her critique of Althusser, "is the space of agency."[107]

Butler's discussion appears as part of a performative analysis of the conditions of possibility for resistance to social interpellation, be it the response to the subjugating hailing of racist or homophobic hate speech or the seemingly benign enforcement of gender and sexual identities. One may ask, what does all this have to do with the framework that makes it possible for a poetic subject's intertextual agency to appear? But note that Butler's analysis is rooted in the most general performative linguistic aspects of discourse (as part of a critical reading of Austin's speech-act theory). Moreover, she herself uses the language of intertextuality—in an argument that is at its core intertextual—in order to both describe the constitution of the subject by the authority and to analyze the possibility of a (circumscribed, necessarily limited yet) resistant response to interpellation. Thus, for example, sexual identity is neither biologically determined nor a matter of personal choice, but rather "the forcible *citation* of a norm,"[108] where, as Sara Salih points out, "citing the norm is necessary in order to qualify as a subject."[109] And since the constitution of the subject is in itself, according to Butler, a matter of linguistic agency,[110] then the very possibility of a "disobedient" response to interpellation,[111] a response that subverts the existing norms, must also be articulated in intertextual terms. In the context of the possibility of a resistant response to hate speech, Butler argues that we need to account for those responses that restage and resignify the injurious speech, or which use the powers of language to expose hate speech for what it is, and thus oppose it.[112] Butler adds:

> Consider for a moment how often such terms are subject to *resignification*. Such a *redoubling* of injurious speech takes place not only in rap music, and in various forms of political parody and satire, but in the political and social critique of such speech, where "mentioning"

> those very terms is crucial to the arguments at hand. . . . [S]uch speech
> has become *citational, breaking with the prior contexts of its utterance*
> *and acquiring new contexts for which it was not intended.*[113]

In such a move of "counter-appropriation," the authority's speech
"can be cited against its originary purposes."[114] But repetition-through-
change of an authoritarian or authoritative text is also a precise and
rigorous description of the workings of radical intertextuality—for example, the iconoclastic allusions to sacred texts in Amichai's poetry.
Beyond Amichai, Butler's description applies with surprising accuracy to the critical intertextual practices that are the hallmarks of the
Hebrew poetry of Dahlia Ravikovitch and Yitzhak Laor, who in turn
provide a secular twist on an age-old religious—but no less radical—
Jewish exegetical tradition of rewriting and textual reappropriation.
Furthermore, among the genres that Butler lists, parody is, of course,
intertextual by definition. The very act of response, as Butler depicts
it, consists of a series of intertextual rewritings, ranging from restaging and resignification all the way to citation and redoubling-through-
change.

An important but insufficiently acknowledged dimension of Butler's notion of resistant agency is the "axis of time," a dimension that is
also central for the diachronic activation of poetic intertextual agency
as it rewrites the authoritative texts of the past. In an interview with
Gary A. Olson and Lynn Worsham, published in 2000, Butler takes to
task the ahistoricity in Lacan's conception of the subject, and presents
as an alternative "the possibility of a temporarily coherent subject who
can act." Butler continues to explain:

> [I]n the answer to the question: "How is it that subordination and
> subjection are the very conditions for agency?" the short answer is
> that I am clearly born into a world in which certain limitations be-
> come the possibility of my subjecthood, but those limitations are not
> there as structurally static features of my self. They are subject to a
> renewal and I perform (mainly unconsciously or implicitly) that re-
> newal in the repeated acts of my person. Even though my agency is
> conditioned by those limitations, my agency can also thematize and
> alter those limitations to some degree . . . [T]he whole scene has to
> be understood as more dynamic than it generally is.[115]

It seems productive to me to return Butler's discourse to its—perhaps prototypically Jewish—intertextual foundation, and to ask not only how the poetic subject is constituted through her interpellation by representatives of the hegemonic literary canon of the past, but also how she reacts to such a subjugating hailing, and to what extent she can refuse to "redouble" it without change. Somewhere along the conceptual continuum between the murderous violence of the Bloomian model and the pleasurable transmission of a replicated textual tradition in Brodsky's approach, there is a third option: the radical and resistant, though limited, resignification of authoritative texts. This, I argue, is precisely the position that Amichai takes.

Intertextuality

The ideological context for influence theories such as Bloom's reversing agency from the precursor to the belated poet is, as I have suggested, both the elitist individualism of American bourgeois capitalism and the neoconservative trend among Jewish intellectuals in the United States. This trend gained force from the 1970s on as a veritable antifeminist and anti-progressive backlash against the more egalitarian spirit of the 1960s. It is interesting to note that an opposite trend developed in France around the same time, in the form of a reaction against (pre-Bloomian) traditional source criticism and its articulation of literary influence. The background and historical and ideological context of what came to be known as the French theories of intertextuality was, of course, the revolutionary egalitarian movements in Europe. Starting with Formalist and anti-Formalist criticism in Eastern Europe in the wake of the October Revolution, this trend culminated in the (post) structuralist approaches that developed some fifty years later, in the radical poetics of the *tel quel* group, and leading up to the May 1968 movement in Paris. Even though it is well known that the innovative term "intertextuality" is Julia Kristeva's important contribution, it is customary to see her account only as a prelude to her teacher Roland Barthes's "Death of the Author";[116] however, in this case the teacher may well have been influenced by the student. The theory of intertextuality that the Bulgarian Kristeva submitted as a thesis to Barthes in 1966, about a year after her arrival in France from Eastern Europe, refracts

Bakhtin's dialogism and his critique of Slavic Formalism and structuralism through the poststructuralist prism of an avant-garde Parisian poetics and a Saussurian linguistics. Kristeva replaces, as I suggested above, Bakhtin's dialogic intersubjectivity with intertextuality, and her account therefore is short on agency, whereas for Bakhtin (intersubjective) agency is precisely what makes the sociolinguistic perspective on literary language possible. Kristeva's interpretation of Bakhtin, as Daniel Boyarin has shown recently, attributes agency "to the language itself or the anonymous and unknown uses of the word that preceded the text. Such a reading produces the Kristevian version or, more broadly, the deconstructive account of intertextuality."[117] Against this, Boyarin presents a different reading of Bakhtin according to which authors "are capable of harboring the word and the word that challenges that word at one and the same time without seeking harmonization, or closure, or decision."[118] Mary Orr argues, by contrast, that Kristeva played a subversive role in importing Russian poetics into the heart of Western poststructuralism, and that her conception of intertextuality has a radical social dimension for the simple reason that it erases the hierarchical authority of the author:

> Prior texts lose special status by permutation with others in the intertextual exchange because all intertexts are of equal importance in the intertextual process. . . . Kristeva's intertextuality as permutation, like Bakhtin's dialogism before it, amply allows for socio-historical "polyphonic" and "carnivalesque" "ideologemes" in order that the status quo will be challenged.[119]

In Kristeva's own words as translated in her *Desire in Language*: "The concept of text as ideologeme determines the very procedure of a semiotics that, by studying the text as intertextuality, considers it as such within (the text of) society and history."[120] There is something both seductive and misleading in Kristeva's formulations since she speaks at one and the same time in her own voice and in that of Bakhtin, performing an act of theoretical ventriloquism, and what I read as a self-conscious mimicry of his dialogism. First it appears that she indeed accepts Bakhtin's focus on intersubjective agency: "The writer's interlocutor . . . is the writer himself, but as reader of another text. The one who writes is the same one who reads." But the next sentence immediately moves from the author as reader to the text itself, in a personifying gesture that will become the basis for the agentless and anonymous conception of intertextuality common to poststructuralism and deconstruction: "Since the interlocutor is a text, he himself is no more than a text rereading itself as it rewrites itself. The dialogical structure [Bakhtin's concept, CK], therefore, appears only in the light of the text elaborating itself as ambivalent in relation to another text."[121] A similarly seductive blurring of the distinction between the reader as a site of intertextual agency and the text itself appears also in Barthes, whose views of intertextuality are based to a large extent, as I suggested above, on Kristeva's *Semeiotiké*.

> A text is made of multiple writings, drawn from many cultures and entering into mutual relations of dialogue, parody, contestation, but there is one place where this multiplicity is focused and that place is the reader, not, as was hitherto said, the author. The reader is the space on which all the quotations that make up a writing are inscribed without any of them being lost; a text's unity lies not in its origin but in its destination. Yet this destination cannot any longer be personal: *the reader is without history, biography, psychology;* he is simply that someone who holds together in a single field all the traces by which the written text is constituted.[122]

Against this background it is hard to understand why it remains so important for critics such as Mary Orr to stress that Barthes too retains some notion of agency—for example, when he insists that in intertextuality there is no authority but only "circular *memory.*"[123] Unfortunately, however, the agency of the rememberers, which is logically implied by the concept of memory, gets all too often written out of poststructuralist accounts of intertextuality in the West, that of the early Barthes included.[124]

Perhaps because of the increasing critical interest in theories of trauma, memory has indeed proven to be a popular way back to a historical, cultural, and collective sense of agency. As Wolfgang Iser observes in his foreword to Renate Lachmann's book *Memory and Literature: Intertextuality in Russian Modernism*, memory is the crucial link between theories of intertextuality and the possibility of sociocultural agency.[125] Lachmann's insight in this book is of particular importance. Intertextuality, she argues, is our only tangible manifestation of cultural memory (a view which brings to mind, not coincidentally, Brodsky's memorable words quoted above). Literature, according to Lachmann, is not a *representation* of cultural memory; it is cultural memory inchoate. In its diverse styles, it enacts the operations of collective memories as they are being created. Miryam Sas, working comparatively with modernist Japanese and French cultural practices while focusing on surrealism, has developed an account of intertextual memory that reinvests the post-structuralist model with historicity and agency; and Lars Eckstein has described intertextuality in African-American literature as performative memory.[126] I don't think that memory quite solves our problem, but I find it interesting—as Lachmann's, Sas's, and Eckstein's examples illustrate—that it is in the non-Western or nonmajoritarian contexts that we find new ways of thinking about intertextuality, which manage to extricate us from the trap of anonymity embedded in the personifications of texts that were the norm in Western (post)structuralism. Typical of these new discussions is an attempt to preserve some notion of socio-poetic agency, whether à la Bourdieu or à la Butler.

While discussions of intertextuality in the context of Asian and Eastern European literatures, like those by Lachmann and Sas, have on the whole retained a notion of agency, the prominent version of intertextuality in the West—which developed out of the Barthes-Kristeva model—has been anonymous, impersonal, and indeed ahistorical. Let me describe here briefly one typical example that I analyze in detail elsewhere.[127] In his discussion of *Casablanca* as a cinematic archetype, Umberto Eco articulates with almost poetic sensitivity a model for a postmodernist conception of intertextuality (which serves also as a manifesto of sorts for his own postmodernist novelistic practice): "Two clichés make us laugh but a hundred clichés move us because we sense dimly that the clichés are talking among themselves, celebrating a reunion." When in later films the dialogue of cinematic clichés becomes a selfconscious act of quotation, it creates an aesthetics marked by what Eco has aptly termed "intertextual collage": "what *Casablanca* does unconsciously, later movies will do with extreme intertextual awareness."[128]

This is an alluringly beautiful account. But what is behind the personification of cinematic texts as having an unconscious? From Eco's description of the viewers' "dim" and passive arousal as they watch the intertextual reunion it is clear that this is no conventional metonymic shift of agency from the director, actors, characters, or audience onto the cinematic dialogue itself. Why, then, should a postmodernist intertextual collage turn the texts themselves (cinematic in this case) into patients who have successfully undergone psychotherapy and therefore have conscious access to what for the text of *Casablanca* was still only unconscious? Moreover, who is that generalized "we" about whose reactions to the dialogue of citations Eco is so omniscient? The consumers of cinematic texts are presented by Eco in utterly universalist terms: they are ahistorical, agentless bystanders, who lack any exegetical involvement, and are devoid of any class, gender, national, or ethnic context, just like Barthes's abstract reader. Such a "we" can only eavesdrop passively, without any critical distance, on the conversation of the reified, personified clichés, as they are having their reunion; Brecht would have been appalled at such an account of the audience's response to the artwork, a response that allows only identificatory, affirmative voyeurism and brackets the possibility of a socially and politically situated critical distance. It is immaterial to Eco's account where in the world these moviegoers are located and what their socioeconomic circumstances happen to be: they could be watching *Casablanca* at the Film Forum in New York or on TV in a housing project in the Bronx; they could be in Eco's castle in Rimini, in a refugee camp in Gaza, or in Casablanca itself—it shouldn't make a difference, or so the argument goes, because the effect or meaning of the intertextual collage is constructed only through the agency, subjectivity, and voice that are the property of the cinematic clichés themselves and their various rewritings, rather than of the viewers and their social contexts (or, for that matter, of the writers or characters represented in the film, or even of language as a social institution constituted by a historically situated speech community). This is a highly problematic universalizing account even for a cult movie like *Casablanca*, let alone for works of novel poetic expression. Yet, it is important to note that Eco's agentless reunion of clichés is not an extreme theoretical mutation but rather a perfectly typical—and logical—1980s development of the 1960s (post)structuralist account of intertextuality, and its common tendency toward what Ducrot and Todorov have described as the "pulverizing" of the subject.[129]

What seems to be behind Eco's position is the trivially correct suggestion that anonymous tissues of citations encompass all textuality. In Kristeva's famous reformulation of Bakhtin: "[a]ny text is constructed as a mosaic of quotations; any text is the absorption and transformation of another."[130] Moreover, for Eco, as for Kristeva and Barthes before him, the general intertextuality of all texts also renders meaningless—at least in their explicit, theoretical pronouncements—any selective, purposeful, and critical engagement with particular articulations of allusion, translation, parody, and so on. As Barthes suggests, this is because "[t]he intertextual in which every text is held . . . is not to be confused with some origin of the text: to try to find the 'sources,' the 'influences' of a work, is to fall in with the myth of filiation; the citations which go to make up a text are anonymous, untraceable, and yet already read (*déjà lu*): They are quotations without inverted commas."[131]

Abandoning the positivistic hunt for sources and the myth of filiation was, to be sure, an important step in the struggle to liberate literary historiography from agonistic authoritarianism. But the (logically) trivial intertextuality of all texts leaves us with a theory that has no explanatory power whatsoever about the specific intertextual practices embedded within this general all-encompassing intertextual condition. For a long time it was thought, under the influence of French (post) structuralism, that the way out of the hierarchical relations between texts or writers, presupposed by influence models, was to smooth over the asymmetrical power relations and remove the figures of authority from the picture in order to create a level playing field. But current trends in literary historiography express a growing awareness of the heavy toll that such a leveling out has exacted: eliding agency, history, and any theoretical analysis of specific cultural practices based on intertextuality.

Slovenian scholar Marko Juvan proposes, in his critical history of the field, a distinction between theories of a generalized intertextuality as the condition of all textuality and theories of what he terms "citationality," the historically and culturally specific "stylistic and poetic features foregrounded in certain literary works, genres, and trends."[132] Citationality is indeed the focus of Israeli theories of allusion and intertextuality, developed by Ziva Ben-Porat on the model of modern

Hebrew poetry and by Daniel Boyarin on the model of midrash. These accounts avoid—each in its own way—the totalizing trap of generalized intertextuality, perhaps because of the centrality of specific radical rewriting practices in the Jewish culture of commentary.[133] These accounts, while definitely siding with egalitarian intertextuality rather than the authoritarian influence models, nevertheless insist on the need for and possibility of unpacking specific citational strategies such as allusion, midrash, parody, and translation. Their paradigmatic examples (iconoclastic allusion in Statehood Generation poetry for Ben-Porat, and midrash in rabbinic literature for Boyarin) embody precisely what Butler will later describe as a disobedient reiteration: a repetition with change that is often radical (in the etymological sense of the term— change that involves a return to the *radix* or radices—the roots).

The bilateral and dynamic nature of rhetorical intertextuality according to Ben-Porat is its most salient feature. Like other aspects of what came to be known as Tel Aviv School poetics, the theory itself is modeled on the historical conditions of Hebrew and its literature during the 1960s and 70s. The Hebrew literary culture of the time, though perhaps more militantly secular than today, maintained, in spite of itself, a sense of continuity with what the late Amos Funkenstein described as a text-oriented, interpretive Jewish tradition in which engaging in intertextual activities such as exegesis and commentary constitutes "a primary religious command and value," and, I would add, a source of aesthetic play and pleasure in literature, as well as in the culture of everyday life.[134] Boyarin's theory of intertextuality analyzes midrash as a model of a polyphonic practice, a "co-reading" or "co-citation" of biblical texts in which what is valued is the diverse ways for generating new readings and meanings within "the ideological intertextual code" of the rabbis.[135] Even though the content of these codes has changed in the modern "secular" reworkings of Jewish intertextuality—and a deviation from readings allowed by the Torah is no longer a transgression or a taboo[136]—the basic structural principle of *bilateral polyphony* remains central in the poetry of the Statehood Generation, which is, after all, what Ben-Porat models her theory on. The intertextual moves that are most representative in her account are precisely those that underscore the distance—in meaning, power relations, authority, and agency—between the modern alluding text and the (typically biblical) evoked texts, so that in the process of "actualization" and mutual modification the reader must reconstitute *both* texts. Indeed, this is the intertextual principle most characteristic of Amichai and his generation, despite important specific differences between Amichai, Ravikovitch, Zach, Ruebner, and Pagis, for example, in the ways they destabilize and reconstitute alluding and evoked texts.

Amichai's work provides a procedure for rescuing Eco's important notion of intertextual collage from the problematics of erasing the poetic subject and canceling out the possibility of any critical and socially situated intertextual agency. Indeed, Amichai's poetry offers one of the most sustained examples of intertextual collage in contemporary poetry. Yet it does this while rejecting—ideologically and rhetorically—the alienated, elitist view of intertextuality as the "burden of encyclopedic expertise," in Eco's words.[137] Amichai's intertextual practices and his metapoetic thematization of these practices (as in the figure of the mother discussed above) thus serve as the basis for my questioning those poststructuralist conceptions of intertextual relations that still cling to an ahistorical totalizing model, just as they helped me critique the agonistic authority of influence models.

The intertextual reunion Amichai's poetry celebrates is infinitely more complex than the one described by Eco, and not because sacred texts rather than cinematic clichés are reunited in the pages of Amichai's poetry. In fact, as we have seen, Amichai often applies the same strategies to ordinary language allusions as he does to the intertextual critique of the topos of the Binding of Isaac or to secular-feminist subversions of the Yom Kippur liturgy. The intertextual collages in his poems serve also to undermine the chauvinism of popular nationalist songs or, indeed, the translatability of old movies (as in the poem "Summer Rest and Words"). What makes his dialogue with precursor texts complex, while appearing rhetorically simple, is, instead, his commitment to reinvest intertextuality with agency, to insist on it as a vital social and personal practice rather than an "impersonal field of crossing texts."[138]

Poem #29 in the 1977 volume *Ha-zman* (*Time*) is a self-critical and meta-intertextual midrash on the radical and iconoclastic uses Amichai himself makes of biblical allusion, rabbinical exegesis, and even midrash itself.

From: Poem #29, Time

From the Book of Esther I filtered the sediment
of vulgar joy, and from the Book of Jeremiah
the howl of pain in the guts. And from
the Song of Songs the endless
search for love, and from Genesis the dreams
and Cain, and from Ecclesiastes
the despair, and from the Book of Job: Job.
And with what was left, I pasted myself a new Bible.
Now I live censored and pasted and limited and in peace.[139]

סִנַּנְתִּי מִתּוֹךְ מְגִלַּת אֶסְתֵּר אֶת מִשְׁקַע
הַשִּׂמְחָה הַגַּסָּה וּמִתּוֹךְ סֵפֶר יִרְמְיָהוּ
אֶת יִלְלַת הַכְּאֵב בַּמֵּעַיִם. וּמִתּוֹךְ
שִׁיר הַשִּׁירִים אֶת הַחִפּוּשׂ הָאֵין סוֹפִי
אַחַר הָאַהֲבָה וּמִסֵּפֶר בְּרֵאשִׁית אֶת
הַחֲלוֹמוֹת וְאֶת קַיִן וּמִתּוֹךְ קֹהֶלֶת אֶת
הַיֵּאוּשׁ וּמִתּוֹךְ סֵפֶר אִיּוֹב אֶת אִיּוֹב.
וְהִדְבַּקְתִּי לִי מִן הַשְּׁאֵרִיּוֹת סֵפֶר תַּנָ"ךְ חָדָשׁ.
אֲנִי חַי מְצֻנְזָר וּמֻדְבָּק וּמֻגְבָּל וּבְשַׁלְוָה.

Amichai both asserts the poet's strong intertextual agency and exposes it as limited in its ability to produce an uninterpellated subject. He deflates the poet's intertextual rewriting of biblical texts and domesticates and "feminizes" it as nothing more than kitchen prep-work (for example, straining soup through a colander to retain the broth)[140] or homey craft (gluing together fabric remnants). The poem starts with a rejection of the bloody last chapters of the Book of Esther, and its nationalistic reading tradition, where the Jews conduct a vengeful massacre against the Persians and the biblical narrator indulges in some serious schadenfreude.[141] *Gasa*, when applied to *simcha* ("joy"), means "vulgar." But the same adjective (*gas*) is returned to its literal meaning of "coarse" or "gritty" in the context of the metaphorical system of writing poetry as straining through a sieve, which the first seven lines develop. As the poem progresses, it's no longer so clear what the speaker is straining out of the biblical text, or how much is left after all that filtering. In the process, the value of his radical rewriting is also increasingly called into question. What, in other words, is the Book of Job without Job, or Ecclesiastes without despair? The catalogue that constitutes the bulk of the poem must also be read as an intra-textual self-critique, a series of internal allusions to other poems by Amichai where the speaker engages critically with the Book of Esther, Jeremiah, the Song of Songs, Genesis, and Job, much as the love poem to Tamar, discussed in section I, took on the erasure of despair from Ecclesiastes. But it is also a critique of the attempts, trendy especially in the United States, to construct a more acceptable "tradition" by picking and choosing the texts that can still produce the desired, comfortable sense of Jewish identity and not "trouble" it with gender or ethical disturbances.

In typical Amichai fashion, the poem changes metaphors—and direction—in the final two lines, in a free-verse variation on the traditional volta in a sonnet.[142] The transitional junction between the two organizing metaphors of the poem—cooking and craft—is the Hebrew *min ha-she'eriyot* in the next to the last line, translated as "with what was left." In the context of the culinary metaphor system, WRITING AS COOKING, *she'eriyot* registers simply as the colloquial modern Hebrew term for "leftovers." But the new metaphorical term *hidbakti li* (I pasted or glued for myself) changes the meaning of *she'eriyot* to "remnants," as in fabric or craft-store lingo, introducing a variation on the metaphorical system TEXT AS TEXTILE. But, of course, both of these meanings deflate the religious-turned-national sense of *she'erit*, the remnant of the exiled nation that carries within it the possibility of redemption. The speaker puts together his new usable Bible from those leftovers/remnants, in a hands-on critical process of cutting and pasting: a literal intertextual collage-making. With one last turn in the final line, we find out that what the speaker has pasted together is not just a usable textual tradition, but also the poetic subject himself: "Now I live censored and pasted and limited and in peace." The Hebrew here draws beautifully on the untranslatable qualities of the dative of reference *li*, which Chana Bloch has subtly rendered into a slightly Yinglish fruitful ambiguity: "I pasted *myself* a new bible" (emphasis added, CK). This is precisely where the self-critical turn can no longer be ignored: From the celebratory rejection of the vulgar joy of Esther, to the logically absurd erasure of Job from the Book of Job, the speaker ends up as the interpellated poetic subject, the always "limited" and "censored" lyrical "I" who can, only under these conditions, live "in peace." Intertextual critique then both subjectifies and subjugates the poetic "I," constituting him—and not just his poem—as an intertextual collage. Amichai's dissident intertextual agent turns the revisionist project of "filtering out" unacceptable biblical precursors into a life-affirming and poetry-enabling process of constructing the kind of imperfect poetic subjectivity he can live with. But the price he pays, as the history of his reception in Israel and abroad illustrates, and as the poet himself was keenly aware and here directly thematizes, is nationalist and religious appropriation: being censored and defined by the domesticated textual remnants as a patchwork of the very religious/national institutions that his radical intertextuality has attempted to do without.[143]

Amichai, as we have seen, reinscribes intertextuality as the practice of a historicized, ordinary human subject engaging with asymmetrical sources of power and authority *as if* they too were just ordinary human subjects, while keenly aware that they are not. His is a personal, critical gesture aimed both inward, toward the Hebraic intertextual traditions that have left him with the prescribed use of a mosaic of quotations (*shibutz*) or ornate stock phrases (*melitza*), as well as the exegetical genres (such as midrash) that are intertextual by definition; and simultaneously also a gesture outward, toward Euro-American modernist and postmodernist views of the poetic text as an impersonal, fragmented, unharmonized tissue of citations. Both Jewish and Western intertextual practices are experienced in this poetry as vital pieces of "an archaeology of the self," in Robert Alter's terms, rather than as anonymous abstractions.[144] Throughout, Amichai insists that the person speak the language, not the language speak the person.[145]

Four Celebrating Mediation
The Poet as Translator

> I went out into my life with willpower seventyfold
> At the gates there stood as-if translators from tongue to tongue
> who helped me. But now that they've gone to sleep
> My heart returns alone to its first abode.
> —Yehuda Amichai, unpublished quatrain[1]

I. The Poetics and Politics of Translation

Amichai's poetry articulates an implicit theory of translation as the intertextual practice of a historical agent, an implicit theory that is poised to provide a new perspective on the critical discourse of contemporary translation studies. A recurring metaphor in his work, which depicts the poet as "mere" translator, goes a long way toward deflating the still-influential romantic aesthetic criteria of originality, individuality, and uniqueness; he places instead special value on translational mediation as emblematic of the creative work of the lyrical "I." Through the prism of Amichai's poetic corpus, and in particular through the way his poetry challenges the dichotomy between writer and translator, it becomes possible to explore the notion of translational/poetic agency while leaving behind any vestiges of romantic ideals of authenticity and authority; and to give up, I hope once and for all, honorific notions about the primacy and purity of the original and derisive views about the secondary, derived, and contaminated status of the translated work.

Exploring the ways in which translation is implicitly and explicitly theorized within the poetry of Yehuda Amichai will allow me to read it, as I read intertextuality in general, not only within the poetic but also within the ethical and political practices that impact cultural exchange. His work celebrates the translational mediation among cultural subjects around the circulation of texts and sees poetry as just one form, not necessarily a privileged one, of this vital circulation. Amichai's poetics of translation foregrounds the historicized, culturally specific ways poets and readers affect and are affected by what he describes as

175

the recycling of words (*michzur milim*). As in the case of radical allusion, the conception of translation in his poetry is not structured on the relationship between a given translator and his or her apologetic and self-deprecating secondariness to some original genius. For Amichai it is always a matter of open and dynamic constellations of historical, cultural, and personal conjunctures that inform the ways poets, translators, and readers use different intertextual discursive strategies. These strategies, for Amichai, are not just models for the poet's work but essential human practices within the social and historical sphere. His poetry presents the recurring figure of the translator as metaphor and metonymy for the limited poetic subject and—by extension—for every human subject, whose very limitations must become a source of strength and a site of resistance.

I recently discovered in the Amichai Archives at Yale's Beinecke Library the unpublished early quatrain I use as the epigraph for this chapter. This quatrain is a moving meditation that describes "as-if translators" (*kemo turgemanim*) as watchmen over the cycle of birth and death and as crucial to the conditions of possibility for poetry in general. Written in the medieval Hebrew and Arabic style, the quatrain uses monorhyme and echoes Ibn Gabirol and Shmuel Ha-Nagid, rather than Fitzgerald's infamously colonial English translations of the *Ruba'iyat*, exactly as Amichai had described his unpublished quatrains to me.[2] The quatrain depicts these as-if translators (*kemo turgemanim*) standing guard at the gates of life, helping the newborn poet to go out into his future. Once the poet has grown up, his guardian translators can finally get some sleep, leaving him to fend for himself as his heart makes its journey toward death. It is a circular journey back to his first "abode," to the earth-as-womb from whose gates he emerged in the opening line.

Amichai builds here on the traditional Jewish metaphorical system, whose biblical locus classicus is the Song of Songs, of the woman's body as a house or home (here translated as "abode," to signal the poem's homage to the Arabic tradition), and more specifically of her womb as the gate.[3] The speaker in this poem describes his birth into life and into poetry as a birth into the multiplicity of human languages (the Septuagint, also known as the Translation of the Seventy, is subtly invoked here).[4] The as-if translators are both guardian angels and midwives, helping the speaker as he goes out into his life. This social and matrilineal modeling of life and of the possibility of poetry is described as a facilitation of the passage from one language to another. The Hebrew term *lashon*, literally "tongue," is not coincidentally embodied, suggesting, as Amichai does in the other poems about translation I will discuss below, an erotics of transmission. For Amichai, the only moment that is free of linguistic mediation, hence of translation, is the return, in the last line, to his "first abode," the maternal womb-turned-tomb. It's the only thing he can do alone, without the translators' help, and without the social multiplicity of linguistic exchange. Upending the notions of an originary language, the return to his "first abode" is precisely that which forecloses the possibility of life and of poetry: *bayit* after all is not only home and metaphorically the mother's body but also, in the rhetoric of medieval Hebrew and Arabic poetry to which this quatrain adheres with great prosodic precision, the first line of a poem. While in modern Hebrew poetics *bayit* signifies a stanza, in the medieval tradition that the genre of the poem follows so strictly it is what we would today call a line, made up of two hemistichs: the first called *delet*, literally "door," and the second *soger*, literally "lock." The first house/line/womb to which the speaker returns ends the poem and locks out the possibility of poetry and of life.

The poem's genre itself is, of course, an act of translational mediation between languages and cultures, offering a Hebrew homage to the illustrious tradition of the Arabic and Persian monorhymed quatrain, which saw also the flourishing of Hebrew poetry in al-Andalus during the medieval Golden Age. The poem's conclusion then becomes a poignant thematization of the impossibility to differentiate between original poet and secondary translator, much as medieval Hebrew poetry was both a rewriting and an original creation. But the poem's genre also underscores the inseparable cultural links between the now-warring Hebrew and Arabic literary cousins. Without cross-cultural translation there is no poetry and there is no life.[5] That the conditions of possibility for poetry and for life are predicated on "as-if translators" is also, however, a self-conscious acknowledgment of what Adorno describes as the "semblance nature" (*Scheincharakter*) of verbal art—the poem's as-if mode of existence, emblematic of art's "negative" or "oppositional" relation to the "empirical reality" that nevertheless constitutes it.[6]

This small example, like Amichai's other poems and notes on translation discussed below, encapsulates a theory of translation as cultural mediation that makes it a model not only for poetry but also for intertextuality itself.[7] In order to set the stage for the relevance of the insights Amichai's poetry provides and the importance of their theoretical implications, it might be helpful to first offer a brief overview of the current state of the field of translation studies. Theories of intertextuality have, as I illustrated in chapter 3, lagged significantly behind the theorizing embedded in the poetics of verbal artists like Amichai. In the early 1990s a new critical direction finally began to catch up with poetic practice, calling for a new blend of influence and intertextuality, informed by new historicist, feminist, and postcolonial criticism, and the general turn toward the political in a globalized rearticulation of literary and cultural studies.

Interestingly, the same period evinced a flowering of the theoretical study of one particular intertextual practice, namely translation. However, construed as part of cultural studies, postcolonial theory, and subaltern studies, and their subsequent transformation into a globalized model of literary circulation, these contemporary discussions of translation rarely even acknowledge that translation needs to be examined qua intertextual practice. I believe that a conceptual analysis of intertextuality would be greatly enriched by many of the recent theoretical insights about translation. Also, conversely, the contemporary discussion of translation would benefit from an analysis of what translation has in common with other intertextual practices, especially those—like allusion—whose structure has been rigorously studied. What I'm proposing here is an integration of the theoretical developments in contemporary translation studies with the specific poetic and political insights provided by theorists such as Ziva Ben-Porat on bilateral radical allusion and André Lefevere on the politics of translation-as-rewriting. As mentioned above, Ben-Porat classified translation as one of many intertextual practices, alongside allusion, parody, pastiche, imitation, and so forth, in her groundbreaking article from 1985 titled "Rhetorical Intertextuality."[8] A few years later, André Lefevere, in a series of important books, laid the foundation for the connection between a historicized—and politically informed—theory and praxis of translation and other formations of intertextuality.[9]

Consequently, in the last twenty years or so we have witnessed an important shift in the theoretical study of translation. The new theories have taken the field beyond the metaphors of fidelity and betrayal, to models of translation as inter-cultural negotiation, paying special attention to the unequal power relations between target and source cultures. The turn in the field has been greatly influenced by Mary Louise Pratt's analysis of the contact zone, where she argues that the diachronic or synchronic arena of translation is situated in "the social spaces where cultures meet, clash, and grapple with each other, often in contexts of highly asymmetrical relations of power."[10] The prototypical examples that serve these cultural and political theories of translation are colonial translations from Sanskrit, Bengali, Spanish, or Native American languages into British English or Imperial Spanish as a means for "civilizing" and interpellating the "native" subjects in the colonial era.[11] In recent discussions within postcolonial and transnational cultural studies, the examples that serve as theoretical paradigms are most frequently translations from minor languages into American English, which is seen as a vehicle in the service of an imperial American globalization. In this context, translations into American English are critiqued for blurring the distinctive or subversive features of the indigenous voices they mediate, and for effacing the writers' critical agency in order to facilitate a smoother, readable—and saleable—English text. At the same time, the opposite trend is also increasingly evident: a greater awareness—and criticism—of the tendency in traditional views of translation to erase the translator's personal and historical agency, and a growing attempt to counter and redress the invisibility of translators, who are described in sociopoetic accounts as some of the most powerless (often female and underpaid) members of the literary community. Thus, even as translation itself is critiqued as a tool of cultural colonization, translators are now valorized for their work. The fact that these translators are the mediators of powerful cultural capital only reinforces the need to distinguish, in theorizing translation and intertextuality in general, between personal and institutional constructions of subjectivity. Various formations of translational agency are now being examined in their relation to intercultural apparatuses of authority, placing in the center the attempt to understand how such formations can constitute and reinforce discursive identities and, at the same time, undermine or destabilize them.[12]

I find much that is useful in these approaches, and indeed adopt a lot of their insights in my readings of Amichai. However, I think the field could benefit from a greater self-critical awareness of the historical and cultural contingencies that produce many of the theories' paradigm examples. For instance, it might be helpful to treat the tenets of postcolonial translation theory not as universal but as most applicable to the particular conditions of British colonialism in the Indian subcontinent, for which these accounts were developed. Furthermore, the preoccupation with what Gayatri Spivak has famously termed "the politics of translation"[13] has all too often resulted in a crass thematicism that has precluded a more rigorous and nuanced *poetics* of translation. Here again I take my cue for the study—and practice—of translation from the explicit and implicit poetics and politics of translation articulated in Yehuda Amichai's poetry.

Amichai's "And Let Us Not Get Excited" ("Ve-lo nitlahev")[14] is one of the earliest examples in his corpus of the translator as a figure for the poet and for human existence historically conceived. Through the figure of the translator, this 1962 poem develops Amichai's critique of traditional notions of the poet as inspired prophet or original creator. Whereas translation enabled the birth of the poet into always multiple—and multilingual—social life in the quatrain, here the poetic subject is directly described as a translator, and as such s/he is not anything to get excited about, nor should s/he take her/himself too seriously.

And Let Us Not Get Excited

And let us not get excited, for a translator
mustn't get excited. Quietly, we pass on
words from one person to another, from one tongue to other lips,

unawares, the way a father passes on
the facial features of his dead father to his son,
yet he doesn't resemble either of them,
he's just the go-between.

We shall remember the things we had in our hands
and dropped,

whatever belongs to us and does not belong to us[15]
And 'tis not for us to get excited.
Calls and their callers have drowned. Or, it is that my beloved
passed on to me a few words, before she went away,
so that I would raise them for her.

And no longer shall we say that which has been said to us
on to other sayers. Silence equals admission. 'Tis not
for us to get excited.[16]

Trans. Chana Bloch and Chana Kronfeld

וְלֹא נִתְלַהֵב

וְלֹא נִתְלַהֵב, כִּי לֹא יִתְלַהֵב
תַּרְגְּמָן. בְּשֶׁקֶט נַעֲבִיר
מִלִּים מֵאָדָם לְאָדָם, מִשָּׂפָה לִשְׂפָתַיִם אֲחֵרוֹת,

וּבְלִי לָדַעַת, כְּמוֹ אָב שֶׁמַּעֲבִיר
קֶלַסְתֵּר פְּנֵי אָבִיו הַמֵּת לִבְנוֹ,
וְהוּא אֵינוֹ דוֹמֶה לִשְׁנֵיהֶם,
הוּא רַק מְתַוֵּךְ.

מִזְּכֹר אֶת הַדְּבָרִים שֶׁהָיוּ בְּיָדֵינוּ
וְנִשְׁמְטוּ,
דְּאִכָּא בִּרְשׁוּתִי וּדְלָא אִכָּא בִּרְשׁוּתִי.
וְאֵין לָנוּ לְהִתְלַהֵב.
קְרִיאוֹת וְקוֹרְאֵיהֶן טָבְעוּ. אוֹ, כִּי אֲהוּבָתִי
מָסְרָה לִי מִלִּים אֲחָדוֹת, בְּטֶרֶם נָסְעָה,
כְּדֵי שֶׁאֲגַדְּלֵן לְמַעֲנָהּ.

וְשׁוּב לֹא נֹאמַר אֶת מַה שֶׁנֶּאֱמַר לָנוּ
לְאוֹמְרִים אֲחֵרִים. שְׁתִיקָה כְּהוֹדָאָה. אֵין
לָנוּ לְהִתְלַהֵב.

In a series of pseudo-biblical commandments to a collective "us," perhaps the poets of his generation, Amichai's speaker upends the romantic conception of the poet as an individual genius. At the same time he
empties out the collectivist pathos of the 1948 Palmach Generation,
invoked parodically in the first-person plural form of his address (in

Hebrew, lit., "and we shall not get excited").[17] In the process, the poem offers one of the earliest articulations of what I have described as Amichai's embrace of mediation or liminality (*beynayim*), which is to become the central principle of his poetic worldview. As we recall, the place of the human—and poetic—subject for Amichai is in "the narrow between" (*ba-beynayim ha-tsarim*), the space of a hyphen between date of birth and date of death, between the grindstones of past and future, between one textual tradition and another. Aware of the inability to ever create anything anew or "to bring a world quite round," to quote Wallace Stevens's "Man with the Blue Guitar,"[18] the poetic subject willingly and without any anxiety of influence accepts his role as a link in a historical/familial chain of transmission. If every text that every poet can produce is always already a recycled version of something else, seeing the poet as "mere" translator underscores the impossibility of originality, the secondariness and mediated nature of all cultural exchange, and—by extension—of human existence itself. It also places the poet/translator in that tenuous and dangerous space between opposing generational, institutional, and historical forces, subject to their pressures and aware of his own unstable position.

"And Let Us Not Get Excited" is constructed as a series of "takes" on the role of the poet as transmitter of other peoples' words, each stanza developing a different set of metaphors for this intermediary status. All of these metaphors, interestingly, involve an implicit but devastating critique of the ways in which the discourse on translation has been structured on traditional patriarchal gender roles within the institutional nuclear family. Note that at the end of the poem's third stanza, after portraying the normative male generational "relay race," it is the female beloved (*ahuvati*) who transmits (*masra*) to him a few words-as-baby-daughters (*milim*, "words," are gendered feminine in Hebrew), before she leaves both him and her verbal offspring, and—in violation of gender expectations—entrusts him with the maternal role of raising them for her. Thus the patriarchal family model of literary transmission is rewritten by Amichai in feminizing terms.

Amichai's critique here prefigures Lori Chamberlain's analysis of the cliché "*tradittore traduttore*" (the translator as traitor) in terms of the marriage contract and its normative emphasis on "a woman's, not a man's fidelity and sexual purity."[19] As Chamberlain points out, the power relation between source and target texts (and their attendant cultures) determines who is gendered female ("marked," in linguistic terms) in the marriage/translation contract. When the source text has the status of a classic or a sacred norm (the Bible, classical Greco-Roman literature), it is the belated translator or target text that is feminized. When, on the other hand, the target text possesses cultural and political capital, as for example in the colonial translation project described by Tejaswini Niranjana,[20] it is the indigenous, native, and subjugated source text that gets feminized. In both cases, however, the metaphors of fidelity and betrayal apply, predictably, only to the feminized party. Chamberlain does not seem to take her own analysis one step further, however, from a feminist to a queer critique that would expose the constructedness of gender itself. This despite the fact that in all of her examples the translator and the translated engage in remarkable gender-bending metaphorics: they keep switching from masculine to feminine, depending on their power relation vis-à-vis the cross-cultural texts they are mediating.

While explicitly dealing with the lack of originality in poetic transmission, Amichai's "And Let Us Not Get Excited" also targets precisely the static, rigid, and essentialist gender hierarchy of the nuclear family model of literary transmission, with each stanza dismantling a different implication of its underlying metaphorical system. The first stanza sets up for the entire poem the overarching metaphor of the poet as translator. It does so by playing with the androcentric model of historiography, thus motivating us to retheorize the position of the poetic subject tout court. Amichai's choice of the term *turgeman* for "translator," and not the more common *metargem,* both in this poem and in the unpublished quatrain, is particularly interesting because it enacts a radical historical intertextual move in a poem whose very subject is the intertextuality of every textual production. William Hallo has traced this term all the way back to Old Assyrian (and perhaps originally to Hittite), as well as to many other variants (*dragoman, turkeman*) throughout the ancient Near East.[21] Later on, Jewish textual culture recasts "*turgeman* as a Talmudic term referring to a rabbinical scholar whose role in the synagogue was to translate either the Torah reading or the rabbi's sermon into Aramaic or Greek, so that *amkha,* the simple folk in the congregation who no longer had a real command of Hebrew, would understand.[22] In a 1972 poets' round-table discussion in Washington, DC, convened by Allen Tate and published under the title *The Translation of Poetry*, Yehuda Amichai explains to the American poets in attendance the technical aspects of the role of the *turgeman* and the Jewish traditions of the *targumim* (translations of the Torah that form the foundation of the culture of textual exegesis). He insists on these historically and culturally specific translation practices as his model for the poet's role, precisely because translation is the ultimate form of interpretation.[23] In notes for this and other lectures I found in the archives, Amichai often reflects on the various traditions of translation, concluding: *tirgum—havana amitit!* ("translation—true understanding!").[24] Thus, in his use of *turgeman* in the poem "And Let Us Not Get Excited," he recovers an egalitarian moment from traditional Jewish textual practices, and anchors in this moment his critique of romantic conceptions of the poet. In the process he reintroduces a truly Bakhtinian intersubjective polyphony into our understanding of translation—and of intertextuality in general.

In stark contrast both to Harold Bloom's deadly duel of poetic father and son and to the faceless dialogue of clichés in poststructuralist accounts of intertextuality (see chapter 3), Amichai's poet-cum-translator explores without judgment but with unmistakable agency a literary family genetics of unoriginality, calmly accepting his role as no more than a go-between. His notes in the archives describe this view of poetry as *tirgum geneti me-chayey acherim* (genetic translation from the lives of others).[25] Paradoxically, however, the closest filiation (father-son) does not imply in his view any overt similarity. As in Jurij Tynjanov's version of literary historiography (and in contradistinction to Shklovsky's avuncular view), "in the struggle with his father the grandson turns out to resemble the grandfather."[26] But note that Amichai's emphasis is not on the oedipal rejection of the father but quite the opposite, on the father as the poet-in-the-middle, whose limited power and liminal position free him up to be different from both his precursor and his follower. The mediating role of the poetic subject as an agent of intergenerational, intertextual translation gives him the liberty to be quite unlike either older or younger poets in his chain of transmission, so long as he accepts the fact that there are no new words in his mouth. Thus, instead of the Bloomian or the Russian Formalist generational struggle, Amichai underscores the physical, intimate joy of textual transmission. The poem provides an erotic literalization of the metonymically implied Hebrew idiom for oral transmission, *mi-pe le-fe*, literally, "from mouth to mouth," which in the context of the traditional role of the *turgeman* may also invoke the concept of *torah she-be'al pe*, rabbinic texts as oral law; literally, the Torah upon the mouth: "Quietly, we pass on / words from one person to another, from tongue to other lips."[27]

Translation as intertextual transmission becomes an act of linguistic kissing, an intimacy that returns language to the body, one *safa* (language/lip) to the *sfatayim* (lips; dual form) of others.[28] What makes the difference here is the agency of human contact, the words' contact with the lips as they move from tongue to tongue, so to speak. This intertextual pleasure, precisely because of its mediated and iterative nature, is described as an embodied, physical experience. Amichai's account is quite reminiscent of Brodsky's response to Bloom, discussed in chapter 3; for Brodsky, as we have seen, as soon as we accept the pleasure of cultural circulation as the norm, it's the bourgeois individualism of the West and its obsession with being first that for once gets relegated to the domain of savagery and nonculture.

In his last book and magnum opus, *Open Closed Open* (*Patu'ach sagur patu'ach* [1998]), Amichai offers a sustained articulation of a novel metaphorical system (in Lakoff's terms): POETRY AS TRANSLATION. This metaphorical system is elaborated in a powerful serio-comic late *poema*, which is unparalleled in his oeuvre (with the possible exception of the 1967 "The Travels of the Last Benjamin of Tudela").[29] Titled "Knasim Knasim: Ha-milim ha-mam'irot ve-ha-dibur ha-shafir" ("Conferences, Conferences: Malignant Words, Benign Speech"),[30] this *poema* is at once a witty spoof on the discourse of academic symposia and a parody of political newspeak (what leftist Hebrew slang describes as "the word laundry" [*makhbesat ha-milim*]),[31] in which the language of war masquerades as the language of peace. But it is also a philosophically nuanced critique of dualism, both Hellenistic-Jewish and Christian, and a profoundly serious meditation on body and soul, life and death:

> A conference on language: colloquial, baroquial, poetic, pathetic.
> And the chance for a new language of war and peace:

Just as nouns and verbs in Hebrew change in the masculine and
    feminine
by adding a syllable or changing a vowel, making the sound longer
or shorter, so will it be with the language of war and, once again,
the language of war. And the final conference,
just me and myself: a panel of my body parts
addressing my soul . . .[32]

כֶּנֶס עַל שָׂפָה מְדַבֶּרֶת, מְזַמֶּרֶת, עוֹבֶרֶת וּמְגַמֶּרֶת,
וְאֶפְשָׁרוּת שָׂפָה חֲדָשָׁה שֶׁל שָׁלוֹם וְשֶׁל מִלְחָמָה:
כְּמוֹ שֶׁבְּזָכָר וּנְקֵבָה יִשְׁתַּנּוּ פְּעָלִים וְשֵׁמוֹת
בְּתוֹסֶפֶת הֲבָרָה, אוֹ בְּשִׁנּוּי הַתְּנוּעוֹת, בְּהַאֲרָכַת הַצְּלִיל
וּבְקִצּוּרוֹ, כָּךְ תִּהְיֶה לְשׁוֹן מִלְחָמָה וּלְשׁוֹן מִלְחָמָה.
וְכֶנֶס אַחֲרוֹן רַק אֲנִי רַק אִתִּי: הַרְצָאַת
חֶלְקֵי גּוּפִי אֶל נַפְשִׁי . . .

In its fourteen sections, the *poema* strings together fragments of reports
from various realist and surrealist international conferences (on inflammations of the eye, skin diseases, the import and export of religions
to Jerusalem, the Book of Job). Six of the sections depict the stress
of the translators (or simultaneous interpreters) at these conferences,
whose role as discursive mediators exposes them to the "malignant
words" of all the speechifiers, which they struggle to render into "benign speech"—words that are connected to the emotional and embodied experiential core of everyday life. After an exhausting day's work
at an "'International Conference on Inflammations of the Eye' / for
those who have cried too much or not cried enough," a conference
where the discourse is utterly cut off from the emotional and physical
sources of crying, the women translators return home at night, wash
themselves clean of all the verbiage, and "with sobs of happiness /
they start loving, their eyes aflame with joy" (*ve-ohavot / be-hityapchut
osher u-ve-eynayim dolkot mi-simcha*).[33] By punning on the same root,
d.l.k. (which Chana Bloch and I have rendered with the two etymo-
logically related words "inflammation" and "aflame"), Amichai underscores the contrast between "inflammation" (*daleket*), the "malignant"
word associated with academic jargon, and the women translators' eyes

"aflame" (*dolkot*) with joy: theirs is a healing alternative to the misuse of language in academia or politics ("the language of war and, once again, the language of war"). Interestingly, the first published poem to express Amichai's conception of the poet as translator, "Ve-lo nitlahev," also focalizes a verb—*le-hitlahev* (to get excited)—whose root, inter alia, has the meaning of "flame" ("*lehava,*" root *l.h.v.*), and is thus synonymous with root *d.l.k.* What the translators try to heal—in their collective metaphorical role as the stand-in for the poet, but also as emblematic of any ordinary creative user of language—is the rhetorical equivalent of an ocular inflammation.

Like the translators of the Septuagint, Amichai's simultaneous interpreters are confined to their isolated cubicles ("Conferences, Conferences," Section 4), but unlike the seventy-two Jewish elders in some of the later Christian appropriations of this legend, the Holy Spirit doesn't do the translating for them. They must toil "like bees" to make "cultured" or "wild honey" "from all the buzz and babble" ("Conferences, Conferences," Section 14). The place of the poetic subject, for Amichai, is thus not with the queen bee but with the workers in the beehive; not with the inspiration of the Holy Ghost, nor on the podium of the speaker (be it a professor or a politician), but in the translators' cubicles; not with the head of the yeshiva or the rabbi sermonizing from the pulpit but with the *turgeman* standing close to the people and interpreting for them.

The lack of originary power that comes with modeling poetry on translation is, paradoxically, what makes its language more meaningful in the universal ecology, drawing the poet/translator closer to the spirit of God in the Genesis creation story:

> The translators sit and recycle it all to another
> recycling plan that has no end, and the spirit of God
> hovers above with the whirring wing-blades of a giant fan
> whipping the air, the words whipped over and over like foam.[34]

וְהַמְתַרְגְּמִים יוֹשְׁבִים וּמְמַחְזְרִים הַכֹּל

לְמִחְזוּר אַחֵר שֶׁאֵין לוֹ קֵץ וְרוּחַ אֱלֹהִים

מְרַחֶפֶת לְמַעְלָה בִּתְנוּעוֹת כַּנְפֵי מְאַוְרֵר עֲנָק

וּמַכֶּה אֶת הָאֲוִיר וְהַמִּלִּים מֻכּוֹת שׁוּב וָשׁוּב כְּמוֹ קֶצֶף.

Rather than a deification of the translator, what we have here is a cutting-down to human size of the Holy Spirit, a move that, as Boaz Arpali has shown, is central to Amichai's poetics from its earliest stages.[35] Amichai's bilateral radical allusion reminds us that God in chapter 1 of Genesis does not actually create the world ex nihilo, as fundamentalist readings would have it, but rather recycles primordial air and water that are already there in a state of chaos (*tohu va-vohu*).[36] In a series of metonymic shifts, the Spirit of God (*ru'ach elohim*, always literalized and embodied in the Hebrew as "the wind of God"), which "hovers above" (*merachefet le-ma'ala*), does not create a world but rather recycles *language* up in the heavens, as the translators do here on earth. In a note from the archives, Amichai asks himself, "Do you need to be a poet in order to translate?" and then answers, "You need to be God" (*tzrikhim li-hyot elohim*; the word *elohim* is doubly underlined, and the word "Septuagint" appears above it in English).[37] Even for *rua'ch elohim* there is no privileged access to a pre-intertextual point of origin, to some "verbal first cause," so to speak. Here Amichai rejects outright the view of the Holy Spirit as the Logos that was there "in the beginning" (John 1:1), and along with it, various Christian appropriations of the Septuagint legend, which in the centuries following Philo began to describe the miracle of the perfect identical translations as performed by the Logos penetrating the cells and bodies of each of the seventy-two translators "from above," thus effecting a unified, monological translation of the Hebrew Bible into Greek.[38] In Amichai's poem, however, the Spirit of God continues to hover up above, and doesn't descend to produce a single authorized text for which the translators are mere vehicles or mediums. Here all that the translators and the Holy-Spirit-turned-wind are left with is the laborious effort of endlessly recycling beaten, whipped words, the way eggs are whipped in baking a cake. What Amichai valorizes here, then, is the creativity of ordinary labor—of creativity *as* ordinary labor— by the nameless translators and the biblical God alike, rather than the special gifts of human or divine inspiration. The metaphor of textual recycling makes us see the Spirit of God first as a giant ceiling fan (with the heavens as the ceiling), and then as a cosmic mixer (with the universe as the kitchen where all the recycled words are whirred and whipped up). This cosmic recycling of words encompasses all textual-

ity, as in Kristeva and Barthes's most orthodox poststructuralist formulations. In Amichai's philosophy of language too, as in theirs, there
is no sense in any search for origins, since intertextuality is a cycle
that has no beginning and no end. But as we have seen, and in utter
contrast with the poststructuralist position, the cyclical and recycled
nature of all discourse does not entail for Amichai impersonality and
erasure of agency, nor does it occasion an epistemological crisis. Quite
the contrary, the agency of the "recyclers" themselves—precisely because it is limited and threatened—serves as both point of departure
and syntactic topic for the whole stanza: "the translators sit and recycle it all."

As the co-translator—with Chana Bloch—of *Open Closed Open*, the
book in which this *poema* appears, I identify especially with the situation described in "Conferences, Conferences," Section 6, a situation
familiar to any translator:

> The translators flee their burning cubicles,
> run out into the streets, crying "Help!"
> and make their way to other, calmer conferences.[39]

הַמְתַרְגְּמִים בּוֹרְחִים מִתָּאֵיהֶם הַבּוֹעֲרִים,
הֵם רָצִים בָּרְחוֹבוֹת וּמַזְעִיקִים עֶזְרָה
וְהוֹלְכִים לִכְנָסִים אֲחֵרִים רְגוּעִים יוֹתֵר.

But, as in the metaphorical conceits of the ceiling fan and the giant
eggbeater, there is a great deal more here than a mock-epic hyperbolic account of the translators' flight from the all-consuming fiery
speeches.[40] This section of the poem upends the New Testament celebration of divine intervention as obviating the need for translation.

Little by little it turns out that the entire *poema*—not just the sections dealing with textual recycling that I've described here—is in close
critical dialogue with some early Christian conceptions of translation.
In the cosmic recycling image ("Conferences, Conferences," Section
2), as we have seen, Amichai reverses Christian appropriations of the
legend of the Septuagint and the role of the Logos in it. And indeed,
the connection between fire and translation, on which the image of
the translators fleeing their burning cubicles is based ("Conferences,
Conferences," Section 6), appears elsewhere in the New Testament

in relation to the Logos. In her book on the history and politics of Jewish-Christian translation, Naomi Seidman discusses this very poem by Amichai as "restaging a (Jewish) retelling of the Pentecost event narrated in Acts 2."[41] This event, as she suggests, is the source of the Christian impulse toward translation. In the New Testament narrative, Seidman points out,

> [t]he apostles who assembled in Jerusalem after Jesus' death experience a theophany in the form of what could be called a miraculous translation performance. The Holy Spirit that descends in tongues of fire among the apostles in Jerusalem is heard and understood "each . . . in his own native language" by a rainbow coalition of pilgrims to the temple: "Parthians and Medes and Elamites and residents of Mesopotamia, Judea and Cappadocia, Pontus and Asia, Phrygia and Pamphylia" etc. etc. (Acts 2:10)[42]

Translation in the New Testament account is not necessary because mutual intelligibility across languages is reached without it. But Amichai's *poema* ironically reverses this miracle of universal linguistic transparency, in which one authoritative version audible to all makes translation altogether superfluous. At the same time the *poema* also upends the early Christian view of the translators—and by extension, of the poetic and human subject in general—as a mere vessel lacking any agency, whose action is completely dependent upon divine power, or upon any other authority for that matter. In Amichai's seriocomic parody, the tongues of fire do not bring down a multilingual Holy Spirit that enables communication despite linguistic difference. Quite the opposite: the intertextual fire chases the translators away from their burning cells. As the fire of divine inspiration gets literalized, it is also emptied out of all redemptive promise—it's just a fire, nothing more, and as such it is dangerous. And the translators, like the addressees of an injurious interpellation in Judith Butler's analysis, have the option to refuse to collaborate with its destructive violence:[43] they can, even must, run away, call for help, or find other texts to translate. This midrash on the right to refuse, which posits the poet himself as resistant translator, is, I believe, at the heart of the theory of translational agency embedded within Yehuda Amichai's poetry.

II. The Two Amichais and the Blessings of Mistranslation

To Yehuda Amichai

Because you are a king and I'm only a prince
without a country
with a people who trust in me
I wander sleepless at night

And you are a king and look on me as a friend
worryingly—how long can you drag yourself
through the world

—A long time Yehuda
To the very end

Even our gestures differ—gestures of mercy
of scorn of understanding
—I want from you nothing but understanding

I fall asleep at a fire with my head on my hand
when night burns out dogs howl and guards go
to and fro in the mountains

Zbigniew Herbert[44]

In the spring of 1994, *Ma'ariv*, the popular, distinctly lowbrow Israeli
newspaper, published the following news flash:

Poet Yehuda Amichai Translated into Many Languages

At a ceremony on May 22, the 70th birthday of the Israeli poet Yehuda
Amihai will be celebrated. Overseas students at the Hebrew University
in Jerusalem will read poems by Amihai in 21 languages.[45] Four of the
translations will be by the students themselves. The languages used for
the translation of the poem "Tourists" will include Japanese, Chinese,
Korean, Slovak, and Italian. His poem "Jerusalem" will be read in
Hungarian, Romanian, Serbian, French, and Arabic. "The Mayor" will
be rendered in Amharic, Croatian, Estonian, Dutch, Czech, and Turkish. And "The Ballad of the Long Hair to [*sic*] the Short Hair" will be
heard in German, Russian, Spanish, Danish, and English.[46]

It is hard to imagine a similar anniversary of an American poet being
covered, say, by *USA Today*. This dry journalistic account of famous

Amichai poems and their diverse languages of translation provides a striking illustration—in an almost Amichaiesque catalogue—of how eminently translatable his poetry has become. Yet this very translatability is perhaps the most puzzling aspect of his poetry. Indeed, as Robert Alter has shown in an article that, like Herbert's poem, was published in honor of the poet's seventieth birthday,[47] the most salient aspects that make up the Hebrew Amichai's poetic signature are precisely those that cannot, almost in principle, be translated: his ongoing linguistic and thematic critique of—as well as his inextricable enmeshment with—the historical layers of the great intertextual echo chamber we know as Hebrew.

The key to the puzzle of Amichai's (un)translatability may lie in what readers in the "target language" (English in our case) are left with—rather than what they lose—in translation. What, in other words, remains when the English inevitably strips Amichai's Hebrew of its virtuoso prosodic and grammatical punning, the force of its iconoclastic allusions to sacred Jewish texts, and its radical, playful disruptions of idioms and collocations? What we are left with, in the case of Amichai, is obviously enough. In this line of thought I follow Amichai's own poetics of translation and his privileging of the imperfect mediation and the imprecise recirculation of texts as the site of poetic agency. In their oral performance of Amichai's poems in twenty one languages, the student-readers, unlike the pilgrims to the Temple in Acts 2, do not magically become mutually understandable, nor are they transformed into the vehicle of a single, penetrating Logos. Instead, in their diverse renditions of the multiple Amichais, these languages produce modern-day *turgemanim* who "help" the poetic subject, each in their own way, to "go out into my life," in the language of the unpublished quatrain discussed above. Thus, paradoxically, the multiplicity of (diminished, inexact, unoriginal) versions of the poem is also, to quote Walter Benjamin, the poem's "afterlife," the very condition of its survival-through-suffering.[48]

That translational "afterlife" (which is also the source text's "endurance") is bound to be different from one language to another, and—following Benjamin yet again—to play a constitutive role in the formation of the target language and its culture, precisely as it deforms and mistranslates the source language. Yet traces of Amichai's poetic signature remain legible, even as each target culture's translation emphasizes those aspects of his poetics that best serve its own needs, rejecting others that may be construed as threatening or that simply become illegible. It's easy enough to imagine, for example, that the poem "Tayarim" ("Tourists"), a devastating political critique of the voyeuristic culture of tourism, would read very differently by American-English and Japanese audiences (who are the stereotypic butts of Amichai's satire), than by Italian audiences (who presumably share a similar distaste for touristic voyeurism). In fact, to account for the mystery of Amichai's translatability we need to acknowledge that the constructions of his poetry are at least as numerous as the translation projects that have enabled his reception into the canon of that slippery entity, "international poetry." Each of these projects significantly and necessarily recasts Amichai's work not only according to the personal tastes and choices of the translator, although those are of course crucial, but also in accordance with the linguistic and literary practices and constraints of the target language, its audiences, and its cultures of reception at that particular historical moment.[49] Indeed, a whole system of implications—political and aesthetic—is invoked by the mere choice of the language of translation.[50] Furthermore, extratextual aspects that concern, for example, the physical production, design, and distribution of Amichai's poetry books are additional factors that shape the reception of his poetry within the target language, yet these factors are often ignored. Thus, as I noted in earlier chapters, Amichai always insisted on the pocketbook format of Hebrew editions of his poems because a book of poetry is something that should fit in everyone's back pocket. However, the very different relation of poetry to the culture of everyday life in American society, not to mention the commercial interests of trade publishers, have typically ruled out this format for American translations, including our own.

Far from attempting to encompass anything like an international perspective on Amichai's translatability, I have limited myself in the rest of this chapter—as in this book as a whole—to the different, even contradictory constructions of Amichai's poetry and poetics within the Hebrew and the Anglo-American cultural contexts. Note that I'm not talking about the Hebrew "original" versus the English translation: if we acknowledge, with Amichai, the ontologically mediated status of all poetry, then the Hebrew and the English are two—already recycled—versions. Clearly, my focus on the English Amichai, to the exclusion of translations into other languages, perpetuates the problematic dominance of "imperial English" in the discourse of translation studies within the current globalized "World Literature" movement. However, it is also the case that, pragmatically speaking, many of the translations into other languages are mediated via the English rather than performed directly from the Hebrew. A focus on the English Amichai thus of necessity redoubles the mediation: first from Hebrew to English and then from English to other target languages.

Even if we limit our purview only to book-length translations of Amichai into English, and exclude the hundreds of individual poems translated over the years in anthologies, the periodical literature, and the popular press, the sheer number and diversity of Amichai translators is remarkable: Assia Gutmann, Harold Schimmel, Dennis Silk, Ted Hughes, Glenda Abramson and Tudor Parfitt, Ruth Nevo, Benjamin and Barbara Harshav, and Chana Bloch and Stephen Mitchell, as well as Chana Bloch and myself. Such a polyphony of translational voices has been nicely captured first in the anthology edited by Ted Hughes and Daniel Weissbort, which brings together in a slim volume twelve different English translators of Amichai; and, more recently, in the comprehensive volume edited by Robert Alter, *The Poetry of Yehuda Amichai*, which includes ten of Amichai's major English translators.[51] Finally, and this again involves Ted Hughes, there is the theoretically intriguing phenomenon of self-translation, which is quite the tradition in Jewish literatures. Significantly, however, Amichai's auto-translations have usually been collaborative, either as Ted Hughes's co-translator of *Amen* and *Time*, or as a behind-the-scenes collaborator (for example, on Bloch and Mitchell's *Selected Poetry*). Some insight into the way Amichai negotiated between auto- and collaborative translation can be gleaned from the books' "outwork" (in Lefevere's terms; or their paratext, in Genette's terms)—front and back matter, introduction, and blurbs that situate the poems for the English reader. *Time* is presented as Amichai's own English poems, without the mention of a co-translator; *Amen*, on the other hand, is described on the inner cover page as "translated from the Hebrew by the author and Ted Hughes." But in the introduction, Ted Hughes's account insists that

> [t]he translations were made by the poet himself. All I did was correct the more intrusive oddities and errors of grammar and usage, and in some places shift about the phrasing and line endings. What I wanted to preserve above all was the tone and cadence of Amichai's own voice speaking in English, which seems to me marvelously true to the poetry, in these renderings. What Pound called the first of all poetic virtues— "the heart's tone." So as translations these are extremely literal. But they are also more, they are Yehuda Amichai's own English poems.[52]

Curiously, however, in conversations with me Amichai always referred to both *Amen* and *Time* as collaborative translations with Ted Hughes; and the translations, contra Hughes, are very far from being literal, nor are the poems simply documents of "Amichai's own voice speaking in English." Thus, it seems that in the way these poems are situated for and presented to an English reader, Hughes's own poetics of direct expression, authenticity, and originality overrides Amichai's emphasis on mediation. *The Selected Poetry* is another interesting case in point, which involved two levels of collaboration: first, between Stephen Mitchell, who translated the early poetry, *Shirim 1948–1962* (1963) and *Akhsav ba-ra'ash* (1968), and Chana Bloch, who translated (what was then) "the later poetry," the books published between 1971 and 1989; and second, between Chana Bloch and Yehuda Amichai, working together in Jerusalem, and Stephen Mitchell and myself working in Berkeley. The "outwork" of the volume includes information about this second level of collaboration in acknowledgments at the end of the book (191) rather than at the beginning, although Amichai himself always highlighted the collaborative nature of this project, at the same time that he insisted that, once translated, the poems are the translators', not his. While Amichai may have been ambivalent about noncollaborative auto-translations, he did, as is the norm among canonical Hebrew writers, translate several works into Hebrew—most notably from the German: Hermann Hesse's *Wanderung*, Rolf Hochhuth's play *Der Stellvertreter*, and the poetry of Else Lasker-Schüler.[53]

Despite rather significant individual differences, my study of the corpus of the "English Amichai" and the history and context of his reception appears to produce consistent and at times quite surprising results. When translation is seen, with Lefevere, as part of a system of cultural rewriting (including not only the translated poetry but also the "outwork," as well as reviews and scholarly interpretations), the English Amichai may appear to be almost a religious poet (in the most traditional sense), as I have suggested in chapter 1, and his thematics may be viewed as predominantly Jewish. This effect, astonishing to Amichai's Hebrew readers, is culturally useful, as we have seen, at least for the Jewish part of the American audience, whose institutions have for decades now regularly appropriated his texts for their own needs of constructing a comfortable religiosity and an uncritical Israel-centered sense of Jewish identity; but, as in other processes of reception, canonization, and appropriation, this imposed religiosity is overdetermined, created also by the differences between the Hebrew and the English language systems in everything from grammatical structure to discursive practices. First, contemporary (normative, white) American English is rather resistant to sarcasm and irony, whereas those are still very much the norms of what Benjamin Harshav has famously termed "Jewish Discourse," norms that live on in Hebrew with little acknowledgment of their origins in Yiddish or other Jewish languages, such as Ladino.[54] Ironic readings are especially resisted in English when the topic is serious or tragic, but it is precisely in such contexts that modern Hebrew—like other Jewish languages before it—tends to be at its most acerbic. Second, American English foregrounds its cultural devaluation of linguistic puns (consider, for example, the collective groan when a witty pun is made in public), where in Hebrew it is highly valued. Various forms of linguistic punning— from paronomasia to pseudo-etymological midrash—are the stock-in-trade of Hebrew poetry historically, as well as of contemporary Israeli humor; and as I have argued throughout this study, these "language games" play a crucial and absolutely serious role in Amichai's stylistics and thematics alike. American English typically frowns upon the insertion of ancient historical layers of English in a modern text, even via parody, and Old or Middle English are often inaccessible to the contemporary American reader. In Hebrew, by contrast, at least up until most recently, even the oldest layers of the language, like biblical Hebrew, have not only been transparent for most readers but have formed an integral part of the intertextual toolkit of any poet as well as of the citational practices in everyday speech. Part of Hebrew speakers' psychological reality and sociolinguistic practice is an acute "component awareness"—the linguists' term for a synchronic and diachronic metalinguistic consciousness that is expressed not only in literary but also in everyday communication: from (often ironic or sarcastic) obsessive quotations and (intentional) misquotations of sacred sources, to arguments about the verbal roots of words, to countless lexical innovations and debates over grammatical purism versus slang and foreign calques. All these discursive practices are doubly motivated by the traditional culture of commentary and by the special conditions of a language with a recent and rapidly changing vernacularization. The particular cultural conditions that distinguish the pragmatics of American English from that of Hebrew coincide with the different ideological needs among Amichai's Israeli and Jewish American readers. As a result, it's nearly impossible to present an English Amichai that will have as much of a counter-theological edge as the Hebrew, no matter how hard the translator tries to underscore the irreverent tone.

Another related finding about the difference between the Hebrew and the English Amichai is equally consistent and intriguing: Many English versions of Amichai—especially in their "outwork" and critical reception—minimize, or even avoid altogether, the Hebrew Amichai's dialogue with non-Judaic cultural materials and literary intertexts, from classical Arabic poetry to American postmodernism. To put it bluntly: English seems to need the Hebrew to be first and foremost Jewish. The opposite tendency seems to be characteristic of the Hebrew representation and reception of Amichai. After an initial period in the 1950s in which critics attack Amichai, alongside the other members of the Statehood Generation, for his "disrespectful" treatment of sacred Jewish sources, Israeli scholarship focuses primarily on his intertextual dialogue with the Anglo-American and European canons, from Rilke and Auden to the English Metaphysical poets and the High Modernists. This is, of course, not coincidental and needs to be read in the context of the cultural agenda of establishing modern Israeli literature as an outpost of Western modernism. Not surprisingly, very little has been done to tease out Amichai's fascinating poetic dialogue with the Hebrew-Arabic Medieval tradition (Tova Rosen's work is an important exception), or with the Palestinian poetry of Mahmoud Darwish, for example.[55]

An excellent case in point illustrating the prominence of Jewish intertextuality in English translations and interpretations of Amichai is Glenda Abramson's chapter "Allusion and Irony" in her *The Writing of Yehuda Amichai: A Thematic Approach*, a work that was groundbreaking at the time (1989) as the first book-length study of Amichai in English, written by a noted English scholar who is fully bilingual.[56] Abramson astutely observes that the poet's "subversive intertextuality" (35) is to be read in the dual contexts of "the aesthetics of orthodoxy" on the one hand (33), and of Anglo-American modernism and their earlier models, the English Metaphysical poets, on the other: "He can be compared to Joyce, Eliot, or John Donne in his employment of classical texts for the purpose of ironic pointedness"; but she agrees with Ted Hughes that in recharting "the map of the sources," Amichai remains "exclusively within his own tradition" (34–35).

I am not arguing here that the "Jewish translation" of Amichai into English is wrong, any more than I believe his Western and international construal in Hebrew to be right; for, following Amichai's own implicit theory of poetry-as-translation, I posit that the Hebrew reader does not have access to an unmediated, authentic, and "unrecycled" Amichai either, but necessarily reads him through culturally and historically situated layers of "rewriting" in Lefevere's terms, or intralingual translation in Jakobson's terms.[57] This cautionary note, furthermore, applies to my own reading-as-rewriting as well. The target texts and their interpretations—like the reading and reception of the source texts—are instead to be taken as "symptomatic" in the Marxist sense: clues to the different cultural needs and pressures brought into dialogue in the translation process, and to the poetics and politics of the negotiations between them at a particular historical conjuncture.

Thus, it is instructive that in her translation and detailed reading of the famous early poem "Ve-hi tehilatekha" ("And That Is Your Glory"),[58] whose opening stanzas were discussed at the beginning of chapter 3, Abramson meticulously identifies the various biblical, liturgical, and kabbalistic allusions that the English reader would otherwise miss, but doesn't address the Western classical and modern ones (and not only, I would argue, because these would be self-evident to the English reader).

In discussing the fourth stanza, significantly the point in the poem where the speaker gives up the apostrophe to the male God of Jewish liturgy, replacing it with an address to his earthbound female lover, Abramson emphasizes the Jewish cultural perspective both in her translation of the stanza and her close reading. First, here is the Hebrew text of this stanza:

אוּלַי כְּמוֹ פֶּסֶל עַתִּיק שֶׁאֵין בּוֹ זְרוֹעוֹת
גַּם חַיֵּינוּ יָפִים יוֹתֵר, בְּלִי מַעֲשִׂים וּגְבוּרוֹת.
פִּרְקִי מִמֶּנִּי אֶת שִׁרְיוֹן וּפְסִיַּתִי הַמַּצְהִיבָה,
נִלְחַמְתִּי בְּכָל הָאַבִּירִים, עַד הַחַשְׁמַל כָּבָה.
וְהִיא תְּהִלָּתִי.

In my literal translation (inflected by the construction of the Hebrew Amichai), this stanza reads:

Perhaps like an ancient statue that has no arms,
our life too is more beautiful without [good] deeds and heroics.
Ungird the armor of my yellowing undershirt,
I have fought all the knights till the electricity went out.
And that is my glory.

Abramson translates this stanza much more poetically, as follows:

Like an ancient statue without arms
Our lives might be improved
Without deeds and derring-do.
Strip off my armor, my faded undershirt,
I fought the mighty until the lights went out.
And this is my praise.

Abramson construes the last three lines of the stanza as intertextually Jewish: "He has been fighting with the mighty [*abirim*, "nobles"], faintly reminiscent of Jacob's struggle with the angel, but finding no glory or ennoblement." Since *abirim* is translated as "the mighty" (according to the term's meaning in classical Hebrew; ibid., 41–42) rather than "knights" (its main meaning in modern Hebrew), then the image in the English Amichai is of a speaker engaged in a hopeless struggle with (Jewish) mystical divine beings. He recognizes his limitations, indeed "asks to be made incomplete by the reduction of his ability to perform anything but the most ordinary acts," and armlessness represents for him "the lack of some requisite spiritual quality," as it does elsewhere in Amichai. The English Amichai is then a modern reincarnation of the traditional Jewish figure of the believer, who seeks God's glory and is devastated when he does not find it.[59]

The Hebrew Amichai, by contrast, foregrounds the speaker's parodic, mock-heroic, and rather funny self-portrayal, yet ultimately reaches a much more life-affirming conclusion than the English one. Yoking together allusions to Jewish sacred texts and to classical Western models, the Hebrew emphasizes the grotesque incongruity between the exhausting struggles of a workaday laborer in the modern world ("yellowing undershirt," "electricity") and the anachronistic vestiges of chivalrous idealizations of masculinity and of war ("knights," "fought," "armor"). Yet, by embracing brokenness as a mark of classical Western icons of beauty and "the beautiful life," the speaker in this construal ends up not in despair but—precisely through his self-directed sarcasm—with an affirmation of the unheroic as a new ethical and aesthetic norm. The stanza starts, in my reading—and translation—with a reinterpretation of Venus de Milo, and of all other armless classical statues that represent perfect beauty in spite—or because—of their imperfect aesthetics, ethics, or prowess ("arms," "[good] deeds"). As in other aspects of his poetics, Amichai's view here is very much in line with Wallace Stevens's major poetic principle: "the imperfect is our paradise."[60] Interestingly, while Hebrew "rewritings" of the poem highlight it as one of many homages to Rilke's "Archaischer Torso Apollos," they tend to minimize the internal allusion to Shaul Tchernichovski's poem, "Nokhach pesel apolo" ("Facing Apollo's Statue," 1899).[61] Finally, the Hebrew emphasizes the clash between these classical Western allusions and the intertextual frame of Jewish High Holidays liturgy, which occurs in this stanza not only in the refrain but also in the allusion to the vaunted prayer *avinu malkenu / chanenu va-anenu / ki eyn banu ma'asim* (Our father / our king, have mercy and respond to us / for we have no [good] deeds). The Jewish concept of *ma'asim* in the sense Amichai invokes here of "good deeds" (rather than "stories" or just the unmarked "deeds") is uniquely identified with the Hebrew liturgy. Amichai's Hebrew thus engenders a typical dialogue between disparate Western (classical and modernist) texts on the one hand and Judaic ones on the other, in order to wrest from these textual fragments an argument in favor of antiheroic, ordinary human existence as the true source of glory. In this new ethics and aesthetics of human imperfection, ordinary people's "lack of [good] deeds" or heroics no longer needs to be atoned for, just as the torso of Venus need not be "improved" by adding arms to it but can be accepted and celebrated as a model of beauty. Indeed, Amichai suggests—via the Hebrew—that there is a correlation between a valorized aesthetics of imperfection and an ethics of compassion for human powerlessness, and for the manual laborer in particular (the socialist context of Israel in the 1950s is crucial for this aspect of the Hebrew reading).

Amichai seriocomically recasts, in the Hebrew of the last three lines of this stanza, the speaker as a modern-day Don Quixote whose only armor is a yellowing sleeveless undershirt, presumably so thick with dried sweat and grime it has hardened into armor. In this modern Hebrew use of *abirim* ("knights"), the stanza sets the stage for the focus on the woman, a modern-day Dulcinea, who becomes from here on in the poem the quixotic speaker's substitute for God's glory (in Abramson's reading, you will recall, the speaker finds "no glory").

The Hebrew Amichai—at least the one constructed by my translation and reading (two of the major forms of rewriting, as Lefevere reminds us)—is the "postcynical" atheist who comes to see—in the second half of the poem—his female lover, rather than God, as glory incarnate. In the poem's title and the refrain as it recurs in the first three stanzas, *ve-hi* retains the sense of "and that" which it had in liturgical Hebrew: "And that is your glory," with God as the addressee. But as the speaker keeps questioning the evidence of "that," the supposed manifestations of God's glory in the world, he also increasingly erodes the medieval liturgical sense of the word *ve-hi* ("and that"). Finally, in the last two stanzas of the poem *ve-hi* comes to be read in its modern Hebrew sense of "and she," the third-person feminine personal pronoun, thus turning the woman into a radical substitution for the liturgical earthly proofs for God's glory. It is, in fact, possible to see this whole poem as a performance of an intralingual translation (in Roman Jakobson's terms) from an older, liturgical layer of Hebrew to a modern, secular idiom; and from allusive deixis to the sacred ("and

that") to an anaphoric pronoun pointing at the flesh-and-blood beloved woman ("and she").

In Stephen Mitchell's translation the poem retains Amichai's epigraph, reminding the English reader, as Amichai did the reader of Hebrew, of the liturgical source of his title, only in order to affect its
radical resignification:

And That Is Your Glory

(Phrase from the liturgy of the Days of Awe)

I've yoked together my large silence and my small outcry
like an ox and an ass. I've been through low and through high.
I've been in Jerusalem, in Rome. And perhaps in Mecca anon.
But now God is hiding, and man cries Where have you gone.
And that is your glory.

Underneath the world, God lies stretched on his back,
always repairing, always things get out of whack.
I wanted to see him all, but I see no more
than the soles of his shoes and I'm sadder than I was before.
And that is his glory.

Even the trees went out once to choose a king.
A thousand times I've given my life one more fling.
At the end of the street somebody stands and picks:
this one and this one and this one and this one and this.
And that is your glory.

Perhaps like an ancient statue that has no arms
our life, without deeds and heroes, has greater charms.
Ungird my T-shirt, love; this was my final bout.
I fought all the knights, until the electricity gave out.
And that is my glory.

Rest your mind, it ran with me all the way,
it's exhausted now and needs to knock off for the day.
I see you standing by the wide-open fridge door, revealed
from head to toe in a light from another world.
And that is my glory
and that is his glory
and that is your glory.[62]

וְהִיא תְּהִלָּתָךְ
מִתּוֹךְ פִּיּוּט לְיָמִים הַנּוֹרָאִים

בִּשְׁתִיקָתִי הַגְּדוֹלָה וּבְצַעֲקָתִי הַקְּטַנָּה אֲנִי חוֹרֵשׁ
כִּלְאַיִם. הָיִיתִי בַּמַּיִם וְהָיִיתִי בָּאֵשׁ.
הָיִיתִי בִּירוּשָׁלַיִם וּבְרוֹמָא. אוּלַי אֶהְיֶה בְּמֶכָּה.
אַךְ הַפַּעַם אֱלֹהִים מִתְחַבֵּא וְאָדָם צוֹעֵק אַיֶּכָּה.
וְהִיא תְּהִלָּתֶךָ.

אֱלֹהִים שׁוֹכֵב עַל גַּבּוֹ מִתַּחַת לַתֵּבֵל,
תָּמִיד עָסוּק בְּתִקּוּן, תָּמִיד מַשֶּׁהוּ מִתְקַלְקֵל.
רָצִיתִי לִרְאוֹתוֹ כֻּלּוֹ, אַךְ אֲנִי רוֹאֶה
רַק אֶת סֻלְיוֹת נְעָלָיו וַאֲנִי בּוֹכֶה.
וְהִיא תְּהִלָּתוֹ.

אֲפִלּוּ הָעֵצִים הָלְכוּ לִבְחֹר לָהֶם מֶלֶךְ.
אֶלֶף פְּעָמִים הִתְחַלַּפְתִּי אֶת חַיַּי מִכָּאן וָאֵלֵךְ.
בִּקְצֵה הָרְחוֹב עוֹמֵד אֶחָד וּמוֹנֶה:
אֶת זֶה וְאֶת זֶה וְאֶת זֶה וְאֶת זֶה.
וְהִיא תְּהִלָּתָךְ.

אוּלַי כְּמוֹ פֶּסֶל עַתִּיק שֶׁאֵין בּוֹ זְרוֹעוֹת
גַּם חַיֵּינוּ יָפִים יוֹתֵר, בְּלִי מַעֲשִׂים וּגְבוּרוֹת.
פָּרְקִי מִמֶּנִּי אֶת שִׁרְיוֹן גּוּפִיָתִי הַמַּצְהִיבָה,
נִלְחַמְתִּי בְּכָל הָאַבִּירִים, עַד הַחַשְׁמַל כָּבָה.
וְהִיא תְּהִלָּתִי.

תָּנוּחַ דַּעְתֶּךָ, דַּעְתֶּךָ רָצָה עִמִּי בְּכָל הַדֶּרֶךְ,
וְעַכְשָׁו הִיא עֲיֵפָה וְאֵין בָּהּ עוֹד עֵרֶךְ,
אֲנִי רוֹאֶה אוֹתָךְ מוֹצִיאָה דָּבָר מִן הַמְּקָרֵר,
מוּאֶרֶת מִתּוֹכוֹ בְּאוֹר שֶׁמֵּעוֹלָם אַחֵר.
וְהִיא תְּהִלָּתִי
וְהִיא תְּהִלָּתוֹ
וְהִיא תְּהִלָּתָךְ.

As Amichai's epigraph suggests, the poem rewrites an ancient liturgical poem (*piyyut kadum*) of the same title, a *Piyyut* for the ten Days of Awe between Rosh Hashanah and Yom Kippur, in which God insists on having human beings sing his praises and provide earthly proof of his greatness, when he could have had the adoration of the heavens and the angels above.[63] Amichai's poem, as we have seen at the beginning of this chapter, starts with a God who is hiding, then conceives of God as a mechanic lying under the world, always fixing something, and ultimately gives up the transcendental divine altogether to find mystical and aesthetic glory in the beloved woman as she performs the mundane motion of opening the refrigerator door: *Ani ro'eh otakh motzi'a davar min ha-mekarer, / mu'eret mi-tokho be-or she-me-olam acher.* In my literal translation: "I see you taking a thing [*davar*, also a prophetic vision!] out of the fridge / illuminated from within it with an otherworldly light." This famous seriocomic epiphany (expressed in the Hebrew in a rhyming couplet), which has become the signature of Amichai's feminist counter-theology, depends for its punch on the Hebrew parody of *Don Quixote*, itself the ultimate Western parody of heroic courtly love epics. But that, I feel, is the whole point of Amichai dismantling the dichotomy between sacred and profane. "I am brought to you [fem. sing.] slow and falling. / Accept me. We have no redeeming angel" (*ani muva elayikh le'at ve-nofel. / kablini. eyn lanu mal'akh go'el.*), the speaker says in the conclusion of "The Two of Us Together, Each of Us Alone."[64] Weary and powerless, flawed yet oddly celebratory, he rejoices in what is real, in what is of the here and now: his female partner illuminated by the mock-mystical refrigerator light, and the food she takes out of the fridge as the only "prophetic vision" (*davar*) he shall ever encounter. The woman thus becomes the iterative subject of the final conjugation of glory: *ve-hi tehilati / ve-hi tehilato / ve-hi tehilatekha*, which now must be read as "and she is my glory / and she is his glory / and she is your glory."

The ideological transformations that Amichai's poetry undergoes en route from Hebrew to English may call into question the tendency formerly prevalent in translation studies to divorce the translation process from its social, historical, and political context in the search for some universal theoretical principles that apply to all literatures at all times—principles that, in Susan Bassnett-McGuire's words, "can be determined and categorized, and ultimately utilized in the cycle of text-theory-text regardless of the languages involved."[65] This underlying search for a universal criterion is, according to Gideon Toury, typical of traditional prescriptive studies concerned with discovering what it is that makes any translation "good" or "bad," "faithful" or "unfaithful." However, in the selection of their principles, many of the more sophisticated or "scientific" descriptive translation theories themselves "also pretend to apply to ahistorical phenomena," to use Toury's own terms, even as they avoid the prescriptives of universal norms.[66]

The international distribution of Amichai's translation (in over forty languages so far), and the literary dialogue his work maintains with contemporary poets from Ted Hughes and Zbigniew Herbert to Charles Simic and Mark Strand,[67] point up the limitations of going to the other extreme in current translation studies: modeling the theory exclusively on colonial and postcolonial cultural domination and subjugation, conflating what Tejaswini Niranjana has described as "the power relations informing translation" with a national—if not nationalist—construction of literature.[68] Translation on this account is either a tool for appropriating and controlling the discursive practices of one nation by another, or—in its resistant, disruptive reappropriations by the native culture—a vehicle in the postcolonial nation-building process. These perspectives, although primarily associated with postcolonial studies, are found, as I suggested above, also within some system-theoretical views of translation, although in a sanitized, depoliticized rhetoric. In their most doctrinaire ideological forms, however, these views consistently restrict the politics of translation to examples and theoretical principles that fit the Indian-British model, excluding the possibility of any transnational or, in Claudio Guillén's terms, "metanational" constructions of the politics and poetics of translation.[69] But it is precisely such constructions that the multiple translated Amichais call for.

In exploring the different versions of Amichai produced by his English translations—a process in which I myself am implicated—and in treating the Hebrew as yet another already mediated version rather than a uniquely authoritative original, I have been trying to present a corrective to these two exclusionary directions. My argument throughout has been that the literary culture and historiographic needs of English as the target language, as well as the transnational literary affiliations in which Amichai and his translators participate, alter significantly what features of his style, thematics, poetic worldview, and tone are considered salient. Thus a different set of characteristics necessarily becomes prominent and is perceived as prototypical of Amichai in English. In this context, mistranslation needs to be treated as a critically and culturally informative practice rather than as a mere "mistake" that needs to be "corrected": it is, to recap, symptomatic in the Marxist sense.[70]

Literary (mis)translation is thus a significant resource in the construction and transference of cross-cultural models. Beyond the clichés about the untranslatability of all poetry, I think we can accept as more or less uncontroversial Roman Jakobson's proclamation in his seminal 1959 essay, "On the Linguistic Aspects of Translation," that in translation "[o]nly creative transposition is possible: either intralingual transposition—from one poetic shape into another, or interlingual transposition—from one language into another, or finally intersemiotic transposition—from one system of signs into another (from verbal art into music, dance, cinema, or painting)."[71] Consistent or systematic departures from the stylistic, semantic, and structural strategies of the "source text," as well as translators' sustained omissions, become interpretable choices, crucial indices of the linguistic/cultural/political grid of the target audience. Although I am quite ambivalent about the general conceptual framework within which each works, I take my cue for this point of theory from Barbara Johnson and Tejaswini Niranjana,[72] who—each in her own way—were among the first to extricate translation studies from the seductive discourse of betrayal and fidelity (of being "faithful" or "unfaithful" to the original). Following these developments, Naomi Seidman in her "Midrash on Jewish 'Mistranslation': Diaspora and the Migration of Meaning"[73] has articulated a cogent programmatic statement of what was then a new approach to the politics of translation:

> The history and phenomenology of translation, then, cannot help exposing its role as mediator not only between languages, between texts,

and between the present and the past, but also between centers of power, and between distances traveled. Translations bear the stamp of border crossings, places one should speak of not so much in terms of true or false currency, but rather of cultural-exchanges, which may be more or less limited, but which always work under some sort of political legislation.

As I am proposing this view of translation, I am aware that it is undoubtedly colored by the fact that I am reading here translation theory through the English renditions of a modern Hebrew poet and not through the Chinese, Arabic, or even French translations mentioned in the 1994 news article from *Ma'ariv* with which this section of the chapter begins. And I am implicated—as Amichai's co-translator—in the very process I am critiquing here. It is indeed the hegemonic and culturally homogenizing "global" literary idiom of English that helps establish the reassuring—but dangerous—illusion that "we" have a universal contemporary language of literary translation at our disposal, on which the theory of translation can be modeled.

Figure 2.   Yehuda Amichai with Chana Bloch and Chana Kronfeld discussing the translation of *Open Closed Open*, Berkeley, California, October 29, 1996. Photo: E. Arnon.

III. The Genders of Grammar and the Grammars of Gender: On Translating *Open Closed Open*

I will close this chapter with a few examples of the challenges and cultural negotiations Chana Bloch and I reflected on as we prepared and then presented to the American audience our translation of Amichai's last book, *Open Closed Open* (2000).[74] We started our translation process in close consultation with Amichai, working from his manuscript, a year before *Patu'ach Sagur Patu'ach* appeared in Hebrew (in 1998), and completed it when he was already gravely ill.[75]

Gender is one of the major issues that comes up for any translation from Hebrew into English, but it receives special significance in translating Amichai's *Open Closed Open*, a book—as Michael Gluzman has pointed out—in which Amichai's feminism is most explicitly imbricated in an extended meditation on the Hebrew language.[76] For the purposes of this last section of the chapter, gender is of course first a question of translation practice: how to convey in English the prominent role that grammatical gender plays in Hebrew, a language that has no neuter and that not only marks both inanimate objects and abstract entities as grammatically masculine or feminine but also often personifies them as males or females.[77] Many of these personifications form part of a native speaker's tacit psychological reality and cultural memory; they become topics for Amichai's metalinguistic reflections in the poems of *Open Closed Open:* "memory" (*zikaron*) and "trace" or "remnant" (*zekher*) are masculine and share a root with the noun that means "male" (*zakhar*), while "forgetting" (*shikhecha*) is feminine/female.[78] Vowels are female and consonants are male because, as Amichai reminds us, the plural noun *tnu'ot* (fem., "vowels") also means "movements," whereas the root meaning of *itzurim* (masc., "consonants") is "stopping."[79] The word "compassion" (*rachamim*, masc.) needs to be feminized if it is to become an ethical principle that guides social life, by returning it to its root meaning of "womb" (*rechem*, fem.), something God too should be reminded of.[80] The grammatical markedness that Hebrew feminine forms share with other languages (where the masculine serves as the universal, "unmarked" or base form) is, however, associated in Amichai's Hebrew with a greater degree of vivid personification for inanimate feminine nouns. This is the case especially with nouns that designate sites of the sacred: from the city (*ir*) in general and Jerusalem in particular[81] to the Sabbath; and from the *tallis* (the ritual prayer shawl traditionally worn only by men) to the Torah—all are grammatically feminine and figured as women in erotically resonant metaphorical systems embedded in Jewish culture that Amichai both invokes and undermines.[82]

The difference between Hebrew and English in the psychological reality of grammatical gender metaphorics is best described perhaps by Yona Wallach (1944–1985) in her poem "Hebrew" ("Ivrit"):

About pronouns and sex English leaves its options open
in practice each *I*
has all the options
she is *he* when it's *you*
I doesn't have a sex
there's no difference between she-*you* and he-*you*
and all *things* are *it*—not man not woman
no need to think before relating to sex
Hebrew is a sex maniac
Hebrew discriminates for and against
forgives, gives privileges
with a big gripe from the exile
[. . .]
Hebrew is a sex maniac
wants to know who's talking
almost a mirror almost a picture
forbidden by the Torah.[83]

בִּשְׁמוֹת מִין יֵשׁ לְאַנְגְּלִית כָּל הָאֶפְשָׁרֻיּוֹת
כָּל אֲנִי – בְּפֹעַל
הוּא כָּל אֶפְשָׁרוּת בְּמִין
וְכָל אַתְּ הִיא אַתָּה
וְכָל אֲנִי הוּא בְּלִי מִין
וְאֵין הֶבְדֵּל בֵּין אַתְּ וְאַתָּה
וְכָל הַדְּבָרִים הֵם זֶה – לֹא אִישׁ לֹא אִשָּׁה
לֹא צָרִיךְ לַחְשֹׁב לִפְנֵי שֶׁמִּתְיַחֲסִים לְמִין
עִבְרִית הִיא סֶקְסְמַנְיָאקִית
עִבְרִית מַפְלָה לְרָעָה אוֹ לְטוֹבָה

מְפַרְגֶּנֶת נוֹתֶנֶת פְּרִיבִילֶגְיוֹת
עִם חֶשְׁבּוֹן אָרֹךְ מֵהַגָּלוֹת
[. . .]
עִבְרִית הִיא סֶקְסְמַנְיַאקִית
רוֹצָה לָדַעַת מִי מְדַבֵּר
כִּמְעַט מַרְאֶה כִּמְעַט תְּמוּנָה
מַה שֶׁאָסוּר בְּכָל הַתּוֹרָה

Wallach, the leading feminist poet of the generation that followed
Amichai's, holds out English as a queer alternative that offers the poet
a refuge from what she sees as Hebrew's gender fixations and maniacal,
idolatrous male and female personifications of inanimate objects. But
Wallach's entire point depends, in self-conscious irony, on the poem exploiting precisely those gendered personifications she protests against,
and specifically on the fact that *Ivrit* (Hebrew) and *Anglit* (English),
like all other language names, are gendered feminine and are always
personified as women. The poem ends with the female speaker's promise to make erotic love to the female language in spite, or because
of her sex-mania: *Ohav ota akhshav beli kesut lashon*—literally, "I shall
make love to her now without the cover of tongue."

While Amichai's speaker typically expresses quite a different affect
from Wallach's, the result, I would argue, is an equally radical critique
of Hebrew's essentializing conflation of gender and sex(uality), and
the categorical division between male and female that underlies it. In
many poems Amichai proceeds from a descriptive meditation on the
normative dualism of masculine versus feminine encoded in Hebrew
and prescribed by patriarchal culture, to uncovering alternatives for
this dualism within the Hebrew language system, often by privileging
various "third options" that Hebrew itself can be made to provide:
nouns that have changing gender (e.g., *shemesh*, "sun," *ru'ach*, "wind/
spirit," which can be both feminine and masculine); morphologically
irregular nouns that make the masculine word look feminine and vice
versa; or slippages between singular, dual, and plural forms. All of
these "irregulars" are construed as an escape from the rigid singularity
of gendered identity that are the norm.

Early on, in his second book, *Two Hopes Away* (*Be-merchak shtey
tikvot*, 1958), Amichai begins to link a desired fluidity of gender with

the plurality or split nature of the singular subject in a poem that uses a geometric theorem as a text for meditation on the slippage between the singular and the dual: "Through Two Points Only One Straight Line Can Pass" ("Derekh shtey nekudot over rak kav yashar echad").[84] The last stanza of the Hebrew reads literally: "Sometimes the sun is masculine, sometimes—feminine, / Sometimes we're two, sometimes more than a myriad, / Sometimes I don't know who will hold us by the hand. / But through two points only one straight line can pass." (*Lif'amim ha-shemesh zakhar, lif'amim—nekeva, / lif'amim anachnu shnayim, lif'amim yoter me-revava, / lif'amim eyneni yode'a mi yachazik otanu ba-yad. / aval derekh shtey nekudot over rak kav yashar echad.*) Mitchell's translation, which preserves the rhyme and tone of the Hebrew, nevertheless focuses on number rather than gender, domesticating Amichai's metalinguistics within English (where "you" can be singular or plural). His solution is to do away with gender altogether, omitting any reference to the sun: "At times *I* stands apart, at times it rhymes / with *you*, at times we's singular, at times / plural, at times I don't know what. Alas, / through two points only one straight line can pass."[85] But it is precisely Hebrew's rare and therefore all the more precious ability to bend gender—in grammar and beyond it—that the Hebrew Amichai holds on to. This gender flexibility is for him perhaps the only positive—even potentially utopian—aspect of the fragmentation of the modern subject, and of the problematic politics of an "I" who is pressured to stand for a collective, national "we" in the Israel of the 1950s. And indeed, the split poetic subject continues, throughout the Hebrew oeuvre, to be associated with a need to acknowledge—and increasingly, to celebrate—the masculine and feminine aspects within every human being, the dual form (-*ayim*) rather than a collective plural.

In the poems of *Open Closed Open* Amichai repeatedly revisits early works in which male and female appear as separate figures only to offer a third, dual-gendered alternative. A typical example is a self-parodic reworking of his early poem "Jacob and the Angel."[86] Written in mock-heroic couplets and with midrashic humor worthy of the most irreverent Yiddish carnivalesque biblical mock-epics, the poem "Our Father Jacob" depicts the patriarch struggling with a gender-shifting angel: "At dawn he wrestles a man to the ground. / The man is a woman. They roll round and round." (*Ve-khol shachar hu ne'evak im ish she-hu isha / achuzim ze ba-ze ba-adama ha-kasha.*)[87] But lest we think that the speaker's own gender remains fixed and his subjectivity intact, the poems of *Open Closed Open* provide numerous variations on anthropocentric articulations of the One and the Many, the masculine and the feminine—all as part of the lyrical "I." Summarizing this perspective in his midrashic retelling of the Flood story, Amichai asserts pointedly: "I am two of a kind, male and female" (*Va-ani shnayim shnayim zakhar u-nekeva*).[88]

For the translator of *Open Closed Open*, the difficulty is not just a matter of the difference between Hebrew and English morphology but the larger question of the pragmatics of language use: how to convey the layers of gendered signification embedded in Jewish religious law and expressed in cultural norms, toward which Wallach gestures? For even when these are not explicitly mentioned in the text, they continue to inform a Hebrew reading of the poems. Indeed, as we shall see, the gendered practices of Orthodox Judaism, and the specific attitudes toward the female and male body associated with them, turn out to be as much part of the translational dynamics as the morphological and syntactic peculiarities of Hebrew. And for Amichai, after all, grammar (*dikduk*) is often the most rigorous source of ethical and political meaning. Thus, the stringent gender binary distinctions of the Hebrew grammar between masculine and feminine, which leave no mediating—or queer—option of a neuter or an "in-between" state, are paralleled, for Amichai, by the strict separation of male from female in rabbinic law, and its numerous ramifications for the life cycle, the regulation of domestic and public space, and the access to sacred texts. This in turn forms part of Amichai's critique of the larger obsession with systems of separation in traditional Judaism, which even if they are no longer observed by the non-Orthodox majority, continue to constitute the collective cultural memory—from dietary laws (*kashrut*) and laws pertaining to the contents of textiles (*sha'atnez*) to the separation between Jews and other nations. All of these binary oppositions are the target of Amichai's ethical critique throughout his oeuvre, as evinced by his insistence on mixing categories and valorizing all forms of inbetweenness (*beynayim*) and mediation, such as—translation. But in *Open Closed Open* this critique often takes on a gendered perspective, which is at once thematic and metalinguistic.

Amichai's metalinguistic thematics, which goes back to an early sonnet about the Hebrew verb patterns,[89] challenges his modern translator to reflect the traditional Jewish textual study-model referred to as
shanyim mikra ve-echad targum—"two words of (sacred, Hebrew) text,
and one of translation." Our translation into English thus mimics, in a
sense, the Jewish exegetical practice of incorporating and foregrounding
bilingualism in the translation. Chana Bloch and I sometimes include in
our English translation key words in Hebrew, followed by our English
gloss, when those words themselves function as an object of meditation
for Amichai's speaker. An English translation that includes the Hebrew
"other" is therefore not only our way of foreignizing English as the
hegemonic target language, with its aspirations for universality, but also
our attempt to reflect the exegetical culture Amichai inhabits in his own
irreverent, heretical way, a culture that is always at least bilingual.

Amichai himself recommends "foreignizing translations" quite explicitly, even to the point of stretching the syntax and word order of
the target language beyond grammaticality. His position, expressed as
early as the 1980s, foreshadows the current trend in translation studies,
evinced by Venuti and others' revival of translation theories from
Friedrich Schleiermacher to Walter Benjamin.[90] In a 1984 interview
with me Amichai asserts that

> [the translator] needs to preserve aspects of the original language
> precisely when these aspects don't work well in the second language.
> For example, word order of transitive verbs and their direct object
> should be rendered the way they are in the original, even if it doesn't
> work grammatically, because it's not a coincidence that the original
> language is set up the way it is.[91]

The challenge to the translation of *Open Closed Open* is redoubled
when the rules of Hebrew grammar are themselves the subject of the
poem. Amichai, as we have seen, is fascinated throughout his oeuvre by
the precision (*diyuk*) of grammar (*dikduk*)—a punning etymology that
is linguistically accurate and not just midrashic. This fascination is predicated on grammar's demonstratively unpoetic nature, distanced by its
dryness from excessive pathos or melodrama;[92] but also on the fact that—
in the verbal root system, as well as in the tendency to gender everything—Hebrew grammar always seems to tell a story, often a love story.

Poem #1 in the series "the Language of Love and Tea with Roasted Almonds" in *Open Closed Open* is such a metalinguistic meditation on the Hebrew language and the love stories it tells.[93] Our translation of this poem illustrates one of the ways in which we apply the Jewish exegetical principle of allowing Hebrew to infiltrate the target language, so that the translated text lays bare its own mediation, while paying homage to a central rhetorical practice in the source culture. Amichai's critique of a dualist ethics that is based on the exclusion of the "other" finds its anchor in the grammatical and ontological paradox of God's singular plurality, as it brings together masculine and feminine, male and female, Jew and Arab:

> *Layla*, night, the most feminine of all things, is masculine
> in Hebrew, but it's also the name of a woman.
> Sun is masculine and sunset feminine,
> the memory of the masculine in the feminine, and the yearning
> of a woman in a man. That is to say: the two of us, that is to say: we.
> And why is *Elohim*, God, in the plural? Because All of Him
> are sitting in the shade under a canopy of vines in Akko,
> playing cards. And we sat at a table nearby and I held your hand
> and you held mine instead of cards, and we too
> were masculine and feminine, plural and singular,
> and we drank tea with roasted almonds, two tastes
> that didn't know each other and became one in our mouth.
> And over the café door, next to the sky, it said:
> "Not Responsible for Items Forgotten or Lost."

לַיְלָה, הַדָּבָר הַנָּשִׁי בְּיוֹתֵר הוּא בִּלְשׁוֹן זָכָר

אֲבָל הוּא גַּם שֵׁם אִשָּׁה. יוֹם הוּא זָכָר וִימָמָה נְקֵבָה

זֵכֶר זָכָר בַּנְּקֵבָה וּכְמִיהַת אִשָּׁה בָּאִישׁ.

כְּלוֹמַר שְׁנֵינוּ, כְּלוֹמַר אֲנַחְנוּ.

וּמַדּוּעַ אֱלֹהִים הוּא בִּלְשׁוֹן רַבִּים, כִּי הוּא יוֹשְׁבִים בְּצֵל

סֻכַּת גְּפָנִים

בְּעַכּוֹ וּמְשַׂחֵק קְלָפִים וּמְשַׂחֲקִים. וַאֲנַחְנוּ יָשַׁבְנוּ

בְּשֻׁלְחָן קָרוֹב וְהֶחֱזַקְתִּי אֶת יָדֵךְ וְהֶחֱזַקְתְּ אֶת יָדִי

בִּמְקוֹם קְלָפִים וְגַם אֲנַחְנוּ הָיִינוּ זָכָר וּנְקֵבָה וְרַבִּים וְיָחִיד

וְשָׁתִינוּ תֵּה עַל שְׁקֵדִים קְלוּיִים, שְׁנֵי טְעָמִים

שֶׁלֹּא יָדְעוּ זֶה אֶת זֶה וְהָיוּ לְאֶחָד בְּפִינוּ.

וּמֵעַל לַדֶּלֶת שֶׁל בֵּית הַקָּפֶה, לְיַד הַשָּׁמַיִם הָיָה כָּתוּב

"לֹא אַחֲרָאִים לַחֲפָצִים נִשְׁכָּחִים וְלִדְבָרִים שֶׁאָבְדוּ".

At the end of chapter 1 I discussed this poem at some length as Amichai's ultimate antidote to all forms of authority-sanctioned divisions. Here let me recap just those aspects that pertain directly to the metalinguistic challenge we faced in translating the poem. The entire point of this poem rests on the fact that a personifying actualization of grammatical gender is ever-present in Hebrew. English, on the other hand, marks very few inanimate objects for gender, even metaphorically ("ship" and "car" are notable exceptions). Some difficulties could not be resolved. For example, "day" (*yom,* masc.) is contrasted in line 2 of the Hebrew with *yemama* (fem.; from the same root as *yom*), a twenty-four-hour-period of night-and-day, a lexeme English does not have. We opted to invoke the English Metaphysical poets (who are important for Amichai's use of metaphor and for Statehood Generation modernism in general) by pairing the "sun," which is metaphorically masculine in English,[94] with "sunset," whose femininity we imported from the Hebrew (where *shki'a* is gendered fem.), following here Amichai's advice to push the target language beyond its comfort zone. Because "sun" is already personified male, we felt we could treat the other part of this minimal pair, "sunset," as feminine/female. We thus opted to "impose" gender personification on English only in order to make it possible for Amichai's rejection of gender separation to be more perceptible.

The poem's key word, *layla* ("night"), in the first line becomes the subject of a metalinguistic meditation on the tension between morphological and grammatical gender in this irregular noun: in Hebrew it "looks feminine" since it has the fem. sing. ending *-ah* but is in fact grammatically masculine. Amichai thus uses the "irregular" in Hebrew grammar to call into question the stability—and ontological veracity—of gender binarism, which is the hallmark of "regular" nouns. This leads him to open up the option of a third, queer and fluid gender dynamics. The poem's opening lines are quite complex in terms of the philosophy of language they posit. On the face of it, the speaker underscores the inconsistency between the femininity of the "thing" (*davar*) and the masculinity of the linguistic term used to express it (*leshon zakhar*), but the fact that night in Hebrew is perceived as "the most feminine of all things" is itself linguistically determined: morphologically *layla* appears to be feminine. In destabilizing the dichotomy between sign and referent, Amichai's poem thus discloses a queer desire that undermines the normative system of separation, and the very notion of the arbitrariness of the sign: "the memory of the masculine in the feminine and the yearning / of a woman in a man" (*zekher zakhar ba-nkeva u-khmihat isha ba-ish*).[95] Grammatical irregularity is for Amichai the way Hebrew registers the remnant of a bisexual, primordial past as a desire for a holistic future. Poignantly, the speaker immediately associates this morphological tension with another, more shadowy semantic one, between *layla* as a noun and as a proper name (*shem*): "but it's also the name of a woman." What the poem does not say—but at least source-culture readers would know—is that it is common as a woman's name in Arabic, not in Hebrew. This, together with the extralinguistic pragmatic context of the poem's staging—a café in the binational coastal city of Akko—associates the speaker's utopian undoing of gender divisions with a utopian dismantling of the divisions between Arab and Jew, as part of this idyllic scene where the language of love makes intimate partners of alien "others."

Amichai boldly violates Hebrew grammar here in order to destabilize dichotomous notions of gender and sexuality, and—by implication—to critique nationalist separatism. This violation has transcendental consequences, which are expressed in the linguistically most experimental move in the poem: an ungrammaticality that not only destabilizes the division between the human and the divine but also returns the monotheistic God of the Hebrew Bible to his pagan plurality. This is achieved by breaking what linguists used to call "strict sub-categorization rules," rules that native speakers supposedly never violate.[96] *Elohim*, one of the common biblical designations for God, and the one used most frequently in modern Hebrew as well, has a morphologically plural ending even though it usually takes a singular verb. By making the noun *Elohim* take a plural predicate, Amichai sets up the God he does not believe in as an imaginative site where the One and the Many unite; at the same time, he implies that the ordinary Jewish and/or Palestinian men playing cards in the café *are* God:

And why is *Elohim*, God, in the plural? Because All of Him
are sitting in the shade under a canopy of vines in Akko,
playing cards.

וּמַדּוּעַ אֱלֹהִים הוּא בְּלָשׁוֹן רַבִּים. כִּי הוּא יוֹשְׁבִים בְּצֵל
סֻכַּת גְּפָנִים

בְּעַכּוֹ וּמְשַׂחֵק קְלָפִים וּמְשַׂחֲקִים.

The literal meaning of the Hebrew—*hu yoshvim*—"He [singular] are sitting [plural]," is as ungrammatical in Hebrew as it would be in English. But in Hebrew, where linguistic norms are in a constant state of flux, academic attempts at purism notwithstanding, a playful ungrammaticality is less jarring than "He are sitting" would be to an English reader today. This is a case where a foreignizing literal translation would run the risk of looking like a typo, rather than registering as a radical move of destabilizing grammar. Furthermore, while biblical Hebrew typically assigns singular verbs to the morphologically plural noun *Elohim* (God), there are cases where it appears in the plural, thus allowing Amichai again to use the exception to undermine the rule. The most notable example of *Elohim* being used with both a singular and a plural verb appears in the first poem in the Hebrew Bible—the first version of the creation story in Genesis 1. This version, echoed as the marker of an intertextual syllepsis in Amichai's poem,[97] can be read as depicting God's "image" (*tzelem*) as combining male and female aspects: "And God said (*va-yomer*, sing.), 'Let us make (*na'aseh*, pl.) a human in our image, by our likeness,' [. . .] And God created the human in his image, / in the image of God He created him, / male and female He created them" (Genesis 1:26–27).[98] Thus, as in the early "Through Two Points Only One Straight Line Can Pass," there is an inextricable link in this late poem between mixing singular and plural and combining masculine and feminine, self and other, although here this link is foregrounded here through a blatant ungrammaticality. We opted in our translation for the bilingual pun "All of Him are sitting," since the pseudo-etymology "Elohim / All of him" is in the spirit of

Amichai's irreverent use of the genre of midrash, drawing attention to the sound and morphology of the Hebrew within the English. This is an example of translational "compensation" (to use the terms of traditional translation studies), since there is no such midrashic pun in the Hebrew of this line but there are many others that we could not render, such as the punning midrash on the term for the women's section (*ezrat nashim*) in the poem "I Studied Love" I discuss below. It also allowed us to press English into service as far as the violation of grammatical rules is concerned ("All of Him/are"), without it appearing as a typographical error.

Ultimately, however, it is not the metalinguistic meditation and its accompanying wordplay but the details of realia, the life outside language, which troubles translation. In linguistic terms, pragmatics trumps syntax, semantics, and phonology in the translational challenges it presents, which is precisely why a domesticating translation that erases the source's cultural specificity would render the Hebrew Amichai completely unreadable in English. The poem is suffused with the sensual textures of local life, the tastes and smells of Akko, and the layered "temporal archaeology" with which Amichai is so fascinated and which he always offers as an alternative to linear chronology. Akko is a binational city in the north of Israel on the Mediterranean coast whose landscape evinces its complex history of conquests and occupations, going back to the Crusades and Napoleonic wars. The Israeli reader would probably know that Amichai is referring to the Palestinian-Arab section of the city (on the waterfront), and might even have a few specific cafés in mind that have outdoor seating under a canopy of vines. But to the English reader, the names "Akko" and "Layla" by themselves would not necessarily convey the crucial extralinguistic information that the poem takes place at the intersection of Arab and Jewish cultures, and that the binary opposition of Arab and Jew is another form of "othering" that "the language of love" aims to dissolve. This language of love is offered, as we have seen, throughout Amichai's oeuvre, as a special "cure" for the devastating consequences of categorical divisions not only between grammatical genders but also between men and women, Jews and Arabs, God and human beings.

Translating gender is similarly as much a matter of extralinguistic cultural norms as it is of grammatical morphology. In one of the most memorable feminist poems in this collection, "I Studied Love,"[99] the Hebrew Amichai relies on his readers' specific and quite precise familiarity with the gender separation mandated by traditional Jewish prayer practices, from the architecture of the synagogue (where the women are separated from the men by a *mechitza*, a partition), to the types of gender-specific prayer required of each. In the absence of this cultural information, the English Amichai could be read as expressing a sweet nostalgic yearning for the women in his childhood synagogue in the Old Country, a nostalgia that blunts the poem's critique. What makes this critique translatable, however, is the fact that it is articulated throughout the poem in terms that are informed by Western feminism: the exclusionary practices of patriarchy and of clericalism affect not only women but also men (and the construction of nascent masculinity in young boys); the prison of the women's section (and the Hebrew repeats four times the verb *k.l.a.*, to "jail," "imprison," or "lock up") becomes also the prison of a woman-less male space:

21

I studied love in my childhood in my childhood synagogue
in the women's section with the help of the women behind the
    partition
that locked up my mother with all the other women and girls.
But the partition that locked them up locked me up
on the other side. They were free in their love while I remained
locked up with all the men and boys in my love, my longing.
I wanted to be there with them and to know their secrets
and say with them, "Blessed be He who has made me
according to His will." And the partition—
a lace curtain white and soft as summer dresses, swaying
on its rings and loops of wish and would,
lu-lu loops, lullings of love in the locked room.
And the faces of women like the face of the moon behind the clouds
or the full moon when the curtain parts: an enchanted
cosmic order. At night we said the blessing
over the moon outside, and I
thought about the women.

לָמַדְתִּי אַהֲבָה בְּיַלְדוּתִי בְּבֵית הַכְּנֶסֶת שֶׁל יַלְדוּתִי
בְּעֶזְרַת הַנָּשִׁים בְּעֶזְרַת הַנָּשִׁים שֶׁמֵּאַחוֹרֵי הַמְּחִצָּה
שֶׁכָּלְאָה אֶת אִמִּי עִם כָּל הַנָּשִׁים וְהַנְּעָרוֹת.
אֲבָל הַמְּחִצָּה שֶׁכָּלְאָה אוֹתָן, כָּלְאָה אוֹתִי מִן הַצַּד הַשֵּׁנִי,
הֵן הָיוּ חָפְשִׁיּוֹת בְּאַהֲבָתָן וַאֲנִי נִשְׁאַרְתִּי
כָּלוּא עִם כָּל הַגְּבָרִים וְכָל הַנְּעָרִים בְּאַהֲבָתִי וּבְכִמְיָהָתִי,
וְרָצִיתִי לִהְיוֹת אִתָּן שָׁם וְלָדַעַת אֶת סוֹדוֹתֵיהֶן
וּלְבָרֵךְ ״בָּרוּךְ שֶׁעָשַׂנִי כִּרְצוֹנוֹ״ אִתָּן. וְהַמְּחִצָּה,
וִילוֹן מַלְמָלָה לָבָן וְרַךְ כִּשְׂמָלוֹת קַיִץ וְהַוִּילוֹן
זָז הָלוֹךְ וָשׁוֹב בְּטַבָּעוֹת וּבְלוּלָאוֹת,
לוּ לוּ לוּ לוּלָאוֹת, לוּ לוּ, קוֹלוֹת אַהֲבָה בַּחֶדֶר הַסָּגוּר.
וּפְנֵי הַנָּשִׁים כִּפְנֵי הַלְּבָנָה שֶׁמֵּאַחוֹרֵי הָעֲנָנִים
אוֹ הַמְּלֵאָה בְּהִפָּתַח הַוִּילוֹן כְּמוֹ בְּמַעֲרֶכֶת
קוֹסְמִית קְסוּמָה. וּבַלַּיְלָה בֵּרַכְנוּ בִּרְכַּת
הַלְּבָנָה בַּחוּץ וַאֲנִי חָשַׁבְתִּי עַל הַנָּשִׁים.

The Hebrew opens with an untranslatable pun that literalizes the traditional idiomatic name for the Women's Section in the synagogue, *ezrat nashim*, through a pseudo-etymological midrash on the rabbinic architectural term *azara* (section of a building), treating it as if it were derived from the root for "help" (*a.z.r.*; both nouns are grammatically feminine in Hebrew!). The pseudo-tautology of the Hebrew (*be-ezrat ha-nashim be-ezrat ha-nashim*) is made to sound like the intoning of an unauthorized prayer. This then is the personal mantra for the boy who refuses to become a normative male by repressing the feminine aspects of his subjectivity, at the same time that he protests the collective discrimination against women in the religious life of the community. This highly expressive stutter— *be-ezrat ha-nashim be-ezrat ha-nashim*—uses the workings of verbal art articulately to undo the silencing of women, whereas in our English translation it is only a message available as semantic content: women's exclusion taught the male child the "language of love," which as we have seen is Amichai's antidote to *acherut* ("otherness"), the institutional and ideological manipulation and separation of one group of people from another.[100]

Some of the most symptomatic difficulties this poem presented to us as translators had to do with the intersection of nonliterary intertextuality and cultural norms. But note that here the negotiations do not correlate simply with the boundaries of language or the nation-state: the same lines would be read very differently by Hebrew and English readers familiar with Jewish textual practice in general and with quotations from the Orthodox *siddur*, the Jewish prayer book, in particular, and by those who are not (and increasingly, many Israeli Hebrew readers would not be familiar with such intertextuality).

Thus, the cultural negotiations triggered by the translation process are never fully coextensive with the source and target languages. As in literary theory in general, the national boundaries of language and state may not always be the relevant parameters for translation studies. For the sake of convenience, I will refer to the two "rewritings" produced along these distinctions as the Jewish versus the non-Jewish Amichai, although of course this does not correspond to the reader's actual religious "identity." Thus, "Blessed be He who has made me according to His will" in line 8—*Barukh she-asani ki-rtzono*—sounds unambiguously pious in a non-Jewish reading. Readers who do not identify this verse as part of the morning prayers recited by women will not recognize just how iconoclastic the Jewish Amichai may be here—first, because the speaker wishes to say the woman's blessing instead of the man's; and second, because the man's blessing happens to be *Barukh she-lo asani isha*, "Blessed be He who has not made me a woman." In C. D. Blanton's terms, the man's blessing functions as "the shadow text"—the part of the allusion that is not included but casts its shadow on the entire poem.[101] In our endnotes to the poems we quote the man's blessing, though we know that this bit of outwork, with its academic connotations and relegation to the end of book, cannot begin to express how that cultural-religious understanding radically alters the way the poem reads.

This is not to say that the difference between a Hebrew and an English reading ceases to be relevant once the negotiations between transnational and translinguistic cultural and religious formations is taken into account. It is, I would argue, always a matter of multiple and partial modeling of (inter)textual communities (as it is with other forms of literary affiliation). Clearly, the Jewish Amichai is often completely transparent within an (Israeli) Hebrew reading, not least because of the political struggle over religious versus civil law in the State of Israel. But in such cases the tensions between a Jewish and a Hebrew reading must also enter into the translational negotiation. Thus, for example, the term *chevra kadisha* that opens the poem "When I Die" ("In My Life, On My Life," #13) is familiar to all Israeli Jews, even if they are otherwise religiously uninformed—and despite the fact that the term is Aramaic rather than Hebrew![102] Within an English or a non-Jewish reading of the poem, the literal rendition, "the sacred fellowship," wouldn't indicate its function, and an explanatory phrase like "the burial society" would suggest neither the sanctity accorded that function in traditional Jewish life nor the political controversy it generates in present-day Israel, where religious burial is mandated by State law. We thus use the Aramaic in our English, incorporating an aspect of the Jewish Amichai into our text via the same foreignizing strategy we use elsewhere. However, the Jewish reading signaled by the rest of our endnote on this poem has again to do with extra-linguistic cultural practices rather than with language proper. It explains that the poem's first line, "When I die, I want only women to handle me in the Chevra Kadisha" expresses a wish that is a scandalous violation of Jewish law, according to which men's bodies must be purified and prepared for burial by men, and women's bodies by women. The Jewish Amichai thus attacks head-on—using traditional rhetorical strategies of irony and irreverent, self-directed humor—what he sees as the grotesque persistence of systematic gender separation beyond the boundaries of life and death:

> When I die, I want only women to handle me in the Chevra Kadisha
> and to do with my body as they please: cleanse my ears of the last
> words I heard, wipe my lips of the last words I said,
> erase the sights I saw from my eyes, smooth my brow of worries
> and fold my arms across my chest like the sleeves of a shirt after ironing.
> Let them salve my flesh with perfumed oil to anoint me King of Death
> for a day . . .

כְּשֶׁאָמוּת אֲנִי רוֹצֶה שֶׁרַק נָשִׁים יְטַפְּלוּ בִּי בְּחֶבְרָה קַדִּישָׁא
וְיַעֲשׂוּ בְּגוּפִי כַּטּוֹב בְּעֵינֵיהֶן הַיָּפוֹת וִינַקּוּ אֶת אָזְנַי מִן הַמִּלִּים
הָאַחֲרוֹנוֹת

שֶׁשָּׁמַעְתִּי וְיָנְגְּבוּ אֶת שְׂפָתַי מִן הַמִּלִּים הָאַחֲרוֹנוֹת שֶׁאָמַרְתִּי,

וְיִמְחֲקוּ מֵעֵינַי אֶת הַמַּרְאוֹת שֶׁרָאִיתִי וְיַחֲלִיקוּ אֶת מִצְחִי מִן

הַדְּאָגוֹת

וִיקַפְּלוּ אֶת זְרוֹעוֹתַי עַל חָזִי, כְּמוֹ שַׁרְווּלֵי חֲלָצָה אַחַר הַגִּהוּץ,

וְיָסוּכוּ אֶת בְּשָׂרִי בְּשֶׁמֶן בָּשׂוּם לִמְשֹׁחַ אוֹתִי לְמֶלֶךְ הַמָּוֶת

לְיוֹם אֶחָד

Moreover, to write "When I die, I want only women to handle me in the Chevra Kadisha" is to dream up a scenario that within a Jewish reading traditionally conceived is strictly unkosher, not because of the explicit nudity and disrespectful tone used to describe the deceased, but because of the audacity—the chutzpah—to imagine the ultimate undoing of the clerical separation, the *mechitza*, between men's and women's bodies. Such a radical reading of the Jewish Amichai is reinforced by the passionate attitudes that fuel the crisis between secular and Orthodox in Israel—and thus by the Hebrew (or Israeli) Amichai—not least as this crisis bears on restrictions on women in key areas that have been controlled since the foundation of the State by religious parties and, hence, by rabbinical law: birth, marriage, divorce, and death.

The speaker in this poem goes on to prescribe the disposition of his genitals after his death:

> and arrange in my pelvic basin as in a fruit bowl
> testes and penis, navel and frizzy hair
> like an ornate still life from some past century,
> a very still life on a ground of dark velvet

וִיסַדְּרוּ בְּאַגַּן יְרֵכַי, כְּמוֹ בְּקַעֲרַת פֵּרוֹת,

אֶת הָאֲשָׁכִים וְאֶת אֵיבַר הַמִּין עִם הַטַּבּוּר וְהַשֵּׂעָר הַמְקֻרְזָל

כְּמוֹ בְּצִיּוּר מְפֹאָר שֶׁל טֶבַע דּוֹמֵם מִן הַמֵּאוֹת שֶׁעָבְרוּ,

טֶבַע דּוֹמֵם מְאֹד עַל רֶקַע קְטִיפָה אֲפֵלָה

For a Western reading of Amichai, the scandal of these lines lies in the explicit treatment of the dead naked body—and of pubic nudity in general—as well as in the shocking literalization of the corpse as a "still life" by adding the quantifier "very" to the mix. The necrophilic

eroticism of the women's handling of the dead speaker's genitalia is thus
equaled by the outrage of the metaphorical mapping of the speaker's
dead pelvis onto an overwrought—and decidedly European—academic
painting of a fruit bowl. Yet attitudes toward nudity and sexuality are
much less prudish for the Jewish Amichai, where the wit of the far-
fetched metaphor and its mock-heroic self-depiction register as humor-
ous rather than outrageous. The outrage, as suggested above, is instead
in the very wish for transgressing gender boundaries and roles in death
as in life, indeed in daring to grant the female touch the ultimate status
of the sacred.

When Amichai himself addresses the task of the translator in his last
book, in the great *poema* "Conferences, Conferences" discussed in section I of this chapter, he in fact also provides a critique of the once-
dominant theory of translation as a process obsessed with finding lexical equivalence. Amichai situates instead the challenge of translation
(and hence, for him, of poetry as well) entirely outside language, in the
realm of human experience and emotional transformation. Ultimately,
for Amichai, translation is the work of turning one propositional attitude (belief, hope, fear, desire) and its attendant performatives into its
opposite; and of bridging the emotional gap between dichotomies, and
emphasizing flow and change, rather than fixing a singular meaning:

> And the translators translate pain to another kind of pain,
> remembering to forgetting, forgetting to remembering,
> curse to blessing and blessing to curse.[103]

וְהַמְתַרְגְּמִים מְתַרְגְּמִים כְּאֵב לִכְאֵב אַחֵר
זְכִירָה לְשִׁכְחָה וְשִׁכְחָה לִזְכִירָה
וּקְלָלָה לִבְרָכָה וּבְרָכָה לִקְלָלָה.

Five   Living on the Hyphen
The Necessary Metaphor

> Metaphor is the greatest invention of humankind; more than the
> wheel and the computer.
>   Yehuda Amichai, interview with author, Jerusalem, 1986[1]

I. Hyphenated States

Despite the diverse modalities of figurative language in Amichai's
early and late work, one thing remains consistent: metaphor, simile,
analogy, and other modes of figuration are accorded a (literally) vital
role within his poetic worldview in all its phases. My discussion in
this chapter focuses on the ways in which metaphor, broadly construed, becomes the central marker of in-between-ness (*beynayim*),
the hyphen of survival and resistance for the poetic subject. As such,
metaphor in Amichai's work must never erase the disparate domains
that it brings together, even while it strives to make the transient, liminal space *in between* them as existentially meaningful as it can possibly
be. The principle for Amichai, whether in figurative language or in
love, is: "The Two of Us Together and Each of Us Alone" ("Shneynu
be-yachad ve-khol echad le-chud"), the title of his early poem that I
discuss briefly in earlier chapters and will return to below.[2] In both
building and drawing attention to the bridges they construct over
semantic, perceptual, and historical distances, Amichai's metaphors set
up arrays of tentative, novel exchange between previously alien domains, all the while maintaining—and communicating to the reader—
a keen awareness of their distinctness.[3]

Underscoring how Amichai's metaphors resist the erasure of difference, I wish to enlist his poetry to dispense with contemporary vestiges
of some poststructuralist attacks on figurative language; these are partially responsible, I believe, for the stagnation over the past thirty or so
years in the once-flourishing literary study of metaphor. One of the specific sources for this stagnation was Paul de Man's attack on metaphor as

225

a "Lucifer of light,"[4] "an error [that] believes or feigns to believe in its own referential meaning."[5] Ironically, the same period evinced an explosion of rigorous scholarly engagement with metaphor in general, and with metaphorical systems in particular, within linguistics. The study of metaphor has been especially productive in those approaches that, like cognitive linguistics, are oriented toward the connection between language and thought but are, unfortunately in my opinion, less interested than they could be in a metaphor's specific sociocultural context. I hope that my discussion will help reinvigorate the once-vibrant dialogue between literature and linguistics in order to reclaim the study of metaphor for a historically nuanced, post-poststructuralist theoretical mindset.

In line with this gesture toward cognitive linguistics, I have placed in the center of the chapter a close analysis of the diverse *image schemas* Amichai develops throughout his poetic oeuvre to thematize metaphor as a hyphenated state linking disparate domains. This analysis is based on my 1996 adaptation of prototype semantics for a historically inflected theory of literary trends.[6] My approach draws especially on the work of George Lakoff and Eve Sweetser and their precursor, Eleanor Rosch.[7] Methodologically, this section helps me to argue for the relevance of cultural, experiential, and cognitive linguistics for contemporary literary theory and cultural studies. More importantly, these tools allow me to explain how Amichai's metaphors, while as novel and surprising as any seventeenth-century Metaphysical poet's,[8] so often strike us—once we can "see" them—as completely "right," as visually familiar, even intuitive and natural.

As we have seen, Yehuda Amichai's poetic worldview disrupts all rigid categorical distinctions, binary or otherwise: from literary genres and intellectual disciplines to historical periods, poetic generations, and territorial borders. Even his early poetry from the 1950s and 60s displayed this sustained practice, foreshadowing—in its focus on the construction of a liminal hybrid subject—literary theories that would develop half a century later. Independently of any postcolonial or subaltern theoretical trajectory, but in implicit dialogue with the same Marxist critical thought that may have inspired both, Yehuda Amichai developed over a period that spans half a century a poetics of the hyphenated state as the location of the human agent. Conceptually, this has entailed writing on the shifting, tenuous border *between* accepted ontological and epistemological categories; rhetorically, it has meant a semantically productive "hovering" on the boundaries or intersections of generational trends and poetic styles, a topic I take up in the next and final chapter. Borderline or interim states are embraced in Amichai's poetry precisely because they hold out no false hope or mystification about identity and possession, although they may, of course, be quite dangerous places:

> The pressure of my life brings my date of birth closer
> to the date of my death, as in history books
> where the pressure of history has brought
> those two numbers together next to the name of a dead king
> with only a hyphen between them.
>
> I hold onto that hyphen with all my might
> like a lifeline, I live on it, . . .[9]

לַחַץ חַיַּי מְקָרֵב אֶת תַּאֲרִיךְ הֻלַּדְתָּה

אֶל תַּאֲרִיךְ הַמָּוֶת, כְּמוֹ סִפְרֵי הַהִסְטוֹרְיָה,

שֶׁבָּהֶם לַחַץ הַהִסְטוֹרְיָה הַצְמִיד אֶת שְׁנֵי

הַמִּסְפָּרִים הָאֵלֶּה יַחְדָּו לְיַד שֵׁם מֶלֶךְ מֵת

וְרַק מַקָּף מַפְרִיד בֵּינֵיהֶם.

אֲנִי מַחֲזִיק בַּמַּקָּף הַזֶּה בְּכָל מְאֹדִי,

כְּמוֹ בְּקֶרֶשׁ הַצָּלָה, אֲנִי חַי עָלָיו,

Living/writing occurs in the ever-narrowing space of the hyphen between date of birth and date of death. I will look closely at the workings of this central image schema below, but at this point let me just illustrate in the most general terms some of the major visual and grammatical variations on the state of in-between-ness in Amichai's metaphorical systems. Amichai often uses the *dual* grammatical form as a morphological thematization, such as *beynayim* (in-between), *reychayim* (grindstones), *arbayim* (twilight)—all nouns ending with the dual plural morpheme -*ayim*.[10]

In "Shneynu be-yachad ve-khol echad le-chud" ("The Two of Us Together and Each of Us Alone"), the image schema of *beynayim* is expressed in the metaphor of the moon-as-saw cutting the clouds into two opposing camps. This figurative scenario serves as a visual parallel to the lovers performing their love on the battlefield down below for the two armies' diversion:

> The moon is sawing the clouds in two—
> Come, let's go out for a love duel.
> Just the two of us will love before the camps at war.
> Perhaps it's still possible to change it all.
> The two of us together and each of us alone.[11]
>
> Trans. Chana Kronfeld

יָרֵחַ מְנַסֵּר אֶת הֶעָבִים לִשְׁנַיִם –
בּוֹאִי וְנֵצֵא לְאַהֲבַת בֵּינַיִם.
רַק שְׁנֵינוּ נֹאהַב לִפְנֵי הַמַּחֲנוֹת.
אוּלַי אֶפְשָׁר עוֹד הַכֹּל לְשַׁנּוֹת.
שְׁנֵינוּ בְּיַחַד וְכָל אֶחָד לְחוּד.

Visually, the image schema, here as elsewhere, involves variations on two halves of one whole. Thematically, as we have seen, in-between-ness is presented through the biblical metaphor of a *duel*. But rather than the European scenario of an individual in a chivalrous duel over honor, what is being invoked here is the ancient Near Eastern image of two warriors, each stepping forward from their camp and doing battle on behalf of the nation or tribe at war. While the European "duel" is *du-krav* in modern Hebrew, the biblical term is *milchemet beynayim,* literally "an in-between war"; Goliath, for example, is described as *ish ha-beynayim,* literally "the in-between man" (1 Samuel 17:23). Since for Amichai love is always performed under the sign of war, the young couple's love (*ahava*) is sarcastically termed here *ahavat beynayim,* in what I have described as a purposeful catachresis, where "love" replaces "war" but "war" still echoes in the background of the expression. Theirs is a love duel as well as an interim love, threatened by and performed for the interpellated warring masses. Thus the lovers in this poem are compelled to perform like gladiators before the powerful camps of army and state, serving as their rulers' bread and circuses.[12]

In another early poem, the speaker tries to insert himself "in the narrow crack" between the two well-matched halves of loving/hating masses who stand in the way of the personal dreams of ordinary people like him, even when those dreams are as mundane as finding housing in the newly built projects of Israel in the 1950s:

From: Half the People in the World

Half the people love,
Half the people hate.
And where is my place between such well-matched halves,
and through what crack will I see
the white housing projects of my dreams
and the barefoot runners on the sand
or, at least, the waving
of a girl's kerchief, beside the mound?[13]

מַחֲצִית הָאֲנָשִׁים אוֹהֲבִים,

מַחֲצִיתָם שׂוֹנְאִים.

וְהֵיכָן מְקוֹמִי בֵּין הַמַּחֲצִיּוֹת הַמְּתָאָמוֹת כָּל־כָּךְ,

וְדֶרֶךְ אֵיזֶה סֶדֶק אֶרְאֶה אֶת

הַשִּׁכּוּנִים הַלְּבָנִים שֶׁל חֲלוֹמוֹתַי,

וְאֶת הָרָצִים הַיְחֵפִים עַל הַחוֹלוֹת

אוֹ לְפָחוֹת אֶת נִפְנוּף

מִטְפַּחַת הַנַּעֲרָה, לְיַד הַתֵּל?

The poetic subject's location is thus in between loving and hating populations, which, in the post-1948 context, necessarily implies people at peace versus people at war. The ambiguity of all present-tense verbs in Hebrew between verbal forms and nominalized adjectives produces an alternative reading: "half the people in the world are lovers / half are haters" (this is, strictly speaking, the only grammatically "correct" reading, otherwise we would have here two transitive verbs that do not have an object). The last four lines in this section of the poem describing the poetic subject's unromantic dreams and aspirations make a wry reference to the severe housing shortage in Israel during that period, a shortage that Amichai's contemporary readers would know was attributed to defense budget priorities. Even the speaker's private love (the girl waving her kerchief) is seen through her proximity to the *tel* (here translated as "mound"), an archaeological site marking the ruins of history, personal and collective, recent and ancient. The inability of the individual lovers to extricate themselves from the pressures of historical and present haters constitutes the geologically unstable layers in Amichai's "archaeology of the self."

In a poignant early quatrain, the speaker positions himself "in the right angle between a dead man and his mourner," sketching out an emotional, yet anti-sentimental, geometry for grief as the liminal place of the poet in the corner between the dead and the living:

Quatrain 46[14]

In the right angle between the dead man and his mourner
will be my life's place from now on, my corner.
The woman sits with me, the girl went up
in a cloud of smoke to the heavens and into my big heart.

בְּזָוִית הַיְשָׁרָה בֵּין מֵת וּבוֹכֶה עָלָיו
תִּהְיֶה פִּנָּתִי, מְקוֹם חַיַּי, מַעֲכָשָׁו.
הָאִשָּׁה יוֹשֶׁבֶת עִמִּי, הַיַּלְדָּה עָלְתָה בְּעַב
שֶׁרֵפָתָה לַשָּׁמַיִם וּלְתוֹךְ לִבִּי הָרָחָב.

"[T]he girl [who] went up / in a cloud of smoke to the heavens" is a clear reference to his childhood love "little Ruth" (Ruth Hanover), who died in the Nazi crematoria. But the visual image for the poet's role—of his "place" in the world—draws on the Jewish concept of a *shomer*, the person guarding the unburied dead body laid out on the floor. He is squeezed into "the right angle" that mediates between the dead man and his mourner, without claiming the halo of victim or survivor for himself ("I Wasn't One of the Six Million" is the insistent title of one of the sections in his last book, *Open Closed Open*).[15] And, as always in Amichai, there is enough room in that corner for the woman to sit guard with him.

In the later poem "Equality" ("Shivyon"), the variation on this schematic positioning of the poetic subject in between existential categories is graphically represented by the speaker's arm (*zro'a*, the secular, quotidian substitute for divine power, *zro'a elohim*),[16] observed by him with a Hemingwayesque detached objectivity: "the hand / that's at the end of my arm."[17] This distanced, objective perspective bridges external and internal, the figs that the speaker holds and his own body.

In this bridging the two are equally important, of equal weight, with
the arm acting as an old-fashioned scale:

Equality[18]

I buy a small bag of figs,
I hold the bag with the hand
that's at the end of my arm.

My arm is the bridge
between the bag of sweet figs
and my body,

The bridge belongs to them both.
The bag of figs and my body are equals.

שִׁרְיוֹן

אֲנִי קוֹנֶה שַׂקִּית תְּאֵנִים,
אֲנִי מַחֲזִיק אֶת הַשַּׂקִּית בַּיָּד
שֶׁבִּקְצֵה זְרוֹעִי,

זְרוֹעִי הִיא הַגֶּשֶׁר
בֵּין שַׂקִּית הַתְּאֵנִים הַמְּתוּקוֹת
וּבֵין גּוּפִי,

הַגֶּשֶׁר שַׁיָּךְ לִשְׁנֵיהֶם.
שַׂקִּית הַתְּאֵנָה וְגוּפִי שָׁוִים.

In Amichai's last book, *Open Closed Open*, this visual schema of *beynayim* becomes the central organizing principle of the book's "modular structure" (his term), and thematically a central marker of the individual's existence in history:

Jewish history and world history
grind me between them like two grindstones, sometimes
to a powder.[19]

הַהִיסְטוֹרְיָה הַיְּהוּדִית וְהַהִיסְטוֹרְיָה הָעוֹלָמִית
טוֹחֲנוֹת אוֹתִי בֵּינֵיהֶן, לִפְעָמִים עַד דַּק
כְּשְׁתֵּי אַבְנֵי רֵחַיִם . . .

The Hebrew uses the dual genitive compound for "grindstones" (*shtey avney rechayim*, "two grindstones"), redoubling the sense of *beynayim* (in-between-ness) both grammatically and visually. The speaker is grist for history's mill; he is being pulverized by the irresolvable tensions between world history and Jewish history. But beyond being the site of injury for the poetic subject, the grindstones are also the ones that turn him—or his poetry—into flour, a staple of human subsistence.

The figurative process, through its numerous variations, but especially as it self-consciously lays bare the act of "seeing as" in simile or explicit analogy, continues to be for Amichai one of the most prototypical linguistic and perceptual thematizations of the existential "in-between-ness" that his poetry is often about. Metaphor, broadly construed,[20] marks both the life of the imagination and the individual struggle for survival in a world of opposing massive and institutional forces. In refusing to erase difference, Amichai's poetic project in general and his metaphorical practices in particular may shed a new, accepting, and even celebratory light—from their "marginally incorrect" Israeli angle—on metaphor, countering the attacks on figurative language in the discourses of postmodernism in Europe and the United States. Specifically, Amichai's poetics of metaphor provides a sustained argument against the still-popular poststructuralist repudiation of figurative language. It calls into question, as I have noted above, those vestiges of deconstruction that remain under the influence of Paul de Man's attack on metaphor in the 1970s and 1980s. "Figurality" (as de Man liked to call it), and metaphors in particular, are often condemned as "aberrant totalizations," delusions, and errors. Metaphor for de Man is the figure that disfigures, erasing difference by asserting that one thing is indeed another:

> Metaphor is error because it believes or feigns to believe in its own referential meaning. . . . Metaphor overlooks the fictional, textual element in the nature of the entity it connotes.[21]

> [T]he figure, the trope, a metaphor as a violent . . . light, a deadly Apollo . . . Lucifer, or metaphor, the bearer of light which carries over the light of the senses and of cognition from events and entities to their meaning, irrevocably loses the contour of its own face or shape.[22]

This, then, is my own "double agenda" in outlining Amichai's valorization of metaphor as a poetics of survival. First, I wish to provide further
support for the argument I make in this book, namely that Amichai's
work presents a complex systematic poetic worldview that remains in
need of serious critical and philosophical study (its popularity, clarity,
and apparent simplicity notwithstanding), a worldview for which metaphor is absolutely crucial. Second, I hope to theorize from within his
poetics a counterexample to the neo-Nietzschean deconstructionist
campaign against metaphor, which has had such a long-lasting chilling
effect on the field. For I still believe, with Wallace Stevens, "It is only
au pays de la métaphore qu'on est poète."[23]

The link between a dedication to figurative language and a poetics of
hyphenation may explain why all phases of Amichai's poetry exhibit a
salient foregrounding of similes, analogies, and overt or elaborate comparisons—all figurative practices that involve the explicit hyphenation of
two domains, which can be construed as involving no deviation from
literal meaning: *a* is like/is analogous to/can be seen **as if** it were *b*,
rather than *a* is *b*. This is not to say that Amichai does not use straight-
forward metaphors proper that "assert" that *a* is *b* in their surface structure, or which elaborate one term of the metaphor only; nor does this
deny the observation, put forth by Nili Scharf Gold, that similes, analogies, and comparisons in his early poetry are different in important ways
from those of the later poetry.[24] What it does mean is that the simile
is Amichai's *prototypical* figure, in terms of the model of poetic prototypes I proposed in *On the Margins of Modernism* (1996). Boaz Arpali
has argued cogently that this is the case not because similes are quan-
titatively the most commonly used figure in the Amichai corpus, but
because they are *symptomatic*: they offer a cluster of figurative practices,
which in their connections to other rhetorical, syntactic, structural, and
thematic features of Amichai's poetics have come to represent his work
most prototypically.[25] What's more—and this is of particular relevance
for the subject of this chapter—similes and other overt comparisons
offer a syntactic as well as a visual-typographic articulation of the hyphenated state, in which the existence of the all-important liminal space
between the two domains ("like," "as," etc.) comes into focus.

The salience of Amichai's simile as the figure of choice may help
account for what many readers describe intuitively as the most recog-

nizable trait of his poetic style. For once the semantically distant fields are figuratively hyphenated, they create a maximal degree of semantic and experiential fit. His metaphors (broadly construed) launch a detailed and systematic mapping of one domain onto another, allowing the reader to see with a certain immediacy how, to use Amichai's own image schema, the two halves are matched, without reducing them to one conjoined sphere or eliminating the space in between them. This great *semantic coherence* is achieved despite the initial distance between the realms of the tenor and the vehicle, even though the terms of the metaphor may be merely juxtaposed rather than grafted onto or embedded within each other. Amichai's network of figurative effects combines a simultaneous impression of novelty and familiarity, strong metaphoricity and strong literality. This seemingly paradoxical effect is made possible in a variety of ways, all of them involving complex interactions of two parameters: first, what I have described as *degrees of collocability* (how *fixed* the components of an expression have become due to conventions of language use and how frequently they co-occur); and second, *degrees of metaphoricity* (how *distant* the domains of the metaphor are from each other, but also how extensive and *salient* the mapped features are within each term). But that is a matter I have dealt with elsewhere.[26] Suffice to say in the present context that Amichai's metaphors typically have a low degree of collocability; or if they do use fixed expressions and idioms, it is only in order to break them up, literalize them, or otherwise render their underlying metaphoricity perceptible again. Concomitantly, the metaphors involve a high degree of semantic distance, but once the domains are mapped onto each other, it turns out that they share many salient features, hence they are semantically coherent. Moreover, not only the rhetorical effect but also the epistemological consequences of this combined novelty and coherence are given a central role in Amichai's poetics.

Many critics have observed that Amichai's metaphor (and again I use "metaphor" here as an overarching term to include simile) serves to organize, albeit temporarily, the fragmented aspects of experience and of the self.[27] What's more, and this bears emphasis, Amichai's poems consistently underscore the separateness of the realms that metaphors juxtapose. He uses metaphor as a means for tentatively bridging or hyphenating chaotically disparate domains of language and experience without harmonizing or conflating them. His poetics of metaphor is thus propelled by an underlying dialogic tension, in the Bakhtinian sense, a tension that both animates and threatens the human subject who must clear a small space for himself in its midst.

It is no accident, I think, that the typical articulations of the principle of existing in-between categories are not offered through direct philosophical or metapoetic statement but take the shape, literally, of variations on a similar visual and spatial image schema, involving experientially and developmentally embodied shapes and forms.[28] Some of the variants include, as we have seen, a line wedged between two poles or points ("Through Two Points Only One Straight Line Can Pass"),[29] the right angle between two sides of a right-angle triangle,[30] or a semiotic hyphen between numbers, signifying "from"–"till" (x–y).[31] These are vivid *verbal* representations of a *graphic* representation of an embodied, experientially grounded poetic worldview. They lay bare the extent to which Amichai's philosophy is anchored in, indeed gets realistically motivated by, a system of primary and concrete image schemas: simple combinations of a line and a circle, the most basic shapes a child first learns to recognize. The developmental primacy of the constituents of these schemas produces an effect of unstudied simplicity in what might otherwise have been a rather "scientific" or "dry" poetics, a complex ontology and epistemology, and an intertextually daunting body of poetry. (A very similar view of metaphor is allowed to create a rhetorical impression of great difficulty and abstraction in the poetry of Wallace Stevens, where the ideology of reading requires no such effect of simplicity and accessibility.)

But when the concrete visual aspects of Amichai's images of the hyphenated state are "actualized by a reader," in the language of Harshav's theory of the text,[32] what emerges is also an ethically and politically powerful *displacement* of the periphery onto the center: the marginal, liminal subject is no longer situated on the visual sidelines but is rather positioned at the center of the image, wedged in-between forces, yet also functioning as their hyphen, fulcrum, hinge, or scales, simultaneously endangered and empowered by his or her critical stance of in-between-ness. This *centrality* of the *liminal* position of the subject is visually thematized in Amichai's early poetry by placing the poetic "I" or the lovers in the middle of the arena (*zira*) or military front (*chazit, sde-krav*), surrounded by bloodthirsty spectators or armies, as, for example, in "The Two of Us Together and Each of Us Alone" ("Shneynu be-yachad ve-khol echad le-chud") discussed above, as well as in "Here" ("Kan"), "The Bull Returns" ("Ha-par chozer"), and "Elegy" ("Elegya").[33] In the later poetry it is approaching death or the pressures of history, alongside "the lost battles for the children's future" (the title of the first section in his post-1982 war book, *From Man Thou Art and Unto Man Shalt Thou Return*,[34] that form the large circles or spheres around the speaker, his beloved, and his children. The circles are typically in motion, closing in, exerting pressure horizontally or vertically on the ordinary people in their center.

In the poem "Inside the Apple" (1985), the speaker and his beloved are portrayed via an implicit, context-dependent metaphor as the lowly worms inside the round fruit, providing a novel extension of his basic image schema. In spite of this marginalizing depiction (playing perhaps on the traditional self-deprecating poetic signature of nineteenth-century poet Rachel Morpurgo, *rima tole'a*, "lowly worm," itself echoing Job 25:6), the speaker and his lover are spatially—and emotionally—situated in the center of the spherically shaped apple, while death is metonymically portrayed as the paring knife that keeps circling closer and closer to the speaker in the middle:

Inside the Apple

You visit me inside the apple.
Together we can hear the knife
paring around and around us, carefully,
so the peel won't tear.

You speak to me. I trust your voice
because it has lumps of hard pain in it
the way real honey
has lumps of wax from the honeycomb.

I touch your lips with my fingers:
that too is a prophetic gesture.
And your lips are red, the way a burnt field is black.
It's all true.

You visit me inside the apple
and you'll stay with me inside the apple
until the knife finishes its work.[35]

בְּתוֹךְ הַתַּפּוּחַ

אַתְּ מְבַקֶּרֶת אוֹתִי בְּתוֹךְ הַתַּפּוּחַ.
אֲנַחְנוּ שׁוֹמְעִים יַחְדָּו אֶת הַסַּכִּין
הַמְקַלֶּפֶת סָבִיב, סָבִיב בִּזְהִירוּת
כְּדֵי שֶׁהַקְּלִפָּה לֹא תִּשָּׁבֵר.

אַתְּ מְדַבֶּרֶת אֵלַי, קוֹלֵךְ מְהֵימָן עָלַי
כִּי יֵשׁ בּוֹ גּוּשֵׁי כְּאֵב קָשֶׁה
כְּמוֹ שֶׁבַּדְּבַשׁ הָאֲמִתִּי יֵשׁ גּוּשֵׁי דֹּנַג
שֶׁל חַלַּת הַדְּבַשׁ.

אֲנִי נוֹגֵעַ בְּאֶצְבְּעוֹתַי בִּשְׂפָתַיִךְ,
גַּם זוֹ מֶחֱוָה שֶׁל נְבוּאָה.
וּשְׂפָתַיִךְ אֲדֻמּוֹת, כְּמוֹ שֶׁשָּׂדֶה שָׂרוּף הוּא שָׁחוֹר.
הַכֹּל אֱמֶת.

אַתְּ מְבַקֶּרֶת אוֹתִי בְּתוֹךְ הַתַּפּוּחַ
וְאַתְּ נִשְׁאֶרֶת אִתִּי בְּתוֹךְ הַתַּפּוּחַ
עַד שֶׁהַסַּכִּין הַמְקַלֶּפֶת תַּשְׁלִים אֶת מְלַאכְתָּהּ.

II. Metaphor as Poetics of Survival

Amichai's later work in general, and his last book *Patu'ach sagur patu'ach* (1998; *Open Closed Open*, 2000) in particular, increasingly thematize the metaphorics of *beynayim*. These volumes contain several poems that can be read as sustained parables on the hyphenated state as both metaphor for and mode of survival. In this section, I offer a closer look at a few of the later poems that articulate this position most explicitly.

Late Marriage

I sit in a waiting room with bridegrooms
much younger than me. If I had lived in ancient times

I would be a prophet. But now I wait quietly
to register my name along with the name of my beloved
in the big book of marriages,
and to answer the questions I still
can answer. I've filled my life with words,
I've gathered enough data in my body to supply
the intelligence services of several nations.

With heavy steps I carry light thoughts
as in my youth I carried thoughts heavy with destiny
on light feet that almost danced from so much future.

The pressure of my life brings my date of birth closer
to the date of my death, as in history books
where the pressure of history has brought
those two numbers together next to the name of a dead king
with only a hyphen between them.

I hold onto that hyphen with all my might
like a lifeline, I live on it,
and on my lips the vow not to be alone,
the voice of the bridegroom and the voice of the bride,
the sound of children laughing and shouting
in the streets of Jerusalem
and the cities of Yehuda.[36]

חֲתֻנָּה מְאֻחֶרֶת

אֲנִי יוֹשֵׁב בַּחֲדַר הַמַּמְתָּנָה עִם חֲתָנִים צְעִירִים
מִמֶּנִּי בְּהַרְבֵּה שָׁנִים. אִלּוּ חָיִיתִי בִּימֵי קֶדֶם,
הָיִיתִי נָבִיא. אֲבָל עַכְשָׁו אֲנִי מְחַכֶּה בְּשֶׁקֶט
לִרְשֹׁם אֶת שְׁמִי עִם שֵׁם אֲהוּבָתִי בַּסֵּפֶר הַגָּדוֹל
שֶׁל הַנִּשּׂוּאִין וּלְהָשִׁיב לִשְׁאֵלוֹת שֶׁעֲדַיִן אֲנִי יָכוֹל
לְהָשִׁיב לָהֶן. מִלֵּאתִי אֶת חַיַּי מִלִּים,
אָסַפְתִּי בְּגוּפִי יְדִיעוֹת שֶׁאֶפְשָׁר לְכַלְכֵּל בָּהֶן
שֵׁרוּתֵי בִּיּוּן שֶׁל כַּמָּה אֲרָצוֹת.

בִּצְעָדִים כְּבֵדִים אֲנִי נוֹשֵׂא מַחֲשָׁבוֹת קַלּוֹת,
כְּשֵׁם שֶׁבִּנְעוּרַי נָשָׂאתִי מַחֲשָׁבוֹת כְּבֵדוֹת גּוֹרָל
עַל רַגְלַיִם קַלּוֹת, כִּמְעַט רוֹקְדוֹת מֵרֹב עָתִיד.

לַחַץ חַיַּי מְקָרֵב אֶת תַּאֲרִיךְ הַלֵּדָה
אֶל תַּאֲרִיךְ הַמָּוֶת, כְּמוֹ סִפְרֵי הַהִסְטוֹרְיָה,
שֶׁבָּהֶם לַחַץ הַהִסְטוֹרְיָה הִצְמִיד אֶת שְׁנֵי
הַמִּסְפָּרִים הָאֵלֶּה יַחְדָּו לְיַד שֵׁם מֶלֶךְ מֵת
וְרַק מַקָּף מַפְרִיד בֵּינֵיהֶם.

אֲנִי מַחְזִיק בַּמַּקָּף הַזֶּה בְּכָל מְאֹדִי,
כְּמוֹ בְּקֶרֶשׁ הַצָּלָה, אֲנִי חַי עָלָיו,
וְנֵדֶר לֹא לִהְיוֹת לְבַד עַל שְׂפָתַי,
קוֹל חָתָן וְקוֹל כַּלָּה וְקוֹל
מִצְהֲלוֹת יְלָדִים בְּחוּצוֹת יְרוּשָׁלַיִם
וּבְעָרֵי יְהוּדָה.

"Late Marriage" ("Chatuna me'ucheret") invokes the problematic of
the contemporary poet as prophet manqué, so common in Amichai's
work, from the brief 1958 mock-prophetic "Dedication to Prophecy
in an Army Camp" ("Hakdasha le-navi be-machane tzva'i") to the
ironic 1998 poem cycle "I Foretell the Days of Yore" ("Ani navi shel
ma she-haya").[37] The lyrical "I" of "Late Marriage" is portrayed in the
dual contexts of his belatedness: he's too late (in historical time) to be
a prophet or a king; and, although he's going through with the bureaucratic wedding arrangements, it feels too late (in personal time)
to be getting married. The metapoetic and densely allusive dialogues
that these two notions of time launch through the intertextual echo
chamber of classical Hebrew literature are carefully camouflaged here,
as they ought to be within Amichai's egalitarian poetics (see chapter
2), while the surface situation deromanticizes the traditional wedding
thematics by placing the speaker in the waiting rooms of a modern-day
bureaucracy. The point of departure for the speaker's meditation, as
in Ha-Nagid's poems (see chapter 3), is thus again an autobiographical event that is made to seem as ordinary and literal as possible (first
stanza). This event gets further fleshed out by some extratextual gossip
that Amichai, given that zero privacy is the norm in Israeli culture,
would have probably expected at least some of his Hebrew readers to
know about: the circumstances under which Yehuda and his second
life-partner Hana, who'd been living together since the 1960s, raising their kids in Jerusalem, were finally able to get married. That this

became possible only after Yehuda's mother died in 1983 is another piece of the story, but the connection of the wedding with death in general and with the mother's death in particular is marked everywhere in this volume of poems.[38]

In a review in *Ha'aretz*, Gershon Shaked cites the image of the hyphen from "Late Marriage" as the ultimate expression of Amichai's special talent to mix humor and poetry, and in the process to push poetic expression beyond its limits.[39] As Shaked points out, the unexpected, witty association of the individual will to live with the "historical hyphen" renders an existential experience concretely perceptible. I wish to add, however, that the hyphen's concreteness and perceptual vividness are enhanced not only by the great *familiarity* of this notational convention but also by the great *novelty* of using it as a metaphor—zeroing in on the hyphen as the marker of mutability rather than on the dates that flank it. Amichai turns the hyphen itself into the visual and figurative site of the tenuous struggle for survival. Thus, mutability—itself a common theme in the tradition of the epithalamium, or wedding poem—is not meditated on, nor described through any conventional literary topoi, but rather invoked through the dry, nonpoetic notational conventions of reference books (d.o.b.—d.o.d.), restraining pathos and tempering sentimentality, as well as avoiding placing royal narratives ("the dead king") in the center. All this while providing a visual, metapoetic parable on metaphor and the struggles of ordinary human beings.

Indeed, in the course of the last two stanzas, mutability—and change in general—become physically (in the sense of the laws of physics) inscribed, as the static image of the hyphenated numbers in the history book is subtly mapped onto image schemas that contain *pressure* and *movement*.[40] Two opposing forces, the date of birth and the date of death, literalize "the pressure of history," depicting it as compressing the hyphen between them. Over the next two stanzas, the hyphen becomes simultaneously both a wooden plank that a drowning person can reach for—literally, in Hebrew, a "rescue plank" (*keresh hatzala*) and a wedge to hold off the walls from closing in on him (as in the famous scene of the shrinking garbage compactor room in *Star Wars*). These two kinetic, dynamic image-schemas allow Amichai's hyphen to become not simply the linking device of its punctuation function but, as his Hebrew has it, *makaf mafrid* (instead of the normative *kav mafrid*), literally, the hyphen that separates, a dash of a hyphen. The brilliant thing about this is that there is no direct mention of the shrinking room in the text (just as the worm wasn't mentioned in "Inside the Apple"): It is part of the poem's visual "shadow text," to quote Blanton's term yet again (see chapters 1 and 3), and forms an overarching, implicit, and entirely context-dependent metaphorical situation. The scenario is put in motion, so to speak, only indirectly, through what is explicitly only a literal similarity statement: Two types of pressure—of individual life and of history—are perceived by the speaker to be alike. But the notational convention of separating date of birth and date of death with a hyphen takes over when physics overtakes history, and the dormant literal meaning of "pressure" is resuscitated in the forces of life and death flanking the hyphen. The mini-narratives that the speaker offers by way of explaining the terms of the explicit comparison don't in themselves make literal sense at all. The fact that the time he has left to live is getting shorter and shorter does not mean that the date of his birth is getting closer to the date of his death, nor is the small distance between the numbers flanking the hyphen "really" a function of history exerting its pressure on notations in history books. The blurring of the semiotic and the referential is not part of some deconstructive move. It makes sense only if we are willing to visualize a metaphorical schema of physical forces exerting pressure simultaneously from opposing directions, and being temporarily held back by a plank wedged between them; in other words, if we supply the implicit scenario of the inward-moving walls (compare the expression, "the walls are closing in on me") as the metaphor's vehicle. But just as the explicit comparison makes sense only if we resort to the *unstated* shrinking-room scenario, the notational metaphor of the historical record can be mapped onto it visually only if we add the one element that Amichai carefully withholds: the parentheses needed to add to the image schema the proverbial walls closing in on the hyphen in the middle.

But now, in the last stanza, the hyphen literally becomes a lifesaver and lifeline. In the transition from "hyphen" to "lifeline" or rescue plank (note again that this is done via simile, not metaphor), the camera moves in closer and closer, focusing on and enlarging that narrow space of in-between-ness. The hyphen turned lifeline and wedged plank grows in dimensions until it fills the spatial and temporal lifespan itself. Moreover, the hyphen replaces religious faith and the ritual of daily prayer: the speaker holds onto it "with all [his] might" (*be-khol me'odi*), as onto God, in ironic reference to the Shema daily prayer.

As always in Amichai, there is room on that wedge for a lover, for someone to help with the holding on and the pushing back. This desperate and obstinate resistance to the pressures of personal life and collective history is ultimately celebrated at the end of the poem as the true "late marriage" of the title: the hyphen as life force for the man and source of livelihood for the aging poet (*ani chay alav*; the Hebrew suggests both literally living/surviving on the hyphen and making a living from the hyphen). In the final analysis, it is the possibility of having someone there with you as the walls are closing in that makes the hyphenated state tolerable. For, by the end of the poem, the belated wedding is indeed enacted in the public spaces (*chutzot*—both streets and public places); Jeremiah's curses have turned to blessings;[41] and the joyful noise of the couple and the children in the cities of Yehuda (a pun on Judah and the poet's name, both the same in Hebrew), make the short time still left to live on the hyphen all the more worthwhile.

III. Accessible Novelty: Comprehending Amichai's Metaphors

Novel, iconoclastic metaphors in Yehuda Amichai's poetry are the ultimate prototypes for the creative use of language. In exploring the role of metaphor in this section I will engage two sets of problems, theoretical and interpretive, using one set of problems to elucidate the other, negotiating theory and close reading as a two-way process. The first set of problems involves the puzzle of metaphor's comprehensibility: How do people understand each other's metaphors, and how do they formulate them in such a way as to make them intelligible to others? Some specific questions derived from this puzzle are, for example: What makes one metaphor striking, surprising, or otherwise salient, and another just barely noticeable? What makes some metaphors more difficult to understand and interpret than others?

The second group of problems concerns the puzzle of Yehuda Amichai's poetry: How can his poetry be at once extremely accessible and extremely difficult? In the Hebrew, as we have seen, the poems often seem totally untranslatable because of their dependence on cultural, geographic, and historical materials. They exemplify a complex acrobatics of language, idiomaticity, biblical, rabbinic, and liturgical intertextuality, as well as a pastiche of popular songs, army slang, and children's games. Yet his work survives even the crudest of translations, of which he has had more than his share. To what extent does the experientially universal basis of Amichai's figurative language have anything to do with that accessibility and translatability? How does even the most surprising untraditional metaphor end up feeling "right," becoming instantly familiar and recognizable in Amichai's hands?

To begin, though, what does it mean for a metaphor to be "easy" or "difficult" within the framework of Amichai's poetry? I have argued above that there is an experiential component to the accessibility of Amichai's metaphors (which is related to its use of primary image schemas). Yet what makes a metaphor "easy" or "difficult" may also be culturally inflected and contextually determined. In the case of a language like Hebrew, where all the historical layers and many of the traditional intertexts are still readily accessible to many readers, a native knowledge of the language and its pragmatics may be sufficient to make even Amichai's many surprising metaphors fully comprehensible:

> Like a newspaper clinging to a fence in the blowing wind,
> so my soul clings to me.
> If the wind stops, my soul will fall.[42]

כְּעִתּוֹן הַדָּבוּק לַגָּדֵר לַגֶּדֶר בְּרוּחַ נוֹשֶׁבֶת

כֵּן דְּבוּקָה בִּי נַפְשִׁי.

אִם הָרוּחַ תִּשַּׁךְ

תִּשֹּׁר נַפְשִׁי מִמֶּנִּי.

Depicting the soul as a discarded newspaper is radically novel—and quite startling—yet I don't think there is any doubt here that the meaning of the metaphor would be apparent to the native speaker of Hebrew, even without any further reference to the context of the entire poem or to any special body of knowledge, whether Jewish liturgy or Hebrew literary history. How is such an easy processing of a totally novel metaphor made possible? In the Hebrew Amichai, the immediacy of this metaphor is enhanced by the diction. *Nefesh*, the Hebrew word for "soul," means, among other things, the embodied "soul-as-throat" in biblical Hebrew, while in postbiblical and modern usage it also designates "spirit," "vitality," "life," or "life force"; *ru'ach*, whose primary meaning in the poem is "wind," also means "spirit" and is thus partially synonymous with *nefesh*, "ghost" and "breath," as in *ru'ach chayim*, "the breath of life." (Note that the Hebrew uses the singular, thus retaining all the possible meanings. *Ruchot*, the plural, would have restricted the meanings to "winds" and "ghosts," but would have eliminated the positive valence of "spirit" and "life force.") Thus, the metaphor may be accessible to most Hebrew readers despite its novelty, simply because of the partial congruence between the meaning of *nefesh* and *ru'ach*, and because of the association of *ru'ach* with breathing. The metaphor remains jarring, however, in its comparison of the spiritual and poetic concept of the soul/spirit to a newspaper sticking to a fence. Amichai achieves semantic coherence in this metaphor *despite* the distance in semantic domain and pragmatic "importance" between the realms of the tenor and the vehicle. Furthermore, elevating the quotidian newspaper to the level of a metaphor worthy of expressing issues of life and death is itself an aesthetic and ethical goal for Amichai, as for his fellow Statehood poets. The two separate domains invoked by the metaphor contain several strong points of contact that focus on features that are *salient* within each scene. Both the word for "wind" (*ru'ach*) and the word that is translated here as "cling" (*davuk*) can apply quite literally to each context. Both "clingings" will cease once the *ru'ach* ("wind" and "breath of life") dissipates; the newspaper will fall from the fence, and the soul will exit the body.

The congruence of the two scenes is, of course, in part an illusion. Amichai creates a realistically coherent image that enhances the vividness and familiarity of the speaker's sense of his own mortality, at the same time that it legitimizes the newspaper as a worthy metaphor. The two frames fit so well together because the *language* of the lines creates an analogy. This completely explicit comparison has the structure:

"just as the *a* is clinging to the *b*, so does the *c* cling to the *d*," where the same predicate "cling" appears in both situations, adding to the semblance of their similarity. The parallel construction also implies that the same *ru'ach* is the instrument of clinging in both scenes. But just as *ru'ach* actually has different meanings in each of the two cases ("wind" and "breath of life"), so also does the word "cling" (*davuk*) change its sense in each part of the simile. The impression that there exists a literal analogy between the newspaper and the embodied soul (*nefesh*), rather than a figurative mapping of the two, is therefore only an illusion. The gap between physical clinging and spiritual clinging is even more obvious in the Hebrew, where the term literally means "glued to," but by lexicalized figurative extension it also denotes "clinging," "being attached to," "devoted to," or even "devotional" (compare the religious notion of *dvekut*, devotion to God). Amichai uses the fact that in contemporary Hebrew "glued" and "cling" are single lexemes (*davuk*) in order to make his mapping together of soul and newspaper less stylistically outrageous, almost as if to say: if you look carefully at the gust of wind that blows a newspaper up against a fence, and if you remember that the minute the wind dies down, the newspaper will fall to the ground, you'll then be able to understand the last minute of your life, to comprehend your own death; it will become as comprehensible, as commonplace, as the newspaper dropping from the fence. The poet working to make his metaphor at once less difficult and less lofty is therefore also the human agent struggling to make issues of life and death more comprehensible.

The general theoretical question of *metaphorical salience* can thus be reformulated in terms of the specific problematics of Amichai's poetry: How is it that metaphors that are daring, novel, or only minimally conventional may be presented as if they were the normal, common, or literal ways of talking about a given subject? This ultimately leads to the further question: Why is this type of metaphor, or metaphor tout court, so central for Amichai in the first place? His poetry creates much of its effect by compelling the reader to make shockingly new kinds of semantic connections, while at the same time impressing upon her the inherent "realism" of these novel, often unorthodox connections. Such a combination of novelty and natural fit applies to all levels of Amichai's poetry, from thematic structure to prosody and

genre preference, but it is most clearly at work in the form and function of his metaphors. The very foundation of metaphor as a rhetorical
strategy is in mapping one domain (of things, words, ideas, experiences, etc.) onto another. It is not merely a matter of comparison, nor
is it—as the post–de Manian critique has it—a *conflation* of the two
domains and an erasure of their distinctiveness. The epistemological
consequences of this metaphorical mapping and its attendant non-
erasure of the separate domains are given a central role in Amichai's
poetics. They provide a tentative, dynamic way of organizing, albeit
temporarily, the fragmented aspects of experience and the bits and
pieces of the self. And yet they stress—and make us *remember*—the
differences between the realms that metaphor brings together. Rather
than point to preexisting shared features, Amichai makes metaphor
reveal or *create* connections that were not noticed or that *did not exist*
prior to the metaphorical act of the speaker or poet. Amichai's poetics
often gives a realistic motivation to this emphasis on acknowledging
semantic distance and then bridging it via metaphor: The speaker's
state of mind and the pressures of external reality upon him implicitly
justify the strength of the metaphors he uses.

So far I have described two major rhetorical strategies that allow
Amichai to have his metaphorical cake and eat it too: first, creating
the impression of a literal analogy or comparison where, "in fact," a
figurative mapping of great semantic distance occurs; and second, creating the impression within the metaphor of (literally) shared features
between the domains when, "in fact," these common features take on
different meanings in the context of the tenor and the vehicle. Bor-
rowing a term from Benjamin Harshav, I refer to this latter practice as
the formation of the lexical or cognitive *junction* (*tzomet*) between the
tenor and the vehicle.[43]

I would like to take a look now at the role these two strategies play
in establishing Amichai's populist poetics of metaphor—either making
difficult metaphors appear easy, or turning strong metaphors into nat-
uralized ones—ways of speaking or thinking that an ordinary human
being (rather than a professional poet) would turn to. My example,
the poem "I've Grown Very Hairy" ("Na'aseti sa'ir"), brings up the
specter of the Shoah without ever mentioning it, through the "shadow
texts" of its metaphorical entailments:

I've Grown Very Hairy

I've grown very hairy all over my body.
I'm afraid they're going to start hunting me for my fur.

My shirt of many colors isn't a sign of love:
it's like an aerial photograph of a railroad station.

At night my body is wide open and awake under the blanket
like the blindfolded eyes of someone who's about to be shot.

I live as a fugitive and a vagabond, I'll die
hungry for more—

and I wanted to be quiet, like an ancient mound
whose cities were all destroyed,

and peaceful,
like a full cemetery.[44]

נַעֲשֵׂיתִי שָׂעִיר

נַעֲשֵׂיתִי שָׂעִיר מְאֹד בְּכָל הַגּוּף,
אֲנִי חוֹשֵׁשׁ שֶׁיָּצוּדוּ אוֹתִי בִּשְׁבִיל פַּרְוָתִי.

לִכְתֹנֶת הַפַּסִּים שֶׁלִּי, אֵין מַשְׁמָעוּת שֶׁל אַהֲבָה.
הִיא כְּתַצְלוּם אֲוִיר שֶׁל תַּחֲנַת רַכֶּבֶת.

בַּלַּיְלָה, פָּקוּחַ גּוּפִי וָעֵר מִתַּחַת לַשְּׂמִיכָה,
כְּמוֹ עַיִן תַּחַת מַחְסוֹם הָאִישׁ שֶׁיְּיָרֶה.

נָע וָנָד אֲנִי חַי
רָעֵב יָמִים אָמוּת.

וְרָצִיתִי לִהְיוֹת שָׁקֵט, כְּתֵל שֶׁכָּל עָרָיו נֶחֶרְבוּ
וְרָגוּעַ כְּבֵית קִבְרוֹת דָּוָה.

Each of the first three couplets elaborates a different metaphor. On the
surface, at least, no attempt is made to link them together. However,
within each metaphor many factors help minimize the prominence of

the figurative effect. The first couplet presents a metaphor that is easily understood and has no poetic salience because it presents itself as a joke, based on hyperbole—not uncommon in the discourse of the average Israeli. Clearly, the speaker is not *literally* afraid to be mistaken for a bear, for example; the realistic context is just as clear: as he grows older (and grows more body hair), his existential fears grow too. The private joke here is that Yehuda's children called him "Dov," a Hebrew proper name that literally means "bear."[45] At this point, however, the speaker's fears are still subsumed by the comical effect, perhaps because they remain unstated. Yet even here, being hunted, or feeling like a hunted animal, is sufficiently marked as a conventional metaphor (in both Hebrew and English) to suggest a sense of persecution (in addition to the "normal" fear of death associated with getting older).[46] All this makes the metaphor not quite consistent with the initial interpretation of a joke about aging.

The second couplet presents Amichai's typical oscillation between the rhetorical effect of literalness and an underlying daring, novel adventure in metaphor. On the surface this couplet is completely literal; it is certainly possible for a speaker's shirt *literally* to resemble an aerial photograph of a railway station (for example, the lines formed by the tracks can be said to look like the stripes on the shirt). But while a literal reading is semantically possible, it remains pragmatically improbable: it is not clear why anyone would want to compare their shirt to aerial photography. The two scenes begin to fit better, but also appear less literal, when we focus in on the *junction words* and their dual function. Here the translation cannot convey the Hebrew Amichai at all, unlike the earlier example of "cling." In modern colloquial Hebrew usage *ktonet pasim* means simply "a striped shirt or tunic" and not "a coat of many colors" (though the allusion to the biblical story of Joseph is, of course, equally crucial in the Hebrew, as I suggest below). However, the image evoked by the railroad tracks is also associated lexically with the word *pasim*, which is a polysemy representing anything stripe- or strip-like. In fact, the Hebrew for "railroad tracks" is the compound *pasey rakevet* (lit., "strips/stripes of train"). In Amichai's couplet, the junction word *pasim* appears explicitly only in reference to the stripes on the shirt. The reader has to supply her own construal, linking the *pasim* on the shirt with the implicit image of the railroad tracks. Once the link or congruence between the scenes is found, the tenor and the vehicle are perceived as more closely related than the initial impression might have suggested.

At this point the second major factor in determining metaphoricity needs to be introduced, namely the tendency of the terms of the metaphor to occur together in set contexts, whether linguistic, cultural, or intertextual. I describe this principle as a figure's *collocability*.[47] All the conventional aspects of a metaphor's use, its history, and its degree of triteness or novelty are included in this dimension, together with the intertextual baggage, which in Hebrew typically involves biblical, rabbinic, and liturgical contexts of use and is, as we have seen, especially important in Amichai's case. In order to understand the full impact of Amichai's metaphor of the "shirt of many colors" in the line "My shirt of many colors is not a sign of love," it must indeed be examined not just semantically but also pragmatically in terms of the history of its use. The most apparent *collocated context* is, of course, the Joseph story, where a *ktonet pasim* was a token of love. Though it is usually translated as "a coat of many colors," in modern Hebrew *ktonet pasim* literally means, as we have seen, simply "a striped tunic or shirt." Amichai works here directly against this biblical allusion, stripping it of its traditional "symbolic" significance. The speaker tells us in so many words that the *ktonet pasim* has lost for him all its special, idiomatic—or national—collocability, its association with love, chosenness, or privilege. He is, in effect, talking metapoetically as well, insisting that the modern poet-as-Everyman, or as hero manqué, can only use the locution quite literally to describe a man's common "striped shirt." Only once he negates the old, privileged, metaphorical meaning can the speaker superimpose upon the traditional expression the modern, antipoetic military image of aerial photography of a railway station. The *negated collocation*, along with its association with the denial of biblical love and chosenness, nevertheless hover in the background, enhancing, by contrast, the speaker's feelings of isolation and fear. At this point the first couplet's comical reference to the fear of being hunted becomes contextually relevant again, but it is no longer just funny or hyperbolic. It generates a radical rereading of both the biblical text and the contemporary situation of the aging speaker. *Ktonet pasim*, the emblem of love, becomes after all for old Jacob a token of fear, the same fear of (his son's) being hunted that the poem's speaker invokes. As in the bilateral use of iconoclastic allusion I discussed in chapter 3, Amichai's metaphor sends us back to the biblical narrative, armed with the new perspective of his irreverent interpretation. And we indeed find, within the Joseph story, the kernel for the same reading against the biblical grain that he proposes.

Culturally, this reading is reinforced by the metonymic association that Amichai's contemporary Israeli readers are bound to make between aerial photography and the danger of war. Aerial photographs (known in Hebrew by the military acronym *tatza*, for *tatzlumey avir*), which recur in many of Amichai's poems, are perhaps so central because, like the archaeological imagery he uses frequently, they represent a static, spatial façade, below which everything is constantly shifting. The railway station, a common metonymy for separation or parting, is another recurring site in Amichai's poetry, offering his own innovative development of the metaphorical system LIFE AS A JOURNEY. But here, in the Jewish cultural context especially, the juxtaposition of a striped tunic with military photography of trains immediately conjures up the transports to the death camps—a reminder that even cognitive mappings in universal metaphors like LIFE IS A JOURNEY are profoundly inflected by culture and history. This historically specific reading becomes more plausible if we consider the linguistic fact that *ktonet* in modern Hebrew also refers to an inmate's (prototypically striped) uniform, and that the next couplet explicitly compares the speaker to a man about to be executed. Being a hunted man thus subtly connects the speaker's personal aging with the historical experience of the Shoah (persecution, trains, striped tunic, inmate, execution). The exquisite subtlety, almost a coded secrecy with which the Shoah is invoked here, is consistent with Amichai's refusal to participate in its exploitation, but it has resulted, as we have seen, in his being faulted for not writing about the Shoah.[48]

Perhaps the most powerful metaphorical couplet is the third one, combining again a *negated allusion*, here one reversing love descriptions in the Song of Songs (and the conventional poetry that has emulated it) with a bold new metaphor that invokes, in vivid detail, the speaker's own anticipation of death. The speaker lies on his bed at night, with his body "open and awake."[49] The Hebrew, in fact, uses for "open" a specific verb that signals the opening of eyes (*p.k.ch.*), which, in juxtaposition with the eye of the second line of this couplet, suggests a horrific, surreal metonymy of the entire sleepless body as a wide-open eye. The mundane insomnia or restlessness of the aging body in the first line becomes a taut anticipation of an execution, as the familiar image of a blindfolded man facing the firing squad is mapped onto the image of the body lying under the blanket. It is the exact fit between the details of the mapping that renders this metaphor so startling: the blindfold mapped onto the blanket, and the open eyes onto the wakeful body. These concrete metaphorical entailments are the bridge on which the urgency of the fear of death is transferred from the man in front of the firing squad to the aging man on his bed at night; the six million murdered Jews shadow and haunt the scene without ever being mentioned. But this cognitive bridge allows the metaphorical mapping to work also in the other direction, from the literal back to the figurative. The all-too-familiar firing squad scene is typically depicted from the outside: we always remain external observers (as in Francisco Goya's famous painting *The Third of May 1808*). Here, however, the perspective is reversed when the body, waiting like an open eye under the blanket, is mapped onto the open eye of the person about to be shot. Poignantly, we are compelled to see the execution scene from the internal perspective of the victim, to experience again Walter Benjamin's "history of the vanquished" from a first-person point of view, albeit through the as-if prism of simile.

Taken together, the three metaphors in these first three couplets present a gradually intensifying sense of persecution and imminent death. A similar analysis of the last two couplets in the Hebrew (which are the last three in the English translation) further develops the same sense, in both archetypal images (Cain) and topographic/archaeological ones (the mound and the cemetery). Ultimately, in a typical move of renunciation, the fearful speaker's hunger for longevity (*re'ev yamim*—lit., "hungry for [more] days") is replaced with the shockingly new simile of a "satiated cemetery" (*ke-veyt kvarot raveh*). Structurally symmetrical, the second line in each couplet introduces death via metaphor, broadly construed. At the same time, the seemingly disconnected details of the first line of each couplet can also be linked to form a concrete, literal situation within which the speaker's metaphorical thinking takes place: A middle-aged man in bed (wearing striped pajamas), contemplating his hairy chest and his insomnia, and thinking about death, ultimately is able to overcome his terror and calmly accept his mortality.

IV. Metaphor, Speech Act, and the Construction of Readerly Critical Agency

I would like to conclude this chapter by reading closely some of the detailed workings of metaphor in a single early poem, "The Smell of Gasoline Ascends in My Nose," one of my favorites in the corpus of Amichai's early work. In this poem, the entailments of the dramatized speaker's metaphors, similes, and analogies systematically undermine his speech act, turning it from reassurance to threat:[50]

The Smell of Gasoline Ascends in My Nose

The smell of gasoline ascends in my nose.
Love, I'll protect you and hold you close
like an *etrog* in soft wool, so carefully—
my dead father used to do it that way.

Look, the olive-tree no longer grieves—
it knows there are seasons and a man must leave,
stand by my side and dry your face now
and smile as if in a family photo.

I've packed my wrinkled shirts and my trouble.
I will never forget you, girl of my final
window in front of the deserts that are
empty of windows, filled with war.

You used to laugh but now you keep quiet,
the beloved country never cries out,
the wind will rustle in the dry leaves soon—
when will I sleep beside you again?

In the earth there are raw materials that, unlike us,
have not been taken out of the darkness,
the army jet makes peace in the heavens
upon us and upon all lovers in autumn.

רֵיחַ הַבֶּנְזִין עוֹלֶה בְּאַפִּי

רֵיחַ הַבֶּנְזִין עוֹלֶה בְּאַפִּי,
אֶת נַפְשֵׁךְ, נַעֲרָה, אָשִׂים בְּתוֹךְ כַּפִּי,
כְּמוֹ אֶתְרוֹג לְתוֹךְ צֶמֶר רַךְ –
גַּם אָבִי הַמֵּת עָשָׂה כָּךְ.

רְאִי, עֵץ הַזַּיִת הִפְסִיק לִתְמֹהַּ –
הוּא יוֹדֵעַ שֶׁיֵּשׁ עוֹנוֹת וְצָרִיךְ לִנְטֹעַ,
גִּנְבִי אֶת פָּנַיִךְ וְעִמְדִי לְיָדִי
וְחַיְכִי כְּמוֹ בַּתַּצְלוּם הַמִּשְׁפַּחְתִּי.

אָרַזְתִּי אֶת חֲלֻצוֹתַי וְאֶת יְגוֹנִי.
לֹא אֶשְׁכָּחֵךְ, שֶׁהָיִית יַלְדַּת חַלּוֹנִי
הָאַחֲרוֹן לִפְנֵי הַשֶּׁטַח, הַשְּׁמָמָה,
שֶׁחַלּוֹנוֹת אֵין בָּהּ וְיֵשׁ בָּהּ מִלְחָמָה.

פַּעַם צָחַקְתְּ וְעַכְשָׁו אַתְּ שׁוֹתֶקֶת,
הָאָרֶץ הָאֲהוּבָה לְעוֹלָם אֵינָהּ צוֹעֶקֶת,
הָרוּחַ יָבוֹא לְרַשְׁרֵשׁ בַּכְּמוֹשׁ –
מָתַי נִישַׁן שׁוּב רֹאשׁ לְיַד רֹאשׁ?

בְּתוֹךְ הָאֲדָמָה יֵשׁ הַרְבֵּה חָמְרֵי גֶּלֶם,
לֹא הוּצְאוּ כָּמוֹנוּ מִתּוֹךְ חֹשֶׁךְ וָאֵלֶם,
מְטוֹס הַסִּילוֹן עוֹשֶׂה שָׁלוֹם בִּמְרוֹמָיו
עָלֵינוּ וְעַל כָּל הָאוֹהֲבִים בַּסְּתָו.

This poem's metaphors—their accessibility or opacity, but also their pragmatic reliability or unreliability within the speaker's speech act—are determined by what we take the literal, concrete situation of the speaker to be. As Boaz Arpali argues in his book, while Amichai's poetry maintains a very tight contact with the "real," external world, it rarely presents a clear realistic situation, even though such a situation can be postulated for most of his poems.[51] At the center of this poetic situation we usually find a human agent, but as this poem illustrates, that agent is often critically and aesthetically distant from the implied author, even as the "rhetoric of autobiography" I discussed in the Introduction creates the illusion that it is simply Amichai talking to his wife before going off to war. Since whatever criticism the poem expresses toward its speaker can be taken as self-criticism, it is harder for the reader to dissociate from it. Thus a narratological critical distance and gap in reliability between speaker and implied author encourages the construction of a readerly critical agency. This distance between speaker and implied author is emphasized here even more than usual, as the poem presents a dramatized "I," and is itself a late modernist adaptation of the genre of the dramatic monologue. Only through this male voice, his associative and digressive speech, can the Hebrew or English reader reconstruct the "world" of the poem and develop a critical attitude toward it. The monologue, in this case, is perhaps one side of a dialogue; the speaker addresses his beloved ("my girl") who is probably also his wife (line 8 makes reference to the family photo). There are indications that the addressee is reacting to the speaker's words, but we are simply not given her side of the dialogue (this is especially evident in the second stanza).

Israeli readers, among whom I have conducted an informal survey over the years, appear quite confident that they understand the poem's expositional situation even though it is only implied: The speaker has just received his orders for the front, and this monologue is therefore part of the last words he speaks before going off to war. The Israeli readers usually take the first line quite literally, suggesting, for example, that the smell of gasoline comes from a military jeep waiting to pick up a reserves soldier from his home. Another prototypical reconstruction I have heard from native readers is that the smell of gasoline anticipates what will take place once the speaker reaches camp. Amichai's Hebrew-speaking audience is all too familiar with the unique smell of war—a blend of gun oil and gasoline that seems to be everywhere when the army is gearing up for battle. Amichai himself relates that the smell of gasoline is exclusively associated with war in the poem's contemporary context and reconstructs the dramatic situation in a similar way to that of his readers:

> The basic situation is that of a man who is saying goodbye to a
> woman and is going off to war. In a world "which has no windows

but has a war," the tragedy is that war begins right outside the home. This is how close it gets. . . . Today, the thing with the smell of gasoline sounds funny. When the poem was written in the early fifties, the smell of gasoline was associated exclusively with war, because you would drive a vehicle only in war time. Who had a car? Today, the smell of gasoline could be a picnic.[52]

But as my informal survey indicates, the smell of gasoline that permeates the country is still prototypically associated with war for Israelis today. The speaker makes many direct and indirect references to war throughout the poem. He is all packed up and ready to go, and he does not know what will happen. These detailed readerly hypotheses, all approaching the poem with a highly naturalistic "reality key,"[53] are themselves significant. It is as though the very situation in which speech takes place within the poem conditions a mimetic reading, and this despite the relatively high degree of stylization and artfulness that this poem displays from the very first line. Note, for example, that, as in "Hadera" (discussed in chapter 3), the speaker's diction (in Hebrew), though peppered with colloquialisms (the mere mention of gasoline in a poem in the Holy Tongue was revolutionary at the time!), is marked by a poetic stylistic register and highly allusive idioms. And unlike the later poetry, this poem's prosodic structure is still quite formal (replacing traditional meter with four speech stresses per line, but employing traditional rhyme throughout). Thus, the speaker says, "The smell of gasoline ascends in my nose," not "I can smell gas" or "everything reeks of gun oil." With the concrete and literal "reality" as backdrop and backbone, the speaker uses utterances that are metaphorical to some degree at least twice in every stanza. In the opening and closing stanzas he develops extended metaphors that articulate much of the poem's complex, if not contradictory meaning:

> Love, I'll protect you and hold you close
> like an *etrog* in soft wool, so carefully—
> my dead father used to do it that way.

These lines are packed with an arsenal of figurative devices that are supposed to convince the speaker's beloved, the poem's addressee, that she will remain protected, even as he is going off to war. He combines metaphor, literalized idiom, simile, and analogy all in one sentence.

This figurative excess, compounding level upon level of metaphoric embedding, marks also his closing couplet:

> The army jet makes peace in the heavens
> upon us and upon all lovers in autumn.

Here he conjoins, as we shall see, metonymic description with a catachresis based on a liturgical allusion, and collocations from military and children's slang. Amichai's simultaneous, "archaeological" layering of different levels of reality and of language reaches its climax in these opening and closing stanzas, piling them up, I would argue, to undermine his own speaker. The very same words participate in contradictory patterns, and yet these patterns remain aesthetically and thematically complementary, performing what Dancygier and Sweetser have described as complex metaphorical mappings.[54]

The first line of the poem establishes most vividly both the concrete background of the dramatic monologue and the central figurative device. I have suggested how the smell of gasoline concisely invokes for native Israeli readers the hurried preparations for war and the atmosphere so typical of a military emergency. But it also establishes the inevitable link between war (line 1) and the separation of lovers (line 2), a central theme of the poem and of Amichai's poetry in general. However, the modern-day, automotive connotations of the smell of gasoline clash with the biblical cadence of the phrase *oleh be-api* (lit., "ascends in my nose") which is commonly associated with God's smelling the *re'ach ha-nicho'ach*, the aroma of ritual sacrifices. The intertextual collision between the ancient phrase and the modern war scene creates an unexpected congruence between the two contexts, a congruence that is enabled by their very contrast. The "smell ascends" in the Bible from sacrifices—the Hebrew *korban* means both "sacrifice" and "victim," which is what the speaker and his female listener are no doubt worried about becoming. He turns the smell of gasoline, inadvertently, into an intertextual metaphor for sacrifice; the metaphor's entailments thus invoke unwittingly the dangers of his own death. In the fourth stanza, similarly, the implied author's serious wordplay (behind his speaker's back, so to speak) on the two meanings of *korban* (victim and sacrifice) is revisited via the odd use of the noun *kemosh* (root *k.m.sh.*, "wither") to refer to the fallen leaves of autumn, thus setting loose an allusion to Chemosh, the Moabite god associated with human sacrifice (line 15). This choice again betrays the speaker's (conscious or subconscious) fears of becoming or causing others to become victims, sacrificed on the altar of war: Hebrew actually has a common term for the romantic *feuilles mortes* of autumn, *shalekhet*, and never uses the term *kemosh* for that purpose. Within this context, the extended metaphor in the first stanza acquires at least two distinct readings. Each reading locates the figurative process on a different level, and each interacts with the other to produce the compound meaning of the metaphor.

The first reading assumes that the speaker really means what he is saying, or at least that he is trying to convince himself, as well as his beloved, of the truth in what he is saying. In this interpretation the figurative process hinges on the semantic impossibility, or "deviance" (to use terms of traditional linguistics), of a literal reading; namely, line 2 offers a novel metaphorical mapping: The speaker says that he is going to put his lover's soul in his palm; the reader knows that this cannot be literally true and therefore resorts to a figurative interpretation. The metaphor is then construed according to its immediate realistic context—the scene of the lovers parting as the man goes off to war. The man tries to reassure his beloved that everything will be all right with them despite the war, and expresses his tenderness toward her by promising to cherish and protect her memory and love (represented by "your soul," *nafshekh*) while he is away in battle. He promises that she will always be with him in spirit, the way a precious object is protected and taken along on a journey by being kept in the closed palm of one's hand. The simile of the Sukkot citron in line 3 is, on this account, aimed to reinforce these feelings of protectiveness and tender adoration, equating the beloved with something as holy and spiritual as an *etrog*, a ritual fruit that is pungent and beautiful to behold but is not to be consumed. In addition, the soft wool protecting the *etrog* is to be seen as analogous— so the speaker hopes—to his own protective palm. The image of the woman's soul nestled in the man's palm receives a secondary metaphorical mapping as it is visually "laid over" the image of an *etrog* nestled in its protective oval box. The visual schema common to both images is meant by the speaker to align the soul with the citron and to map the closed palm onto the oval box lined with soft wool. Thus, both domains are made to share the salient features of shielding a delicate, precious thing from harm. Finally, drawing the analogy between the woman and the speaker's father ("my . . . father used to do it that way"; line 4) is intended by him to suggest the preciousness of love's memory as well as to establish a sense of continuity and rootedness in the face of separation and danger. According to this unironic reading, the "that way" of the last line of the stanza (*kakh*) is syntactically ambiguous, referring either to the father's religious practices (he too observed the sanctity of the *etrog* and protected it), or to his attitude toward his own loved ones (the father also remembered and protected them when he faced similar circumstances).

Clearly, this reading takes into account only the details of the opening stanza that fit its unironic point of departure, or the speaker's conscious communicative intentions, leaving several important aspects of the text unaccounted for. A case in point is the mention of the father's death: If all the speaker wishes to convey is a sense of continuity and reassurance, why would *avi ha-met* ("my *dead* father") be the relevant feature to mention here? The process of reading the poem as it unfolds—or listening in on the speaker's monologue as he gets further entangled in it—deepens not only the gap (in terms of narratological point-of-view) between the first-person speaker and the poem's implied author but also the ironic tension between the speaker's direct and indirect speech-acts.[55] The similes, analogies, idioms, and metaphors proper that he keeps enlisting in his attempts to reassure his partner end up interrupting the reader's uncritical identification, which the poem's all-too-familiar and emotionally charged context would otherwise elicit. Instead, the reader is increasingly led to develop an awareness that, while the speaker's locutions take the form of a series of promises and reassurances, their illocutionary force is actually that of a threat, or at least of a series of expressives that bespeak worry and fear. At this point another question becomes crucial for the construal of the poem's figurative language—and therefore, as we shall see, for the reader's becoming an active decoder of the poem's political critique: Are these ironic or sarcastic reversals, where "irony" and "sarcasm" are used in the technical sense of the terms—irony involving a gap of knowledge or awareness at least in one point in the communicative process, while in sarcasm all parties are aware that what is meant is the opposite of what is being said. (And note that in this technical sense, sarcasm has none of the implications of contempt or bitterness associated with it in American colloquial usage.) The reader's critical agency is enlisted to the construal of the poem's metaphors—and thus to calling into question the reassurances mouthed by the poem's speaker, which repeat those supplied by the state apparatus that interpellated him. It becomes increasingly unclear whether the speaker actually believes what he is saying or whether he is in fact aware of the extent to which the *figures of speech* he keeps choosing upend the illocutionary force of his utterances, turning promise into threat and reassurance into warning. Significantly, this is a point on which Amichai refuses to "close off" the poem's meaning: While the naïve reading is quickly shown to be untenable (by the end of the first stanza), the tension between irony and sarcasm, or between conscious and unconscious self-undermining speech acts, is left open almost till the monologue's end.

Read ironically, the process of the poem is the gradual process through which the reader moves from seeing the speaker as "buying into" the reassurances that it's all going to be all right, and furthermore that going out to war is necessary, to reorienting (in the final stanza) the lovers' world around the threat—indeed, around a different kind of war—waged by the army against them, a war in which "all lovers in autumn" – no matter which side they are on — are bound to lose. But it is also possible to read the entire poem as suggesting that both the man and the partner he addresses—and by implication, the reader as well—are aware throughout of the futility of his attempts to reassure her that there is nothing to worry about; in other words, to offer a sustained sarcastic reading where there is no gap in understanding or awareness between reader, implied author, speaker, and addressee. On this reading, the poem starts with the speaker going through the motions, pretending to play the role of a stereotypical male protecting his woman, but actually choosing expressions that reveal his sense that their lives and love are threatened. This interpretation bases the figurative process that launches his speech act in the second line on collocational "deviance," the deviant use of a common Hebrew idiom. Amichai has the speaker break up an idiom by violating its normative syntax, thus causing it to be literalized and in the process reverse its meaning. For the native speaker, line 2, *et nafshekh, na'arah, asim be-tokh kapi*, literally: "your soul, girl, I'll put inside my palm," echoes the (figuratively collocated, idiomatic) expression *asim nafshi be-khapi*, which means "I shall endanger myself; I shall face danger" (similar to, but not quite identical in meaning, with the English "take your life in your [own] hands").[56] Again, this is a reader-centered move on Amichai's part, since this idiom was part of the required Hebrew proficiency curriculum in Israeli schools. A high-school reference grammar on the proper uses of idioms that prepared students for the matriculation exams (*Ve-dayek*, by Ya'akov Bahat and Mordekhai Ron),[57] presents the following paradigm sentence: *hu sam nafsho be-khapo ve-yatza li-sde ha-krav* ("He took his life in his [own] hands and went out to battle"). Despite Amichai's violation of the anaphoric structure of the idiom ("*I* shall put . . . *your* soul . . . into *my* hand"), the idiom is definitely echoed in the background of the utterance, as in the other purposeful uses of catachresis I discussed earlier. Read according to its idiomatic sense, the line has the exact opposite meaning it would have when read as a novel metaphor, without its collocational history. If the speaker is at this point unaware of the inversion, then—in H. Paul Grice's terms—the sentence meaning is "I shall endanger you," while the utterer's meaning is "I shall protect you."[58] Thus, an ironic reading would suggest that at least at this stage in the poem, even though he means to comfort her, his choice of idioms and metaphors betrays his worries unbeknownst to him; a sarcastic reading would imply that speaker, addressee, as well as implied author and reader all know that this speech act of reassurance actually expresses fear. The omnipresence of danger is thus inevitably and continuously expressed in the speaker's choice of phrase. In terms of speech-act analysis, the promise unwittingly becomes an indirect speech-act of threat, as collocated-idiomatic and novel-metaphoric meanings clash, requiring the reader to be aware of that incongruity in order to comprehend the poem's figurative language.

This reinterpretation of the idiomatic meaning also affects the reading of the simile in the third line. The comparison of the woman to an *etrog* (citron) now centers not so much on the fruit's beauty and sanctity as on its fragile and vulnerable nature; *etrogim* are often rendered unfit for ritual use because their stems (the *pitam*) break so easily. Since they may not be eaten, a citron with a broken stem becomes utterly useless, and is deemed *pasul* ("unfit" or "null and void"). Following the ironic or sarcastic readings to the last line of the first stanza, the analogy to the speaker's father now centers on his being dead. It is as if the speaker is saying: "Yes, my father did all the right things for God and Country, and a lot of good that did him; he died." The syntactic ambiguity created by the deictic expression "that way" (*kakh*) in the last line of the stanza may now be taken to mean (again, consciously or subconsciously, sarcastically or ironically): "My dead father, just like me, though he wished to protect those he loved, actually endangered them by being such a hero. He died, and I may die too." Any reader familiar with Amichai's poetry will recognize this theme, so frequently echoed, for example from the first sonnet in the sonnet cycle "We Loved Here" ("Ahavnu kan"), "My Father Spent Four Years Inside Their War" ("Avi haya arba shanim be-milchamtam").[59]

It is important that no conclusive meaning for the metaphors of the first stanza can be found in either of these readings alone, but rather that the illocutionary force of the poem emanates from their interaction. However, as the poem progresses it becomes increasingly clear to both addressee and reader that the speaker too is—or is becoming—aware of these reversals. Whereas the first attempt to reassure his beloved fails because his use of *language* undermines his intention, his second attempt fails because of his choice of *referents*. In the first line of the second stanza, the old biblical and poetic device of taking an example from nature is on the face of it meant to help the woman accept their parting and the impending reality of war:

> Look, the olive-tree no longer grieves—
> It knows there are seasons and a man must leave.

(Literally, these lines read: "See, the olive tree stopped wondering / it [he] knows there are seasons and one must go [travel].") Despite the respectable tradition of such examples, for instance in biblical Wisdom Literature, it seems that we are bound, indeed expected, to find this example lacking in wisdom, if not patently ridiculous. Olive trees are quite unaffected by seasonal changes and they certainly don't travel. For an Israeli Jewish audience during the early 1950s they were, if anything, paradigmatic examples of native Middle Eastern stability, of literal and figurative rootedness, and—poignantly in the context of war against an Arab enemy—suggestive of the Palestinians' rootedness in the land, by contrast with the recently arrived Israeli Jews. Evergreen and therefore unaffected by seasonal changes, what does it mean for them to know that "there are seasons and [one] must go"? Olive trees are of course the symbol of peace, not war, and they are immune to going anywhere—their uprooting for political reasons is a practice that became notorious only after 1967. Thus using them as paradigms for a stoic acceptance of the necessity to go off to war and of human mutability in general is semantically incongruous, and politically subversive. That the woman and not only the reader remain unconvinced by this *exemplum* is evident from the speaker's attempt to calm her down immediately in the next line: "dry your face now / and smile as if in a family photo." This line implies clearly that she has started crying and is far from being comforted by her lover's self-defeating, growing catalogue of metaphors and analogies. After this point the speaker himself stops pretending, and irony and sarcasm blend indistinguishably. The dangers of war and the fear of separation and death are now explicitly expressed, and his optimism can no longer be feigned.

Furthermore, it would have been clear to an Israeli contemporary reader that both man and woman do not actually believe that being a true patriot means not protesting; this reverses the assertion in stanza 4 that "the beloved country never cries out." In fact, the line clearly alludes to Alan Paton's 1948 book that condemns South African racist policies, *Cry, the Beloved Country*, which was well known in Israel at the time the poem was published. Paton's title issues a command that directly reverses the speaker's admonition.[60]

In the rest of stanzas 3 and 4, which I will not discuss in detail, a tone of growing disillusionment and consciousness of danger is established by merging a metaphorical mapping with another of Amichai's signature rhetorical strategies, the intertextual collage. In addition to the antiracist *Cry, the Beloved Country*, these stanzas conjoin a radical rewriting of a World War I marching song ("Pack up your troubles in the old kit-bag / and smile, smile, smile") with a biblical allusion to "If I forget thee, O Jerusalem," in which a literal woman—the speaker's addressee—replaces Zion. All these combine to enlist the reader in a series of resistant responses to the reassuring national narrative: to the false promise of a just "war to end all wars," to placing love of (literal)-country-as-(metaphorical)-woman above love of (literal)-woman-as-(metaphorical)-country. The radical address to the literal woman—rather than to Jerusalem—as the one who must not be forgotten joins forces with the legitimation of protest as a patriotic response on the part of the country-as-woman in the allusion to Paton's 1948 book. Taken together, the reader is compelled to draw uncomfortable analogies between 1948 in Israel and South Africa.

The tone of the final stanza is, I believe, most unambiguously sarcastic. The reversal of meaning and speech-act is now openly understood by all parties: speaker, addressee, implied author, and reader. The three components that interact in the extended metaphor that closes the poem all converge around the charged junction word *shalom*. The first concept of peace is introduced along with the jet plane. Both the internal context of the poem and the social context of Israeli military reality in the early 1950s, when the poem was written, are invoked here. Jet planes were used at that time exclusively by the Air Force (Mitchell's English translation wisely adds "army" to the term "jet" to make that clear). Thus the reference to peacemaking in the sky is just a newspeak description of war. The second component of the metaphor is metonymically linked to this armed policing of "peace." It uses a collocation common in children's language: *la-asot shalom*, "to wave hello or goodbye." Some familiarity with the folklore of Israeli pilots is required in order to understand the function of this collocation within the then-new military culture. The Israeli pilots of the period were notorious for showing off before their townspeople or kibbutz members by "waving hello" with the wings of the plane when passing over them. The third, sanctified, and cherished concept of *shalom* as heavenly peace is deflated by the first two components of the metaphor: first by reducing it to the tenuous and godless security of a "peace" imposed by an air force; and second by emphasizing the dangerously childish aspect of those same air force "angels of peace." The greatest and most complex deflation of all is created by the iconoclastic allusion flaunted in the third component of the metaphor: the contrast between jet planes and the prayer *oseh shalom bi-mromav* ("He who makes peace in His Heights").

Characteristically, the most powerful metaphoric effects in Amichai's oeuvre bring together the figurative and the intertextual. And indeed, this metaphor hyphenates contemporary Israeli security issues and a significantly modified version of the last words of the *Kaddish*, the prayer for the dead (although this prayer is said numerous times in other contexts as well, the *Kaddish* is its most paradigmatic use): "May He who makes peace in His heights establish peace over us and over all Israel." Thus the only mention of lasting peace in this poem is within the context of death. Not only does the wording of the prayer change, but the very fact that peace is invoked only as part of the *Kaddish* prayer triggers a tragic and sacrilegious reversal of meaning. The jet plane becomes, in the modified allusion, a mock-god, just as the gasoline replaced heavenly scents in the opening of the poem. The change of wording from "over us and over all Israel" to "over us and over all the lovers in the fall" marks Amichai's typical deflation of the national-religious ethos and the formation of an alternative sense of community, an "us" that is not Jews or Arabs but lovers on both sides of the proverbial fence. This move also performs his sanctification of love as an alternative to all the reigning ideologies. It is the inevitable fate of lovers of this time and of this place—wherever they are in the Middle East, whosoever war machine "makes peace" over them—to live in constant danger of war, with the jet plane rather than divine providence as their horrific guardian. The traditional romantic symbol of the fall season as the end of love and of life is invoked here to redefine that end in terms of the lovers' common enemy, for the mock-god of the air force jet plane makes "peace" by dropping bombs over them and "all lovers"—Jewish and Arab alike—who find themselves in its range.

＊

"The Smell of Gasoline Ascends in My Nose," like the other poems I discussed above, provides just a small window into the intricate metaphorical network developed throughout Amichai's poetry, which, while novel, daring, and iconoclastic, also consistently absorbs the figurative into a familiar, lifelike, and literal frame. One of the principal methods used to maintain this dual effect is the simultaneous activation of the semantic and the collocative potential of the metaphor. Amichai "normalizes" or mitigates his most salient, daring, and novel metaphors through a variety of linguistic junctions, literal or realistic frames, and experientially primary image schemas; but he also de-automatizes and de-conventionalizes his collocations (idioms, fixed expressions, stock quotations, and familiar or sacred allusions) in order to release their dormant metaphorical potential and use them to undermine their ossified linguistic, national, or religious authority. Amichai's poetics requires both rhetorical strategies for reasons that may be as epistemological and political as they are aesthetic. Metaphors have to appear normal, "collocated," or literal—they are not the privilege of the rarified poetic genius but form the common speaker's "hyphen" of everyday struggles against institutional power. The playful, creative, and revolutionary potential of language is one of the few tools a person has in order to resist—at least in his or her imaginative acts—the pressures of history and the coercive forces of religion and the state. Conventions, whether linguistic, literary, religious, or national, are meaningful only inasmuch as they are challenged or upended by the human agent confronting them, metaphor in hand.

Six   Double Agency
Amichai and the Problematics of
Generational Literary Historiography

> My divided fate has willed it so that I should be planted in between two
> generations, a sort of double agent.
> > Yehuda Amichai, "Generations in the Land" speech, 1968[1]

I. Amichai and the Statehood Generation

Yehuda Amichai's poetics is, as we have seen, the expression of a hybrid, liminal poetic subject who extols and privileges his freedom to oscillate between ontological and epistemological categories. By way of conclusion I want to explore some of the ways Amichai positions himself in the interstices of generational trends and poetic styles, on the margins of affiliation, calling into question in the process the underlying assumptions of generational literary historiography. I do not mean to imply here, as some critics have, that he is in any sense poetically a member of the 1948 generation.[2] His 1968 speech that I quote in the epigraph of this chapter and discuss in the Introduction makes it clear that although he is chronologically of the age of the Palmach Generation, poetically he shares very little with them. As he states further on in the same speech: "Even though 'biographically' I belong to that generation . . . from a 'literary' point of view I belong to the next generation of writers [*kotvim*] that arose in the 1950s."[3]

I believe that Amichai's self-marginalizing position vis-à-vis the Statehood Generation writers, with whom he professes to share the most poetically, is an important part of his critique of any such affiliation as an institutionalizing, reifying process that reduces the poetic flux to ossified coteries. This is the context in which I wish to interrogate in this chapter the tensions between Amichai's centrality within Israeli and "Western" literary cultures and the self-consciously marginal stance he maintained within established literary movements beginning in the 1950s. In the process, I will contrast his work with the group poetics of *Likrat*, the first Statehood Generation modernist circle in Israel, its belated affiliation with Anglo-American imagism, and Amichai's ambivalent orientation toward both. The result may be to complicate our understanding of the generational profile of the Statehood Generation, a move that would be a natural development from the theory of marginal prototypes proposed in my 1996 book, *On the Margins of Modernism*.

The ambivalence toward modernism marks a contradictory set of orientations in Amichai's work. One orientation places anti-elitism at the center of his poetics. As we have seen, Amichai reduces both God and the sacred muse to life-size dimensions, and succeeds in generating a truly popular poetic voice able to reach people in their workaday world. Yet an opposite orientation within his poetry embraces much of the poetics of Anglo-American modernism, including the complexity of classical allusion, multilayered figurative language, and syntactic fragmentation. These imported modernist prototypes in Amichai's poetry would appear to deny or at least clash with the possibilities for a truly accessible populist poetics. But Amichai does not simply oscillate between these two orientations; rather, he harnesses together—as we have seen in his treatment of intertextuality and metaphor—both the accessible and the difficult within a systematic yet open-ended poetics that problematizes trend affiliation in general and the boundaries of modernism in particular. In this way, he helps me make the case for the marginal as prototypical, at least as far as transnational modernisms are concerned. Thus while Amichai is the most central poet Israeli modernism has produced, throughout his life he chose to remain on the margins of his poetic generation. How do these two contradictory orientations, simplistically construed as modernist and antimodernist, coexist, and how do they combine in his actual poetic practice?

In the poem "Ve-hi tehilatekha" ("And That Is Your Glory")—one of the poems, like "The Travels of the Last Benjamin of Tudela," that I revisit throughout this study—the picture of God as a *garagenik*, a mechanic lying on his back underneath a world that keeps breaking down as if it were a lemon of a car, creates a quotidian image that is at once antimodernist in its populism and modernist in its iconoclasm. Let us return then to the poem's famous second stanza:[4]

From: And That Is Your Glory

Underneath the world, God lies stretched on his back,
always repairing, always things get out of whack.
I wanted to see him all, but I see no more
than the soles of his shoes and I'm sadder than I was before.
And that is his glory.

אֱלֹהִים שׁוֹכֵב עַל גַּבּוֹ מִתַּחַת לַתֵּבֵל,

תָּמִיד עָסוּק בְּתִקּוּן, תָּמִיד מַשֶּׁהוּ מִתְקַלְקֵל

רָצִיתִי לִרְאוֹתוֹ כֻּלּוֹ, אַךְ אֲנִי רוֹאֶה

רַק אֶת סֻלְיוֹת נְעָלָיו וַאֲנִי בּוֹכֶה.

וְהִיא תְּהִלָּתוֹ.

Framed by its title and refrain, the last line of each stanza of this poem alludes, as we have seen, to a relatively obscure piece of ancient liturgy for the Days of Awe (the ten days between Rosh Hashanah and Yom Kippur) that the average Jewish reader may not recognize, since it is not found in all the versions of the *Machzor*, the High Holidays prayer book used in synagogue. Amichai alerts the reader to the evoked text and its context in a parenthetical epigraph—"(from the liturgy for the Days of Awe)"—but he does not tell us where to find it, nor who the liturgical poet is. Furthermore, the title and refrain require not only the identification of this allusion but also a scholarly "excavation" of the rare paradoxical meaning of *tohola* ("fault," "imperfection," as in Job 4:18), alongside the normative sense of *tehila* ("praise," "glory"; the tendency of Semitic languages to derive opposite meanings from the same root is well documented): God's glory is also his imperfection or even his infamy. Combining the domestication of God with an intertextual, etymological critique of the divine is Amichai's typical stance—a stance that dismantles the very dichotomy between the sacred and the profane.[5]

This bivalent position has led critics and readers alike to observe that Amichai's poetry is at once easy and difficult, accessible and elusive, familiar and strange.[6] Ironically, the simultaneity of such contradictory poetic positions is commonly associated transnationally with the conceptual structure of the category modernism. But Amichai's particular form of ambivalence leads him in part away from the modernism of his—and his generation's—Anglo-American prototypes. This further complication adds two interesting questions to an investigation of the trends of Amichai's poetics. First, how can the very ambivalence toward the modernist prototypes embedded in his poetry point to Amichai's own modernist affiliation? And, second, does it make sense to talk about his modernism if the very turning away from its formations can itself be seen as a typically modernist practice? A closer examination of what it means for Amichai to be or not to be affiliated with Hebrew and international modernism might help shed some light on the particular ways in which he has come to serve as a paragon of his generation while remaining situated—in important ways—on its margins.

As it turns out, this bivalence is not unusual within the implicit poetics of most other Statehood Generation poets, their manifestos and historiographic reception notwithstanding. The works of almost all the Statehood poets, with the possible exception of the early poetry of their self-appointed spokesperson, Natan Zach, demonstrate an ambivalent position toward the various formations of high modernism that are supposedly their model. The explicit poetics (manifestos, public proclamations) of Amichai's generation proclaimed it to be a late modernist, neoimagist grouping. However, the implicit poetics, reconstructed from the poets' actual works, ranging from Amichai and Dahlia Ravikovitch to Dan Pagis and David Avidan, contains many traits that either subvert or go beyond this group's official modernist positions—be they the prescribed reaction against the *moderna* of the pre-Statehood Generation or the embrace of the newly legitimated Anglo-American modernist poetry (associated until 1948 with the British colonial occupier), which Zach studied in graduate school (at Sussex) and helped import to Israel. These contradictory trends are manifested most fully, I believe, in Amichai's poetry.

Modernism was always a self-referential (set of) literary movement(s), although this fact does not make self-reference itself into a sufficient condition for modernism.[7] The choice of affiliation among modernists was usually quite deliberate and often entailed the compulsion either to join or to form groups of like-minded artists, in what Douwe Fokkema has termed the "sociocode of modernism."[8] Each group would then usually provide public declarations of its explicit poetics to distinguish itself from other groups. Not only do the iconoclastic manifestos of Filippo Tommaso Marinetti and the Italian Futurists before World War I set the stage for this type of writing, but the Futurists remain perhaps the most salient example of the self-conscious, manifesto-producing literary group; after the war that role fell to the dadaists, who made the manifesto into a full-fledged literary genre that embodied—again self-referentially—its own necessary and imminent destruction. These modernist groups were intent on supplying readers as well as critics with programmatic credos stating their aesthetic and ideological goals, goals they often deviated from—in significant, even systematic, ways—the poetics implicit in their own literary practice.

Amichai's generation of Hebrew modernist poets, led by what I describe in *On the Margins of Modernism* as the "activist paragon," Natan Zach, followed this familiar pattern, and perhaps because of the trend's belatedness—and Zach's own scholarly interest in Anglo-American imagism, on which he wrote his thesis—their explicit poetics often read like self-referential allusions to the famous "high modernist" manifestos. Given all this, Amichai's participation in the formation of Statehood Generation groupings remains highly ambivalent. His poems were published in *Likrat* from the second issue on, and his first poetry book was published by *Likrat* press in 1955.[9] But while he was one of the founding members of the group, he was never among the manifesto-writers or activists in it. Amichai recalls: "In the beginning of the 1950s we established *Likrat*. This was a literary group that also published a magazine. Among us were [Benjamin] Hrushovski [Harshav], Moshe Dor, Arie Sivan, David Avidan, Natan Zach, Moshe Ben-Shaul, and others. I never turned my poetry into a manifesto. The *Likrat* group was all about manifestos. They were always writing poetic and critical manifestos. I was writing poems."[10] Thus while Amichai describes himself as part of the group that launched *Likrat* ("**we** established [it]"), he immediately adds that he was a nonparticipant in its explicit poetics ("**They** were always writing poetic and critical manifestos. **I** was writing poems"; emphases added). The only metapoetic genre he favored throughout the years was the interview, because it was modeled on ordinary human conversation.

Amichai's ambivalent relation to *Likrat* is acknowledged even by Zach. Always quite keen on the manifesto as a metapoetic genre, Zach points to Amichai as a salient prototype of Statehood Generation poetics, at the same time that he has to acknowledge that Amichai deviates from what he, Zach, describes as the group's principles. Zach's major manifesto of 1966, titled "On the Stylistic Climate of the Fifties and Sixties in Our Poetry," better known as "Tet-vav ha-nekudot" (the Fifteen Points), is actually the fifth in a series of six essays serialized in *Ha'aretz* between July 1 and August 12, 1966 (unfortunately, most scholars read only the "Fifteen Points," thus missing some of the more interesting and subtle counterpoints, if not contradictions in his argument). In this fifth manifesto, Zach attempts to provide a checklist of necessary and sufficient conditions for the poetry of his generation, modeling them quite self-consciously on Pound's "A Few Don'ts by an Imagiste."[11] In his manifestos throughout the 1960s, Zach describes a belligerent objection to the previous generation's *moderna* as one of the most important common features linking together the Statehood Generation, an objection that for him centers around his famous attacks on Nathan Alterman. Amichai, like Dahlia Ravikovitch, never accepted that belligerent stance and, as we have seen, claimed Goldberg, one of the major *moderna* poets, as his literary mother. Furthermore, in a 1976 interview I cite below, in response to a question about the rebellion of one literary generation against another, Amichai explicitly asserts that in his view there was no sharp break (*mifne chotekh*) between the Statehood Generation and their *moderna* precursors. He relates this observation to a more general conception of intergenerational historiography: on the one hand there is always more continuity with the immediately preceding generation than the contemporary poets are willing to acknowledge; and on the other, the dominant trends of the previous generation or two often include marginal members who already practice what comes to be considered as revolutionary by the new generation. While Zach would accept the second tenet, offering for example David Fogel and Esther Raab as proleptic paragons for his own generation, he obviously rejects the first. Amichai proposes here—as in his implicit poetics—a nonlinear, nonsequential view of literary dynamics and of the interaction of margins and center, and his view has served as one of the major models for my theory of "marginal prototypes" (1996). Since this 1976 interview is one of the rare occasions on which Amichai explicitly articulates his metapoetic historiographic principles, I would like to quote his answer in full. The interviewer, Aviva Barzel, asks: "To what extent is the new modernist phase [in poetry] a turning point, and to what extent does it continue previous periods?" Amichai answers:

> I don't think there is a sharp break. Actually, our poems are continuous [*hemshekhiyim*], and only **on the surface** do they appear as a great innovation. Shlonsky wasn't a great rebel against Bialik either. But in Shlonsky and Alterman's generation too, and even in Bialik's, there were already poets like Fogel and Lerner, who wrote in a simple and non-bombastic language about themselves, their personal experiences within their historical frameworks, both the individual and the national. Shlonsky and Alterman were great suns [*shmashot gdolot*] who wrote about "the we" [*al "anchnu"*] even when they were writing about themselves, and they overshadowed those other poets, but they [those other poets] were nevertheless there. Nowadays most poets tend to express themselves as part of historical events. There is more individualization within the ideational collective. Perhaps the deviations from the "we" may also be attributed to the doubt that started gnawing immediately after the War of Independence and was already expressed in the poetry from the 1950s on, and perhaps it is this doubt that is the differentiating factor, one turning point in our poetry.[12]

Zach is not unaware, in his manifestos, of the extent to which the historiographic picture he paints does not fit many of the poets of his group, most of all the one he repeatedly holds up as a model, Yehuda Amichai. With perhaps a touch of self-irony, Zach finds himself in his "Fifteen Points" at once citing Amichai as the group's internal paragon (playing the role of an Eliot to his Pound), and as the most salient example of Statehood Generation modernism, at the same time that he acknowledges time and again Amichai's deviation from the various strictures of the Fifteen Points. Zach's fifteen-point catalogue is revealing precisely because this type of checklist definition cannot work for modernism or for any literary trend, as I've suggested elsewhere.[13]

A couple of examples should suffice to illustrate the stylistic practices at issue here. In point 1 of his fifteen-point manifesto, Zach prescribes: "Opposition to the quatrain, because of its excessive symmetry and static nature." Zach then cites Amichai as an exception that never-theless proves the rule, because he manages to use the quatrain form while successfully breaking the "squareness" of the line.[14] But Amichai clearly and consistently privileges the "square" four-line stanza, not only in his early poetry, to which Zach refers in the 1966 manifesto, but also in his liturgically parodic later work, and maintains an affin-ity for it even when he switches to free verse. Zach is then forced to qualify his very first principle by saying that Amichai finds ways to undo the static symmetry of the quatrain, especially through the use of enjambment, a modernist technique Zach himself has mastered. Zach encounters similar trouble when he states in point 4 that free verse should be embraced as a rule and adopted as a guideline for the gen-eration's poetic goals. But he immediately qualifies the prescription by saying that Amichai's rhythms continue to be free even though, in this early period, they are often based on more or less regular tonic-syllabic metrical schemes. Zach cannot minimize the importance of Amichai within the late modernism of the 1950s and 60s, but he is forced to ac-knowledge that Amichai's implicit poetics provides a limit case for the explicit poetics that he, Zach, is trying to establish as the prescribed mainstream of the trend.

While Amichai's poetry underwent many changes, his later work presented equally complex challenges to any orthodox notions of liter-ary affiliation. Furthermore, as I have argued in chapter 1, Amichai's commitment from the very start to political poetry as part of a cri-tique of ideology is in itself a departure from the Zachian modeling of Statehood Generation's "apolitical," individual-universalist poetry, a modeling that became the normative literary-historiographic concep-tion of the period, even though very few of the poets actually followed it. Ironically, Zach's later poetry itself seems to follow Amichai (and Dahlia Ravikovitch's) example, and return to the political, though its aesthetic success has been called into question by many.

As an important critical reexamination of the poetics of the State-hood Generation is currently underway, scholars increasingly turn to poets such as Amichai, David Avidan, Dahlia Ravikovitch, Moshe Dor, and Dan Pagis, as well as to hitherto overlooked aspects of Zach's own early work. This reexamination is part of an attempt to move the dis-cussion beyond the parameters set up in the 1950s and 60s for the reception of these poets by critics who took Zach's polemics at face value, and saw the heterogeneous poetic production of the entire generation through that narrow lens.[15]

Zach's appropriation of Amichai's poetry has largely gone unchallenged because, as we have seen, not only does Amichai not write—or sign—manifestos but he rarely makes poetry the explicit subject of his poems (as part of the egalitarian poetics I explore in chapter 2). This fact in itself, however, points to Amichai's ambivalent modernism since poems about poetry have often been considered by poets and readers alike as the quintessential modernist gesture; modernist poets have made poetry, modernity, or poetic language in general the subject of their poems. From Paul Verlaine's "Ars Poètique" to Wallace Stevens's "Of Modern Poetry," modernists have used their poems to explore the aesthetic, philosophical, and even the most technical metapoetic concerns, such as the use of rhymes and metaphor. Zach, similarly, makes the "right poem" (*ha-shir ha-nakhon*) the central thematic focus of many of his early poems.[16] In the entire corpus of Amichai's work, by contrast, only a handful of poems explicitly thematize the poetic process; and even these few first appear as if they don't.

II. Ordinary Language Poetics

While Amichai shuns the openly metapoetic use of poetry, he does compensate for it, as we have seen, with a meditative concern for language—ordinary language, especially the kind that is traditionally considered quite unpoetic. Grammatical constructions, everyday trite phrases, and word etymologies are commonly thematized by the speaker in Amichai's poetry. But despite this concentration on the possibilities of language, Amichai's speaker rarely presents himself as a poet contemplating the possibilities of poetic language. For Amichai, language as theme never goes beyond the quotidian, the palpable expression of the everyday and the colloquial. Rather than make metapoetic assertions, Amichai's speaker consistently takes on the character of an ordinary human being thinking about ordinary speech. And given that component-awareness and metalinguistic reflection continue to be culturally common among Hebrew speakers, there is nothing odd or elitist about this. His demystification of the written word and the concomitant privileging of mundane discourse explain why for Amichai the poem about language replaces the poem on poetry, just as the journalistic interview—with its emphasis on colloquial speech, dialogue, and direct communication between people—replaces the manifesto as metapoetic genre. "To write a poem is to speak," Amichai told me in a 1986 interview.[17] "The poet," he elaborated in a seminar at the University of California, Berkeley during the same visit, "is of measly importance" (*pchut erekh*); but not being more important than anyone else is "the highest achievement any poet could possibly strive for." He went on to tell my stunned students that he only wrote poetry because he was "too lazy to do anything more difficult." For the poet, as for the reader, poetry should be easy, he explained; it is ordinary language—not any privileged poetic diction—that is magical, inexhaustible, and, if one only pays attention, infinitely complex.[18]

The privileged and complex status accorded to ordinary language is brilliantly exhibited in the early poem "Sonet ha-binyanim" ("The Verb-Pattern Sonnet").[19] In this poem, Amichai offers a virtuoso—and literally untranslatable—account of life as a series of changing grammatical conjugations. It is significant that he chooses the genre of the sonnet in order to endow the Hebrew grammar with the emotional and poetic charge traditionally associated in the West with love poetry. The Judeo-Arabic traditional love for grammar is thus thematized paradoxically via the choice of the most prototypically Western poetic genre. The second-person addressee in the poem, who is both the reader and the self-addressing speaker, is described as caught within the structure of language, but not in the postmodernist sense associated with the emptying out of the possibility of reference. Rather, he is confined surrealistically within the morphological architecture of the Hebrew verb forms, as its seven verb patterns (*binyanim*, lit., "buildings") lay out his life story. Ordinary language, not poetry, is thus the building in which the life of its speakers evolves in a series of stops and starts; a *Bildungs*-poem contained within the grammatical building. The poem follows the addressee as he makes the rocky journey from youthful activity to aged passivity, from full agency to agentlessness, with a final, self-fulfilling rest stop in (self-)reflexivity. Note again that this is a love poem to grammar, rather than a version of the poststructuralist cliché about being trapped within the sign. Neither is this poem merely a series of puns on the traditional names of the patterns that Hebrew verbs fall into (derived from the verbal root *p.a.l.*, "to act"). Rather, through sustained verbal play on the correlation between the name of a grammatical pattern and its epistemological and ontological significance, Amichai seems to suggest, with perfect seriousness, that dry, ordinary language is the ultimate source of humanitarian wisdom and expressive power.

The tri-consonantal roots and the verb patterns "built" around them are the very core of the grammar of the Hebrew language. In this grammar—its precision, nuances, and modulations—Amichai finds true poetry, material for the late modernist revival of the Hebrew sonnet, which flourished in Italy even before Petrarch. (As we have seen on several occasions, he often uses throughout his oeuvre the adjective "precise," *meduyak*, derived from the same root as "grammar," *dikduk*, as a poetic—even romantic—compliment.) Taking a few basic roots through the multiple transformations that make up Hebrew verb patterns, he also tells the story of a human life. I will not attempt a real translation here, not only because in this case I believe it to be truly impossible, but also out of respect for the poem's refusal to exceed the confines of the Hebrew language. Chana Bloch and I supply instead a prose paraphrase, and I've added a transliteration, which, although it cannot of course convey the poem's philosophical content, serves as an acoustic illustration of the prosodic virtuosity Amichai is able to draw out of grammatical conjugation patterns. This formal virtuosity, when combined with the poem's unabashed regionalism and resistance to universalization, is, I think, a particularly powerful example of Amichai's ambivalent stance vis-à-vis international modernism:

The Verb-Pattern Sonnet

To write, to drink, to die, and that's the easy part [= the *kal* pattern].
And already you are acted upon [= the *pa'ul* passive participle],
    beloved, written up.
Until they make you: you are enacted [= the *nif'al* verb pattern]:
Created, broken, finished, found and again

Your exploits are growing so much stronger:
Till the [intensive active] *pi'el* pattern: play [music], speak, shatter.

The world of action will get so entangled:
The [intensive passive] *pu'al* pattern, shattered, in-gathered, just that
   once.

You make others act [= the causative *hif'il* pattern]: Others are acting
And again [you're] acted upon [= the passive *hof'al* pattern] in an
   exchange of miracles,
Overseeing, overseen, spurred to action, being spurred.

And only in the end do you return to yourself
And get clarified and exchange whispers, it's all returned,
[In the state of being] amazed [= in the reflexive and mutual *hitpa'el*
   pattern] and enfolded till it ends.
                              Paraphrase by Chana Bloch and Chana Kronfeld

Sonet ha-binyanim

li-khtov, li-shtot, la-mut. ve-ze ha-kal.
u-khvar ata pa'ul, ahuv, katuv.
ad she-osim otkha: ata nif'al:
nivra, nishbar, nigmar, nimtza ve-shuv

alilotekha mitchazkot kol-kakh
ad la-pi'el: nagen, daber, shaber.
olam ha-ma'asim ko yesubakh:
pu'al, shubar, kubatz, beli chozer.

ata maf'il: ha-acherim osim
ve-shuv mof'al be-chilufey nisim,
mashgi'ach u-moshgach, malhiv, molhav.

ve-rak ba-sof ata chozer el atzmekha
u-mitbarer u-mitlachesh, ha-kol mochzar,
be-hitpa'el ve-hitkapel ad she-nigmar.

סוֹנֶט הַבִּנְיָנִים

לִכְתּוֹב, לִשְׁתּוֹת, לָמוּת. וְזֶה הַקַּל.
וּכְבָר אַתָּה פָּעוּל, אָהוּב, כָּתוּב.
עַד שֶׁעוֹשִׂים אוֹתְךָ: אַתָּה נִפְעָל:
נִבְרָא, נִשְׁבָּר, נִגְמָר, נִמְצָא וְשׁוּב

עֲלִילוֹתֶיךָ מִתְחַזְּקוֹת כָּל־כָּךְ
עַד לַפָּעַל: נֻגַּן, דֻּבַּר, שֻׁבַּר.
עוֹלָם הַמַּעֲשִׂים כֹּה יָסֻבַּךְ:
פֻּעַל, שֻׁבַּר, קֻבַּץ, בְּלִי חוֹזֵר.

אַתָּה מַפְעִיל: הָאֲחֵרִים עוֹשִׂים
וְשׁוּב מֻפְעָל בְּחִלּוּפֵי נִסִּים,
מַשְׁגִּיחַ וּמַשְׁגָּח, מַלְהִיב, מָלְהָב.

וְרַק בַּסּוֹף אַתָּה חוֹזֵר אֶל עַצְמְךָ
וּמִתְבָּרֵר וּמִתְלַחֵשׁ, הַכֹּל מָחֲזָר,
בְּהִתְפַּעֵל וְהִתְקַפֵּל עַד שֶׁנִּגְמַר.

The poetic function of conjugation does not rest on the accuracy of the grammatical insight. After all, it is a gross oversimplification to suggest that there is an automatic, predictable correlation between verb pattern and syntactic-semantic function in Hebrew. (Thus, while *hif'il* verbs are prototypically causative, there are many which are not, e.g., *hu hiskim*, "he agreed"). The main point of the poem is that "mere" grammar can be made to tell such a nuanced story about life's processes. Drawing attention to the beauty and wisdom embedded in the "dry" skeleton of the linguistic medium, and orienting the reader toward the signification that resides within the signifier rather than the signified, are avant-garde gestures common in many of its trends and articulations (e.g., Russian symbolism and Futurism). Through a particularly modernist defamiliarization of semantic features within Hebrew, the poem compels the Hebrew reader—and only him or her—to perceive grammar in a new, philosophically charged way (though it would be interesting to see if the poem could go into Arabic, for example, which has equally complex root-based verb patterns). Amichai abandons standard thematic presentation here in favor of an expressive thematization of grammar that follows a mimetic paradigm and calls into question the arbitrariness of the sign—and with it, some of the foundational tenets of modern linguistic theory, not the least of which is the claim for a universal grammar. He thus both upholds and subverts basic aspects of modernity, and not only of literary modernism. The valorization of

language, its ability to express the most nuanced philosophical statements and convey ontological truth *in its very structure*, goes against
some modernist disenchantments with language's ability to signify (a
position that Zach represents consistently).

Amichai's view that poetic language is no more creative and insightful
than grammatical forms and the discourse of ordinary people is a central feature in another early poem, "El maleh rachamim" ("O God Full
of Mercy"), which has served as one of my touchstone poems throughout this book.[20] Looking at the second stanza now in this metalinguistic
context, with its implications for Israeli and international modernism, I
believe that its speaker's assertions need to be read a bit more carefully:

O God Full of Mercy

If God were only not so full of mercy
There would be mercy in the world, not just in Him.
I, who used to gather flowers on the mountain
And gaze at all the valleys,
I, who carried corpses down from the hills,
Can tell you: the world is empty of mercy.

I, who was King of Salt by the sea,
Who stood undecided at my window,
Who used to count the footsteps of angels,
Whose heart lifted pain-weights
In those terrible competitions,
I, who use only a small part
Of the words in the dictionary;

I, who must solve riddles in spite of myself,
Know that if God were only not so full of mercy
There would be mercy in the world
And not just in Him.

Trans. Chana Bloch and Chana Kronfeld[21]

אֵל מָלֵא רַחֲמִים

אֵל מָלֵא רַחֲמִים,
אִלְמָלֵא הָאֵל מְלֵא רַחֲמִים
הָיוּ הָרַחֲמִים בָּעוֹלָם וְלֹא רַק בּוֹ.

אֲנִי, שֶׁקָּטַפְתִּי פְּרָחִים בָּהָר
וְהִסְתַּכַּלְתִּי אֶל כָּל הָעֲמָקִים,
אֲנִי, שֶׁהֵבֵאתִי גְּוִיּוֹת מִן הַגְּבָעוֹת,
יוֹדֵעַ לְסַפֵּר שֶׁהָעוֹלָם רֵיק מֵרַחֲמִים.

אֲנִי שֶׁהָיִיתִי מֶלֶךְ הַמֶּלַח לְיַד הַיָּם,
שֶׁעָמַדְתִּי בְּלִי הַחְלָטָה לְיַד חַלּוֹנִי,
שֶׁסָּפַרְתִּי צַעֲדֵי מַלְאָכִים,
שֶׁלִּבִּי הָרִים מִשְׁקָלוֹת כְּאֵב
בַּתַּחֲרֻיּוֹת הַנּוֹרָאוֹת.
אֲנִי, שֶׁמִּשְׁתַּמֵּשׁ רַק בְּחֵלֶק קָטָן
מִן הַמִּלִּים שֶׁבַּמִּלּוֹן.

אֲנִי, שֶׁמֻּכְרָח לִפְתּוֹר חִידוֹת בְּעַל כָּרְחִי
יוֹדֵעַ כִּי אִלְמָלֵא הָאֵל מָלֵא רַחֲמִים
הָיוּ הָרַחֲמִים בָּעוֹלָם
וְלֹא רַק בּוֹ.

Amichai deals here, quite self-consciously, with the relations of the poet to language, especially concerning the issue of *difficulty* that is critical within a modernist context. He cannot do so directly, for the explicit situation concerns the ways in which the Everyman speaker's wartime experiences have affected—or are reflected in—his use of language. At one important and yet subdued moment at the end of stanza 2, the speaker says of himself: *Ani, she-mishtamesh rak be-chelek katan / min ha-milim she-ba-milon* ("I, who use only a small part / Of the words in the dictionary"), adducing his linguistic minimalism as somehow related to his experiential knowledge that God's mercy is nowhere to be found in the world. This simple declaration has always been taken at face value, as a description of Amichai's poetic style, but I think it actually reveals his ambivalent and complex attachment to modernism, as well as to his own literary generation. The *speaker's* professed lexical minimalism and his refraining from stylistic plenitude are actually quite far from being true of the *poet*, especially if one considers Amichai's complex biblical and rabbinic intertextuality, his novel metaphors, and his typical blend of high and low registers.

And it's definitely not true of the early Amichai, whose use of slang and colloquial idiom is often sharply juxtaposed within the same text against highly stylized lexical and prosodic choices. The statement needs, I think, to be read first and foremost as part of the poem's specific situation, as relating to the speaker—and his generation's—war trauma.[22] But it is also an expression of his protest and rage against the beautiful, mellifluous words of the prayer said over the open grave, which assert the doctrine of *tziduk ha-din*, justifying people's death by pointing to divine judgment as a higher criterion we mortals cannot fathom. This religious requirement to accept divine judgment is issued by the eulogizing rabbi at a moment when the speaker—and people experiencing loss everywhere—may feel no such justice or mercy exist. Metapoetically, however, "I, who use only a small part / of the words in the dictionary" is an endorsement of minimalist formations of Hebrew modernism, usually associated with precursor women poets like Rachel [Bluwshteyn] and Esther Raab and described as a poetics of *dalut*, meagerness, and with a rejection of a poetics of plenitude and pathos. Existentially, this is also an articulation of Amichai's "great renunciation" of hope (*ha-vitur ha-gadol*) discussed in the context of the poem "Not Like a Cypress," for example, in chapter 2. Therefore, it is not the actual size of Amichai's lexicon that is at issue here, but the metaphysical implications of the need, indeed the ethical necessity, to renounce the "riches of vision," refusing to aestheticize the political by flaunting the artist's verbal arsenal. That is, as he says in another poem, what he has learned in the wars.[23]

Through the protesting stance of the speaker in this central poem, Amichai communicates his objection to the poetics of difficulty common to many modernist trends, from German expressionism to Anglo-American high modernism, and from Avot Yeshurun to Natan Zach's (very different) forms of hermeticism. He presents himself as just another member of the speech community, whose experiences with human loss and God's absence have taught him that he is ethically required to avoid elitism and obfuscation and to privilege simple, ordinary language over lofty poetic diction. He has learned from those experiences, as the title and first three lines of the poem suggest, to take the familiar, collocated idiom *el maleh rachamim* (God full of mercy) of the sacred prayer literally, thereby revealing its inverse meaning. A literal translation of the Hebrew opening lines would read: "God filled with [*el maleh*] mercy, / If God weren't so filled with [*il-male ha-el mele*] mercy / There would be some mercy [left] in the world [*ba-olam*] and not just in him." The paranomasia creates a heretical pseudo-midrashic explanation for the lack of divine justice here on earth. The speaker uses the Talmudic counterfactual conditional *ilmale* ("had it not been the case that") to suggest that, since God has taken all the mercy *to himself* (*el maleh*), the language of the prayer actually proves the absence of God's mercy in the world.

In his later work, Amichai abandons rhyme, meter, and traditional poetic forms in favor of a rhetoric of plain speech that radically challenges the very distinction between various forms of language—ordinary, prosaic, scientific, poetic—and between linguistic action and action in the world. In the poem "Ba-yom she-bo nolda biti lo met af ish" ("On the Day My Daughter Was Born No One Died"), Amichai expresses this challenge by obscuring the typographic distinction between poetry and prose in a poem that thematically engages with the prosaics of poetry and the poetics of prose. In the process, Amichai also dismantles the dichotomy between artist and scientist as he reverses the conventional metaphor of the poem as the poet's "baby":

On the Day My Daughter Was Born No One Died

On the day my daughter was born not a single person
died in the hospital, and at the entrance gate
the sign said: "Today *kohanim* are permitted to enter."
And it was the longest day of the year.
In my great joy
I drove with my friend to the hills of Sha'ar Ha-Gai.

We saw a bare, sick pine tree, nothing on it but a lot of pine cones.
Zvi said trees that are about to die produce more pine cones than
healthy trees. And I said to him: That was a poem and you didn't
realize it. Even though you're a man of the exact sciences, you've
made a poem. And he answered: And you, though you're a man of
dreams, have made an exact little girl with all the exact instruments for
her life.[24]

בְּיוֹם שֶׁבּוֹ נוֹלְדָה בִּתִּי לֹא מֵת אַף אִישׁ

בְּיוֹם שֶׁבּוֹ נוֹלְדָה בִּתִּי לֹא מֵת
אַף אִישׁ בְּבֵית הַחוֹלִים וְעַל שַׁעַר הַכְּנִיסָה
הָיָה כָּתוּב: "הַיּוֹם הַכְּנִיסָה לַכֹּהֲנִים מֻתֶּרֶת."
וְזֶה הָיָה בַּיּוֹם הָאָרֹךְ בְּיוֹתֵר שֶׁל הַשָּׁנָה.
וּמֵרֹב שִׂמְחָה
נָסַעְתִּי עִם יְדִידִי אֶל גִּבְעוֹת שַׁעַר הַגַּיְא.

רָאִינוּ עֵץ אֹרֶן חוֹלֶה וְחָשׂוּף מְכֻסֶּה רַק אִצְטְרֻבָּלִים אֵין
סְפֹר. וּצְבִי אָמַר שֶׁעֵצִים הָעוֹמְדִים לָמוּת מַצְמִיחִים יוֹתֵר
אִצְטְרֻבָּלִים מִן הַחַיִּים. וְאָמַרְתִּי לוֹ: זֶה הָיָה שִׁיר וְלֹא
יָדַעְתָּ. אַף עַל פִּי שֶׁאַתָּה אִישׁ הַמַּדָּעִים הַמְדֻיָּקִים, עָשִׂיתָ
שִׁיר. וְהֵשִׁיב לִי: וְאַתָּה, אַף עַל פִּי שֶׁאַתָּה אִישׁ חֲלוֹמוֹת
עָשִׂיתָ יַלְדָּה מְדֻיֶּקֶת עִם כָּל הַמִּתְקָנִים הַמְדֻיָּקִים לְחַיֶּיהָ.

The poem takes the form of a reported conversation between the
speaker, whose wife has just given birth to their daughter, and his scientist friend, Zvi. Within this dialogue, the poem builds an important
analogy between the aging poet, who is still producing both poems
and babies, and—on the hills at the outskirts of Jerusalem[25]—some
dying pine trees that, as a matter of botanical fact, produce more pine
cones than young, healthy trees do; interestingly, the analogy is built
as an extended poetic metaphor (in which the tenor is implied rather
than stated). But in the dramatic situation of this poem, the poetic
qualities of the metaphor are attributed to the spontaneous speech of
Zvi, the scientist, who knows the correct botanical facts about trees,
and not to the conventions of the literary institution within which
the reader ultimately finds this figurative language—namely, the poetic
text. This reversal—on the level of theme—of the traditional roles of
poetic and nonpoetic discourse is echoed closely in the generic structure of the text.[26]

The typographically poetic first stanza invokes matter-of-factly and
without recourse to metaphor or poetic diction the rabbinical law that
prohibits members of the priestly class (kohanim) from coming in contact with the dead, since the impurity of death is ritually "contagious"
and contaminating. Thus the fact that no one died in the hospital on

the day his daughter was born, and hence the sign says "Today *kohanim* are permitted to enter," associates his daughter's birth with an all-too-temporary victory over mortality. This *prosaic poetics* gives way to a *poetic prosaics*, as the poem typographically switches into prose and the spontaneous speech of the scientist subverts the lyrical ruminations of the old poet. There is no interest here in a professionalization of the language of poetry, or any sense that poetic discourse needs to be difficult or special; the point of this prose strophe is expressed clearly and meaningfully by a scientist, who within traditional norms of categorization is the opposite of the poet, but whose language for Amichai is precisely the model for the poetic.[27] Zvi's response provides the corollary to the speaker's assertion that a scientific observation—in the truth and simplicity of its language and its insight—is an unconscious form of poetry ("that was a poem and you didn't realize it"). Not only does the scientific become a source of poetry, but the poetic agent (thinly veiled here as "a man of dreams")—when acting in his capacity as an ordinary human agent—can produce exact, precise science—the perfectly formed newborn. But this symmetrical analogy must not be mistaken for a romantic endorsement of the power of poetic expression in the tradition of "beauty is truth, truth beauty." Such a move would undermine both the "wisdom of camouflage" and Amichai's refusal to assign the poetic any special privileges. It is thus not anything the poet *says* or *writes* but the baby girl he has *made* that is the perfect aesthetic object, "an exact little girl with all the exact instruments for her life." (This is yet another instance where the adjective *meduyeket* [exact, precise, fem.], from the same root as *dikduk* [grammar], functions as one of Amichai's highest aesthetic attributes, indeed as a marker of perfection.) The creative act—common to poets and ordinary human beings—is both "poetry in action" and a work of exact science; in the liminal space between them, all dichotomies fall away. Amichai arrives at an egalitarian view that blurs the distinction between the poet and the ordinary person on the one hand, and between poetic language and ordinary or scientific language on the other. Ultimately, however, it is the distinction between poetry and life that is blurred, if not dismantled altogether.

This view is much more characteristic—within the Anglo-American models for Statehood Generation poetry—of the work of the antimodernist critics of elitist modernism: W. H. Auden, George Orwell, Philip Larkin, and others. At the same time, the blending of poetry and prose is also a mark of modernist experimentation, from symbolism on. In addition, Amichai's modernist/antimodernist redefinition of the poet's status may be motivated as much by specific reactions to intrinsic traditional poetic models within the Hebrew literary system as by an ambivalence about international modernist trends. In Bialik's neoromantic verse, the poet is seen not only as a prophet but also as a mother, giving birth to the poetic baby that is also his (mother's) tear and his (own) prophetic vision. Amichai works against precisely this type of romanticist poetic model: he simply inverts the terms of Bialik's tenor and vehicle, as he does in "To the Mother," and here in "On the Day My Daughter Was Born No One Died," turning the ordinary and literal mother into a poet and prophet, or the flesh-and-blood baby girl into the perfect poem, and not vice versa.[28] But Amichai equally distrusts the concept of the poet qua linguistic magician, a view that continued to predominate in the work of poets of the *moderna* like Nathan Alterman and Abraham Shlonsky. While Amichai rejects Zach's dictum that Statehood Generation poets must repudiate the work of their modernist predecessors, the *moderna* poets of the 1930s and 40s, it is in Goldberg's then-marginalized and more minimalist poetics, and not Shlonsky's or Alterman's, that, as we have seen, he finds his lineage. Ironically, Amichai rejects the elitism of a Pound and even a late Eliot, with all its subsequent links to fascism and anti-Semitism, for the same reasons that bring him to deny the special powers that the Hebrew poet claims in the exhibitionistically artful uses of the Holy Tongue within an early nationalist or modernist framework. After treating me to a hilarious parody of Pound's hermeticist *Cantos*, Amichai commented: "It's an aristocratization of art. I don't believe in it."[29]

By showing the "influence" of Rilke and Auden on Amichai, Shimon Sandbank has pointed to the poetic complications that arise as a result of these conflicting models.[30] The specific qualities that can be associated with Rilke and Auden in Amichai's work demonstrate the ways in which the *selective modeling* of modernist and antimodernist prototypes that I described in *On the Margins of Modernism* helps form Amichai's particular type of ambivalent modernism. Rilke is the paragon who represents Amichai's orientation toward modernist poetics, while Auden represents his tendency toward an antimodernist critique. Instead of creating a homogenized unity from the combined models of his predecessors, Amichai maintains the individual strands of each; the differences between them become a source of tension that informs and enriches his own discursive strategies. Thus Amichai's need to maintain a rhetorical impression of accessibility remains consistent with the Auden prototype, while his emphasis on figurative innovation, semantic reversals, and radical intertextuality stays true to the Rilke prototype. Amichai's use of Auden is clearly interwoven with his use of Rilke, and not in the least because, as Sandbank has shown, Auden himself, though critical of Rilke, was also greatly "influenced" by him.

III. Revisiting the Hand Grenade

The long autobiographical *poema* "Travels of the Last Benjamin of Tudela" that I have revisited periodically at different stages in this book thematizes many of the issues that Amichai faces as both a modernist and an antimodernist. It offers many examples of his ambivalence of affiliation through his use of metaphorical collage. This type of metaphor, in effect, is the overarching principle of the poem's organization and a substitute for the narrative required by the poem's genre: a fragmented, simultaneous journey of the adult protagonist into "everything that I had," a nonlinear spiritual autobiography that is also, as I have argued in the opening of this book, an autobiography of the world. This journey to the past of the speaker and of his culture is modeled metaphorically, as we have seen, on the travels of the medieval Benjamin of Tudela, and Amichai self-consciously places himself at the end of this generic tradition, following in the footsteps of Abramovitch (Mendele's) satirical parody of the travelogue in his *The Travels of Benjamin the Third*. This parodic point of departure is significant, for in its intertextual cycles the very possibility of presenting a life—or a literal journey—in linear fashion is denied, at the same time that it is attempted over and over again. Thus the fragmentation of linear narrative, replacing narrativity with metaphoricity, and the real with the surreal—all combine to anchor this major work squarely within the modernist tradition, even as its autobio-

graphical, mock-heroic reinterpretation of the *poema* form align it more
with anti- or even postmodernist trends. At the conclusion of this study
I wish to revisit a metaphorical collage that appears at the beginning of
this *poema*, a collage that I discussed in *On the Margins of Modernism*.
I will reexamine it in the light of Amichai's response to my reading of
it, and suggest some implications for the need to theorize modernist
affiliations as both partial and multiple.

In the middle of the second strophe, as the narrator tries for the first
time of many to describe his early childhood and recapture a toddler's
point of view, Amichai presents us with a complex catalogue of juxtaposed similes that superimpose in collage fashion the perspective of the
adult narrator onto the child's:

> But even then I was marked for annihilation like an orange scored
> for peeling, like chocolate, like a hand-grenade for explosion and
>   death.[31]

אַךְ כְּבָר אָז הָיִיתִי מְסֻמָּן לִכְלָיָה כְּתַפּוּחַ
לְקִלּוּף, כְּשׁוֹקוֹלָדָה, כְּרִמּוֹן־יָד לְפִצּוּץ וָמָוֶת.

The fragmented metaphorical collage articulated in this catalogue of
similes is indeed prototypical within modernist trends like expressionism and imagism in its focus on what the Formalists would describe
as the simultaneous, paradigmatic aspects of language rather than on
a linear, syntagmatic, and logically coherent sequence. Furthermore,
the striking semantic and stylistic distance between the domains of the
tenor and the first two vehicles within the catalogue enhances the initial incongruity of the two lines, following—if you will—the model
of a juxtaposition-effect exemplified by Pound's famous "In a Station
of the Metro": the apparent incongruity between Pound's title, first
line, and second line have since come to represent the introverted,
minimalist (imagist) branch of modernism, with which the Statehood
Generation has been so strongly identified.[32] Other typically modernist
moves evident here include the selection of the colloquial *shokolada*
and *tapuz*, rather than their more formal equivalents, *shokolad* and
tapu'ach zahav, for "chocolate" and "orange," respectively, which
contrast with the grand and tragic verb phrase *mesuman li-khlaya*
("marked for annihilation"). The mixing of high and low registers and

the use of "un-poetic" referents as the point of departure for philosophical meditation are all familiar from various transnational formations of the avant-garde. Switching mid-metaphor to metonymy with the third vehicle (a hand grenade) further complicates the figurative structure of the catalogue. The hand grenade—the instrument of death—is described as if it were the victim of explosion and death, not its cause, implying perhaps that the child is destined not just to be killed but also to kill. This switch also clues us in that we are perhaps moving from experimental figurative artistry to history and politics.

What first appears fragmented and distant—and ultimately modernist in its apparent incongruity and lack of cohesion—actually becomes closely integrated via intricate image schemas that mitigate or bridge the semantic distance between the domains of the metaphor (as we have seen in chapter 5). Various thematic and linguistic clues absorb the vehicles into a quasi-literal frame and thus, subverting modernist tendencies, make the metaphor perceptually simple and visually accessible and coherent, despite its fragmentation and radical novelty: the first two items in the catalogue are mapped onto each other to produce the third (see Fig. 3).

When I showed Amichai the schema in Figure 3, after I had included it in *On the Margins of Modernism*, his reaction took me by surprise. I guess I expected him to wince at the pseudo-scientific reduction of his art to a graphic, or—as many poets do—to say he was

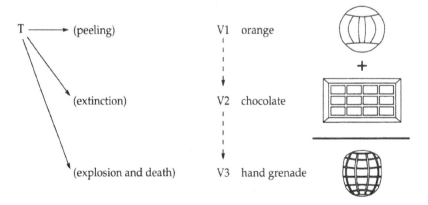

Figure 3. Amichai's composite image schema (T = Tenor; V = Vehicle).

not consciously trying to do anything of the sort. Instead, without skipping a beat, he nodded and said:

> I only meant to make the thing more precise [*le-dayek et ha-davar*]. . . . The chocolate bar is marked in order for it to break more easily, and the hand grenade is marked in order to be more effective. . . . What's important is not to paint a sweet picture but to show that this [similarity] is the true repugnance—the marked lines, the utility in the production: either for blowing up or for eating. And when you look at a hand grenade [*rimon yad*] it reminds you that it is both a grenade and a pomegranate [*rimon*], and that it involves someone's hand [*yad*]. . . . The hand grenade is war's version of ingenuity. It was invented to produce more shrapnel, to kill more people. A hand grenade that is marked like chocolate is called "defensive," while an offensive hand grenade is smooth. A smooth hand grenade makes more noise but is much less lethal.[33]

Thus, Amichai describes in fact how he uses the visual and associative cohesion within the various metaphoric vehicles—orange, chocolate, and hand grenade; indeed, how he mobilizes the composite structure of the visual collage in its entirety not only to link distant domains but to suggest the horror of that linkage. The mapping of one image (the chocolate bar divided into little squares) onto another image from the same domestic realm (the orange scored for peeling) produces a visually realistic motivation for the unexpected, deadly item in the catalogue (the hand grenade). The hand grenade is thus sarcastically introduced as "simply" a precise "mapping" of the chocolate bar around the surface of the orange scored for peeling, an inviting-looking chocolate orange. Though the child does not understand it yet, the adults are powerless in their foreknowledge that the young child they are hovering over will eventually die, and moreover that he will kill or be killed. In typical fashion, Amichai enhances the shocking perceptibility of this metaphorical collage through the use of *junction words*, polysemies that apply literally—in their different senses—to the domain of the tenor and of the vehicle: the verb *k-l-h* ("finish off") is used with reference to both chocolate and life.

The metapoetic message seems to be that ordinary language, not the poet's privileged sensibility, brings together the mundane and the philosophical, the autobiographical and the historical. Even more poignant is the use of *rimon yad,* a junction term that Amichai explicitly explains in his response to me, returning it to its literal meaning ("hand grenade" in Hebrew literally means "pomegranate of the hand"); thus, for one "repugnant" moment (Amichai's term!), the hand grenade becomes yet another food item on the list.

The larger context of these charged lines enhances the verisimilitude of using such radical figures of speech. The items in the catalogue are, for the most part, selected from the immediate experiential field of a child but seen from the perspective of the adult's present in post-1967 Israel. Thus the semantic distance between the vehicles in this catalogue of similes is "simply" a realistic expression of the simultaneity of these two points of view, the child's and the adult's, so common in the anti- or postmodernist genre of autobiography. In the end, the combination of surprise and simplicity, or the attempt to present the novel and the shocking as simple and readable, produces a uniquely cohesive metaphorical punch that is effective precisely because hand grenades and oranges or chocolate bars are *not* to be conflated. Amichai's metaphors, as we have seen in chapter 5, follow this same, three-step process, oscillating between ease and difficulty throughout his poetry: at first glance, a wild, often playfully violent conjoining of heterogeneous semantic material; then a sense that the combination is so natural that we begin to wonder why no one has made it before; and finally an often shocking realization of the ethical toll of conflating these dissimilar domains, and the insistence on maintaining the hyphen of distance between them.

*

Hovering on the borders of poetic affiliation, embracing modernist radicalism yet critiquing its elitism, Amichai seeks for the poet an in-between state that, like twilight time in Jewish mysticism (and the title of his 1983 book), is the Hour of Grace (*she'at ha-chesed*).

Notes

Introduction

1. ‏"מַה נִּשְׁאָר לוֹ לָאָדָם / אֶלָּא לְנַתֵּר עַל עַצְמוֹ בְּאֹשֶׁר / לִתְרֹם אֶת דָּמוֹ וְאֶת‏
‏כְּלָיוֹתָיו / לִתְרֹם אֶת לִבּוֹ וְאֶת נַפְשׁוֹ לַאֲחֵרִים / לִהְיוֹת שֶׁל אַחֵר, לִהְיוֹת‏
‏אַחֵר."‏

From "Deganya," *Gam ha-egrof haya pa'am yad ptucha ve-etzba'ot* (The Fist, Too,
Was Once the Palm of an Open Hand, and Fingers), 97. Translation mine, but I
had a lot of help: I wish to thank Maya Kronfeld, Margaret Larkin, and Ma'ayan
Sela for their input into the translation of this challenging passage. Given the
context of a poem whose title names a kibbutz, the difference between the Hebrew and English sense of "donate," *li-trom*, needs to be acknowledged up front.
Li-trom has much more of a sense of contributing to one's community than the
primarily financial connotation of the English word "donate." Fortunately, both
languages use the same term to describe blood and organ donors.

2. See, for example, "Ka-anashim ha-bodedim" ("Like the Lonely People") in
the title poem of this study, "Be-khol chumrat ha-rachamim" (To the Full Severity
of Compassion), in Amichai, *Shirim 1948–1962*, 219; translation mine. The post-
humously published Hebrew edition of his collected poetry, titled *Shirey Yehuda
Amichai* (*The Poetry of Yehuda Amichai*) (5 vols.) is a scanned boxed set replete
with errors. I have therefore cited in this book from earlier editions of his Hebrew poetry. See discussion of this poem in chapter 3. And see also the lines,
"metos ha-silon oseh shalom bi-mromav / aleynu ve-al kol **ha-ohavim** ba-stav," in
"Re'ach ha-benzin oleh be-api," *Shirim 1948–1962*, 22. In Stephen Mitchell's translation: "The army jet makes peace in the heavens / upon us and upon all *lovers*
in autumn," in "The Smell of Gasoline Ascends in My Nose," *Selected Poetry of
Yehuda Amichai*, 3 (henceforth, *Selected Poetry*); emphases added. See discussion
in chapters 5 and 6.

3. Amichai used this term on many occasions. See, for example, Amichai's statement in a 1992 interview with Lawrence Joseph in the *Paris Review*: "I've often
said that I consider myself a 'postcynical humanist.' Maybe now, after so much
horror, so many shattered ideals, we can start anew—now that we are all armored
for disappointment." "Yehuda Amichai: The Art of Poetry," 239. In an earlier in-

terview with me at his home in Jerusalem in the summer of 1986, Amichai explains: "The concept of postcynical humanism grew out of a series of lectures I've given this year." Throughout this book I cite from a series of interviews with Amichai I conducted in person between 1984 and 1996 at his house and at the King David Hotel in Jerusalem, at New York University (NYU) during his sabbatical there, and at our Berkeley home, as well as at the University of California, Berkeley.

4. Hebrew original in *Shirim 1948–1962*, 226–27; English translation by Stephen Mitchell in *Selected Poetry*, 40. For a close reading of this poem, see chapter 3.

5. A similar point is made by Sidra DeKoven Ezrahi about the reception of another poet of the Statehood Generation, Dan Pagis. See her "'Atem sho'alim keytzad ani kotev?': Dan Pagis ve-ha-proza shel ha-zikaron" ("You Ask How Do I Write?" Dan Pagis and the Prosaics of Memory). As I argue below, the same point can be made about other poets of the Statehood Generation as well. In this sense, my book is part of a larger project of reevaluating the historiography, reception, and appropriation of *dor ha-mdina* poetry.

6. See Althusser, "Ideology and Ideological State Apparatuses," 127–88.

7. See the poem "Ma lamadeti ba-milchamot" (What Have I Learned in the Wars), in Amichai, *Gam ha-egrof*, 15–16; translated by Barbara and Benjamin Harshav as "What Did I Learn in the Wars," in their *Yehuda Amichai: A Life of Poetry* (henceforth, *A Life of Poetry*), 412–12; and discussion of this principle in my article, "'Wisdom of Camouflage,'" 469–91.

8. Amichai, *Shirim 1948–1962*, 76–77; *Selected Poetry*, 12–13.

9. On becoming-other, see also Deleuze, *Essays Critical and Clinical*. An application of this theoretical framework to modern Hebrew literature was first proposed by Eyal Bassan in his Master's thesis, "Gnessin: Likrat sifrut minorit" (Gnessin: Toward a Minor Literature).

10. *Shirim 1948–1962*, 156. Translation mine. For Mitchell's translation, see *Selected Poetry*, 31.

11. "Shneynu be-yachad ve-khol echad le-chud" (The Two of Us Together and Each of Us Alone), *Shirim 1948–1962*, 13. Set to music by Hanan Yovel. Previously untranslated. Translation of this poem by Chana Bloch and me is forthcoming from Farrar, Straus & Giroux in Robert Alter, ed., *The Poetry of Yehuda Amichai*.

12. "Ani lo hayiti echad mi-sheshet ha-milyonim. u-ma meshekh chayay? patu'ach sagur patu'ach," #1, and "Ani navi shel ma she-haya," #8, in *Patu'ach sagur patu'ach*, 126, 47; "I Wasn't One of the Six Million: And What Is My Life Span? Open Closed Open," #6, and "I Foretell the Days of Yore," #7, in *Open Closed Open*, 7, 13.

13. *Rak shneynu nohav li-fney ha-machanot* (just the two of us will love before the [warring] camps), in "Shneynu be-yachad ve-khol echad le-chud"; see n. 11 above.

14. "Beynayim," in *Gam Ha-egrof*, 35; "Between," *Selected Poetry*, 173–74.

15. *Ha-zman* (Time), #29; *Selected Poetry*, 124.

16. Butler, *Excitable Speech*.

17. In "Menuchat kayitz u-milim," *Gam haegrof*, 65–66; "Summer Rest and Words," *A Life of Poetry*, 428–29.

18. Spivak, "The Politics of Translation," 179–200.

19. "Chatuna me'ucheret," in *Me-adam ata ve-el adam tashuv* (From Man Thou Art and Unto Man Shalt Thou Return), 75. "Late Marriage," in *Selected Poetry*, 163–64.

20. "Dorot ba-aretz (ne'um bi-ve'idat ha-sofrim)" ("Generations in the Land," speech at writers conference), *La-merchav*, May 3, 1968. Cited in Weissbrod, *Ba-yamim ha-acherim: tmurot ba-shira ha-ivrit beyn tasha'ch le-tashka'ch* (In Other Days: Shifts in Hebrew Poetry between 1948–1967), 327.

21. "Mas'ot Binyamin ha-acharon mi-Tudela" (Travels of the Last Benjamin of Tudela), in *Akhshav ba-ra'ash* (Now in the Earthquake), 109, 114; *Selected Poetry*, 67, 70.

22. *On the Margins of Modernism*.

23. But see Kurzweil, "Sipurey Yehuda Amichai" (The Stories of Yehuda Amichai); "He'arot le-lo me-akhshav lo mi-kan" (Remarks on *Not of This Time, Not of This Place*); 221–30, 246–57; Zach, "Sipurav ha-shiriyim shel Yehuda Amichai" (The Poetic Stories of Yehuda Amichai), 26–30; Sandbank, "Ha-ga'agu'im el ha-patu'ach" (The Longings for the Open), 94–101; Kramer, *Re'alism u-shvirato: Al mesaprim ivriyim mi-Gnessin ad Applefeld* (Realism and Its Decline: On Hebrew Writers from Gnessin to Applefeld), 197–202; Shaked, "Hoy dori ha-atzuv ve-ha-mukeh" (Oh, My Sad and Beaten Generation), 89–124; Friedman, "Olam ha-dimuyim ve-ha-tadmiyot shel Yehuda Amichai: Iyun be-ba-ru'ach ha-nora'a ha-zot" (Yehuda Amichai's World of Similes and Imagery: A Study of *The World Is a Room*), 311–12; Pelli, "Ha-nefesh ha-mefutzelet bi-mtzi'ut chatzuya le-achar ha-Shoah: Iyun ba-roman shel Yehuda Amichai" (The Divided Soul in a Split Post-Shoah Reality: A Study of Yehuda Amichai's Novel), 492, 509; Abramovitch-Ratner, "Beyn ha-mesaper le-veyn shiro: Le-sugiyat ha-korelatzya she-beyn shira le-veyn siporet" (Between the Storyteller and His Poem: The Problem of Correlation between Poetry and Prose), 227–46; Milner, *Ha-narativim shel sifrut ha-Shoah* (Narratives of Holocaust Literature). For a theoretically sophisticated recent study of the different poetics of Amichai's short fiction and novel, see Bassan, "Metaphorization vs. Interpellation."

24. Amichai, *Lo me-akhshav, lo mi-kan*. The English translation by Katz (*Not of This Time, Not of This Place*, published in 1968) unfortunately omits large sections of the Hebrew. In conversations with me, Amichai would often talk wistfully about the 200 pages or so of the original Hebrew manuscript that were cut by Dan Miron, the book's editor for Schocken at the time, and the fact that no other copy of the full manuscript has survived. Miron told me the manuscript is unfortunately no longer in his possession.

25. For Grossman's acknowledgment of his debt to Amichai in a different context, see chapter 1. Yoram Kaniuk is another antirealist exception to the documentary norm. It is interesting that Hebrew poetry never adhered to this criterion.

On the intricacies of "documentation as art" and the norm of "concentrationary realism," see Sidra DeKoven Ezrahi's pioneering study *By Words Alone: The Holocaust in Literature*.

26. Amichai's sharpest critique of the theological account is provided in the poem "After Auschwitz, No Theology" ("Acharey Auschwitz eyn te'ologya"), which starts by rewriting Adorno's famous dictum in order to blast—via the metonymies of white versus black smoke—both the Catholic Church's conduct during the Nazi genocide and the Jewish notion of a divinely chosen people, and leads up to the surreal and shockingly macabre assertion: "the numbers on the forearms / of the inmates of extermination / are the telephone numbers of God, / numbers that do not answer / and now are disconnected, one by one" (*Ha-misparim al amot asirey ha-hashmada / hem misperey ha-telefon shel ha-elohim / misparim she-eyn mehem tshuva / ve-akhshav hem menutakim, echad, echad*). In "Elim Mitchalfim, hatfilot nish'arot la-ad," #27, *Patu'ach sagur patu'ach*, 18–19; "Gods Change, Prayers Are Here to Stay," #23, *Open Closed Open*, 46–47. And see on this question Bloch and Kronfeld, "Amichai's Counter-Theology: Opening *Open Closed Open*."

27. Bernstein, *Foregone Conclusions: Against Apocalyptic History*, III, 125–26 ff.

28. Gold's biography, *Yehuda Amichai: The Making of Israel's National Poet*, is discussed critically below in the context of Amichai's rhetoric of autobiography.

29. The title of this section is a paraphrase of the title of Benjamin and Barbara Harshav's anthology of Amichai's poetry. See n. 7.

30. Alter, "Israel's Master Poet."

31. Felstiner, "Writing Zion: An Exchange between Two Great Poets." For comparative analyses of Amichai and Celan, see Eshel, "Eternal Present: Poetic Figuration and Cultural Memory in the Poetry of Yehuda Amichai, Dan Pagis, and Tuvia Rübner"; and Rokem, "German-Hebrew Encounters in the Poetry and Correspondence of Yehuda Amichai and Paul Celan," 97–127. The full extent of the literary dialogue between these two great Jewish poets merits further exploration and is the subject of a book-length study by Rokem (in preparation).

32. "Bo ty jesteś król a ja tylko książę." Published in David Weinfeld's Hebrew translation in *Ha'aretz*, May 13, 1994. The Hebrew version presents the poem as dedicated to Amichai on the occasion of his seventieth birthday. The English version does not mention this occasion. See Herbert, "To Yehuda Amichai," 489. For the full English text of the poem see chapter 4. Robert Alter uses a specifically Hebraic royal analogy when he suggests that "Yehuda Amichai . . . is the most widely translated Hebrew poet since King David." See his "The Untranslatable Amichai," 28. For a discussion of this point, see DeKoven Ezrahi, "Yehuda Amichai: paytan shel ha-yomyom" (Yehuda Amichai: Liturgical Poet of the Quotidian), 143–67.

33. From the blurb to *Selected Poetry*.

34. Amichai kept a record of his budding friendship with these poets in a notebook dated 1966–1967. Inter alia, Amichai refers to Ginsberg as "a cowardly Rasputin" and expresses surprise to discover that Berryman speaks some Hebrew and admires his poetry. See Amichai archives at the Beinecke Library, Box 43,

Folder 1486. The importance of Auden's poetry for Amichai's work predates this notebook. One of Amichai's rare essays about poetry dates from the mid-1950s and is titled "Auden kore mi-shirav ha-acharonim" (Auden Reads from His Latest Poems), *La-Merchav/Masa*, December 2, 1955. During his first visit to the United States in 1955, Amichai heard Auden read in New York. I am grateful to Hana Amichai for this information. On the complex genre of this essay and its role in theorizing influence in the poetry of Yehuda Amichai, see discussion in chapter 3, n. 63.

35. Simic and Strand, *Another Republic: 17 European and South American Writers*, 18–19.

36. "International Books of the Year," 8–14. Many sources erroneously date this to December 1998, though Hughes died in October of that year.

37. See, for example, Scharf Gold, *Yehuda Amichai*, 10; and Michael Karpin's film, *"Jerusalem Is Full of Used Jews": Yehuda Amichai's Poems of Jerusalem*, 2006; documentary film synopsis, http://www.michaelkarpin.com/Documentaries/Doc4/Michael_Karpin_Docs4.html.

38. *Poems by Yehuda Amichai*. See her biography by Koren and Negev, *Lover of Unreason: Assia Wevill, Sylvia Plath and Ted Hughes' Doomed Love*, esp. 166–69. Gutmann (Wevill's) biographers follow the accepted narrative that the translations were more Hughes' than hers, disregarding the fact that she was the one who, having lived in Israel, knew Hebrew. Furthermore, having been born in Germany and maintaining her love of German literature and art even after the Nazi genocide, like so many other *Yekes* (German-born Israelis), she was very much in tune with Amichai's modernist German models. Since the poetics of her translation seems quite different from that of Hughes's own poetry or of his subsequent translations of Amichai (with the poet's collaboration), I remain skeptical about this translation being primarily his. See Amichai's poem written shortly after her death, "Mota shel Assia G.," in *Ve-lo al menat li-zkor* (Not for the Sake of Remembering), 102; "The Death of Assia G.," in *A Life of Poetry*, 216. I found in the Amichai archives at Yale University's Beinecke Library thirteen pieces of correspondence directly between Assia Gutmann and Amichai, quite apart from his extensive correspondence with Hughes; these letters to and from Gutmann discuss specifics of the translation. See Box 5, Folder 210. It is true, however, that as coeditor and founder, with Daniel Weissbort, of the journal *Modern Poetry in Translation*, Hughes included some poems by Amichai (in Gutmann's translation!) in the very first issue (1965) and thus helped introduce him to the English-reading public.

39. Though Amichai would cringe at such a characterization. "No Greek tragedies," he told my collaborator Chana Bloch during her last visit with him, when she was visibly shaken by how ill he looked in his hospital bed.

40. I wish to thank Sasson Somekh and Hana Amichai for their help with the dating of this award.

41. And not, as Natan Zach claims, in 1978, after Zach supposedly rejected it for political reasons. Interviews that the poet's widow, Hana Amichai, conducted with the Israel Prize Committee unambiguously refute this account. See conversa-

tion with her by Na'ama Lensky in *Israel ha-yom*, April 8, 2011; and Hana Amichai's article "Al menat li-zkor: Yehuda Amichai, Natan Zach ve-uvdot she-ra'uy le-hatzig" (For the Sake of Remembering: Yehuda Amichai, Natan Zach, and Facts That Should be Presented), 27–33.

42. Interview conducted at the Amichais' home in Yemin Moshe, Jerusalem in summer 1986.

43. *Kmihat isha ba-ish*, in "Leshon ahava ve-te al shkedim kluyim," #1, in *Patu'ach sagur patu'ach*, 92; "The Language of Love and Tea with Roasted Almonds," # 1, *Open Closed Open*, 93.

44. In a series of three articles in *Ha'aretz* commemorating the fifth anniversary of the poet's death: "Yehuda Amichai: Mahapekhan im aba" (Yehuda Amichai: A Revolutionary with a Father).

45. Interview in Amichai's Bleecker Street apartment, NYU Housing, New York City, July 26, 1984.

46. See Amichai's description of the father's decision to leave Germany after he witnessed, as an honorary member of the Burial Society (the *chevra kadisha*), the deadly results of the brutal beatings of two rural Jews by Nazis. Interview with Arye Arad, "Pa'amonim mevasrim ra'ot" (Ominous Bells). A year earlier there was also an attack on the young Ludwig and his friend Ruth Hanover by Hitler Youth. Ruth, who had lost a leg in an accident and was wearing a prosthesis, was thrown to the ground together with Ludwig by three or four of the young thugs. "I heard the prosthesis make a metallic sound. That sound has remained with me more than all the books about Auschwitz," he said in an interview with his good friend, poet Dan Omer. See "Ba-aretz ha-lohetet ha-zot, milim tzrikhot li-hyot tzel" (In This Scorching Land, Words Must Provide Shade), 4.

47. See the essay by Hana Amichai that accompanies two diary pages of Amichai's about Little Ruth excerpted from the Beinecke Archives, "'Ruth ha-ktana hi Anna Frank pratit she-li'" ("Little Ruth Is My Own Private Anne Frank"), *Ha'aretz*, December 9, 2010. As Hana Amichai points out, the girl was called "Little Ruth" by family and friends to distinguish her from her stepmother's older daughter, also Ruth, and that is how she is often named in the poems.

48. *Patu'ach sagur patu'ach*, 126–29; *Open Closed Open*, 3–8.

49. *Patu'ach sagur patu'ach*, 20, 138–39; *Open Closed Open*, 31, 131–32.

50. A Russian genre that was very common in modern Hebrew poetry from the Enlightenment (Haskalah) on, but to which Amichai gives a decidedly unconventional avant-garde twist, blending it with the fictional Jewish travelogue and the modernist epic. See discussion in chapters 2 and 6.

51. *Selected Poetry*, 60–86. Mitchell translated only part of the *poema*. See *Akhshav ba-ra'ash*, 95–139. And see the excellent translation by Ruth Nevo of the entire *poema*, titled *Travels*.

52. In an unpublished paper.

53. Bernstein, *Foregone Conclusions*, 126.

54. See my analysis of Amichai's account of this discovery in chapter 3 as a par-

able on intertextual agency. For a different version of the same story, see Amichai's interview with Eilat Negev, "Ani navi ani she-chozer ba-tzohorayim ha-bayta" (I Am a Poor Prophet Who Returns Home for Lunch), in her *Sichot intimiyot* (Intimate Conversations), 226.

55. As he reports, for example, in his interview with Dan Omer. The poem, a sonnet, was published in the military newspaper *Ha-Gilgal* under the auspices of the British Mandate authorities on January 18, 1945. See interview with Omer, "Ba-aretz ha-lohetet ha-zot," 5. I thank Giddon Ticotsky for his astonishing help with archival work on Amichai, for locating this poem, and for sharing this and other findings with me. And see his article, "'Be-ozvi et chayay, karati bo, va-tov li': Yehuda Amichai ha-tza'ir kotev le-Leah Goldberg" ("'When I Left My Life, I'd Read It, and All Was Good': The Young Yehuda Amichai Writes to Leah Goldberg"), 216n2. Scharf Gold contradicts her own claim that Amichai hid the fact that he started writing and publishing before 1948 by acknowledging his account in this interview with Omer. See *Yehuda Amichai: The Making of Israel's National Poet* (2008, 158). Amichai clearly asserts in this interview that his first poem was published before the establishment of the state. As my book is going to press, Raquel Stepak has just published seven newly discovered poems by Amichai from 1943–1946. Stepak reveals that Amichai sent these poems to literary scholar Dov Sadan, who never responded, and they ended up in the file of "censored and uncensored documents" of the *Davar* newspaper, whose literary editor at the time was Sadan. As Stepak points out, the poems already bear the stylistic and thematic signature of Amichai's mature work. "Ma le-shirim shel Amichai u-le-tik ha-tzenzura shel iton 'Davar'" (What Are Amichai's Poems Doing in the *Davar* Newspaper's Censor File), *Ha'aretz*, September 9, 2014. I am grateful to Yishai Boyarin for bringing these discoveries to my attention.

56. See, for example, Scharf Gold, *Yehuda Amichai: The Making of Israel's National Poet*, 205–6ff. Hebraizing names was a culturally common move at the time, which cannot be divorced from its Zionist implications. But note that the particular names he chose, roughly translated as "Judea," pronounced *Yuda* in colloquial Hebrew (which makes it very close phonetically to the German for "Jew," *Jude*), and "my folk lives," emphasize the Jewish rather than the antidiasporic identification common in the naming practices of the period. Thus, his choice of "Yehuda Amichai" deviates from the then-fashionable "Canaanizing" trend in naming, which was explicitly associated with an erasure of the Jewish deterritorialized past (compare the pagan, ancient Near Eastern or martial Hebraized names of some of his fellow writers of the Statehood Generation: Tammuz, Keynan, Sivan, Ratosh, Oz, etc.). The name "Amichai" was invented (as a first name) by the grandfather of my late husband, Amichai Kronfeld, the teacher and composer Mordekhai Honig, who named his son Amichai Honig. The "original" Amichai became the first Eretz-Israeli pilot in the British Royal Air Force and was killed in action during World War II.

57. *Shirim 1948–1962*, 21; *A Life of Poetry*, 10.

58. In her Introduction to *Selected Poetry*, xii.

59. *Shirim 1948–1962*, 42-59. Only four sonnets were included in "We Loved Here," *Selected Poetry*, 8–9; and six sonnets were included in "Here We Loved," *A Life of Poetry*, 23–26.

60. "An Irish Airman Foresees His Death" starts: "I know that I shall meet my fate / Somewhere among the clouds above; / Those that I fight I do not hate; / Those that I guard I do not love." *Collected Poems of W. B. Yeats*, 145.

61. Bernstein, *Foregone Conclusions*, 126.

62. See Ticotsky, "'Be-ozvi et chayay, karati bo, va-tov li,'" 216.

63. See the attack by Tzemach in "Matzevet ve-shalakhta" (an untranslatable reference to Isa. 6:13); also included in his *Shti va-erev* (Woof and Warp), 216–35; and see my discussion in chapter 2. For Goldberg's favorable reviews see her "Gefen ha-yayin be-kharmey zarim" (A Wine Vine in Foreign Vineyards); and her "Ad barzel" (Unto Iron), *Al Ha-mishmar*. Both are included in Goldberg's collection of essays, *Ha-ometz le-chulin* (The Courage to be Secular), 220–27, 217–19.

64. *Likrat: Bita'on pnimi shel chug sofrim tze'irim* (Likrat: Internal Mouthpiece of a Young Writers' Circle), 9, 13.

65. *Akhshav u-va-yamim ha-acherim* (Now and in Other Days). Amos Levin, however, in his study of the group, gives the publication date as October 1954! The official notice disbanding *Likrat* is dated September 21, 1954. See Amos Levin, *Bli Kav* (No Line).

66. At our home in Berkeley, California in the spring of 1986. For a detailed discussion of this point, see chapter 6.

67. Box 35, Folder 1230. This 37-page seminar paper (for which Amichai received an "A") is erroneously indexed as Shirman's own work.

68. "'Kemo be-shir shel Shmuel Ha-Nagid': beyn Shmuel Ha-Nagid li-Yehuda Amichai" ("As in a Poem by Shmuel Ha-Nagid": Between Shmuel Ha-Nagid and Yehuda Amichai), 83–106. DeKoven Ezrahi discusses these connections in "Yehuda Amichai: paytan shel ha-yomyom." See also my discussion in chapter 3.

69. Interview in Amichai's Bleecker Street apartment, NYU Housing, New York City, July 26, 1984.

70. "Be-tokh ha-tapu'ach," *Me-adam ata ve-el adam tashuv*, 37; *Selected Poetry*, 164. For a close reading of this poem, see chapter 5.

71. Cited by Ari Brookman in his online essay, "Yehuda Amichai," Fall 2001, https://scholarblogs.emory.edu/postcolonialstudies/2014/06/09/amichai-yehuda/.

72. "Bni mitgayes," # 2, *Patu'ach sagur patu'ach*, 162; "My Son Was Drafted," # 2, *Open Closed Open*, 155.

73. See, e.g., "Chatuna me'ucheret," "imi meta be-Shavu'ot," and the section "Mot imi ve-ha-kravot ha-avudim al atid ha-yeladim" (My Mother's Death and the Hopeless Battles for the Children's Future), all in *Me-adam ata ve-el adam tashuv*, 75, 15–16, 7–21; and "Ba-yom bo nolda biti lo met af ish," in *Shalva Gdola: She'elot u-tshuvot* (A Great Tranquility: Questions and Answers), 44; and the section "Bni

mitgayes" in *Patu'ach sagur patu'ach*, 162–68; English versions: "Late Marriage," "My Mother Died on Shavuot," and "On the Day My Daughter Was Born No One Died" in *Selected Poetry*, 163–64, 161, 131–32, and the section "My Son Was Drafted" in *Open Closed Open*, 153–59.

74. Rosen was the first to explore this meditative elaboration of the personal in her comparison of Amichai and Ha-Nagid. See "'Kemo be-shir shel Shmuel Ha-Nagid.'"

75. See chapters 3 and 6.

76. In the unauthorized biography mentioned above, *Yehuda Amichai: The Making of Israel's National Poet*, Nili Scharf Gold argues that the fact that Amichai's poems do not directly document his German childhood "proves" that he was trying to hide his German origins so as to situate himself more effectively in his "desired role" as Israeli National Poet. First, Scharf Gold takes literally the autobiographical rhetorical impression his poetry creates, not noting that this is part of Amichai's progressive/feminist critique of the elitist formations of Anglo-American modernism. She then feels cheated by the fact that "his poems *seem to be* the personal diary of an authentic 'I' who is documenting his life in his writing" (10, emphasis added), but turn out to be neither diaries nor documents! She proceeds to accuse Amichai's poetry of hiding the poet's German past, and uses his metapoetic concept of "the wisdom of camouflage" as evidence of his sustained attempt to "suppress" his childhood. Quite apart from this claim being factually wrong (many poems do engage major biographical way-stations, including the German past!), it reveals her problematic presuppositions about the way lyrical poetry engages history, including personal history. As Robert Alter asks, in an uncharacteristically scathing review of Scharf Gold's book, is it the task of the poet to represent his life directly and in full? He adds: "Do we say that Wallace Stevens or T. S. Eliot suppressed his childhood because there is not much evidence of it in his poems?" "Only a Man," *New Republic*, December 31, 2008, http://www.newrepublic.com/article/books/only-man.

Chapter 1

1. Adorno, *Aesthetic Theory*, 40. Sections of this chapter were included in two joint essays with Chana Bloch. See Chana Bloch and Chana Kronfeld, "On Translating Amichai's *Open Closed Open*," *American Poetry Review* (March/April 2000): 15–19; and "Amichai's Counter-Theology: Opening *Open Closed Open*," *Judaism* 49, no. 2 (spring 2000): 152–67. I am grateful to Chana Bloch for her inspiring collaboration.

2. *Ahava amitit*, perhaps a reference to the title of Dahlia Ravikovitch's 1986 collection of poems, *True Love*, a collection that is often credited with Israeli poetry's return to the political. The Amichai archives at the Beinecke Library at Yale University are filled with fan mail from ordinary people for whom his poetry has become indispensable and who address him with intimacy and directness even when they don't know him personally. One Happy New Year's card points up, with

typical Israeli irony, his work's importance in a reality that seems heartless: "Know that your poems touch everyone's heart, even [the heart] of those who need a transplant." Box 13, Folder 629.

3. At the top right of the poster is the salon's name, which puns on the refrain of a famous Amichai poem, as discussed below. Under the hair model's Godiva-like photograph, the ad copy reads: "Midnight Salon, Tel Aviv's new 'in' trend, chez Ilan Rubin, Mondays 5pm–12am." As of summer 2012, the hair salon by this name is still in the same location.

4. *Shirim 1948–1962*, 110. Unfortunately, this influential poem is not included either in the Harshavs's or in Bloch's and Mitchell's translations of Amichai into English, perhaps because of the poem's heavy reliance on grammatical gender and rhyme. Chana Bloch and I translated it for Alter's forthcoming *The Poetry of Yehuda Amichai*. On the use of Samson's sheared hair as a metaphor for military induction qua emasculation, see discussion of "I Want to Die in My Bed" below. As Sidra DeKoven Ezrahi pointed out to me, it is possible that this ballad is in dialogue with Celan's "Todesfuge," first published in 1948. On Amichai's connection with Celan, see Introduction, n. 31.

5. In the rest of the poem, the third line of each stanza quotes one of the lovers in alternating order (but gives more text to the woman), expressing their struggle to maintain a connection; this struggle is thematized by the third lines rhyming across stanzas: In the first stanza, "*Eyneni shoma'at otkha ba-ra'ash ha-gover*" ("I can't hear [fem.] you [masc.] in the rising noise"); in the second stanza, "*Chazarti elayikh. Aval hayiti acher*" ("I came back to you [fem.]. But I was [a] changed [man]"); in the third stanza, "*Ha-geshem yored. Bo ha-bayta maher*" ("Rain is falling. Come [masc.] home right away"); and again the woman speaking in the fourth stanza, "*Kivanti she'oni. Matay ata chozer*" ("I set my watch. When are you [masc.] coming back?"). This rhyme scheme reinforces prosodically the destructive symbolic valence of the sheared hair, encapsulated by the last word of the refrain, *ha-katzer* (the short [hair]). Thus, the ad puns on the central rhythmic and thematic focalizing sound pattern of the poem. On focalizing sound patterns, see Harshav, *Explorations in Poetics*, 140–60.

Like many other poems by major Hebrew poets, this ballad gained in popularity when it was set to music and performed as a dramatic video clip on TV. Music by Moni Amarilio; adapted for television by me, under my former name, Chana Kaufman. This is just one example of the extent to which Hebrew culture of everyday life integrates canonical poetry into it, and can count on consumers' recognition of allusions to canonical texts both ancient and modern.

6. "Yehuda Amichai: Ha-mavet ha-yafe" (Yehuda Amichai: The Beautiful Death), *e-mago*, last modified October 5, 2005: 1, www.e-mago.co.il/e-magazine/amichai.html.

7. On the importance of intertextuality as a discursive feature of everyday life, see chapter 3.

8. *Shirim 1948–1962*, 76–77; *Selected Poetry*, 12–13.

9. See discussion in the context of Amichai's poetic philosophy in chapter 2.

10. "Amichai va-anachnu" (Amichai and Us), *Ha'aretz*, October 22, 1999.

11. See *Gam ha-egrof*, 65–66; *A Life of Poetry*, 428–29. See also my discussion in chapter 3.

12. From "Ve-hi tehilatekha," *Shirim 1948–1962*, 72; "And That Is Your Glory," *Selected Poetry*, 11. See discussion in chapters 3 and 4.

13. My research in the present study is limited to these two loci. The work on Amichai's reception/appropriation in the numerous other languages into which his poetry has been translated remains to be done.

14. I wish to thank Sidra DeKoven Ezrahi for this wording.

15. In fact, Amichai's work initially came under attack quite regularly by establishment critics for its lack of Zionist or Jewish "values." See the important summary of his early reception history in Tzvik, *Yehuda Amichai: Mivchar ma'amarey bikoret al yetzirato* (Yehuda Amichai: A Selection of Critical Essays on His Writings), especially her introduction: "Yetzirat Amichai bi-r'i ha-bikoret" (Amichai's Oeuvre in the Mirror of Its Criticism), 7–60.

16. A different version of this section of the present chapter appears in my article "Beyond Thematicism in the Historiography of Post-1948 Political Poetry," 180–96.

17. Rafi Man, "'Amichai hu meshorer metzuyan aval me'od mesukan'" ("Amichai Is an Excellent Poet, but Very Dangerous").

18. *Ha'aretz*, July 29, 1966, 10, 13.

19. Tsamir, *Be-shem ha-nof: le'umiyut, migdar ve-subyektiviyut ba-shira ha-yisre'elit bi-shnot ha-chamishim ve-ha-shishim* (In the Name of the Land: Nationalism, Subjectivity, and Gender in Israeli Poetry of the Statehood Generation).

20. In the sonnet cycle "Ahavnu kan" (We Loved Here; 1955), in *Shirim 1948–1962*, 48–49. Chana Bloch and I translated this poem for Alter's forthcoming *The Poetry of Yehuda Amichai*. When you add to these fifteen the numerous poems that invoke 1948 only intertextually or metaphorically, that presence is greater yet. On the problematics of using purely thematic criteria for the political in poetic verbal art, see below.

21. *Shirim 1948–1962*, 167–68; translation by Chana Bloch and me forthcoming in Alter, ed., *The Poetry of Yehuda Amichai*.

22. *Shirim 1948–1962*, 219; for a reading of the workings of intertextuality in this poem, see chapter 3.

23. See Benjamin, "Theses on the Philosophy of History," 253–64. Amichai may have also been familiar with this concept through the works of Bertolt Brecht, who was of course in dialogue with Benjamin. Brecht was a central model for the Israeli leftist intelligentsia and literary culture in particular during the 1950s and 60s. See the allusion to Benjamin in Brecht's acerbic statement: "Always / the victor writes the history of the vanquished," in his *The Trial of Lucullus*, 386. In notes I found in the Amichai Archives dated January 7, 1985, for a speech at an event titled "Israel '85: For Peace and Social Justice," Amichai describes himself as having "a bit of the psychology of a Brechtian army veteran" (*chayal meshuchrar*

Brechti; lit., a Brechtian liberated soldier), who is "suspicious of the establish-ment and [its] words." He adds in pencil: "even when it's a matter of wars that are called just" (*afilu be-milchamot ha-kruyot tzodkot*). Beinecke Library, Box 35, Folder 1216.

24. But these critiques, like Hamutal Tsamir's, for example, make an exception for the women poets of *dor ha-mdina*. See n. 19 above.

25. Characteristically, as soon as the Israeli parliament placed legislative restric-tions in 2011 on the use of the term *Nakba*, it gained a special cachet and became much more prevalent, especially in intellectual and academic circles.

26. *Shirim 1948–1962*, 274–77. The poem was first published in the inaugural issue of the avant-garde journal *Yokhani* 1 (1961):14–16 under the title "Shirim al kfar natush" ("Poems on an Abandoned Village").

27. See, esp., Boaz Arpali, *Ha-prachim ve-ha-agartal; shirat Amichai: mivne, mashmau't, po'etika* (The Flowers and the Urn: Amichai's Poetry 1948–1968), chap. 4, 85–100.

28. An important exception to the critical marginalization of this poem is Haggai Rogani's detailed analysis in his *Mul ha-kfar she-charav: Ha-Shira ha-ivrit ve-ha-sikhsukh ha-yehudi-aravi 1929–1967* (Facing the Ruined Village: Hebrew Poetry and the Jewish-Arab Conflict 1929–1967), 197–202. Boaz Arpali discusses the poem only briefly in terms of narrative point of view in his *Ha-Prachim ve-ha-agartal*, 155. Yochai Oppenheimer goes out of his way to deny the elegy's political protest be-cause, according to him, "an aesthetic point of view" and a poetic voice that main-tains a "distance" cannot be truly ethical or political. This is precisely the problem, as I argue below, with the reduction of the political to the thematic in discussions of poetry in general and of Amichai in particular. Suffice to say at this point that by Oppenheimer's criterion, all of Brecht's oeuvre should be denied political and ethical meaning since critical distance and the *Verfremdungseffekt* (the alienation effect) are two of its key principles. See Oppenheimer, *Ha-Zkhut ha-gdola lomar lo: Shira politit be-Israel* (The Great Right to Say No: Political Poetry in Israel), 274.

29. *Selected Poetry*, 42–43.

30. *Shirim 1948–1962*, 276. Emphasis added. Translation mine, CK. Mitchell's translation minimizes both the ethics of protest and the Shakespearean allusion by rendering the line as follows: "The rest is not simply silence. The rest is a screech"; *Selected Poetry*, 42. And see Rogani for an analysis of this allusion, as well as other radical allusions to Bialik and Ezekiel in the poem that help define the Palestinian experience in terms of the Jewish history of loss and displacement; *Mul ha-kfar she-charav*, 200–201.

31. *Shirim 1948–1962*, 277. This haunting presence brings to mind Celan's poetry in its depiction of the spectral existence of "that which was."

32. Ibid.

33. In an interview with Dalia Karpel, which she titled "Mekave le-Nobel" (Hoping for the Nobel Prize).

34. Probably the *Hamsin*, the hot, dry wind of the local summer. The first line of the poem describes the lovers drinking *yeyn tamuzim*, translated by Mitchell as "the wine of August" (*Selected Poetry*, 42), a translation that neutralizes the unusual use of the plural for the Hebrew month's name *Tammuz*. The odd plural revives the month-name's literal, ancient Near Eastern reference to the Sumerian God whose cyclical death in the heat of summer is mourned by women (see Ezekiel 8:14).

35. Although Mitchell's translation de-Arabizes the mourners, rendering *yelel nashim* as the more universal "the wailing of women," it acknowledges their status as professional keeners with the verb "hire." *Selected Poetry*, 42.

36. An extreme but symptomatic case in point is Nili Scharf Gold, who describes the poem as one of Amichai's greatest achievements only to deny its political valence. She starts her extensive discussion with an acknowledgment that "in the 1950s the word '*kefar*' (village) was almost exclusively used to describe Arab settlements—small Jewish communities were dubbed kibbutz, *moshav*, or *moshava*." Moreover, she admits that "Amichai's choice of the word *natush* recalls the term's post–War of Independence usage in the expression *rekhush natush*, which denoted property that had been abandoned by Arabs who had either escaped the country or been driven away" (*Yehuda Amichai: The Making of Israel's National Poet*, 315). All of this does not prevent Gold, however, from rejecting altogether the poem's analogy between Jewish and Palestinian loss, right after acknowledging that the poem's language asserts it. The rest of her reading simply erases the poem's ethical and political focus on the Palestinian *Nakba*, and argues instead, on the basis of some love letter by Amichai from 1948, that the abandoned village (*kfar*) is an evacuated Israeli kibbutz, where he stayed for a few days during a military assignment. Gold argues that Amichai's claim that the poem is about an abandoned Palestinian village, and not as she would have it about a kibbutz, forms part of his "attempt to prove his political correctness," boasting (her term!) "that in the 1950s he wrote 'anti-war poems'" (ibid.). See her detailed reading of the poem in ibid., 314–23.

37. Interview conducted at the Amichais' home in Yemin Moshe, Jerusalem in summer 1986.

38. Harshav, "On the Beginnings of Israeli Poetry and Yehuda Amichai's Quatrains: A Memoir," in *The Polyphony of Jewish Culture*, 178; "Hirhurim ishiyim al Amichai: ha-shira ve-ha-mdina" (Personal Reflections on Amichai: Poetry and State).

39. See, for example, Morris, *The Birth of the Palestinian Refugee Problem 1947–1949*, esp. 162–65, 183–85, 291–92.

40. Thus, for example, Mahmoud Darwish describes Amichai as "the greatest Hebrew poet" who supplied him with a much-needed counterpoint to the nationalist Hebrew poetry, which Israeli Palestinians of his generation were compelled to study in school. Darwish goes on to say that "Amichai is greatly admired among the Palestinian elite and among the Arab elite. They read him in English, though there are some Arabic translations." Interview with Adam Shatz, "A Love Story between an Arab Poet and His Land," 73. See also the series of interviews in

the Arabic-language magazine published in London, *al-Wasat*, 191–93. In a post-humously published Hebrew interview with his Israeli friend Yosef Algazi, Darwish says that when he reads "the Hebrew writers who exhibit excellence of form and content like the poets Yehuda Amichai and Dahlia Ravikovitch" he gets a "sort of injection of hope that there are people in the Land [*ba-aretz*; the Hebrew term for referring to Israel] who have preserved the ethical measure of understanding the Other." "Le-zikhro shel Mahmoud Darwish" (Mahmoud Darwish, in Memoriam), *Ha-gada ha-smalit: Bama bikortit le-chevra ve-tarbut* (The Left Bank: Critical Forum for Society and Culture), August 16, 2008, http://www.hagada.org.il/hagada/html/modules.php?name=News&file=print&sid=6108. For a comparison of the two poets that ignores, however, their intertextuality and real-life contacts, see Bernard-Donals, "'If I Forget Thee, O Jerusalem': The Poetry of Forgetful Memory in Palestine," in his *Forgetful Memory: Representations and Remembrance in the Wake of the Holocaust*, 41–55; see also Khaled Mattawa's Ph.D. dissertation for a description of Darwish's acknowledgment of his appreciation for Amichai's poetry, whom he read already while he was still living in Israel (until 1970); "When the Poet Is a Stranger: Poetry and Agency in Tagore, Walcott, and Darwish," 227. The complex intertextual dialogue between Darwish and Amichai is the subject of a current project I have embarked on in collaboration with my colleague, Arabic literature scholar Margaret Larkin. I am grateful to Kareem Abu-Zeid for his expert assistance with the research. Special thanks also to Sasson Somekh of Tel Aviv University and Abdul-Rahim Al-Shaikh of Birzeit University for their generous help.

41. *Ktivat pe'ula*, Laor's own term; in Laor, "Preda min ha-sifrut ha-ivrit" (Farewell to Hebrew Literature).

42. "*Shirey asham*," Dahlia Ravikovitch's term; in an interview with Dalia Karpel, "Od sefer: Ahava amitit" (Another Book: *True Love*). See also discussion in Ilana Szobel, "'La-chasof et ha-avel be-makom she-hu kayam': Edut, ashma ve-acharayut ba-shira ha-politit shel Ravikovitch" ("Unearthing Wrongdoing Wherever It Exists": Testimony, Guilt, and Responsibility in Ravikovitch's Political Poetry), in *Kitmey Or: Chamishim shnot bikoret u-mechkar al yetzirata shel Dahlia Ravikovitch* (Sparks of Light: Essays about Dahlia Ravikovitch's Oeuvre), 444–69.

43. Setter, "'Noshekh yonek mar'il lash motzetz madbik': al leshon ha-hitnagdut ha-ivrit be-shirato shel Yitzhak Laor" (On the Language of Resistance in the Poetry of Yitzhak Laor), 163–90.

44. Adorno, *Notes to Literature*, 43.

45. Adorno, *Aesthetic Theory*, 327.

46. In his "Notes on Kafka," in *Prisms*, 256. See discussion in the context of Kafka's modernism in Eysteinsson, *The Concept of Modernism*, 42. Eysteinsson was among the first critics to reclaim Adorno for a new reading of transnational modernism.

47. Kaufman, *Negative Romanticism*. See also his "Poetry after 'Poetry after Auschwitz,'" in *Art and Aesthetics after Adorno*, 116–81.

48. C. D. Blanton, *Epic Negation: The Dialectical Poetics of Late Modernism*, 10, 18.

49. *Shirim 1948–1962*, 82–83. Translation forthcoming in *The Poetry of Yehuda Amichai*.

50. This move may have been the model for David Grossman's much later re-writing of the figure of Samson as a diasporic weakling; see Grossman's psychological essay, *Dvash arayot: Sipur Shimshon*; English version appeared as *Lion's Honey: The Myth of Samson*.

51. Amichai's critique of military bureaucratese echoes the debate in the early years of the State over the constitution of the IDF as an established, professional army that replaced the 1948 folk militia, whose elite units were named the *Palmach*. This criticism, directed at Ben-Gurion, and expressed in numerous public debates was captured in the discourse of the 1950s by the question: "Lama perku et ha-Palmach?" (Why Did They Dismantle the *Palmach*?). See, for example, Gelber's study by that name.

52. *The Koren-Jerusalem Bible*, bilingual edition. All subsequent biblical quotations in the discussion of this poem are from this edition because it comes closest to echoing the Hebrew text of Joshua that Amichai alludes to in the poem in the context of 1948. Perhaps not coincidentally, Amichai's first published poem appeared in the paramilitary journal named for this very campaign by Joshua, *Ha-Gilgal*, in 1945. See Introduction, n. 55.

53. See Michal Arbell, "Abba Kovner: The Ritual Function of His Battle Missives (*Dapey krav*)." In a draft of the poem I found in the Amichai Archives at the Beinecke, one line reads: *Ani Shimshon hafukh* ("I am a reverse/upside-down Samson"), Box 30, Folder 1108. This may also be an allusion to a rhyming Yiddish put-down (known at the time to speakers of Hebrew as well) used to mock would-be heroes: *Shimshen ha-giber/mitn tokhes ariber* (Samson the Hero / with his ass upside-down).

54. Agamben, *The State of Exception*; and *Homo Sacer: Sovereign Power and Bare Life*. "To live in the lion's maw" (*li-chyot be-lo'a ha-arye*) was an idiomatic expression in 1950s and 60s Hebrew for life in Israel; the meaning is roughly equivalent to that of the English idiom "life in the shadow of a volcano." I thank Carol Redmount for her help on this point.

55. As Uri Sh. Cohen has pointed out to me, the Hebrew pun on *la-mut* ("to die") and *mitati* ("my bed," but also a homophone for "my death") reinforces this reading. Dying in one's bed is considered a blessing, a death brought about by the Kiss of God (*mot neshika*) that only the righteous attain.

56. See, e.g., Ravikovitch's poem "Kmo Rachel" ("Like Rachel"), in *Kol ha-shirim*, 155. *Hovering at a Low Altitude: The Collected Poetry of Dahlia Ravikovitch*, 156–57.

57. Eyal Bassan; in conversation.

58. Hirschfeld, "Ravikovitch acharey asor" (Ravikovitch after a Decade), *Yedi'ot Acharonot*, January 9, 1987. Hirschfeld himself would probably disagree with this statement today.

59. See, e.g., Avraham Blatt's review of the book, in which he accuses Amichai of not participating in "everybody's celebration of the reunification of Jerusalem," and engaging instead in "vaudevillian wise cracking" (*hitchakmut vodevilit*); "Shirat Amichai: Be-sha'ar Yerushalayim" (Amichai's Poetry: At the Gate of Jerusalem). See also Cahim Be'er's review in which he pans the book for not acknowledging the "perfection" produced by Jerusalem's "wholeness" (he is punning here on *shlemut*, which can have both meanings in addition to sharing a root with the city's biblical name, Shalem). He implies that this "failure" may be a result of a "refugee's labored learning" (*lemidato ha-yege'a shel palit*) how to love the city, as opposed to the natural, harmonious "rootedness" (*shorshiyut*) of the love of a native son (like himself, presumably; Be'er is a Jerusalem-born writer. To be fair, today Be'er himself would probably reject his youthful disdain for the "diasporic" Amichai). See his article "Akhshav ba-ra'ash li-Yehuda Amichai" in *Ha'aretz*. And compare Tzvia Ginor, "Ha-mapal ha-pnimi shel ha-milim" (The Internal Cascade of Words).

60. On the other hand, the Harshavs opt for "Now in the Din before the Silence," after the book's title poem, a poem of love in the shadow of war that takes a powerfully political turn in its final stanza. As far as I know, this turn has been completely ignored by Amichai scholars: *Ve-akhshav mukdam miday le-arkhe'ologya / u-me'uchar miday le-taken et ha-na'aseh* (183). While the Hebrew insists that the injustice that can no longer be mended is still present as ongoing acts (*ha-na'aseh*; "that which **is being done**"), and the Hebrew verb *le-taken* has obvious biblical and kabbalistic ethical valences, both the Harshavs and Mitchell neutralize the ethical and render what is too late to heal or mend as an impossible "repair" of a past or completed action. Compare "And now it's too early for archaeology / and too late to repair **what was done**," *A Life of Poetry*, 143; and "And now it's too early for archaeology / and too late to repair **what has been done**," *Selected Poetry*, 59. Emphases added.

61. As of this writing, Ravikovitch's letter is still misfiled in the Beinecke Archives among fan mail rather than correspondence with fellow writers. Box 10, Folder 450.

62. "Yehuda Amichai's Exilic Jerusalem," 222; emphasis his.

63. The poem was first published in the literary supplement of *Ha'aretz* on November 24, 1967. I am grateful to Eyal Bassan for his help with the dating. Included as the opening sequence of *Akhshav ba-ra'ash*, 9–20; *Selected Poetry*, 47–55. In addition to the book's title and the title poem discussed above, which suggest that 1967 was an earthquake and that it entailed an ethical breach that cannot be healed, other poems in this volume also express antiwar and anti-Occupation sentiments; among them: poems #7, 8, 12, 13, 17, 22 in the same sequence, *Jerusalem 1967*, 9–20 (*Selected Poetry*, 47–55); "Yaldi nodef shalom," 21 ("My Child

Wafts Peace," *A Life of Poetry*, 88); "Nora hu le-zahot," 28 (It's Terrible to Iden-
tify); "Shir shalom sheni," 35 (Second Peace Poem); "Machshavot le'umiyot," 38
("National Thoughts," *Selected Poetry*, 57); "Shir eres," 48–49 (Lullaby); "Tiyul
im isha," 80 (Trip with a Woman); "Ani akhshav shilo'ach," 83–84 (I Am Now the
Shilo'ach Stream); "Elegya," 92–93 (*Selected Poetry*, 58); sections of "Mas'ot Binyamin ha-acharon mi-Tudela," 130–33 ("Travels of the Last Benjamin of Tudela,"
Selected Poetry, 81–83); "Im eshkachekh yerushalayim," 171–72 ("If I Forget Thee,
Jerusalem," *Poems*, trans. Assia Gutmann, 52); "Rimu otanu," 184–85 ("They Lied
to Us," *A Life of Poetry*, 144; "They Fooled Us," trans. Bloch and Kronfeld, forthcoming in Alter, ed., *The Poetry of Yehuda Amichai*). Translations indicated whenever available.

64. Abramson, whose reading of the *Jerusalem 1967* poem sequence is the most
comprehensive available to date (see below), nevertheless rejects those interpretations that emphasize "the spokesman's need for expiation before the Arab . . .
bearing in mind that the encounter takes place on Yom Kippur." She argues instead that "[t]he Arab shopkeeper has been the inspiration for a day spent" in
silent "peaceful contemplation of his own past and memories of his father. . . . If
the speaker is indeed expiating a sin it is not against God but against himself and
his father." Abramson, *The Writing of Yehuda Amichai: A Thematic Approach*, 131;
and see Omer-Sherman, "Yehuda Amichai's Exilic Jerusalem," 223–27.

65. "Yehuda Amichai's Exilic Jerusalem," 225.

66. *Akhshav ba-ra'ash*, 12; *Selected Poetry*, 49. Emphases added.

67. *The Writing of Yehuda Amichai*, 130.

68. The fact that Amichai biographically stayed within the "national consensus" did not prevent him, nor in fact most other writers of the Statehood Generation, from consistently taking an anti-Occupation stance. Thus, for example, the
Amichai Archives at the Beinecke Library contain many notes for speeches Amichai gave at various peace rallies. Together with one such batch of notes I found
a letter to the Ministry of the Interior protesting the deportation of a female
Palestinian teacher alongside a flyer demanding an end to "offences against and
degradation of the non-Jewish inhabitants of Silwan" on the outskirts of Jerusalem. Box 35, Folder 1205.

69. "Mas'ot Binyamin ha-acharon mi-Tudela," *Akhshav ba-ra'ash*, 97–139;
"Travels of the Last Benjamin of Tudela," sections included in *Selected Poetry*,
60–86.

70. "Between Memory and History: Les Lieux de Mémoire," 7–24.

71. The first two, unlike Abramovitch's Benjamin, are historical figures: the
original Benjamin of Tudela (second half of the twelfth century), whose *Book of
Travels—from Northern Spain to the Holy Land and to Mesopotamia* became a
model for the Jewish travelogue; Benjamin the Second (1818–1864), a Romanian
explorer and writer who self-consciously "decided to emulate the Medieval traveler Benjamin of Tudela" and "styled himself Benjamin the Second." *Encyclopedia
Judaica*, 526–27, 535–58. This blurring of the fictional and the historical is enhanced

by the biographical fact that Amichai lived on Binyamin Mi-Tudela Street in Jerusalem in the 1960s.

72. For a discussion of this *poema* in the intertextual context of the Jewish travelogue, see Sidra DeKoven Ezrahi, *Booking Passage*, 51 ff.

73. See discussion in chapter 2.

74. Interview with author conducted in Amichai's Bleecker Street apartment in New York City, during his sabbatical at New York University, July 26, 1984.

75. *Mi yitneni malon* (Would I Had a Lodging Place). Untranslated.

76. See, e.g., his "Sovereignty and Melancholia: Israeli Poetry after 1948," 180–96.

77. François, *Open Secrets: The Literature of Uncounted Experience*; Eyal Bassan, "Fictions of the Non-Conflictual" (Ph.D. diss., University of California, Berkeley, forthcoming).

78. In conversation.

79. "Mas'ot Binyamin ha-acharon mi-Tudela" ("Travels of the Last Benjamin of Tudela"), *Akhshav ba-ra'ash*, 109, 114; *Selected Poetry*, 67, 70. See discussion in chapter 2.

80. From the end of section 44 through section 47; lines 821–909;130–33.

81. In a meeting of the committee of the Hebrew Writers Union with "a group of Arab writers" that included Mahmoud Darwish, on January 3, 1970 at Beyt Ha-sofer in Tel Aviv, toward the end of the War of Attrition (1967–1970), Amichai talked about the shattered hopes for a joint free and egalitarian society for Jews and Arabs in the Middle East. He asked: "Why has this hope been brought to naught? I allow myself to say, neither Jews nor Arabs are to blame for this but someone who has succeeded very well in stirring the pot and still continues to stir it: the two super-powers."

82. In his classic study *The Fantastic: A Structural Approach to a Literary Genre*.

83. *Akhshav ba-ra'ash*, 130–33; *Selected Poetry*, 81–82.

84. In conversations with me, as well as with Robert Alter and Chana Bloch, Amichai would often use these terms to refer to particular figures in Israel and the United States. In a 1995 interview with Laura Blumenthal, Amichai draws on one of his favorite activities, cooking, to elaborate a metaphor parodying sentimental poetry about his beloved city, Jerusalem, as well as to poke fun at cheap poetic exploitation of the Shoah. What may be hard for the American reader to stomach but is standard fare for macabre Israeli humor is the acerbic way he works the Shoah—zeugma-style—into the mix: "A recipe for a poem about Jerusalem: . . . . All you need is an olive tree, a few nuns, a muezzin screaming, a little bit of Holocaust, falafel and some Sabbath candles. . . . Put it together and cook, and you have a poem. It helps to have a dead grandfather in Poland." See her "Irreverent Poet of Jerusalem." Another, equally sarcastic version of the same "recipe," specifically directed at American poets, appeared in an interview he gave David Montenegro in 1991. See "Yehuda Amichai," in Montenegro's *Points of Departure: International Writers on Writing and Politics*, 219.

85. In *Me-adam ata ve-el adam tashuv*, 51–52; "From Man Thou Art and Unto Man Shalt Thou Return," in *Selected Poetry*, 165–66. Chana Bloch and I have modified here Bloch's translation in *The Selected Poetry* to give a more accurate, literal sense of the Hebrew.

86. A few years earlier, in a 1981 article, Shimon Sandbank summarized—in a tone typical of Hebrew sarcasm—the critical response in Israel to Amichai's late poetry: "To pan a new book . . . by Amichai has become a popular hobby. And indeed, the opportunities for panning seem to be readily available: first of all—an important, successful poet who has received numerous translations and become almost a synonym for Hebrew poetry abroad, and that is simply aggravating. Second—an astonishingly prolific poet . . . and third—and perhaps foremost—[a poet] who writes in his own language, always in his own language, and remains himself just out of spite." Originally published as an article titled "Li-She'elat ha-shir ha-kal" (On the Question of the Easy Poem). Reprinted in *Ha-shir ha-nakhon* (The True Poem), 92–97.

87. *Ani av zaken shomer bi-mkom ha-el ha-gadol / ha-mitgander la-netzach bi-ne'urav ha-nitzchiyim.* In *Me-adam ata ve-el adam tashuv*, 51. ("I'm an old father keeping watch in place of the great God / who struts around forever in his eternal youth." Translated by Chana Bloch and Chana Kronfeld.)

88. *Me-adam ata ve-el adam tashuv*, 51; Translated by Chana Bloch and Chana Kronfeld.

89. For a discussion of this section of the poem in terms of family sociology, see Wolf, *Beyond Anne Frank: Hidden Children and Postwar Families in Holland*, 340.

90. See especially her *Landscapes of Memory*; see also her *Still Alive*. Few critics have written on Amichai's poetry (rather than prose fiction) in the context of its engagement with the Shoah. Important exceptions are DeKoven Ezrahi, "From Auschwitz to Temple Mount: Binding and Unbinding the Israeli Narrative," 291–313; Guy, "Yehuda Amichai," in *Holocaust Literature: An Encyclopedia of Writers and Their Work*, 25. And see discussion of Guy in Omer-Sherman, "Yehuda Amichai's Exilic Jerusalem," 217.

91. See Zertal, *Ha-umah ve-ha-mavet* (Or Yehuda: Dvir, 2002), translated as *Israel's Holocaust and the Politics of Nationhood*, trans. Chaya Galai; and DeKoven Ezrahi, "From Auschwitz to Temple Mount: Binding and Unbinding the Israeli Narrative."

92. See, for example, Ezekiel 45:7–10; Jeremiah 4:9 ff.

93. *Me-adam ata ve-el adam tashuv*, 52; Translated by Chana Bloch and Chana Kronfeld.

94. For a similar apocalyptic image in the context of the Exodus from Egypt, see "Tanakh, Tanakh, itakh, itakh, u-midrashim acherim," #29, *Patu'ach sagur patu'ach*, 40; "The Bible and You, The Bible and You and Other Midrashim," #15, *Open Closed Open*, 25.

95. Ashmedai, King of Demons, is first mentioned in the apocryphal book of Tobias, Chapter 3 v. 8-17. For the midrash evoked by Amichai see *Tractate Gittin* 68b.

96. *Ha'aretz*, October 22, 1999.

97. http://www.confederationhouse.org/index.php?page=29. *Beit ha-konfed-eratzya*, Jerusalem, July 25, 2010.

98. Yehuda Amichai, *Me-achorey kol ze mistater osher gadol* (Behind All This a Great Happiness is Hiding), 7–30; see esp. section 4, 23–24; only partially translated as "Songs of Zion the Beautiful," *Selected Poetry*, 105–14, see esp. section 4. And see *Amen*, trans. Yehudi Amichai and Ted Hughes, 26–40 for a larger selection titled "Patriotic Songs." An early draft of the poem cycle that I found in the Amichai Archives at Yale's Beinecke Library bears the title "Hafgana neged ha-avel" (A Demonstration against the Injustice). Box 29, Folder 1042. Although Amichai was never a member of any political party and rarely gave political speeches, he did participate in protests against the Occupation. See, e.g., the Beinecke Archives for his 1991 speech at a demonstration against new settlements. Box 35, Folder 1205. Prof. Galit Hazan-Rokem of the Hebrew University asked Amichai in late summer of 2000 to read a poem in a rally for Jerusalem as the capital of two states. Amichai, who by then was terminally ill, couldn't attend but requested that she read his poem that starts: "Ani, alav ha-shalom, ani ha-chay omer alay ha-shalom / ani rotze shalom kvar akhshav be-odeni chay," *Patu'ach sagur patu'ach*, 114; "I, May I rest in peace—I, who am still living, say, / May I have peace in the rest of my life." *Open Closed Open*, 112.

99. *Me-achorey kol ze*, 8; *Selected Poetry*, 106.

100. The expression *yesh elohim* (There is a God), cited ironically here, is typically chanted by crowds of sports fans when their favorite team wins, and contains, therefore, a built-in deflation of the sacred that is part of Hebrew slang usage.

101. *Me-achorey kol ze*, 8; *Selected Poetry*, 107.

102. *Me-achorey kol ze*, 19. My translation, CK. For a different version, see *Amen*, 34. On Jerusalem as a site of political ambivalence and deterritorialized spiritual yearnings rather than nationalist-expansionist fulfillment, see DeKoven Ezrahi, *Booking Passage: Exile and Homecoming in the Modern Jewish Imagination*, esp. 20–23, 184–85, 234–36; and her "'Tziyon ha-lo tish'ali': Yerushalayim ke-metafora nashit" ("Zion, Dost Thou Not Ask?": Jerusalem as a Female Metaphor)," in *Rega shel huledet: Mechkarim be-sifrut ivrit u-ve-sifrut yiddish li-khvod Dan Miron* (A Moment of Birth: Studies in Hebrew and Yiddish Literature in Honor of Dan Miron), 674–85. English version published as "'To What Shall I Compare You?': Jerusalem as Ground Zero of the Hebrew Imagination." See also Arpali, "Yerushalayim chatranit: Yerushalayim ke-tzomet mefarek mitosim be-shirat Yehuda Amichai" (Subversive Jerusalem: Jerusalem as a Myth-Busting Juncture in the Poetry of Yehuda Amichai), 1–27.

103. *Yerushalayim ir namal al sfat ha-netzach*, "Yerushalayim 1967," #21, in *Akhshav ba-ra'ash*, 19; "Jerusalem is a port city on the shore of eternity," *Selected Poetry*, 54. See Dan Miron, "*Patu'ach sagur patu'ach*: Yehuda Amichai—ha-nusach ha-elegi" (*Open Closed Open*: Yehuda Amichai—the Elegiac Version). See also DeKoven Ezrahi, "Tziyon ha-lo tish'ali," 680–85; and her "'To What Shall I Compare You?': Jerusalem as Ground Zero of the Hebrew Imagination."

104. See, for example, http://www.jerusalem.muni.il/jer_sys/sr/postersr
out4/open_4.html. This site of official celebration, ironically enough, includes
the poem cycle "Jerusalem, Jerusalem, Why Jerusalem?" from *Open Closed Open*;
a cycle that demystifies and lampoons the city's chosenness. See also "Exploring
Jerusalem through the Poetry of Yehuda Amichai" among the recommended activities for *Yom Yerushalayim*, WUJS website/activities index.

105. *Yedi'ot acharonot*, May 18, 2007. The title is an allusion to Amichai's poem
cycle mentioned in n. 104 above.

106. Grinberg (1896–1981) was a great modernist poet and an unabashed ultranationalist, whose work, marginalized for decades alongside Jabotinsky's "Revisionist Zionism," became part of the official culture only after the right-wing
Likud Party first came to power, routing the Labor government in 1977.

107. Nationalist song made famous in the context of the 1967 war. Lyrics and
music: Naomi Shemer.

108. *Yedi'ot acharonot*, May 18, 2007.

109. "These I Shall Remember," *Kol Ha-neshama: Machzor la-yamim ha-
nora'im* (Kol haneshamah: Prayerbook for the Days of Awe), 899. The same poem
appears on the Israeli government website *Atar O'ach* as recommended reading
for the Memorial Day for Fallen IDF Soldiers. See www.owl.education.gov.il

110. *Me-achorey kol ze*, 26; *Selected Poetry*, #34, 113.

111. *Me-achorey kol ze*, 7–30 is the opening cycle, as noted above.

112. *Me-achorey kol ze*, 107; *Selected Poetry*, 8.

113. See Amichai's self-conscious reference to this form of "containment" in
poem #29 from the book *Ha-zman* (Time); "From the Book of Esther I Filtered
the Sediment," *Selected Poetry*, 124. See close reading in chapter 3.

114. *Kol Ha-neshama*, 899.

115. And compare the nearly identical translation by the Harshavs: "Let the
Garden-In-Memory-Of remember." *A Life of Poetry*, 241.

116. In accordance with rabbinic law, civilian dead are buried in a shroud without a coffin.

117. "Ro'e aravi mechapes gdi be-har Tziyon," in *Shalva gdola: She'elot u-tshuvot*, 14; "An Arab Shepherd Is Searching for His Goat on Mount Zion," *Selected
Poetry*, 138.

118. The same poem segment is posted as part of the reading for Tish'a Be-
Av, the mournful fast-day commemorating the destruction of the Temple, on the
website "Storahtelling." See http://www.storahtelling.org. Amichai's critique of
the conflation of religion and nationalism continues to be central to his poetics
through the 1980s and 1990s. In a commencement speech at the Hebrew University delivered on June 11, 1989, in the midst of the first Intifada, Amichai exhorts
his students to "think about the concept 'the altar of the homeland'" (*mizbach
ha-moledet*; part of the idiomatic expression for the fallen soldiers as sacrificed on
the altar of the homeland). He adds: "Our reality would demand of us true and
correct words. Whoever refers to 'the altar of a homeland' sins against [= distorts

the meaning of] the sacred religious concept 'altar' and also sins against the new human concept 'homeland'. . . . In blurring the distinction they turn life and words into a lie." Amichai Archives, Beinecke Library, Box 35, Folder 1206.

119. *Patu'ach sagur patu'ach*, 177; *Open Closed Open*, 171.

120. Amichai told me several times that he felt this book would be his last, even many months before his illness was diagnosed.

121. *Patu'ach sagur patu'ach*, 176; *Open Closed Open*, Poem #6, 171.

122. On this subject, see Hannah Naveh's pioneering study, *Bi-shvi ha-evel: ha-evel bi-r'i ha-sifrut ha-ivrit ha-chadasha* (Captives of Mourning: Mourning as Mirrored in Modern Hebrew Literature).

123. See Pierre Nora, "Between Memory and History: Les lieux de mémoire," 7–24. Strangely, in a self-exoticizing move, the Jewish Nora suggests that his theory of national sites of memory does not apply to the Jewish nation. See esp. 8, 16, 22.

124. The poet Haim Gouri's famous song "Bab El Wad," whose lyrics are sung in typical Palmach Generation fashion from the point of view of the fallen soldiers, alternates between first-person singular and plural, exhorting the site *Bab el Wad* itself to "remember our names forever." The song, which has attained a status that approaches that of a sacred national text, is as much in the intertextual background of Amichai's poem as the actual site and the (then) newly disclosed facts about its "maintenance."

125. At the time Israel held the dubious record for the most car crashes per capita in the world. A few years after the poem was published, the relics were vandalized during "iron robberies" (*shod barzel*) and sold for scrap metal, a fact that caused a national scandal. This is acknowledged, inter alia, on the Israeli government's conservation website, www.shimur.org, in an entry titled "The Armored Vehicles on the Road to Jerusalem" (Hebrew). The official Israeli website http://inature.info, in an entry titled "National Site: Armored Vehicles at Sha'ar Ha-gay" (Hebrew), states unequivocally that "the wrecks [*gruta'ot*] present at the site today are not the relics of the original armored vehicles but models [*dgamim*] placed [there] during the 1960s." The website further discloses that "during 2008–2009 the armored vehicles were anchored to the ground in the shape of a convoy (consisting of 7 vehicles), painted khaki, and night lighting was added." As of summer 2012, this was still the state of the site.

126. *Patu'ach sagur patu'ach*, 173; *Open Closed Open*, 169.

127. *Patu'ach sagur patu'ach*, 174; *Open Closed Open*, 169.

128. *Atar zikaron ve-atzma'ut shel misrad ha-chinukh, minhal tikshuv u-ma'arkhot meyda* (The site for memorialization and independence of the ministry of education, the administration for teleprocessing and data-systems). http://ramat-gan.info/pisgaRG/Resources/הזכרון+יום/ומועדים+חגים.html.

129. *Atar hantzacha le-chaleley ma'arkhot yisrael, Misrad ha-bitachon* (The eternal commemoration site for the fallen in Israel's campaigns, ministry of defense). http://www.izkor.gov.il/.

130. *Tekes ha-zikaron le-chaleley magav* (The memorial ceremony for fallen sol-

diers of the border patrol), 2008. The poem is cited here in a speech by the then Minister of Public Security Avi Dichter, former head of the Shin Bet, Israel's Security Service.

131. *Yom ha-zikaron le-chaleley ma'arkhot yisrael u-f'ulot eyva, ma'agar matal be-mikhlelet Kay Be'er Sheva* (The memorial day for the fallen in Israel's campaigns and hostilities, educational program database, KAY community college, Beer Sheba). http://kaye7.school.org.il/zikaron2.htm?findWords=עמיחי.

132. See his *Translation, Rewriting, and the Manipulation of Literary Fame*, esp. 59–72.

133. Harshav, *Meaning of Yiddish*; see esp. "The Semiotics of Yiddish Communication," 89–118.

134. In conversation.

135. Miron, *Ha-tzad ha-afel bi-tzchoko shel Shalom Aleykhem* (The Dark Side of Sholem Aleichem's Laughter).

136. I owe this point to Sidra DeKoven-Ezrahi.

137. Indeed, study groups devoted to Amichai's poetry are quite common in such congregations, from North Carolina to California. A full survey of the role of Amichai's poetry—and of Israeli poetry in general—in the ritual and textual study practices of diverse Jewish American congregations is beyond my scope here. Let me just say that in interviewing rabbis and congregation members on this topic I have encountered a diversity of positions, including a reform rabbi's (accurate!) statement that "Amichai is too blasphemous to be included in the liturgy," although he described himself as a fan of his poetry. Nevertheless, in my own experience and unscientific survey—which are clearly not statistically valid—the norm remains the uncritical, decontextualizing inclusion of Amichai in the Jewish American discourse of religiosity and nationalism (exemplified here by the Reconstructionist *Machzor* and the actress's pathos).

138. *Shirim 1948–1962*, 69–70; *A Life of Poetry*, 31; *Patu'ach sagur patu'ach*, 8; *Open Closed Open*, 41. See discussion of these heretical poems in chapters 2, 5, and 6, as well as below.

139. On this topic, see Bloch and Kronfeld, "Amichai's Counter-Theology: Opening," *Open Closed Open*, 152–67, on which my discussion here draws heavily.

140. *Patu'ach sagur patu'ach*, 8; *Open Closed Open*, 41.

141. Following George Lakoff, I use caps when referring to a metaphorical system rather than to any of its specific entailments. See Lakoff and Johnson, *Metaphors We Live By*; Lakoff and Turner, *More Than Cool Reason*.

142. This also echoes a sarcastic chant popular in Israeli socialist circles in the years after the great disillusionment with Stalin and the Soviet Union: *Ima Rusya, aba Stalin, ha-levay ve-hayinu yetomim* ("Mother Russia, Father Stalin, we wish we were orphans").

143. *Patu'ach sagur patu'ach*, 6; *Open Closed Open*, 39.

144. *Akhshav ba-ra'ash*, 160. See discussion of this ambiguity in chapter 2.

145. In an undated speech draft in support of the separation of "church" and

state that I found in the Amichai Archives at the Beinecke Library, Amichai writes: "I want to express here the outcry of the true Judaism as I saw it in my parents' home. That was an Orthodox Judaism that observed every commandment but was open to an all-human culture (*ha-tarbut ha-klal-enoshit*) and saw no contradiction between the two. . . . An extremist, uncompromising minority cannot distort the image of Judaism, its values and its vision. . . . And I am sure there is a majority among religious and observant Jews who think that a separation of religion and state would be a blessing both to our religion and to our state." Box 13, Folder 629.

146. *Polyphony of Jewish Culture*, 178.

147. *Patu'ach sagur patu'ach*, 92; *Open Closed Open*, 93. See further discussion in chapters 4 and 6.

148. See, e.g., the untranslatable "Sonet ha-binyanim" (The Verb-Pattern Sonnet), *Shirim 1948–62*, 64–65; I discuss this poem in chapter 6. See also the poem "Isha meduyeket," in *She'at ha-chesed*, 112; "A Precise Woman," *Selected Poetry*, 154.

149. At the King David Hotel in Jerusalem, July 7, 1995. As Michael Gluzman has argued in one of the few favorable reviews of *Open Closed Open* in the Israeli press, there is actually something quite radical in the meditation on the Hebrew grammar that serves as the point of departure for this poem, and for other poems in this book: "Amichai was always interested in the internal 'order' of language, in the potential of grammar to be meaningful. . . . But in *Open Closed Open* his interest in grammar received a gendered dimension." Gluzman, "Mi-shirey ha-navi he-ani" (From the Poems of the Impoverished Prophet). Dan Pagis is the other member of the Statehood Generation poets for whom grammar is a consistent source of metapoetic and ethical reflection. The "gender bending" evinced in this poem seems to be in dialogue with the poetry of Yona Wallach (1944–1985).

Chapter 2

1.   "בֵּינַיִם עֵינַיִם בֵּין עֵרוּת לְשֵׁנָה. / בֵּינַיִם עַרְבַּיִם, לֹא יוֹם, לֹא לַיְלָה."

Chapter title and epigraph from "Beynayim," *Gam ha-egrof*, 35; "Between," *Selected Poetry*, 173. This chapter has benefited greatly from input by Maya Kronfeld.

2. In an interview with me at his home in Jerusalem (summer 1986). From about the mid-1980s on, Amichai used this label to characterize his poetic worldview (*hashkafati ha-shirit*). See also his notes for a commencement speech at the Hebrew University, Jerusalem, June 11, 1989, Amichai Archives, Beinecke Library, Box 35, Folder 1206.

3. In the same 1986 interview with me.

4. In the poem "Ma lamadeti ba-milchamot," in *Gam ha-egrof*, 15–16; translated as "What Did I Learn in the Wars," *A Life of Poetry*, 411–12. Below I discuss this poem, which I translate as "What Have I Learned in the Wars." I first explored Amichai's "poetics of camouflage" in my article "'The Wisdom of Camouflage': Between Rhetoric and Philosophy in Amichai's Poetic System." The present chapter expands on points I made there. Nili Scharf Gold, in her biography of Amichai, appropriates this metapoetic term to name Amichai's purported concealment of

his German past. The poetics of camouflage is one of the central concepts in her book. See, for example, *Yehuda Amichai: The Making of Israel's National Poet*, 5–25, 47–56, 313–23. As I show below, "What Have I Learned in the Wars" is a poem about the dangers of flaunting the splendors of the poet's artistry and the need to keep his verbal virtuosity sheltered under the cover of ordinary language. The poem has absolutely nothing to do with Germany or with Amichai's European childhood, as Scharf Gold claims.

5. "Lo ka-brosh," in *Shirim 1948–1962*, 76–77; *Selected Poetry*, 12–13. See close reading below.

6. Sandbank, "Amichai: ha-mischak ve-ha-shefa," in his *Ha-shir ha-nakhon*, 81–91. See also his "Li-she'elat ha-shir ha-kal," ibid., 92–97. Unlike the critics who were later to use Amichai's own statements about the poet as Everyman to pin facile labels on him, Sandbank presents a descriptive argument based on careful and nuanced readings of the poems. Interestingly, some of the most flippant perceptions of Amichai as a playful, easy poet originate with members of his own poetic generation. For example, David Avidan (1934–1995), Amichai's fellow member of the Statehood Generation group of poets of the 1950s and 60s, referred years later to Amichai as a "Santa Claus, a poetic toy manufacturer who markets figurative equations made especially for young or even very young audiences, fit almost for any need or occasion" (*Yedi'ot acharonot*, November 22, 1985). Abandoning any semblance of critical impartiality, Amichai's contemporary, the poet and scholar Arye Sachs (1932–1992), declared also in 1985 in an article in *Ha'aretz* (November 29), that "Amichai's love for sweets is evident in his poetry . . . both in its similes and in the emotional fabric of his language." Sachs goes on to say that one of the most "charming" properties of Amichai's verse is "its feather-light humor." He claims further that Amichai necessarily fails whenever he tries to deal with any real *koshi*, invoking here all three senses of the term in Hebrew: difficulty, hardness, and weightiness. According to Sachs, any apparent conceptual difficulty in Amichai's poetry is ultimately revealed to be quite easy: heavy burdens are actually quite light, and hard human pain is in fact quite soft. Although Avidan and Sachs clearly mean their remarks to diminish the stature of their internationally successful contemporary (the 1980s marked in many ways Amichai's coming into his own as a renowned poet abroad), they may have inadvertently stumbled upon some of the central principles of his poetic system.

7. Sandbank, "Amichai: ha-mischak ve-ha-shefa," in his *Ha-shir ha-nakhon*, 83.

8. Most notably, the late Boaz Arpali in his book *Ha-prachim ve-ha-agartal*; see also his "Amichai, Yehuda" (Hebrew) in *Encyclopaedia Hebraica*, 907–8. Although I disagree with Arpali on some major points, I have learned a lot from his research on Amichai's early work. I am also indebted to Robert Alter, who argues in an unpublished lecture titled "Mischak ve-chazon be-shirato shel Yehuda Amichai" (Play and Vision in the Poetry of Yehuda Amichai), delivered at the Jewish Theological Seminary on October 28, 1979, that the visionary dimension is central to Amichai's poetry and, moreover, that the visionary is intimately linked to the

playful in his oeuvre. Other critics who attempt to describe—with varying degrees of rigor—Amichai's poetic and philosophical system include Hillel Barzel, especially in his books *Meshorerim bi-gdulatam* (Poets in Their Greatness), 353–77; and *Meshorerey bsora* (Poets of Mission), 318–33. The section on Amichai from the latter book is also included in *Yehuda Amichai: mivchar ma'amarey bikoret al yetzirato* (Yehuda Amichai: A Selection of Critical Essays on His Writing), ed. Yehudit Tzvik, 115–37. In the same volume Tzvik herself provides an important if all-too-brief account of Amichai's philosophy of time; ibid., 95–104. Gavriel Moked, who hosted both literally and metaphorically the Tel Aviv branch of the Statehood Generation poets, as well as their younger successors, sketches out what he refers to as Amichai's "humanist, nausea-free existentialism" in his book *Arba'a meshorerim* (Four Poets), 32–40.

9. Sandbank, "*Nof ha-nefesh: Rilke, Auden, Amichai*" (The Landscape of the Mind: Rilke, Auden, Amichai), in *Shtey brekhot ba-ya'ar* (Two Pools in the Forest), 196. Sandbank's statements (see also n. 6 above) have become, since their initial publication in the late 1960s and early 1970s, the hallmark of critical opinion on the subject. For a history of the reception of Sandbank's views see Tzvik's survey, "Yetzirat Amichai bi-r'i ha-bikoret" (Amichai's Work in the Mirror of Its Critics), in her *Yehuda Amichai: mivchar ma'amarey bikoret al yetzirato*; see esp. 30, 42, 50–52.

10. Abramson, *Writing of Yehuda Amichai*, 225, 227, and jacket blurb.

11. Emphasis added. Joseph Lichtenboym (1963), quoted in Tzvik, "Yetzirat Amichai bi-r'i ha-bikoret," 23. See also the prophetic wrath of Shlomo Tzemach's famous essay "Matzevet ve-shalakhta" (an untranslatable reference to Isa. 6:13), originally published in *Davar*, June 28, 1955; included in his *Shti va-erev*, 216–35; also in *Yehuda Amichai: mivchar ma'amarey bikoret al yetzirato*, 70–78. For a more ambivalent evaluation, see Kurzweil's article, "Shira otobiyografit 'ba-midbar ha-gadol'" (Autobiographical Poetry in "the Big Desert"), included in ibid., 79–94. Of the early reviews not included in Tzvik's anthology, the most typical treatments are by David Aran in two articles in the socialist paper *Al ha-mishmar* (June 16, 1961 and June 23, 1961); and, most importantly, by Gid'on Katznelson in his reviews collected in the book *Le'an hem holkhim?* (Where Are They Going?); and by Adir Cohen's reviews, collected in *Ha-shira ha-ivrit ha-tze'ira* (Young Hebrew poetry).

12. See "Ve-kir ha-ne'umim akhshav nivka" (And the Wall of Speechifying Has Now Been Breached). This is the closing (untranslated) sonnet in the magnificent sonnet-cycle "We Loved Here," Ahavnu kan, sonnet 23, in *Shirim 1948–1962*, 58–59. Breaching the wall of ideological verbiage is seen in the poem as a precondition for peace, described as the child's finger crossing national borders on the map because for the child these geopolitical divisions are nothing but "merry patches of color" (*ktamim alizim*).

13. Menachem Ben, "'Ki kol ha-adam edim'" (For All Man Is Vapors), *Yedi'ot acharonot*, January 3, 1986; "flattening of the world" is perhaps a snide reference to the end of the fourth poem from "Shirey eretz tziyon yerushalayim" (Songs of Zion the Beautiful) in *Me-achorey kol ze*, 8, the very poem whose appropria-

tions in Israel and the United States I describe in chapter 1. To recap, this section of the poem cycle, all of which was published in the wake of the 1973 Yom Kippur War, starts with the declaration, *eyn li ma lomar al ha-milchama / eyn li ma le-hosif, ani mitbayesh* ("I have nothing to say about the war, nothing / to add. I'm ashamed"); it ends with a series of sarcastic mock-affirmations:

> And because of the war I repeat,
> for the sake of a last, simple sweetness:
> The sun goes around the earth, yes.
> The earth is flat as a lost drifting plank, yes.
> There's a God in Heaven, yes.

(*Selected Poetry*, 106–7). Ben's review is thus a veiled attack on Amichai's antiwar poetry. And see Natan Zach's emphatic response in his column "Daf chadash" (New Page), in *Ha-olam ha-ze*, March 14, 1986. Zach's response reveals the generational nature of the new nativist/nationalist attacks on Amichai in the 1970s and 80s. As a self-appointed spokesperson for the Statehood Generation poets, Zach correctly identifies Ben and his contemporaries' criticism of Amichai as an attack on the decidedly leftist leanings of the major Statehood poets (in addition to Amichai and Zach, also Dahlia Ravikovitch, David Avidan, and Moshe Dor, all on the dovish margins of the "national consensus").

14. Ortzion Bartana, "Pninim ba-efer" (Pearls in the Ashes), *Ma'ariv*, November 23, 1989. Ironically, these remarks are part of an article in which Bartana begins to recant some of his earlier total rejection of Amichai's poetry and thought. This recanting reaches a zenith in the immediate aftermath of Amichai's death some eleven years later, when Bartana appropriates Amichai—as most mainstream Israeli institutions had done by then (see chapter 1)—as a spokesperson for Bartana's own nationalist causes, and devotes an article in a settlers' journal to mourning the loss of our "last national poet" (*ha-meshorer ha-le'umi ha-acharon*). See his article "Mahapekhan simpati: Yehuda Amichai—sikum beynayim" (A Likable Revolutionary: Yehuda Amichai—An Interim Summary). This journal is published by the West Bank settlers' "Ariel Center for Policy." For earlier unmitigated attacks by Bartana on Amichai and his generation in the name of some missed opportunities for creating a truly nationalist/nativist poetic tradition, see his article, "Amichai: She'elot u-tshuvot" (Amichai: Questions and Answers), *Yedi'ot acharonot*, April 25, 1980; and his books *La-vo cheshbon* (Settling Accounts) and *Zehirut, sifrut eretz-Yisre'elit* (Watch Out, Land of Israel Literature). For an interesting analysis of the ideological roots of Bartana's attack on Amichai and other Israeli writers, see Balaban's "Ha-mayim ve-ha-yayin" (The Water and the Wine). Bartana bases many of his conclusions on a master's thesis by Amos Levin, published in book form under the title *Bli kav* (No Line/Direction). Levin's study provides a sociocritical account of the origins of Statehood Generation poetry in the *Likrat* group of the early 1950s, of which Amichai was a founding though marginal member. For more on Amichai's ambivalent affiliation with *Likrat*, see chapter 6.

15. On the notion of a proleptic paragon, see my *On the Margins of Modernism*, 159–60, 172–76, 184–88.

16. While I don't agree with Laor's conflation of Amichai the person and the poet as far as politics are concerned, Laor's nuanced account of Amichai's poetics is exemplary. See Laor, *Anu kotvim otakh moledet* (Narratives with No Natives; English title, which is not a literal translation of the Hebrew, is supplied by the author on the jacket), 192–223; and see also Laor's retrospective assessments of Amichai in "Ma she-rechem em mavti'ach ve-elohim lo" (What a Mother's Womb Promises and God Doesn't), *Ha'aretz*, August 6, 2004; and the second article in the same series, "'Ha-shiva ha-nitzchit' shel Yehuda Amichai" (Yehuda Amichai's "Eternal Return"), *Ha'aretz*, August 13, 2004. In the latter Laor declares: "No educational system can truly destroy this abundance or make it homogenous."

17. See for example Ronny Someck, "Be-derekh he-afar, be-shira shel tzavaron kachol" (On the Dirt Road, in Blue-Collar Poetry), September 22, 2000, www .ynet.co.il/articles/1,7340,L-130088,FF.html. Shammas uses lines from a politically charged poem by Amichai as the epigraph for a chapter in his novel *Arabeskot* (Tel Aviv: Am Oved, 1986), 67; *Arabesques* (New York: Harper and Row, 1988), 75.

18. Arpali, *Ha-prachim ve-ha-agartal*, 136.

19. Tzvik, "*Yetzirat Amichai bi-r'i ha-bikoret*," 50. "The man with the shopping bags" refers to the poem "Tayarim" ("Tourists") in *Shalva gdola: She'elot u-tshuvot*, 80; *Selected Poetry*, 137.

20. "Pney ha-sifrut nimchatzot bi-r'i" (The Face of Literature Squashed in the Mirror).

21. See, for example, Naomi Brenner's discussion of the importance of the poetic persona in Hebrew and Yiddish literary traditions in her PhD. dissertation, "Authorial Fiction: Literary and Public Personas in Modern Hebrew and Yiddish Literature." On the persona in Yehuda Amichai's poetry see also Feldman, "The Metaphor of the Persona," in *The Experienced Soul: Studies in Amichai*, 71–75.

22. In an interview with me in his office at New York University, July 27, 1984.

23. Amichai used this expression quite often in conversation to refer to self-important, dominant literary figures, about whom he always had some choice words. In a somewhat different context this expression, which echoes the Russian Formalists' critique of bourgeois literary history, is quoted in Robert Alter's *New York Times Magazine* article, "Israel's Master Poet."

24. *Mefulag* is a highly marked ambiguous adjective, meaning both "branching out" (like a river) and physically "divided"; the noun *peleg* means "creek," whereas *peleg guf* means "body part."

25. Yehuda Amichai, *Dorot ba-aretz* (Generations in the Land) (lecture, Writers' Association Conference, 1968); discussed in Tzvik, "Yetzirat Amichai bi-r'i ha-bikoret," 8, 52. The speech was published in the newspaper *La-merchav* on May 3, 1968, in the wake of the 1967 war and the nationalist euphoria that accompanied it. This adds to the political poignancy of the words Amichai chooses here:

the loaded metaphor of a "double agent" (literally, a double spy) cannot but be read as politically subversive. Amichai describes himself as a transitional figure on many other occasions. Most interestingly, this liminal position has allowed him to be conceived by at least one young poet, Eyal Meged, during the height of the attacks on Amichai, as a herald of the postmodernism of the 1980s and 90s. Meged singles out Amichai's self-consciously fictional uses of autobiography and his refusal to abdicate political poetry even in the early days of the supposedly "apolitical," individualist poetry of the Statehood Generation. See Meged, "Yehuda Amichai: Li-krat ha-sof ata na'ase yoter pashut" (Yehuda Amichai: Towards the End You Become Simpler).

26. Amichai's post-1967 speech also calls into question the historiographic debate between Dan Miron and Yitzhak Laor as to whether Amichai is a member of the 1948 generation (*dor ha-palmach/dor ba-aretz*) or the Statehood Generation (*dor ha-mdina*) and offers a third possibility that embraces a partial affiliation with both, and a commitment to neither. See Miron, *Mul ha-ach ha-shotek: Iyunim be-shirat milchemet ha-atzma'ut* (Facing the Silent Brother: Studies in the Poetry of the War of Independence), 273–313; and Laor, *Anu kotvim otakh moledet*, 192–223.

27. Bargad, "Children and Lovers: On Yehuda Amichai's Poetic Works," 50.

28. This was recognized early on by Roseline Intrater; see her "Yehuda Amichai and the Interrelatedness of All Things," 39–42.

29. *Shirim 1948–1962*, 69–70. This translation is published here for the first time. The tendency to read this poem—including the position of the speaker in it—as validating some vague sense of Jewish religiosity simply because it cites a prayer is typical of the uncritical reception of Amichai as a poet of pious faith by some of his American Jewish readers. For a sober reassessment of the poem's heretical tone, see Bloch, "Yehuda Amichai's 'O God Full of Mercy,'" in *Into English: An Anthology of Multiple Translations* (forthcoming).

30. Forthcoming in *Into English* (see n. 29 above). For different translations see *A Life of Poetry*, 31; and Alter, ed., *The Poetry of Yehuda Amichai*.

31. Geldman, "'Tacharuyot nora'ot'" ("Terrible Competitions"), 121–22, 123.

32. The paronomasia empties out the prayer because in terms of logical structure it turns an affirmation into a condition, and in terms of semantics it turns an attribute into a lack. I thank Maya Kronfeld for this observation.

33. A classic example of this type of poem is "Bikur malkat shva" in *Shirim 1948–1962*, 111–19; "The Visit of the Queen of Sheba," *Selected Poetry*, 21–27. On the relation of playful and visionary poetics in this central poem, see Alter, "*Mischak ve-chazon*," 1–6.

34. At his home in Yemin Moshe, Jerusalem, summer 1986.

35. Quoted here from the interview with Eyal Meged, "Yehuda Amichai: Li-krat ha-sof ata na'ase yoter pashut." Amichai also said much the same to me in the 1986 interview cited above, and to Hillit Yeshurun in an interview titled "Yehuda Amichai: Eykh ata magi'a la-shir?" (Yehuda Amichai: How Do You Get to the Poem?).

36. Interview with Michael Miro, titled "Ktiva hi pri atzlanut nifla'a" (Writing Is the Fruit of a Wondrous Laziness).

37. See *Shirim 1948–1962*, 25–26; *Ve-lo al menat li-zkor* 55, 102, 106; *Patu'ach sagur patu'ach*, 135–36. English versions in *Selected Poetry*, 5–6; *The Early Books of Yehuda Amichai*, 53; and *Open Closed Open*, 130, respectively. The poem "Leah Goldberg Died" remains untranslated, as far as I know.

38. Barzel, "Yehuda Amichai: le-hakdim 'sof' le-'eynsof': Iyun bi-tfisat ha-shir shel ha-meshorer" (Yehuda Amichai: Putting "End" before "Endlessness": A Study of the Poet's Conception of the Poem), 21.

39. Ibid., 21–22.

40. This tension between the poet's necessity and his ineffectuality is in dialogue with the poetics of Wallace Stevens, although for quite different aesthetic and philosophical reasons. While Stevens never shies away from self-consciously difficult or metapoetic poetry, the analogy between the two poets is sustained by their sense of play and the similarly crucial role their poetics attribute to metaphor as essential for the life of the mind and even for human survival. For both of them, metaphor—that momentary rapport between reality and the imagination, which quickly degenerates into cliché—is absolutely vital: only metaphor can bridge the gap between the insufficiency and the indispensability of the poetic. For more on that subject, see chapter 5.

41. In *Akhshav ba-ra'ash*, 160. Untranslated. And see also interview with Ya'akov Beser in *Si'ach meshorerim al atzmam ve-al ktivatam* (Poets Talk about Themselves and Their Work), 52–53.

42. *Likrat* (Tel: Aviv: Dov Guterman Press, 1953) [first typeset issue], 2.

43. "Yoman," 18–23. As Arpali has shown in *Ha-prachim ve-ha-agartal* (140–41), Amichai's diary too needs to be treated as a fictional genre. The published diary segments are clearly meant to present the autobiographical and nonpoetic text as the aesthetic and rhetorical equal of the more traditionally poetic works.

44. See "Sonet ha-binyanim" (The Verb Patterns' Sonnet), *Shirim 1948–1962*, 64–65 (previously untranslated, but see literal rendition; and discussion of this poem in chapter 6 below).

45. Amichai's critics sometimes fail to distinguish between a thematization of (ordinary) language as a model for poetry in his poems (expressed through the poems' stylistic and rhetorical practices) and an explicit metapoetic thematics. See, e.g., Levy, "Elements of Poetic Self-Awareness in Modern Hebrew Poetry," 18–33; and Sokoloff, "On Amichai's *El male rahamim*," 127–28. This conflation becomes especially problematic if one automatically applies modernist clichés about the inability of language to communicate to a poetry that often valorizes the communicative and expressive possibilities of ordinary (and scientific!) language, while deflating traditional conceptions of poetic diction.

46. This interview was held in summer 1986 in the King David Hotel in Jerusalem.

47. See, respectively, *Akhshav ba-ra'ash*, 97–139, *Shirim 1948–1962*, 269–83, *Akh-*

shav ba-ra'ash, 92, *Patu'ach sagur patu'ach,* 155–61; *Selected Poetry,* 60–87, 42–47, 58 and *Open Closed Open,* 146–51.

48. Tzvik, "Yetzirat Amichai bi-r'i ha-bikoret," 50.

49. *Shirim 1948–1962,* 76–77; *Selected Poetry,* 12–13.

50. Mitchell's translation, reproduced here, while poetically powerful, deviates from the literal and idiomatic Hebrew original in many significant ways. Below I only point out those differences that are immediately relevant to my discussion.

51. All these are interpretations that have been put forward by different readers. For the poem as a critique of accepted norms see Arpali, *Ha-prachim ve-ha-agartal,* 27–29; as a series of personal wishes: Gad Keynar, "Lo ka-brosh" (Not Like a Cypress), *Masa/La-merchav,* November 28, 1969; as lacking a concrete referent: Teres-Tzukerman, "Al shir echad shel Yehuda Amichai" (On One Poem by Yehuda Amichai), 25–26; as the poet's perception of his art: Shlomo Yaniv, "Beyn tzura u-mahut" (Between Form and Essence), 139–44. Whereas Yaniv places this perception at the thematic center of the poem, most of the others at least acknowledge the possibility of a metapoetic reading. This is the title poem and metaphorical model for Amichai's poetry in Nili Scharf Gold's book *Lo ka-brosh: gilguley imajim ve-tavniyot be-shirat Yehuda Amichai* (Not Like a Cypress: Transformations of Images and Patterns in Yehuda Amichai's Poetry).

52. Sidra DeKoven Ezrahi, "*Yehuda Amichai: paytan shel ha-yomyom,*" 151ff.

53. With one crucial exception, the pronominal suffix *-i* in *lo kuli* ("not all of me"), line 2.

54. Parali, *Ha-prachim ve-ha-agartal,* 29.

55. This has not prevented readers from trying to impose a narrative miniplot on the poem's sequence, a tendency which Amichai's poetry often elicits and, almost as often, frustrates. For an ingenious attempt at constructing a personal autobiographical narrative out of the poem, see Keynar, "*Lo ka-brosh.*"

56. Kalderon, "Hitraptut" (Becoming Worn Out). Kalderon's article marked the beginning of the second wave of critical attacks on Amichai in the 1970s. While I don't at all see how this purported looseness applies to the actual structure of Amichai's poems, and I certainly don't think it applies to his early work, his last book, *Patu'ach sagur patu'ach* (1998), *Open Closed Open* (2000) was structured purposefully as a modular book-length composition ("modular" is Amichai's term, in discussions with Chana Bloch and me; Berkeley 1996). This modular composition, however, refers to the concatenation of the poem sequences in the volume and the resistance to linearity in the book's sections as a whole, not to the internal coherence of each poem.

57. To quote Joseph Frank's seminal concept; see his *The Idea of Spatial Form.*

58. Jakobson and Jones, *Shakespeare's Verbal Art.* Jakobson famously conducted similar analyses of poems by Baudelaire.

59. The Hebrew is ambiguous: it could also be parsed as "the great plain of renunciation."

60. *Shirat Rachel,* 128. See Gluzman, *The Politics of Canonicity: Lines of Resis-*

tance in Modernist Hebrew Poetry, 100–140. It is the rest of the poem—describing the ant's being squashed by a giant hand that prevents "her" (*nemala*, fem. in Hebrew) from reaching the treetop—that the speaker proceeds to identify with and protest against. But only the self-deprecating first lines get remembered and recited.

61. On the role of primary visual and embodied image-schemas in Amichai's use of metaphor and other figurative strategies, see chapter 5.

62. See Saul's description (1 Samuel 9:2) as "a choice young man, . . . from his shoulders and upward . . . higher than any of the people." This is only a very sketchy account of two very complex images. In other respects, the biblical Saul is like the hiding children in Stanza I. The ambivalence with respect to Saul is syntactically represented in the ambiguity of the first two lines of Stanza II. Note, also, that the Hebrew, unlike the English translation, identifies Saul only relationally, as "son of Kish."

63. This point is discussed in an unpublished paper by Abby Goldgeier.

64. Scharf Gold, *Yehuda Amichai: The Making of Israel's National Poet*, 308. See also her article "The 'Feminine' in Yehuda Amichai's Poetics," in *The Experienced Soul*, 57–69. I take issue, however, with the essentializing of gender and biography in her reading of this poem. She argues, for example, that "Not Like a Cypress" reveals some "feminine strain [that] was a deep-seated part of his personality expressed in his romantic relationship" (*Yehuda Amichai: The Making of Israel's National Poet*, 308). Nor do I see any textual basis for her attempt to force this poem into her thesis about Amichai's purported concealment of his German roots. She reads the speaker's desired inconspicuousness as an expression of the German immigrant's "desire to assimilate" in Israeli society "in order to establish himself as an Israeli [national] poet," by camouflaging "the remnant of his past" (ibid., 311). For Amichai's matrilineal modeling of literary historiography, see chapter 3 below.

65. Arpali, *Ha-prachim ve-ha-agartal*, 29.

66. Since Mitchell's English translation says "statesman" here, the local sarcasm of this analogy may be lost. *Sar mitpater* (a government minister resigning) is a cultural zeugma, an item in the catalogue that does not cohere, which increases the impression of a loosely put-together or chaotic structure, and introduces a note of satire in its very incongruity (zeugma is, of course, typical of the satirical and mock-heroic modes). Already in the 1950s, Israeli government ministers were notoriously loath to leave their posts, even when involved in some scandal; it is thus quite comical to use them as a typical example of a quiet exit, *bli tru'ah* (idiomatically, "without much fanfare"; lit., "without *shofar*-blasts" or "without a blaring sound").

67. Keynar, "Lo ka-brosh."

68. Tzukerman-Teres, "Al shir echad shel Yehuda Amichai," 26.

69. Yaniv, "Beyn tzura u-mahut," 141.

70. Amichai is forever pointing out the interconnectedness of promise and threat, as for example in bringing together Genesis's "Like Sand" and Daniel's "writing on the wall" in the title poem of the present study, "Be-khol chumrat ha-rachamim" ("To the Full Severity of Compassion"), *Shirim 1948–1962*, 219; *Selected Poetry*, 38.

71. As in an abstract expressionist painting. I owe this last point to Maya Kronfeld.

72. Sidra DeKoven Ezrahi describes "the great plain of renunciation" as foreshadowing Amichai's metapoetic critique in "The Poet of the Song of Songs" in *Open Closed Open*. See her *"Yehuda Amichai: paytan shel ha-yomyom,"* 154–56.

73. Selections from this book in Chana Bloch's translation appear in *Selected Poetry*, 171–183. Barbara and Benjamin Harshav's translation of most of the book appeared in 1991 as *Even a Fist Was Once an Open Palm with Fingers*. The book's title needs to be understood in the historical context of its publication in the wake of the first Intifada and the IDF's "iron-fist" policy of repressing the Palestinian uprising (lit., *mediniyut ha-yad ha-kasha*, the hard-handed policy).

74. As Sidra DeKoven Ezrahi noted, both "Ima!" ("Mommy!") and "Elohim!" ("God!") are common exclamations in Hebrew, and are by definition non-referential (personal communication).

75. While "wisdom" is the common modern sense of the term *chokhma*, biblical Hebrew adds the meanings of "art" and "craft," and rabbinic Hebrew extends the meaning of *chokhma* to include "philosophy," "field of knowledge," and "science" (in a sense close to *Wissenschaft*).

76. *Gam ha-egrof*, 16. The translations of this and all other poems cited from *Gam ha-egrof* are my own, unless otherwise specified. For an alternative translation, see *A Life of Poetry*, 411–12.

77. The Hebrew uses throughout an elliptical, third-person plural form, usually expressing public opinion. This form is unavailable in English.

78. Lit., a "live fence."

79. Also: "to prepare a house for a blackout in anticipation of an air-raid," and "to overshadow someone."

80. For a discussion of these romantic and early-modernist attitudes toward the land, see my *On the Margins of Modernism*, 103–9.

81. In his "Jeremiah and Ezekiel," *The Literary Guide to the Bible*, 195.

82. "What did I learn in the wars" is an ironic paraphrase of the common Hebrew parental question: "What did you learn in kindergarten today?" (*ma lamadeta ba-gan ha-yom?*). That wars replace school in the Israeli reality is brought to dramatic-ironic relief in Amichai's famous poem "Elohim merachem al yaldey ha-gan" ("God Has Pity on Kindergarten Children"), *Shirim 1948–1962*, 14; *Selected Poetry*, 1. This poem has been so thoroughly co-opted for ceremonial purposes in Israel that its irony is now barely legible.

83. Zach, *Shirim shonim* (Various Poems), no pagination. The comparative discussion of Zach and Amichai's metapoetics that follows below is entirely Setter's. For more on Zach and Amichai's different articulations of modernism, see chapter 6.

84. "Beynayim" ("Between"), *Gam ha-egrof*, 35; *Selected Poetry*, 173. See discussion of the image schemas that represent this in-between state in chapter 5.

85. *Shirim 1948–1962*, 167. *Selected Poetry*, 33.

86. *Shirim 1948–1962*, 13. And on bread and circuses (*lechem ve-sha'ashu'im*)

see the sarcastic "Avinu malkenu" ("Our Father, Our King") in *Patu'ach sagur patu'ach*, 8; *Open Closed Open*, 41.

87. See Yehudit Tzvik's discussion of this topic in "Ba-derekh el ha-shalva ha-gdola" (En Route to the Great Tranquility), in *Yehuda Amichai: mivchar ma'amarey bikoret al yetzirato*, 95–104. And see especially the poems in the closing series "U-mi yizkor et ha-zokhrim" ("And Who Will Remember the Rememberers?") in *Patu'ach sagur patu'ach*, 173–78; *Open Closed Open*, 168–71.

88. But it is found within the sonnet genre itself, where Amichai constructs, following inter alia Leah Goldberg's example (as well as Rilke's), a blend of the Petrarchan and Elizabethan models.

89. *Gam ha-egrof*, 33 (untranslated), 42, and 104, respectively. *A Life of Poetry*, 418; *Selected Poetry*, 171–72, respectively.

90. Compare "Beynayim," *Gam ha-egrof*, 35; *Selected Poetry*, 173–74; and see also 9, 12, 13, 19, 21, 22, 46, 72–74, 88, 94–95, 97–98, 116–18, 128, 144–47 in the same volume. Only a few of these poems have been translated: *A Life of Poetry*, 409–10, 413–14, 420, 433–34, 443–44, 451, 469–71. *Selected Poetry*, 178, 179–80, 181. The botanical imagery is further developed in many of the sequences of Amichai's last book *Patu'ach sagur patu'ach*, especially in "Chayay hem ha-ganan shel gufi," 128; "My Life Is the Gardener of My Body," *Open Closed Open*, 5.

91. "Atzvut ve-simcha" (Sadness and Joy) in *Gam ha-egrof*, 33 (untranslated).

92. "*Ha-nefesh*," *Gam ha-egrof*, 42; "The Soul," *A Life of Poetry*, 418.

93. "Eyze min adam," *Gam ha-egrof*, 105; "What Kind of Man," *Selected Poetry*, 171.

94. In her "Yehuda Amichai: paytan shel ha-yomyom," 151 ff.

95. At his home in Yemin Moshe, Jerusalem, summer 1986.

96. Peckham, *Man's Rage for Chaos: Biology, Behavior and the Arts*, xi. See discussions by E. H. Gombrich and Frank Kermode in the context of the debate on modernism and postmodernism in Bernard Bergonzi, ed., *Innovations: Essays on Art and Ideas*.

97. "Mas'ot Binyamin ha-acharon mi-Tudela" ("Travels of the Last Benjamin of Tudela"), *Akhshav ba-ra'ash*, 109, 114; *Selected Poetry*, 67, 70.

98. *Gam ha-egrof*, 48. Alternatively, the last line can read: "let the world return to chaos," since *yachzor* in this fronted position can be either future or jussive-subjunctive. For a poetic translation, see *Selected Poetry*, 176.

99. See, e.g., "Ani rotze le-valbel et ha-tanakh" ("I Want to Mix Up the Bible"), in *Gam ha-egrof*, 131–32; *Selected Poetry*, 49. And compare the sections from "Mas'ot binyamin ha-acharon mi-Tudela" ("The Travels of the Last Benjamin of Tudela") discussed below.

100. This is expressed elsewhere in the poetry on a political level. The inability of the speaker in "Jerusalem 1967" (*Akhshav ba-ra'ash*, 11–12; *Selected Poetry*, 49) to communicate with the Palestinian in a common language ironically aborts—and calls into question—his personal attempt at atonement and reconciliation.

101. *Akhshav ba-ra'ash*, 99–140; *Selected Poetry*, 60–86. For a full translation of this autobiographical *poema*, see *Travels of a Latter-Day Benjamin of Tudela*.

102. See also discussion in psychobiographical terms in Abramson, *The Writing of Yehuda Amichai*, 18–22.

103. *Akhshav ba-ra'ash*, 109; *Selected Poetry*, 67–68.

104. See Alter, "Mischak ve-chazon"; and Tzvik, "Ba derekh el ha-shalva ha-gdola."

105. *Mas'ot binyamin*, 122–23; *Selected Poetry*, 76.

106. The Hebrew *chelkey chalof* is an untranslatable portmanteau pun, brilliantly combining "spare parts" (*chelkey chiluf*) with "mutability" (*chalof*).

Chapter 3

1. The chapter title quotes the title of the poem "Ani rotze le-valbel et ha-tanakh," *Gam ha-egrof*, 131 (translation mine).

The opening epigraph is from a fragment of a poem I found in the Amichai Archives, Beinecke Library, Box 29, Folder 1072:

"שברי עגל הזהב / ושברי לוחות הברית / בערמה אחת מתערבבים".

(trans. Chana Bloch and Chana Kronfeld).

2. For the dominant view regarding the status of the divine and the mundane in Amichai, see, e.g., the chapter "Allusion and Irony" in Abramson, *The Writing of Yehuda Amichai*, 33–49; and Nili Scharf Gold, *Lo ka-brosh*, 98 ff. DeKoven Ezrahi describes with great nuance and theoretical sophistication Amichai's "holistic" and "post-dialectical" resistance to the binary opposition of "sacred" and "profane," an opposition that is presupposed by those who make a point of how Amichai reverses it ("Yehuda Amichai: Paytan shel ha-yomyom"). My own understanding of this aspect of his poetics has evolved as a result of a fruitful ongoing dialogue with her on the status of the sacred in Amichai's poetry. I am grateful to Sidra for her generosity in sharing her research with me.

3. See, for example, my discussion of the *poema* "Conferences, Conferences" in chapter 4.

4. *Patu'ach sagur patu'ach*, 126; *Open Closed Open*, 7.

5. See his "The Death of the Author," in *Image-Music-Text*, 142–48. And see also in the same collection "From Work to Text," 160, emphasis his.

6. See Sandbank's article, "*Li-she'elat ha-shir ha-kal*," in his *Ha-shir ha-nakhon*, 92–97.

7. In his book *Marginal Forces/Cultural Centers*, esp. 1–61.

8. This is not to say that the public intellectual and the academic cannot be one and the same; in fact, in order to have an impact on what Dan Miron, following Simon Halkin and Albert Thibaudet, has termed "the Hebrew literary republic" (and also make a decent living), Israeli academics often function as reviewers and engage in prescriptive criticism in the popular press and other public forums, side by side with their scholarly pursuits. While the increasing Americanization of Israeli culture has been gradually eroding the status of the public intellectual, writers and occasionally critics are still called upon to weigh in on topical issues in the mass media.

9. "Derekh shtey nekudot over rak kav yashar echad," *Shirim 1948–1962*, 80–81; *Selected Poetry*, 13–14. Music: Shlomo Artzi, 1972.

10. On this topic see Fishelov, "Yehuda Amichai: A Modern Metaphysical Poet," 178–91.

11. While this episode occurred in the 1970s, and academics nowadays regularly bemoan the death of Israeli poetry, Israeli popular music, be it Middle Eastern or Western in style, still draws heavily on canonical poetry for its lyrics. Indeed, the genre of *shirey meshorerim* (poets' songs) is as popular today as ever. On the connection between pop songs and canonical poetry in Israeli culture see Ben-Porat et al., *Lirika ve-lahit* (Lyrical Poetry and the Lyrics of Pop). On the blurring of the distinction between canonical poetry and rock music in Israeli culture in recent years see Kalderon, *Yom sheni: Al shira ve-rok be-Yisra'el acharey Yona Wallach* (A Second Day: On Poetry and Rock Music in Israel after Yona Wallach).

12. The Hebrew literally describes God as always busy with *tikkun*. This is, of course, the kabbalistic term for the mending of the broken vessels of creation, referring to the ethical charge of humanity, not of God. Christian models of God's involvement in creation (as opposed to his image as the "absentee landlord") are invoked here as well. But that is a matter for a different discussion.

13. "Ve-hi tehilatekha," *Shirim 1948–1962*, 71; "And That Is Your Glory," *Selected Poetry*, 11.

14. Ibid.

15. On the complex connections between religious and poetic meditation in Anglo-American poetry, see the classic studies by Martz, *The Poetry of Meditation: A Study of English Religious Literature of the Seventeenth Century*, and Bevis, *Mind of Winter: Wallace Stevens, Meditation, and Literature*. And see the more recent study by Sharpe, *The Ground of Our Beseeching: Metaphor and the Poetics of Meditation*. Amichai's dialogue with this tradition is mediated via the Anglo-American modernists' revival of seventeenth-century Metaphysical poetry and the radical ways the Metaphysicals appropriated Christian meditation in their love poetry. It goes without saying that Amichai is also, at the same time, invoking the Jewish meditative structure of a biblical verse followed by exegetical or narrative elaboration, modeled on the psalms and common to both rabbinical literature and medieval Hebrew poetry.

16. *Gam ha-egrof*, 99–100; *A Life of Poetry*, 445.

17. Colloquial Hebrew often employs a penultimate stress pattern in proper names, whereas literary Hebrew typically retains the stress on the final syllable.

18. On Amichai's treatment of place in his later poetry, see Shemtov, "Between Perspectives of Space: A Reading in Yehuda Amichai's 'Jewish Travel' and 'Israeli Travel,'" 141–61.

19. "'Kemo be-shir shel Shmuel Ha-Nagid': beyn Shmuel Ha-Nagid li-Yehuda Amichai" ("As in a Poem by Shmuel Ha-Nagid": Between Shmuel Ha-Nagid and Yehuda Amichai), 93.

20. At his Bleecker Street apartment, NYU Housing, New York City, July 26, 1984.

21. On foundational metaphorical systems such as "LIFE AS A JOURNEY," of which "the road of life" is one important entailment, see Lakoff and Johnson, *Metaphors We Live By*, and Lakoff, *Women, Fire and Dangerous Things: What Categories Reveal about the Mind*, esp. 439. For a recent comprehensive account of metaphorical systems in the framework of cognitive linguistics, see Barbara Dancygier and Eve Sweetser, *Figurative Language*. For the workings of this metaphorical system in literature see Turner, *The Literary Mind: The Origins of Thought and Language*, esp. 88.

22. Travel directions (*hora'ot li-nsi'a*) are in themselves a recurring **intra**textual pattern in Amichai's poetry since its earliest stages, starting with a poem by that name in *Shirim 1948–1962*, 170; translated in *A Life of Poetry* as "Instructions for Her Voyage," 53.

23. *Gam ha-egrof*, 65–66; *A Life of Poetry*, 428–29.

24. In the Amichai Archives I found a note in which Amichai urges himself to "from time to time return to Rabbi Hanover," the biographical rabbi of his childhood (and father of his childhood love, "Little Ruth"), and to keep asking: "What did the rabbi say?" [*ma amar ha-rav?*]. Beinecke Library, Box 31, Folder 1116.

25. On translation as one of Amichai's models for radical intertextuality and for the poetic process itself, see chapter 4.

26. Numbers Rabbah 22:4.

27. *Shirim 1948–1962*, 226–27; *Selected Poetry*, 40. For an earlier reading of this poem, see my *On the Margins of Modernism*, 109–12.

28. See Harshav, *Explorations in Poetics*, esp. 2–8, 38–40.

29. With the exception of the reference to dawn and knowing the name of the other.

30. But in doing so he is also invoking—and secularizing—a classical artistic representation of this biblical narrative. As Ilana Pardes has reminded me (in conversation), not only does Rembrandt's *Jacob Wrestling with the Angel* (1660–1661) depict the angel as a woman but also the scene it portrays looks more like lovemaking than wrestling. Furthermore, as Daniel Boyarin has observed (again, in conversation), in Jewish textual tradition the cherubs are turned toward each other and are often depicted as having sex!

31. See n. 21 above.

32. In the song, a soldier encounters a woman without knowing her name. Later, as he lies dying from his battle wounds, that same woman turns out to be the nurse who takes care of him in his final hours, and "When he goes and won't come back and she remains all pale / she remembers that he forgot to ask her for her name." The refrain is: *Hu lo yada et shma / Aval ota tsama / halkha ito le-orekh kol ha-derekh* ("He didn't know her name / But that braid of hers / Went with him all along the way"). Lyrics: Haim Hefer, music: Sasha Argov. I am grateful to Miri Kubovy for dating this song for me. Translation mine, CK.

33. I am grateful to Shaul Setter for this last point.

34. And is the basis for the prohibition to eat the part of the kosher animal that corresponds to this spot, *gid ha-nasheh*, translated by the KJV as "the sinew . . . on

the hollow of the thigh." Yehudit Tzvik cites the ways in which Amichai activates here an awareness of the erotic semantic potential present already in the rabbinic debates over the meaning of the struggle between Jacob and the Man. Thus, for example, Rabbi Ephraim of Lontchich in his exegesis *Kli Yakar* reads the verse *Va-ye'avek ish imo* (lit., "and a man struggled with him") as *nizdaveg elav* (lit., "he copulated with him"), and Nahmanides reads *Va-ye'avek* as *va-yechabek* (lit., "and he embraced [him]"). Tzvik, however, insists that the rabbis' interpretations "don't have a trace of erotic flavor!" (*belo kol nofekh eroti!*; exclamation point in the original). See her "Li-vchinata shel ha-intertextualiyut be-shirat Amichai: ha-tavnit ha-makifa" (On the Question of Intertextuality in the Poetry of Yehuda Amichai: The Comprehensive Pattern); see esp. 58–59.

35. *Shirim 1948–1962*, 219.

36. Forthcoming in *The Poetry of Yehuda Amichai*, ed. Robert Alter (New York: Farrar, Straus, & Giroux; in press).

37. From *"El maleh rachamim"* in *Shirim 1948–1962*, 69–70; "God Full of Mercy," *A Life of Poetry*, 31. See discussion in chapters 2 and 6.

38. Tzvik discusses this poem as an instance of what she terms "comprehensive intertextual patterning." See her "Li-vchinata shel ha-intertextualiyut be-shirat Amichai," 63–65. On the biblical narrative type-scene, see Alter, *The Art of Biblical Narrative*, 47–62.

39. This has developed in later times into a belief that it's bad luck to count people. Thus, even this less familiar biblical use of *mene* resonates with a common folk-belief and is therefore culturally recognizable without necessitating knowledge of the narrative from Chronicles. To this day, when counting people, the tradition among Jews is to say: "not one, not two, not three," in order not to tempt the evil eye. Conversely, the equally common belief that God is always counting our deeds is also invoked here. Thus, for example, the liturgy for Yom Kippur repeatedly describes God as counting (same root, *m.n.h.*) human deeds, judging them (root *d.i.n.*, as in the poem's last stanza and the original idiomatic expression echoed in the title), and determining who will live and who will die. Compare the text of the central prayer, *u-netaneh tokef*. And see also the horrifying image of God as conducting a "selection" of sorts in the poem "And That Is Your Glory," where "one" is seen standing at the end of the road, pointing to those who will live and those who will die (*omed u-moneh . . . et ze ve-et ze ve-et ze*, "stands and picks . . . this one and this one and this one and this"). *Shirim 1948–1962*, 71; *Selected Poetry*, 11.

40. *Ha-jesta shel ha-shir tzrikha li-hiyot muvenet. Zo ha-mechva*. He is punning here on the two meanings of the Hebrew *mechva* as designating both a gesture and an homage (at his home in Jerusalem, summer 1986).

41. In German, *Menetekel* is used as a common noun designating a threatening portent, without the expression necessarily registering as translingual. I am grateful to Simone Stirner for pointing this out to me.

42. See Benjamin, "Theses on the Philosophy of History," in *Illuminations:*

Essays and Reflections, 253–64. And see discussion of Amichai's possible Brechtian link to Benjamin in chapter 1.

43. *Shirim 1948–1962,* 274–77. *Selected Poetry,* 42–43.

44. "Ha-gibor ha-amiti shel ha-akeda," in *She'at ha-chesed,* 21; "The Real Hero," *Selected Poetry,* 156–57.

45. Nanette Stahl, for example, has characterized the link and conflict between promise and jeopardy as "central to all . . . biblical liminal moments," such as the Sinai narrative. See her *Law and Liminality in the Bible,* 71ff.

46. See Spiegel's epoch-making study, *The Last Trial: On the Legends and Lore of the Command to Abraham to Offer Isaac as a Sacrifice: The Akedah.*

47. This section of the chapter has benefited greatly from an ongoing dialogue with Margaret Larkin on (re)theorizing intertextuality in Arabic and Hebrew poetry. I consider myself extremely fortunate to have this erudite interlocutor as a dear and generous friend. Margaret Larkin, "Abd al-Wahhāb al-Bayātī's 'Mawt al-Mutanabbī': A Case Study in Arabic Intertextuality" (forthcoming). Some of the arguments in this and the next sections of the chapter have appeared in my Hebrew article "Sokhnut intertextualit" (Intertextual Agency), in a Festschrift dedicated to my teacher, Ziva Ben-Porat. Ben-Porat's pioneering work on allusion and intertextuality informs my entire project. For a discussion of her theory, see section III of this chapter.

48. Christian, "The Race for Theory," 67–79. It is a mistake, in my opinion, to read this essay as an attack on theory (which is the way it tends to be remembered). Rather, it is a call to reconfigure the work of theorizing as a text- and context-dependent verb rather than a universal noun.

49. Bloom, *The Anxiety of Influence: A Theory of Poetry,* and Bloom, *A Map of Misreading.*

50. Barthes, "The Death of the Author," in *Image-Music-Text,* 142–48.

51. Bloom, *A Map of Misreading,* 17, 19.

52. See Jonathan Culler's famous critique along these lines in his "Presuppositions and Intertextuality," in *The Pursuit of Signs: Semiotics, Literature, Deconstruction,* 100–118, and see also n. 128.

53. Kristeva, *Semeiotikè: Recherche pour une semanalyse;* cited from the English translation in *Desire in Language: A Semiotic Approach to Literature and Art,* 65–66. Emphasis hers.

54. In the French original it is even more pronounced, since Kristeva uses reflexive verbs throughout ("se construit," "s'installe," "se lit"): "[T]out texte se construit comme mosaïque de citations, tout texte est absorption et transformation d'un autre texte. A la place de la notion d'intersubjectivité s'installe celle d'*intertexualité,* et le langage poétique se lit, au moins, comme *double.*" *Semeiotikè,* 146. Emphases in the original.

55. Eckstein, *Re-Membering Black Atlantic: On the Poetics and Politics of Memory,* 5.

56. Bakhtin, *Problems of Dostoevsky's Poetics;* Bakhtin, *The Dialogic Imagination.*

On the tensions between authorial and social agency in Bakhtin, see Bhabha, *The Location of Culture*, 245–82.

57. Clayton and Rothstein, *Influence and Intertextuality in Literary History*, 7.

58. Juvan, *History and Poetics of Intertextuality*, 54.

59. See her "Weavings: Intertextuality and the (Re)Birth of the Author," in Clayton and Rothstein, 152. See also her "Migration, Encounter, and Indigenisation: New Ways of Thinking about Intertextuality in Women's Writing." I have benefited from my dialogue with her on these issues in the context of modernism.

60. This despite the fact that Clayton and Rothstein highlighted his critique in the Introduction to their volume, *Influence and Intertextuality in Literary History*, 6.

61. Michael Baxandall, *Patterns of Intention: On the Historical Explanation of Pictures*, 58.

62. The scholar who has done the most groundbreaking work in exploring the connections between Amichai and Rilke—without limiting his purview to an influence model—is Shimon Sandbank. See mainly his three studies: "Nof ha-nefesh: Rilke, Auden, Amichai," in *Shtey brekhot ba-ya'ar*; "Amichai: ha-mischak ve-ha-shefa," in *Ha-shir ha-nakhon*; and "'Mistovev, omed, mitmahameha': Rilke, Amichai ve-ha-mabat le-achor" ("Turns Back, Stands, Lingers": Rilke, Amichai, and the Backwards Gaze), in *Ha-kol hu ha-acher* (The Voice Is the Other), 90–98.

63. Amichai attended a poetry reading by Auden in New York in 1955, but did not meet him then. He describes that reading—and discusses the difference between Auden's late and early poetry—in an experimental prose sketch, "Auden kore mi-shirav ha-acharonim" (Auden Reads from His Latest Poems). This sketch combines the genres of a biographical essay, short story, and poetry translation (it includes Hebrew versions of some Auden poems!) and was later included in revised form under the title "Erev kri'at shirim" (a poetry reading) in Amichai's collection of short stories, *Ba-ru'ach ha-nora'a ha-zot* (Merchavya: Sifriyat Po'alim, 1961), 215–27; not included in the selection of Amichai's short stories in English translation, *The World Is a Room and Other Stories by Yehuda Amichai*. About a decade later, late in Auden's life, when Amichai was already gaining a substantial international presence, the two met at poetry festivals and became friendly. Auden died in 1973. In 1955 Amichai also visited Dylan Thomas's mother and home in Wales, about two years after the poet's death. He recorded that trip in another prose piece written in the style of a personal pilgrimage narrative and published in the same venue. See "Bikur be-nofo shel Dylan Thomas" (A Visit to the Landscape of Dylan Thomas), *La-Merchav/Masa*, October 14, 1955. The piece includes both direct and coded references to key Thomas poems. A revised version under the title "Nofo shel meshorer" (A Poet's Landscape) was also included in *Ba-ru'ach ha-nora'a ha-zot*, 201–11; English translation not included in *The World Is a Room*. The importance of Thomas for Amichai's poetry remains to be explored but certainly cannot be accounted for in terms of any direct influence exerted by Thomas upon Amichai.

64. From a summer 1987 interview with me in the Amichais' home in Yemin Moshe, Jerusalem. Variations on the same narrative appear in many other interviews.

65. Anyone who knew Amichai has similar stories about the allusive wit and associative metaphors of his most ordinary conversations. It may, therefore, be no overreading to analyze stylistically his oral discourse.

66. See, e.g., "Hakdasha le-navi be-machane tzva'i" ("A Prophet's Initiation in an Army Camp"], in *Shirim 1948–1962*, 74–75; and Quatrains 1 and 43 from the cycle "Be-zavit yeshara" (In a Right Angle), in *Shirim 1948–1962*, 120, 129; *Selected Poetry*, 27, 28.

67. In 1935 Eliot proposed that Michael Roberts, associated with the younger poets of the Auden Group, edit a survey of modern poetry, resulting in *The Faber Book of Modern Verse*. The anthology constructed a lineage for Anglo-American high modernism, from Hopkins to Dylan Thomas, which was to become canonical.

68. *The Sacred Wood: Essays on Poetry and Criticism*, 49–50. Typical of the impersonal spirit dominant in Anglo-American modernism, Eliot talks here about works and not poets. He avoids any language that attributes agency, and in the process models for future generations of critics—from New Criticism to Deconstruction—the tendency to focus on the agency of the *texts*. This move enacts what was to become the normative personification of the text or the metonymic shift from the poetic subject to the text itself. In that sense, Eliot's modernist literary history prefigures not only Bloom's model of influence, with its shift of agency to the belated poet, but also Kristeva's impersonal notion of intertextuality.

69. From "Sisha shirim le-tamar," *Shirim 1948–1962*, 24; "Six Poems for Tamar," *A Life of Poetry*, 13.

70. See discussion of Amichai's self-description as a double agent in chapter 2.

71. Literal translation of Ecclesiastes 1:1. Robert Alter's new translation revives Kohelet's agency both as a proper name and as a poetic subject: He calls the text "The Book of Qohelet" and renders the first verse as "The words of Qohelet son of David." See his *The Wisdom Books*, 344–45.

72. On de-creation as an avenue toward redemption, see discussion in chapter 2.

73. Gluzman, *The Politics of Canonicity: Lines of Resistance in Modern Hebrew Poetry*, 102–3; and Gluzman, "The Exclusion of Women from Hebrew Literary History."

74. Or, according to Tinjanov's version, "in his struggle against his father, it turns out that the grandson resembles the grandfather," in *Arxaisty i novatory*, cited in Victor Erlich, *Russian Formalism: History, Doctrine*, 259. For more on the problematic gender politics of Shklovsky's literary historiographic metaphor, see Naiman, "Shklovsky's Dog and Mulvey's Pleasure: The Secret Life of Defamiliarization." And see Shklovsky's essayistic perspective in *Knight's Move*.

75. I am grateful to Daniel Boyarin for his insights on this point.

76. Amichai describes the affiliation with Lasker-Schüler as an intertextual memory that is imprinted upon his body and arises from the most mundane embodied gestures: "I lifted my hand to my forehead / to wipe off the sweat /

and found I have accidentally raised up / the ghost of Else Lasker-Schüler," in the poem cycle "Jerusalem 1967," *Selected Poetry*, 54; *Akhsav ba-ra'ash*, 19. And see also the *poema* "Leah Goldberg meta" (Leah Goldberg Died; untranslated) in *Ve-lo al menat li-zkor*, 55–57. And compare the poems "Shtey meshorerot be-Mexico" (Two Women Poets in Mexico; untranslated), "Elizabeth Swados" ("Elizabeth Swados," in *A Life of Poetry*, 400), "Susan Tichy—meshoreret mi-Colorado" (Susan Tichy—A Woman Poet from Colorado; untranslated), all in *Me-adam ata ve-el adam tashuv*, 81–82, 90, 104.

77. See Arpali, "On the Political Significance of Amichai's Poetry," and Scharf-Gold, "The 'Feminine' in Yehuda Amichai's Poetics," both in Abramson, *The Experienced Soul*, 27–50, 77–92.

78. Lasker-Schüler, *Shirim*; the posthumously published Lasker-Schüler, *Ve-eynay tipot kvedot va-afelot* (And My Eyes Are Heavy and Dark Drops); Lasker-Schüler, *Selected Poems*; and Goldberg, *Selected Poems*. Amichai also wrote a very brief introduction to Rachel [Bluwshteyn]'s poems in English translation; see *Flowers of Perhaps: Selected Poems of Ra'hel*.

79. Lasker-Schüler, *Hebrew Ballads and Other Poems*, x. Amichai collaborated with playwright Motti Lerner on the Hebrew play *Else*. The play was performed at Ha-Bima National Theater in Tel Aviv in 1990, as well as in translation internationally (its English title was *Exile in Jerusalem*). In the Amichai Archives at the Beinecke Library I found a correspondence between Lerner and Amichai dated November 23, 1989 regarding the production of the play and the publication of the text by Or Am Press. Box 7, Folder 344.

80. Huss, "Al shirat Amichai ve-Galay" (On the Poetry of Amichai and Galay). The only scholarly discussions of this issue I am aware of are Sandbank's "Al shirey tzmadim u-modulariyut: Amichai ve-Else Lasker-Schüler" (On Couplets and Modular Structures: Amichai and Else Lasker-Schüler), in *Ha-kol hu ha-acher*, 72–89; and Weissbrod, *Ba-yamin ha-acherim*, 374–75. And see the comparative discussion of Amichai and Goldberg's translations of a Lasker-Schüler poem in Feldman, Shlesinger, and Shedletzky, "Five Hebrew Translations of Else Lasker-Schüler's Poem 'An Mein Kind,'" 176–98.

81. This letter, like Amichai's interview with Dan Omer (see Introduction), provides a much earlier dating for Amichai's first poems than was commonly believed. I am grateful to Giddon Ticotsky for sharing this and other archival findings with me. The beginning of Amichai's letter to Goldberg makes it clear that there had been no contact between them before this letter. Amichai starts by introducing himself to the poet, and apologizes for mailing the letter to Café Herlinger in Jerusalem, which she was known to frequent, because he doesn't know her address. See *Gnazim Archives* (The Goldberg Archives), Collection 275: 5644/1. In the poem "Leah Goldberg Died," Amichai writes: "In the battles of the Negev her little book / *From My Old Home* in my knapsack always. / Its pages were torn and glued together / with band-aids, but I knew by heart / all the words, the hidden / and the revealed." *Ve-lo al menat li-zkor*, 55, parentheses his, translation mine.

These archival findings were subsequently published by Giddon Ticotsky. See his article "Be-ozvi et chayay, karati bo, ve-tov li."

82. Goldberg, *Selected Poems*, 9.

83. *Shirim 1948–1962*, 43; *Selected Poetry*, 8.

84. *Gnazim Archives* (The Goldberg Archives), collection 274: 11787/4, 49. The dedication reads: "For Leah, dear, kind, and understanding, with profound gratitude, Yehuda Amichai, Passover 1958."

85. Goldberg, "Gefen ha-yayin be-kharmey zarim" and "Ad barzel" in *Ha-ometz le-chulin*.

86. Miron, "Yehuda Amichai: Patu'ach sagur patu'ach" (Yehuda Amichai: Open Closed Open), 401–4.

87. She coined this key concept as early as 1986. See her article "Changing the Subject: Authorship, Writing, and the Reader," 102–20.

88. See Bourdieu, *The Field of Cultural Production*, esp. chap. 6, 176–91. And see an interesting application of Bourdieu's theory to a critique of the androcentric historiography of Hebrew poetry in Schachter, "A Lily among the Bullfrogs: Dahlia Ravikovitch and the Field of Hebrew Poetry," 310–34.

89. On this issue, see my "Reading Amichai Reading."

90. Bourdieu, *In Other Words: Essays Towards a Reflexive Sociology*, 9. For the classic articulation of the notion of interpellation, see Althusser, "Ideology and Ideological State Apparatuses."

91. "La-em," *Shirim 1948–1962*, 91–92. On the opening simile see also my "Reading Amichai Reading," 313–15.

92. See, e.g., *yad chazaka* (divine might, heroism), Exodus 13:9, and the alternate title for Maimonides' *Mishne tora*: *Ha-yad ha-chazaka*. The collocation *yad adonay* + the preposition *al* designates divine inspiration (descending on the prophet; compare Ezekiel 37:1); by contrast, the collocation *yad adonay* + the preposition *be* usually indicates the onset of divine retribution or punishment (compare Exodus 9:3, Deuteronomy 2:15). The question as to whether *yad* is a metaphor or a metonymy/synecdoche has to do with the relationship between anthropomorphism and revelation, or between *yad* and *ma'ase merkava*. On the contradictory traditions on this anthropomorphism in biblical and rabbinic literature, see Boyarin, "The Eye in the Torah: Ocular Desire in the Midrashic Hermeneutic." On the relation between metaphor, metonymy, images of the hand, and the figure of the mother in other poems by Amichai, see Miron, *Mul ha-ach ha-shotek*, 289ff.

93. I owe this observation to Daniel Boyarin. As we recall, Don Quixote attacks the windmills with his spear because he is convinced they are giants and that their blades are arms/hands (both *yad*). The adventure concludes with one of these hands—parodically representing the divine—hurling Don Quixote and his horse Rocinante all the way to the adjoining field. Amichai's allusion is thus bilateral here as well: it engenders a rereading of *Don Quixote* that highlights Cervantes' parody of the use of fervent religious rhetoric in the knightly epic allusion.

94. *Akhshav ba-ra'ash*, 47. The second stanza reads: "Every year on the Ninth of Av [the fast day commemorating the destruction of the Temple and, symbolically, all other historical Jewish catastrophes], my mother scrabbles around / among the photos of her dead and her pre-dead [*meteha ve-terem meteha*], / those ruined houses of my life." My translation, CK.

95. "La-em," 92.

96. See, e.g., the chapter on metaphorical coherence in Lakoff and Johnson, *Metaphors We Live By*, 87–96. For a fascinating recent integration of Conceptual Metaphor Theory with an analysis of metonymy, see Dancygier and Sweetser, *Figurative Language*, 100–126.

97. See, e.g., Tractate *Avoda Zara*, 18.

98. Bloom's outrageous pronouncements on this matter are legendary. A small and particularly horrifying example should suffice: "Most feminist poetry, of course, is like most black poetry. It isn't poetry. It isn't even verse." Bloom in Moynihan, *A Recent Imagining*, 30. It is astonishing that quite a few feminist and postcolonial critics have nevertheless strained to adapt Bloom's model of influence to fit the needs of women and minority writers.

99. Gilbert and Gubar, *The Madwoman in the Attic: The Woman Writer and the Nineteenth Century Literary Imagination*; *No Man's Land: The Place of the Woman Writer in the 20th Century*, see esp. 1:130, 160, 167, 170–71, 199–200; repudiated by Kolodny, "A Map for Misreading: Gender and the Interpretation of Literary Texts," in *The New Feminist Criticism: Essays on Women, Literature, and Theory*, 46–62. And see Toril Moi's famous critique of this desire for inclusion, for example in "Feminist Literary Criticism," in *Modern Literary Theory: A Comparative Introduction*, 204–21. For a recent intervention on this issue, see the special issue of the online journal *Women's Writing: Beyond Influence*, Jennie Batchelor, ed. 20:1 (March 2013). http://www.tandfonline.com/toc/rwow20/20/1.

100. See, e.g., Cixous, "Sorties: Out and Out: Attacks/Ways Out/Forays"; and the discussion in Showalter, "Feminism and Literature," 179–202.

101. See, e.g., Cowart, "Tradition, Talent, and 'Stolentelling,'" in his *Literary Symbiosis: The Reconfigured Text in Twentieth Century Writing*, 1–26; Stewart, "The Pickpocket: A Study in Tradition and Allusion"; Lonsdale, "Gray and 'Allusion': The Poet as Debtor," 31–55. And compare Eliot's famous witticism: "Immature poets imitate; mature poets steal," in *The Sacred Wood*, 72.

102. Burnett, "Cultural Continuities?" in *Intertextuality and Modernism in Comparative Literature*, 43.

103. Brodsky, "A Footnote to a Commentary," in *Rereading Russian Poetry*, 184.

104. See, e.g., Murphy, "Jazz Improvisation: The Joy of Influence."

105. See Boyarin, *Intertextuality and the Reading of Midrash*; and Ben-Porat, "The Poetics of Literary Allusion."

106. "Ideology and Ideological State Apparatuses," 170–86.

107. Butler, *Excitable Speech: A Politics of the Performative*, 129. For the larger context of her discussion, see ibid., 1–41, 127–63.

108. Butler, "The Lesbian Phallus and the Morphological Imaginary," in *Bodies That Matter: On the Discursive Limits of "Sex,"* 232, emphasis added.

109. Salih, "Introduction to 'The Lesbian Phallus and the Morphological Imaginary," in *The Judith Butler Reader*, 140.

110. Butler, *Excitable Speech*, 2.

111. Salih, *The Judith Butler Reader*, 140–41.

112. Butler, *Excitable Speech*, 14.

113. Ibid., 13–14. Emphases added.

114. Ibid., 14.

115. "Changing the Subject: Judith Butler's Politics of Radical Resignification," in *The Judith Butler Reader*, 333–34.

116. Barthes, "The Death of the Author," in *Image-Music-Text*.

117. Daniel Boyarin (unpublished).

118. Boyarin, *Socrates and the Fat Rabbis*, 200ff.

119. Orr, *Intertextuality: Current Debates*, 28, citing Kristeva, *Desire in Language*, 37.

120. Kristeva, *Desire in Language*, 37.

121. Ibid., 86–87.

122. Barthes, "Death of the Author," 148. Emphasis added.

123. Orr is conflating here the early and late Barthes, invoking his *The Pleasures of the Text*, 36. Bloom, on the other hand, "refuses to accept social and cultural contexts as relevant intertextual fields of meaning for literary texts," as Graham Allen has observed. See his *Intertextuality*, 140.

124. But the late Barthes seems to value a very personal notion of agency as, for example, in his *Camera Lucida*.

125. Iser, "Foreword," in Renate Lachmann, *Memory and Literature: Intertextuality in Russian Modernism*, vii–xvii. Iser, like other Reader Response critics, has always resisted an agentless version of intertextuality. However, the historical specificity and situatedness of readerly agency remains largely undifferentiated on these accounts. This is true also of Michael Riffaterre's early account of intertextuality, an account that is also reader- rather than text-focused, since for him an "implied reader's" recognition of a textual syllepsis forms the crucial "ungrammaticality" which he or she needs in order to identify particular intertextual practices. Like Ben-Porat and Boyarin, Riffaterre too focuses on specific intertextual modalities rather than on intertextuality as a general condition of all textuality. See, e.g., his "Syllepsis," 625–38; and his "Intertextual Representation: On Mimesis as Interpretive Discourse," 141–62

126. Sas, *Fault Lines: Cultural Memory and Japanese Surrealism*. Eckstein, *(Re-)Membering the Black Atlantic*.

127. Kronfeld, "Reading Amichai Reading," 311–23.

128. Eco, "Casablanca: Cult Movies and Intertextual Collage," 208–9.

129. Ducrot and Todorov, *Encyclopedic Dictionary for the Sciences of Language*, 361.

130. Kristeva, *Desire in Language*, 66.

131. See n. 5 above. As Susan Stanford Friedman points out, Barthes's insistence on the difference between intertextuality and any influence studies itself betrays a kind of anxiety of influence: "Refusing the influence of influence, intertextuality is a concept that denies its filiation to its precursor, influence." See her "Weavings: Intertextuality and the (Re-)Birth of the Author," 150ff. She adds that Barthes and Kristeva posit a "mosaic" or "tissue" of "quotations without quotation marks, without a preexistent author . . . exercising agency in the construction of that text" (ibid.). In my opinion, the problem, however, is not only the erasure of *authorial* agency, but the erasure of *any* poetic agency except for that of the personified text. Interestingly, Barthes's argument here echoes both in its content and in its very articulation, of all things, Bloom's version of the influence model: "[T]he meaning of a poem can only be . . . another poem—a poem not itself . . . any central poem by an indisputable precursor, even if the ephebe never read that poem. Source study is wholly irrelevant here;" Bloom, *Anxiety of Influence*, 70. This sounds almost like a Barthesian pronouncement in the way it equates the meaning of a text with a generalized sense of intertextuality. Hastening to separate themselves clearly from traditional source criticism, both Barthes and Bloom erase the possibility of any localized intertextual formations, even though in their own critical practice they go on to focus on specific relations between texts (Barthes and Kristeva) or poets (Bloom). This was pointed out by Jonathan Culler already in 1981. See his *The Pursuits of Signs*, 103–7, and see a detailed discussion of this point in my "Theories of Allusion and Imagist Intertextuality: When Iconoclasts Evoke the Bible," in my *On the Margins of Modernism*, 120–22.

132. *History and Poetics of Intertextuality*, 8.

133. See Ben-Porat, "Beyn textualiyut retorit" (Rhetorical Intertextuality), 170–78 (this seminal essay has unfortunately not been translated); and Boyarin, *Intertextuality and the Reading of Midrash*. A discussion of the differences between his approach and that of the poststructuralists appears on 135n2. And see my comparison of poststructuralist and Tel Aviv neoformalist views of intertextuality in "Theories of Allusion and Imagist Intertextuality: When Iconoclasts Evoke the Bible," 114–40.

134. Funkenstein, "Intellectuals and Jews," 13–14.

135. Boyarin, *Intertextuality and the Reading of Midrash*, 17.

136. Ibid., 16–17, 35–38, 70.

137. Eco, "Casablanca: Cult Movies and Intertextual Collage," 209.

138. In Clayton and Rothstein's formulation of the poststructuralist position. *Influence and Intertextuality in Literary History*, 32n7. In their excellent Introduction they nevertheless present a totally uncritical view of Eco's essay on *Casablanca*. I am grateful to Ron Helstad for sharing his ideas on this important volume with me.

139. Yehuda Amichai, *Ha-zman*, 29; *Selected Poetry*, 124.

140. Making soup was one of Yehuda's favorite activities, as was cooking in

general. In the Amichai Archives I found an unpublished handwritten poem called "Making Jam" (*asiyat riba*), Box 27, Folder 885. And see my discussion in chapter 1 of making preserves as Amichai's metaphor for the inseparability of remembering and forgetting.

141. See Esther 9.

142. Even though this poem is, of course, not a sonnet, it evokes the structural model typical of Amichai's special blend of Shakespearean and Petrarchan sonnets, a blend that in turn was an homage, as we have seen, both to Leah Goldberg and to Rilke. See, for example, "Ahavnu kan," *Shirim 1948–1962*, 42–59; "We Loved Here," *Selected Poetry*, 8–9. The volta in these blends of Shakespearean and Petrarchan sonnets, as in Amichai's #29 pseudo-sonnet, comes in the last two lines, forming here a free-verse couplet.

143. For a very different reading of this poem, and of Amichai's biblical intertextuality in general, see Jacobson, *Does David Still Play before You: Israeli Poetry and the Bible*, 74–76ff.

144. Alter, "Play and Vision in the Poetry of Yehuda Amichai" (unpublished).

145. I am grateful to Daniel Boyarin for this wording.

Chapter 4

1.   "יצאתי אל חיי בשבעים כח רצון / ליד השערים עמדו כמו תורגמנים

מלשון ללשון / שעזרו לי. אך עכשיו כשהם שכבו לישון / שב ליבי לבדו

אל ביתו הראשון".

Translation mine, CK. Unpublished quatrain; date unclear; manual typewriter copy-format indicates it is early. Amichai Archives, Beinecke Library, Box 28, Folder 972. An earlier, abbreviated version of this chapter appeared in Hebrew as "Hameshorer ki-metargem be-shirat Amichai" (The Poet as Translator in Amichai's Poetry), *Ot* 3 (2013): 5–20. I am grateful to Michael Gluzman and Michal Arbell for their feedback on the article, and to Eyal Bassan and Caroline Brickman for their comments on the chapter draft.

2. Over the years Amichai told me numerous times that he was in the habit of writing quatrains "in the classical Arabic style," with the intention that they be published only "after 120," as he put it (see chapter 6, n. 14). I was surprised, therefore, to find in the Archives only two extant quatrains, of which the above quoted poem is one. It is published here for the first time, so far as I know. It is possible that other quatrains are located in the portion of the archives that have not yet been made accessible to the public. The earliest translation of Omar Khayyám into Hebrew directly from the Persian, rather than via Fitzgerald's English which Amichai would have had access to, is Ben-Tzion Ben-Shalom's volume of the *Rubai'yat* (*Meruba'im* in Hebrew). While I have not been able to verify that Amichai did indeed read the *Rubai'yat* in this translation, to the best of my knowledge this was the version used in Prof. Shirman's classes at the Hebrew University. See the Introduction for further discussion of Amichai's studies of medieval poetry with Shirman.

3. See Song of Songs 5. For the rabbinic allegorical interpretation of Queen Esther's home/body as a figure for the Temple, see midrash Esther Raba, Prologue A:5. *Bayit* in Hebrew is also short for *beyt ha-mikdash*, the Temple. I'd like to thank Mandy Cohen and Marina Zilbergerts for their important insights on this section.

4. In the narrative describing this first Greek translation there were "actually" seventy-two translators. In the typewritten manuscript of this quatrain Amichai crossed out (in pen) the word *shloshim* ("thirty"), which would have linked birth and death more explicitly (the first memorial for the dead traditionally takes place after thirty days and is called *shloshim*), and replaced it with the handwritten *shiv'im* (seventy).

5. My reading of this quatrain benefited greatly from an interpretive dialogue with Shaul Setter.

6. See Theodor Adorno, *Aesthetic Theory*, 142–43. And see earlier articulations in his *Negative Dialectics*, esp. 404–5. Amichai's poetics of metaphor, discussed in terms of Lakoff's theory in chapter 5, is the most developed articulation in his oeuvre of the Adornian aesthetics of "as-if." This, however, is a subject for another study.

7. Juvan explores in some detail the primarily Central and Eastern European theories that "place translation among intertextual phenomena." *History and Poetics of Intertexuality*, 33.

8. *Ha-sifrut* 34:1, 70–78, untranslated.

9. See, for example, his *Translation, Rewriting, and the Manipulation of Literary Fame*; and *Translating Literature: Practice and Theory in a Comparative Literature Framework*. Though informed by system-theoretical accounts of translation like those developed by Itamar Even-Zohar and Gideon Toury, Lefevere's work opened up the historical and political turn in translation studies, taking it beyond both poststructuralism and neoformalism. For Even-Zohar and Toury's contributions, see, e.g., Even-Zohar, "The Position of Translated Literature within the Literary Polysystem" and "The Role of Russian and Yiddish in the Making of Modern Hebrew," in his *Polysystem Studies*, 45–51, 111–120; and Toury, *In Search of a Theory of Translation*; and Toury, *Descriptive Translation Studies and Beyond*.

10. "Arts of the Contact Zone," in *Ways of Reading*, 584. A different version appeared as the Introduction to her *Imperial Eyes: Travel Writing and Transculturation* (London: Routledge, 1992).

11. I am grateful to Rebecca Whittington for her helpful comments on this matter.

12. One of the first studies in this vein was Niranjana, *Siting Translation: History, Post-Structuralism, and the Colonial Context*; and a series of studies by Lawrence Venuti: *Rethinking Translation: Discourse, Subjectivity, Ideology*; *The Translator's Invisibility: A History of Translation*; and his edited *The Translation Studies Reader*. See also the important anthology *Nation, Language, and the Ethics of Translation*, ed. Sandra Bermann and Michael Wood. For a global perspective that focuses on French and Francophone translations, see Apter, *The Translation*

Zone: The New Comparative Literature; and Tranquille and Nirisimloo-Gayan, *Rencontres: Translation Studies*.

13. Spivak, "The Politics of Translation."

14. *Shirim 1948–1962*, 231.

15. The original is a rewriting of the Aramaic words uttered during the ritual of purifying the house of the *chametz* before Passover. (*Chametz* refers to food products made from wheat, rye, and other grains that are forbidden during the holiday). Literally: "that which is in my possession and that which is not in my possession," may it be considered null and void.

16. Forthcoming in Alter, *The Poetry of Yehuda Amichai*. For an alternative rendition, see *A Life of Poetry*, 61.

17. An early partial draft of the poem that I found in the archives shows Amichai experimenting with this parody of a collectivist voice, writing first the very colloquial *eyn lanu ma le-hitlahev*, and finally settling on the biblical *ve-lo nitlahev* in the poem's first two stanzas and the rabbinic Hebrew *ve-eyn lanu le-hitlahev* ("'tis not for us to get excited") in the poem's last two stanzas, in both cases echoing the syntactic structure of a legal injunction. Amichai Archives, Beinecke Library, Box 42, Folder 1451.

18. Stevens, "The Man with the Blue Guitar," *The Palm at the End of the Mind: Selected Poems and a Play*, 133.

19. Chamberlain, "Gender Metaphorics in Translation," 94. See also a different version from 1988 in Venuti, *The Translation Studies Reader*, 312–29.

20. In *Siting Translation: History, Post-Structuralism, and the Colonial Context*.

21. See Hallo, *Origins: The Ancient Near Eastern Background of Some Modern Western Institutions*, esp. 163. I am grateful to Bill Hallo for sharing his erudition on this matter with me in conversation as well.

22. *Palestinian Talmud*, Tractate *Megila*, 75:50, for instance. As Daniel Boyarin pointed out to me, one of the more mundane functions of the *turgeman* in Talmudic times was simply to repeat the words of the sage more loudly, without interlingual translation, thus performing a pure form of mediation via repetition. In later periods variations on the term *dragoman* are used to describe the role of official translators in the various regions of the Ottoman Empire, and it becomes associated with proficiency in Turkish (*Turkeman*). On the diplomatic uses of *turgeman* see Lewis, *Middle East Mosaic: Fragments of Life, Letters, and History*, esp. 130.

23. Amichai Archives, Beinecke Library, Box 40, Folder 1393.

24. Amichai Archives, Beinecke Library, Box 84, Folder 2082.

25. Ibid. This is followed by a downward pointing arrow, and the statement: "your words" (*milim shelkha*), below which is another arrow, pointing to the statement: "foreign words" (*milim zarot*). Thus, Amichai's notes illustrate graphically the connection between literary genealogy, intergenerational intertextual transmission, and translation, highlighting visually the intermediary and necessarily unoriginal status of the poet's own words.

26. Erlich, *Russian Formalism: History/Doctrine*, 259ff; Tynjanov, *Arxaisty i novatory.*

27. Amichai may be providing here a secular restaging of Rabbi Yohanan's account of Moses being given the Torah at Sinai as an act of divine kissing. This is Rabbi Yochanan's allegorical reading of the opening verses of the Song of Songs, *yishakeni mi-nshikot pihu*, "Let him kiss me with the kisses of his mouth" (KJV, 1:2); Song of Songs Rabbah 1:2. As Daniel Boyarin pointed out to me, the traditional origins of this erotics of transmission already contains a literalization of a metaphor.

28. This is quite different from translation figured as the exposure of high-modernist sexual secrets. See Masiello, "Joyce in Buenos Aires," 55–72.

29. See discussion in Introduction and chapters 2 and 6.

30. *Patu'ach sagur patua'ch*, 155–61; *Open Closed Open*, 145–51.

31. See chapter 1.

32. Section 3, *Patu'ach sagur patua'ch*, 156; *Open Closed Open*, 148.

33. *Patu'ach sagur patua'ch*, 155; *Open Closed Open*, 147.

34. Section 2, *Patu'ach sagur patua'ch*, 156; *Open Closed Open*, 147.

35. See Arpali, *Ha-prachim ve-ha-agartal*, esp. 114–19 and 174–84.

36. I wish to thank Chana Bloch for her insights on this point.

37. Amichai Archives, Beinecke Library, Box 84, Folder 2082.

38. And see a fascinating discussion of the different versions and appropriations of the Septuagint legend in the first chapter of Naomi Seidman's book, *Faithful Renderings: Jewish-Christian Difference and the Politics of Translation*; see esp. 47–63. On the negative impact of the Septuagint as a model of perfect translation, see Norich, *Writing in Tongues: Translating Yiddish in the Twentieth Century*, 3–21.

39. Section 6, *Patu'ach sagur patua'ch*, 158; *Open Closed Open*, 149.

40. And see Sonnet 23, the last sonnet of Amichai's first sonnet cycle, "We Loved Here" ("Ahavnu kan"), for a similar critique of what was called in the slang of the Statehood Generation *na'emet*, "the speechifying disease" or "speech-ifitis"—this invented noun uses, as I suggest in chapter 2, the grammatical pattern of disease names: "And the wall of speechifying has now been breached" (*ve-kir ha-ne'umin akhshav nivka*). *Shirim 1948–1962*, 58–59; untranslated.

41. Seidman, *Faithful Renderings*, 21.

42. Ibid. Acts 2:4 reads: "And they were all filled with the Holy Ghost, and began to speak with other tongues, as the Spirit gave them utterance." Seidman cites here Assman, "The Curse and Blessing of Babel, or, Looking Back on Universalism," in *The Translatability of Cultures: Figuration of the Space Between*, 89. Even though Seidman mentions the story of the "Tongues of Fire" in the context of Amichai's *poema*, she relates it only to Section 2, in which the Holy Spirit helps the translators recycle words, but not to Section 6, which, as we've seen, evokes the fire directly.

43. Butler, *Excitable Speech*, esp. 129. See detailed discussion in chapter 3.

44. The Polish poet Zbigniew Herbert (1924–1998), who in Poland acquired the title "the Prince of Poetry," spent time in Israel in 1991 when he was awarded

the Jerusalem Prize and befriended Yehuda Amichai. This poem was translated from Polish into Hebrew by David Weinfeld and published in *Ha'aretz*, May 13, 1994, under the title: "To Yehuda Amichai for His Seventieth Birthday." This dedication is missing from the English. Herbert, "To Yehuda Amichai," *The Collected Poems 1956–1998*, trans. and ed. by Alissa Valles, 489. See Introduction on the use of regal imagery in other poets' descriptions of Amichai.

45. Until his retirement Amichai taught in this program.

46. *Ma'ariv*, May 17, 1994. Cited from the online English edition. Amichai has since been translated into over forty languages by now.

47. Alter, "The Untranslatable Amichai." A revised version will appear as the Introduction to his forthcoming volume, *The Poetry of Yehuda Amichai*.

48. Benjamin's terms "afterlife" or "survival," in his classical essay "The Task of the Translator." In Harry Zohn's "original" translation, both Benjamin's *Fortleben* and his *Überleben* are rendered as "afterlife." But I believe that like other terms in Benjamin—as in Celan!—their full meaning results from an interlinguistic pun on the gap between the German and the Yiddish *faux-amis*: *iberlebn* in Yiddish means "to suffer," "to endure," and "to live through hardship." See Benjamin, "The Task of the Translator," cited here from *The Translation Studies Reader*, 1–23; and see Steven Rendall's important commentary on Zohn's translation in Venuti's first edition, ibid., 23–25, correcting several errors that invert the meaning. The full potential of a Benjaminian reading of Amichai's view of translation still remains to be explored.

49. On the constraints in the theory of translation, see Darwish, *The Transfer Factor: Selected Essays on Translation and Cross-Cultural Communication*. On this issue see also Even-Zohar, "The Position of Translated Literature within the Literary Polysystem"; and Toury, *In Search of a Theory of Translation*.

50. This is not to say that there is a one-to-one correspondence between the poetic and the political implications of language choice. On this matter see Norich, "Under Whose Sign? Hebraism and Yiddishism as Paradigms of Modern Jewish Literary History," 774–84. And see also my "The Joint Literary Historiography of Hebrew and Yiddish," in *Languages of Modern Jewish Culture: Comparative Perspectives*.

51. Alter, *The Poetry of Yehuda Amichai*. For Hughes's and Weissbort's anthology, see *Yehuda Amichai: Selected Poems*; after Hughes's death in 1998, Weissbort brought the anthology to completion by himself, using notes left behind by Hughes for the Introduction. Weissbort died in 2013.

52. Yehuda Amichai, *Amen*, 15; *Time: Poems by Yehuda Amichai*. A more complicated co-translation produced *The Selected Poetry of Yehuda Amichai*, as I suggest below. A new edition, published without the translators' knowledge(!), came out in 2014.

53. Hesse, *Nedudim*; Hochhuth, *Memale ha-makom*; Lasker-Schüler, *Shirim*; and Lasker-Schüler, *Ve-eynay tipot kvedot va-afelot*.

54. See, e.g., Harshav's *The Meaning of Yiddish*, reissued in the *Contraversions*

series (Stanford: Stanford University Press, 1999). And see my discussion in chapter 1 in the context of the appropriations resulting from the erasure of the tones of Jewish Discourse.

55. Sandbank, "Nof ha-nefesh: Rilke, Auden, Amichai"; Fishelov, "Yehuda Amichai: A Modern Metaphysical Poet"; Rosen, "'As in a Poem by Shmuel Ha-Nagid': Between Shmuel Ha-Nagid and Yehuda Amichai"; Kronfeld and Larkin, "Intertextuality in Amichai and Darwish" (in preparation).

56. Pages 33–49. I am grateful to Maya Kronfeld for her methodological input on this section.

57. Jakobson, "On Linguistic Aspects of Translation," 428–35.

58. Yehuda Amichai, *Shirim, 1948–1962*, 71–72; *Selected Poetry*, 11–12. See also discussion in chapter 3.

59. Amichai as a God-seeking modern poet is typical of other Anglo-American academic construals of his work. See, e.g., Sokoloff, "On Amichai's *El male rahamim*," 127–40; and Jacobson, *Does David Still Play Before You: Israeli Poetry and the Bible*, 74–76ff.

60. Stevens, "The Poems of Our Climate," 158. On the connection between Amichai's and Stevens' poetic worldviews, despite important differences, see chapter 2.

61. See, e.g., Sandbank, "Nof ha-nefesh: Rilke, Auden, Amichai"; Arpali *Ha-prachim ve-ha-agartal*, 114–19.

62. Yehuda Amichai, *Shirim, 1948–1962*, 71–72; *Selected Poetry*, 11–12. Note that Stephen Mitchell, with whom I worked as native informant on this poem (and to whom I explained the transition from the first *ve-hi* to the last), chose not to translate the final lines as "and she is my/his/your glory," opting to retain the traditional "and that." Thus, in my opinion, the point of the poem's radical transformation of the divine into the earthly feminine is missed in the English.

63. See "Ve-avita tehila," also known as *asher eymatkha be-er'eley omen*, an ancient *piyyut* attributed to Kalir or to Yanay (sixth and seventh centuries), included in some of the Ashkenazi *Machzorim*, prayer books for the High Holidays.

64. *Shirim 1948–1962*, 13. Translation mine.

65. Bassnett-McGuire, *Translation Studies*, 11. See critique in Niranjana, *Siting Translation: History, Post-Structuralism, and the Colonial Context*, 59.

66. Toury, *In Search of a Theory of Translation*, 92. A very sophisticated example within this scientific tendency is Gutknecht and Rölle, *Translating by Factors*.

67. See discussion of Herbert and Hughes earlier in this chapter. See Introduction for Simic and Strand on Amichai as model for young American poets.

68. *Siting Translation*, 59. The recent global turn in translation studies has unfortunately not improved this selective modeling so far.

69. *Challenge of Comparative Literature*.

70. See Althusser and Balibar, *Reading "Capital."*

71. "On Linguistic Aspects of Translation," 434.

72. Johnson, "Taking Fidelity Philosophically," in *Difference in Translation*, 142–48; and *Siting Translation*.

73. 1994, unpublished. For more on this topic, see her *Faithful Renderings*, 155–64.

74. Parts of this section are based on a brief essay cowritten with Chana Bloch, "On Translating Amichai's *Open Closed Open*," *American Poetry Review* (March/April 2000): 17–19. My title is an homage to Jakobson's *Poetry of Grammar and Grammar of Poetry* (vol. 3, *Selected Writings*).

75. During 1996–1998 we communicated with Amichai both in person (in Berkeley and Jerusalem) and by fax, translating from his handwritten revised drafts of the Hebrew. Fortunately, Amichai lived to see the translation in print. Yehuda expressed to me several times during that period—and before his terminal illness was diagnosed—a fear of finishing the Hebrew book because he had a premonition that when the book would end, so would his life: *ke-she-ha-sefer yigamer, ani egamer*. He described the book to Chana Bloch and me as having a "modular structure" (*mivne modulari*), and therefore indicated that we need not retain the section order of the Hebrew. He also thought that less than half the poems would be translatable because so many of them depend entirely on Hebrew language-play and culturally idiosyncratic references. While we indeed changed the order of some sections, most notably of the opening one, we translated many more poems than Amichai originally suggested. But since, sadly, this turned out to be Amichai's last book, and by many accounts his *magnum opus*, we decided to prepare for the new comprehensive volume *The Poetry of Yehuda Amichai*, edited by Robert Alter, a translation of nearly all the poems we'd originally left out of *Open Closed Open*, and to restore the section order of the Hebrew. Thus, *Open Closed Open* appears nearly in complete form in Alter's new volume. What remain untranslated are poems like "Ve-hayu shirim" (And There Were Songs) from the section *Tiyul Yisra'eli* (Israeli Travel), #5 (68–69), which strings together titles of various pioneer-era songs, and where the meaning of the poem's intertextual collage depends entirely on the reader "hearing" the uncited sections of the various songs' lyrics, as well as their melodies. Alter's volume also includes our renditions of many previously untranslated poems by Amichai, among them some of the early rhymed work (Farrar, Straus & Giroux, in press).

76. Gluzman, "Mi-shirey ha-navi he-ani."

77. See discussion of grammatical gender in the poetry of Esther Raab in my *On the Margins of Modernism*, 71–78.

78. See, for example, poem #7 in "Ha-dvarim she-hayu me-olam": *Lo zakhar ve-lo nekeva / lo zekher ve-lo shikhecha, Patu'ach sagur patu'ach*, 62, untranslated.

79. See, for example, poem #9 in "Batim batim ve-ahava achat": *Chilaknu beynenu et ha-safa, at lakacht et ha-tnu'ot / va-ani et ha-itzurim ve-hayinu yachad safa achat / u-dvarim rabim, Patua'ch sagur patu'ach*, 90; "We divided the language between us: you took the vowels / and I the consonants, and together we were one language / and many things," trans. Chana Bloch and Chana Kronfeld, in the section "Houses (Plural); Love (Singular)," *The Poetry of Yehuda Amichai*, ed. Robert Alter (in press).

80. See discussion later in this chapter of poem #14 in "Be-chayay, be-chayay," *Patu'ach sagur patu'ach*, 115; "In My Life, on My Life," #13, *Open Closed Open*, 113.

81. All place names, as well as the terms for "land" (*aretz*) and "earth" (*adama*), are gendered feminine and form part of an elaborate metaphorical system (LAND/CITY/NATION AS WOMAN), which has its origins in the prophetic books of the Hebrew Bible.

82. See the section "Yerushalayim, Yerushalayim, lama Yerushalayim?" esp. the parody of Lamentations' depiction of the mourning Widow of Zion in poems #3 and #13; Jerusalem as a carousel or seesaw-woman from which the traumatized child begs God-the-Father to let him get off (*karusela, nadneda*; both fem.), #6; *Patu'ach sagur patu'ach*, 140–54; *Open Closed Open*, "Jerusalem, Jerusalem, Why Jerusalem?" 135–44, poems #3, #6, and #12. For the *tallis* as both towel (*magevet*; fem.) and an erotic object for kissing and hugging "close and slow" (*tzamud tzamud*), see #19 in "Elim mitclalfim, ha-tfilot nish'arot la-ad," *Patu'ach sagur patu'ach*, 13–14; *Open Closed Open*, "Gods Change, Prayers Are Here to Stay," 44, poem #16. For the Torah as beloved woman see, for example, "David melekh Yisrael chay ve-kayam: Ata ha-ish," #6, *Patu'ach sagur patu'ach*, 54; *Open Closed Open*, "David, King of Israel, Is Alive: Thou Art the Man," 52–53, poem #5; and for the Sabbath and the Torah scrolls feminized as a bride and as women wearing petticoats and velvet dresses, respectively, see # 26 in "Elim mitchalfim, ha-tfilot nish'arot la-ad," *Patu'ach sagur patu'ach*, 18; *Open Closed Open*, "Gods Change, Prayers Are Here to Stay," 47, poem #22.

83. "Ivrit," in *Tzurot*, 17–19; "Hebrew," trans. Lisa Katz, in *The Defiant Muse: Hebrew Feminist Prose from Antiquity to the Present*, 189–91.

84. Included in *Shirim 1948–1962*, 80–81; *Selected Poetry*, 13–14.

85. *Selected Poetry*, 14.

86. "Ya'akov ve-ha-mal'akh," in *Shirim 1948–1962*, 226–27; *Selected Poetry*, 40. See discussion in chapter 3.

87. In "Tanakh tanakh, itakh itakh u-midrashim acherim," #11, *Patu'ach sagur patu'ach*, 33; "The Bible and You, the Bible and You, and Other Midrashim," #8, *Open Closed Open*, 23.

88. In "Tanakh tanakh, itakh itakh u-midrashim acherim," #4, *Patu'ach sagur patu'ach*, 29; "The Bible and You, the Bible and You, and Other Midrashim," #3, *Open Closed Open*, 20.

89. "Sonet ha-binyanim," *Shirim 1948–1962*, 64–65, untranslated; see literal translation and discussion in chapter 6.

90. Benjamin, "The Task of the Translator," trans. Steven Rendall, and Friedrich Schleiermacher, "On the Different Methods of Translating," trans. Susan Bernofsky, both in *The Translation Studies Reader*, 43–63, 75–83.

91. During his sabbatical at New York University. Interview conducted in his Bleecker Street apartment, New York City, July 26, 1984.

92. Amichai shares this preoccupation with grammar as an inoculation against sentimentality with his fellow poet of the Statehood Generation, Dan Pagis, for

whom grammar offers a rhetorical and ethical solution to restraining the pathos in writing the Shoah. See, for example, "Targilim be-ivrit shimushit," in *Kol Ha-shirim*, 211–13; "Exercises in Practical Hebrew," trans. Peter Cole, in *Hebrew Writers on Writing*, 185–87.

93. "Leshon ahava ve-te al shkedim kluyim," #1, *Patu'ach sagur patu'ach*, 92; "The Language of Love and Tea with Roasted Almonds," #1, *Open Closed Open*, 93. See discussion in chapter 1.

94. As in John Donne's "The Sun Rising." The Christian pun "sun"/"son" may be in the background of its masculine metaphorical gendering in English.

95. Interestingly, even when discussing his own bilingualism, Amichai uses the same concept of gender fluidity to reject the suggestion that while German was his Mother Tongue, Hebrew was his Father Tongue: "I wouldn't say now that such a distinction is necessary. It implies a contrast of masculine versus feminine, where sensitivity and sentimentality are supposedly classified as feminine, while masculinity is tough and realistic. I don't think so. It's simply that my father knew Hebrew and my mother did not. She knew the prayers so in that sense she turned the father tongue into a divine tongue. The point is that over time [the two sources] blend together. And just as we have both feminine and masculine elements in our body and soul, so is it with language." (Interview with me, King David Hotel, Jerusalem, summer 1986.)

96. But avant-garde poets of course do; compare e. e. cummings's "he danced his did," from "[anyone lived in a pretty how town]," in *Complete Poems 1913–1962*, 515.

97. As we recall, Riffaterre describes syllepsis as an ungrammaticality that alerts the reader to an intertextual pattern. See his "Syllepsis," and "Intertextual Representation."

98. In Robert Alter's translation, *The Five Books of Moses*. For a queer reading of the first version of the creation story, see Hendel, Kronfeld, and Pardes, "Gender and Sexuality," in *Reading Genesis: Ten Methods*, 71–91. God's plurality is retained also in modern Hebrew exclamations such as *Elohim adirim* (lit., "mighty Gods"; idiomatically close to "Good God" in English).

99. "Elim mitchalfim, ha-tfilot nish'arot la-ad," #25, *Patu'ach sagur patu'ach*, 17–18; "Gods Change, Prayers Are Here to Stay," #21, *Open Closed Open*, 46–47.

100. Compare "Ha-acherut harga et Ruth," "Otherness Killed Ruth," his childhood love who perished in the Nazi genocide. *Pa'am katavti, akhshav u-va-yamim ha-acherim, kakh overet ha-tehila kakh ovrim ha-tehilim*, #1, *Patu'ach sagur patu'ach*, 20; "Once I Wrote *Now and in Other Days:* Thus Glory Passes, Thus Pass the Psalms," #1, *Open Closed Open*, 30. *Shemot shemot: shemot shemot ba-yamim ha-hem ba-zman ha-ze*, #14, *Patu'ach sagur patu'ach*, 138; "Names, Names, in Other Days and in Our Time," #10, *Open Closed Open*, 131–32.

101. Blanton, *Epic Negation: The Dialectical Poetics of Late Modernism*, 10, 18.

102. "Be-chayay be-chayay," #13, *Patu'ach sagur patu'ach*, 114; "In My Life, on My Life," #13, *Open Closed Open*, 113.

103. "Knasim, Knasim," *Patu'ach sagur patu'ach* #4, 157; "Conferences, Conferences," *Open Closed Open* #4, 149.

Chapter 5

1. The quote is from my interview with Amichai at the King David Hotel, Jerusalem, summer 1986. An earlier version of parts of this chapter appeared as "Hyphenated States: Metaphor as Poetics of Survival in the Poetry of Yehuda Amichai."

2. *Shirim 1948–1962*, 13. Translation by Chana Bloch and me to appear in Alter, ed. *The Poetry of Yehuda Amichai*.

3. As Sidra DeKoven Ezrahi points out, Amichai warns against the poet's taking his own metaphors and similes too literally—against believing their literal truth—in the poem "Meshorer shir ha-shirim," "Tanakh tanakh, itakh itakh: u-midrashim acherim," #32, in *Patu'ach sagur patu'ach*, 42–43; "The Singer of the Song of Songs," "The Bible and You, The Bible and You: And Other Midrashim" #18, *Open Closed Open*, 27. See DeKoven Ezrahi, "'Tziyon ha-lo tish'ali': Yerushalayim ke-metafora nashit"; English version published as "'To What Shall I Compare You?': Jerusalem as Ground Zero of the Hebrew Imagination."

4. de Man, "Shelley Disfigured," 119.

5. de Man, *Allegories of Reading*, 151.

6. See my *On the Margins of Modernism*.

7. See Lakoff and Johnson, *Metaphors We Live By*; Lakoff, *Women, Fire, and Dangerous Things*; Lakoff and Turner, *More Than Cool Reason: A Field Guide to Poetic Metaphor*; Lakoff, *Philosophy in the Flesh*; Sweetser, *From Etymology to Pragmatics: Metaphorical and Cultural Aspects of Semantic Structure*; Dancygier and Sweetser, *Figurative Language*; Sweetser, "Regular Metaphoricity in Gesture: Bodily-Based Models of Speech Interaction"; Sweetser, "'The Suburbs of Your Good Pleasure': Cognition, Culture, and the Bases of Metaphoric Structure," 4:24–55; Sullivan and Sweetser, "Is 'Generic Is Specific' a Metaphor?" In the context of Hebrew literature and culture, see the work of Sovran, especially *Relational Semantics and the Anatomy of Abstraction*; and Shen, "Schemata, Categories and Metaphor Comprehension"; Shen, "Metaphors and Categories"; Shen, *Cognition and Figurative Language*; Shen, "Cognition and Poetic Figures," 295–307.

8. See Fishelov, "Yehuda Amichai: A Modernist Metaphysical Poet."

9. Yehuda Amichai, "Chatuna me'ucheret," *Me-adam ata ve-el adam tashuv*, 75; "Late Marriage," *Selected Poetry*, 163–64.

10. See discussion of the poem "Between" in chapter 2.

11. *Shirim 1948–1962*, 13. Poetic translation by Chandra Bloch and me in Alter, *The Poetry of Yehuda Amichai*.

12. The image of "bread and circuses" as the epitome of distracting entertainment—or of war as distraction—provided by institutionalized religion and the state recurs throughout Amichai's poetry. Its final and most poignant articulation may be found in "Our Father, Our King" ("Avinu malkenu"), a radically iconoclastic inversion of the celebrated prayer, known especially from its use in the High Holidays: in this poem, God, "like any king," provides people with "bread and

nostalgia . . . for a better day," in the name of which they are asked to sacrifice themselves. See "Elim mitchalfim, ha-tfilot nish'arot la-ad," #7, *Patua'ch sagur patu'ach*, 8; "Gods Change, Prayers Are Here to Stay," #7, *Open Close Open*, 41. And see discussion in chapters 1 and 6.

13. Yehuda Amichai, "Machatzit ha-anashim ba-olam," *Shirim 1948–1962*, 82; "Half of the People in the World," *Selected Poetry*, 14.

14. "Ba-zavit ha-yeshara (Machazor meruba'im)," *Shirim 1948–1962*, 130. Translation by Amichai Kronfeld.

15. "Ani lo hayiti echad mi-sheshet ha-milyonim. U-ma meshekh chayay? Patu'ach sagur patu'ach," in *Patu'ach sagur patu'ach*, 126–29; "I Wasn't One of the Six Million: And What Is My Life Span? Open Closed Open," in *Open Closed Open*, 5–8.

16. See discussion of *zro'a/yad* (arm/hand) in chapter 3.

17. This might in fact be an allusion to Hemingway's *The Old Man and the Sea*, where the old man's hand has an objective ontological status like that of any other object in nature. Amichai was a high-school literature teacher during the period when this book was part of the curriculum.

18. Yehuda Amichai, "Shivyon," *Gam ha-egrof*, 117; "Equality," trans. Chana Bloch and Chana Kronfeld, in Alter, *The Poetry of Yehuda Amichai*.

19. In "Ani lo hayiti echad mi-sheshet ha-milyonim. U-ma meshekh chayay? patu'ach sagur patu'ach," # 1, *Patu'ach sagur patu'ach*, 126; "I Wasn't One of the Six Millions: And What Is My Life Span? Open Closed Open,"#6, *Open Closed Open*, 7.

20. Following current practice in linguistic and literary theories of metaphor, I use "metaphor" here as a superordinate category that encompasses not only metaphor proper but also simile and analogy. See discussion following in the chapter. On superordinate vs. basic-level categories, see Lakoff, *Women, Fire, and Dangerous Things*, 91–104. But see also Dacygier and Sweetser for an analysis of recent debates in cognitive linguistics over the characterization, construction, and mapping of simile. *Figurative Language*, 137–50.

21. de Man, *Allegories of Reading*, 151.

22. de Man, "Shelley Disfigured," 64, 66.

23. (It is only in the Land of Metaphor that one is a poet.) Stevens, "Miscellaneous Notebooks," in *Opus Posthumous*, 204.

24. See Scharf Gold, "Images in Transformation in the Recent Poetry of Yehuda Amichai."

25. Arpali, *Ha-prachim ve-ha-agartal*, 267.

26. In my Ph.D. dissertation "Aspects of Poetic Metaphor" (University of California, Berkeley, 1983); and see my article, "Novel and Conventional Metaphors: A Matter of Methodology."

27. Arpali, *Ha-prachim ve-ha-agartal*, 260–76; Scharf Gold, *Lo-kabrosh*, 11–30; Fishelov, "Amichai: Metaphysical Poet"; Sadan-Lovenstein, "*Tavniyot imajistiyot be-shirat Amichai*" (Image Patterns in the Poetry of Amichai); Shamir, "The Conceit as a Cardinal Style-Marker in Yehuda Amichai's Poetry," 17–26; Feldman, "The Metaphor of the Persona," 71–76.

28. On the relationship between image schemas and metaphorical systems, see Lakoff, *Women, Fire and Dangerous Things;* Lakoff and Johnson, *Metaphors We Live By;* Lakoff and Turner, *More Than Pure Reason;* and chap. 2.3, "How Mappings Are Grounded in Experience," in Dancygier and Sweetser, *Figurative Language,* 21–34.

29. *Shirim 1948–1962,* 80–81; *Selected Poetry,* 13;

30. Ibid., 130; trans. Amichai Kronfeld.

31. "Chatuna me'ucheret," *Me-adam ata ve-el adam tashuv,* 75; "Late Marriage," *Selected Poetry,* 163.

32. Harshav, *Explorations in Poetics.*

33. *Shirim 1948–1962,* 13, 245–46; *Akhshav ba-ra'ash,* 30, 92; *Selected Poetry* "Here," 21, "The Bull Returns," 55, "Elegy," 58. Alter, *The Poetry of Yehuda Amichai:* "The Two of Us Together and Each of Us Alone" (in press).

34. See discussion and n. 38 below.

35. "Be-tokh ha-tapu'ach," *Me-adam ata ve-el adam tashuv,* 37; *Selected Poetry,* 164. In *By Words Alone* (84ff.), Sidra DeKoven Ezrahi discusses Ilona Karmel's use of a similar metaphor in Karmel's 1969 novel, *An Estate of Memory,* where the apple (and the implicit knife paring it) depict a woman's perilous existence in a concentration camp: "Her head felt like an apple with its head pared off" (218. I don't know whether Amichai was familiar with Karmel's work).

36. *Me-adam ata ve-el adam tashuv,* 75; *Selected Poetry,* 163.

37. *Shirim 1948–1962,* 74–75; no translation. *Patu'ach sagur patu'ach,* 44–50; *Open Closed Open,* 9–16.

38. Thus, for example, the first section of the book is called "Mot imi ve-ha-kravot ha-avudim al atid ha-yeladim" (My Mother's Death and the Lost Battles for Our Children's Future); section title does not appear in the *Selected Poetry.* Amichai told me he had originally planned to use this as the title of the whole book.

39. Shaked, "Masa shel tachanot" (A Station Voyage). See also Sarna, "Chay al ha-makaf. Yehuda Amichai" (He Lives on the Hyphen. Yehuda Amichai), *Yedi'ot Acharonot,* March 19, 2012.

40. "Change Is God and Death Is His Prophet" ("Ha-shinuy hu ha-elohim, ha-mavet nevi'o"), declares Amichai in the name of one of the sections in *Open Closed Open,* paraphrasing the Muslim prayer (*Patu'ach sagur patu'ach,* 116–25; *Open Closed Open,* 115–31). But in various places throughout the book Amichai changes this statement about change, inverting it by self-consciously applying the principle of changeability to itself.

41. Three out of the four times the expression *kol sason ve-kol simcha, kol chatan ve-kol kala* appears in Jeremiah it is in the context of cursing Zion for its sins—e.g., "Behold, I will cause to cease out of this place in your eyes, and in your days, the voice of mirth, and the voice of gladness, the voice of the bridegroom, and the voice of the bride" (Jeremiah 16:9). Today this expression has lost its negative edge entirely and has become a common wedding greeting and song; but Amichai is clearly aware here of its opposite biblical illocutionary force.

42. "Yesh milchama gdola," *Me-achorey kol ze mistater osher gadol*, 76–77; translated as "My Soul," *Amen*, 60; translation by the author and Ted Hughes.

43. See Harshav, *Explorations in Poetics*, 180, 183, 263.

44. "Na'aseti sa'ir," *Me-achorey kol ze*, 40–41; *Selected Poetry*, 97.

45. When I last checked, the Amichai Archives at the Beinecke Library still had a folder of letters and cards from Amichai's children to their father classified as "Letters to Dov," even though I pointed the error out to them several years ago.

46. On the conventional cultural understanding of violence toward humans as slaughter of animals, see Dancygier and Sweetser, *Figurative Language*, 141.

47. In my "Aspects of Poetic Metaphor."

48. For example, by Geoffrey Hartman at the Yale Conference in Amichai's memory, "Poetics and Politics in Yehuda Amichai's World," convened by Dr. Nanette Stahl (2007). See conference videos at http://www.library.yale.edu/judaica/site/conferences/Amichai/. Similar accusations are made throughout Scharf Gold's biography, *Yehuda Amichai: The Making of Israel's National Poet*.

49. He is either unable to fall asleep, or asleep while his body is awake with a sense of mortality. Amichai is employing here the two alternative scenarios of the evoked text from the Song of Songs (which he reverses from the context of love to that of death, and from female to male speaker). Compare Song of Songs 5:2: "I sleep, but my heart waketh"; and 3:1: "By night on my bed I sought him whom my soul loveth."

50. "Re'ach ha-benzin oleh be-api," *Shirim 1948–1962*, 21–22; "The Smell of Gasoline Ascends in My Nose," *Selected Poetry*, 3. See also Introduction.

51. *Ha-prachim ve-ha-agartel* (The Flowers and the Urn).

52. In an interview with me at his home in Jerusalem, summer 1986.

53. Harshav, *Explorations in Poetics*, 13, 68, 260.

54. *Figurative Language*, 43–58.

55. See Searle, *Speech Acts: An Essay in the Philosophy of Language*; and "Indirect Speech Acts," in *Expression and Meaning*, 30–57.

56. Mitchell's translation chooses not to use the English idiom, thus resulting in a univocal speech-act of romantic promise and reassurance: "Love, I'll protect you and hold you close"; *Selected Poetry*, 3.

57. Bahat and Ron, *Ve-dayek* (Be precise); thirty-six editions were published.

58. On the distinction between "speaker's meaning" and "utterance meaning" see Grice, "Utterer's Meaning, Sentence Meaning, and Word-Meaning"; and Grice, "Meaning Revisited," 223–43.

59. *Shirim 1948–1962*, 42–43; *Selected Poetry*, 8.

60. Translated as *Za'aki, eretz ahuva* (echoed almost verbatim in the poem), the novel became a successful play in the Ha-bima National Theater in 1953. Azriel Carlebach, the founder of *Ma'ariv* newspaper, published in the same year a sharply critical article, using Paton's book to draw an analogy between Israel's policy toward the Palestinians and South African repression of the black population. See discussion in Eyal, "*Za'aki eretz ahuva, girsat 1953*" (Cry the Beloved Country, the

1953 Version), in *Ma'ariv* online at NRG, http://www.nrg.co.il/online/1/ART2
/048/465.html, published February 2, 2010.

Chapter 6

1. "'רצה גורלי המפולג שאהיה שתול בתוך שני דורות, מעין ׳מרגל כפול'". "Dorot ba-aretz
(ne'um bi-ve'idat ha-sofrim)" ("Generations in the Land," speech given at the
writers conference; published in *La-merchav*, May 3, 1968). Cited and discussed
in Weissbrod, *Ba-yamim ha-acherim*, 327. Some parts of this chapter appear in an
earlier version in my *On the Margins of Modernism*.

2. See esp. Miron, *Mul ha-ach ha-shotek*, 273–313. .

3. "Dorot ba-aretz (ne'um bi-ve'idayt ha-sofrim)."

4. "Ve-hi tehilatekha," *Shirim 1948–1962*, 71–72; "And That Is Your Glory,"
Selected Poetry, 11–12. In chapter 4 I discuss this poem in the context of (mis)
translation.

5. See Arpali, *Ha-prachim ve-ha-agartal*, 114–19; DeKoven Ezrahi, "Yehuda
Amichai: paytan shel ha-yomyom"; and my discussion in chapter 3.

6. See Tzvik, "Yetzirat Amichai bi-r'i ha-bikoret," 12–14, 29–30.

7. Compare, e.g., the importance of self-reference as a poetic principle
within romanticism (especially romantic irony) and—famously now—within
postmodernism.

8. *Literary History, Modernism and Postmodernism*, 11–12.

9. While Zach has asserted over the years in various venues that he had edited Amichai's first book and made cuts that supposedly greatly improved it, this
account, repeated by a number of scholars, is contradicted by historical evidence
that his role was limited to that of a publisher. In an interview titled "Monolog
shel ze'ev boded" (Monologue of a Lone Wolf), Amichai says: "My book *Now
and in Other Days* was published at my own expense by the *Likrat* publishing house. The *Likrat* publishing house was actually Natan Zach himself, who
took from me the poems which were written out in a very bad handwriting
and brought them to press [*ve-hevi'am el beyt-ha-dfus*, a Hebrew idiom that
means to bring to press], proofread them and saw to their publication [*da'ag
le-hotza'atam la-or*]." In *Ha-olam ha-ze*, June 30, 1976. For more on the controversy surrounding Zach's role in the publication of Amichai's first book, see
Hana Amichai, "Al menat li-zkor: Yehuda Amichai, Natan Zach ve-uvdot she-
ra'uy le-hatzig."

10. "Monologue of a Lone Wolf."

11. *Poetry* (March 1911).

12. Emphasis in the original. Yehuda Amichai, "Sicha im Yehuda Amichai"
(Conversation with Yehuda Amichai), interview by Aviva Barzel, 326. It is perhaps
no accident that Amichai chose a decentered diasporic venue like *Ha-Do'ar* (published in New York) to express these views.

13. See *On the Margins of Modernism*.

14. Literally, the "square" stanza (*ha-bayit ha-meruba*); Zach cannot resist the

pun, enlisting 1960s youth culture's critique of "squares" for his attack on traditional verse forms. But note also how this wording erases the Middle Eastern origin of the form, so crucial for Amichai. Amichai singles out the quatrain in its Persian, Arabic, and Hebrew medieval *ruba'iyat* form as a regional poetic ideal. He regards the quatrain as a challenge precisely because of its prosodic symmetry and iterative rhyme. In an interview with me Amichai was quite emphatic and unusually technical: "I think the quatrain [*ruba'iyat*] actually plays the role here [in the Middle East] that the sonnet played in Western culture, a set form into which one pours contrary things. So for me the quatrain is the wisdom of monotony, as in Middle Eastern music. The use of monorhyme [*charuz mavri'ach*] is actually the artistic challenge. The form is a challenge and it also helps me. Even today, though today I wouldn't publish them [the quatrains] because I speak a different language and maintain a different dialogue with the world; but I still compose quatrains for myself, for the drawer [*la-megera*]. After 120 [= after I'm gone] you'll get to read them." Interview at our home, Berkeley, California, spring 1986. And see discussion in chapter 4 on Amichai's unpublished quatrain.

15. This reevaluation started with research inspired by postcolonial and feminist theory, but has recently moved beyond those parameters. See esp. Hever, "The Grey Historians of the Brain: Nativism in the Poetry of Moshe Dor," 41–65; and Hever, *Sifrut she-nikhtevet mi-kan: Kitzur ha-sifrut ha-Yisra'elit* (Literature Written from Here: A Précis of Israeli Literature), 46–69; Tsamir, *Be-shem ha-nof*; Tsamir and Hess, *Kitmey Or*; Weisman, "Zman u-tnu'a be-shirat David Avidan" (Time and Movement in the Poetry of David Avidan); Stav, *Aba ani koveshet: Avot u-vanot ba-shira ha-ivrit ha-chadasha* [lit., "daddy, I'm an occupier/charmer"; title translated as "Reconstructing Daddy: Fathers and Daughters in Modern Hebrew Poetry"], 85–159; and the special issue of *Jewish Social Studies* 18, no. 3 (spring/summer 2012), "History and Responsibility: Hebrew Literature Facing 1948," edited by Amir Eshel, Hannan Hever, and Vered Karti Shemtov. My work is in close dialogue with recent reevaluations of Statehood Generation poetry by Michael Gluzman, who is preparing a monograph on the subject, and see his "'Le-ha'atzil alegantiyut la-sevel': al mekoma shel Dahlia Ravikovitch be-shirat dor ha-mdina," in *Kitmey Or*, 578–99; and "Sovereignty and Melancholia: Israeli Poetry after 1948," 64–79. See also Hirschfeld, "Locus and Language: Hebrew Culture in Israel," 1011–60; Eshel, "Eternal Present: Poetic Figuration and Cultural Memory in the Poetry of Yehuda Amichai, Dan Pagis, and Tuvia Rübner," 141–67; Eshel and Presner, "Introduction," 607–14; Shemtov, *Miktzavim mishtanim: Likrat te'oria shel prozodia be-heksher tarbuti* (Changing Rhythms: Towards a Theory of Prosody in Cultural Context), 116–23; Setter, "After the Fact: Potential Collectivities in Israel/Palestine" (Ph.D. dissertation, University of California, Berkeley, 2012); and Ophir, "Why Read Poems in Such Hard Times? Sociopolitical History and Aesthetic Commitment in Modern Hebrew, Yiddish and German Poetry" (Ph.D. dissertation, University of California, Berkeley, 2013).

16. This is the title of one of his most famous and programmatically metapoetic poems, in *Kol he-chalav ve-ha-dvash* (All the Milk and Honey), 68.

17. At our home in Berkeley, California, spring 1986.

18. From notes taken during a question and answer session in my Hebrew literature seminar in spring 1986. I discuss the philosophical and political implications of this point in the Introduction and chapter 2.

19. *Shirim 1948–1962*, 64–65.

20. *Shirim 1948–1962*, 69–70; for different translations see *A Life of Poetry*, 31; and Alter, *The Poetry of Yehuda Amichai*. See discussion in chapter 2.

21. Unpublished.

22. This aspect of my argument is in conversation with Michael Gluzman's work on trauma and melancholia as underlying psychological dimensions of State-hood Generation poetry. See n. 15 above.

23. See discussion of the "wisdom of camouflage" in chapter 2.

24. "Ba-yom she-bo nolda biti lo met af ish," *Shalva gdola: she'elot u-tshuvot*, 44; "On the Day My Daughter Was Born No One Died," *Selected Poetry*, 131–32.

25. In *Sha'ar Ha-Gay* (Gate of the Valley), where burnt vehicles from the 1948 war are still "lying dead" as a roadside monument (in the words of the famous song "Bab el Wad"). It is significant that the speaker in the poem wanted to take a trip to that place, of all places, right after the birth of his daughter; it is there that he points to the dying pine trees' great productiveness. On the constructedness of the Bab el Wad monument in *Open Closed Open*, see chapter 1. Biographically, it should be noted that the wooded area above *Sha'ar Ha-Gay* was indeed one of Amichai's favorite areas to hike and picnic, and Zvi is the real name of one of Amichai's close friends. Emanuela, Amichai and Hana's daughter, was indeed born in 1978. In other words, this poem practices on many levels the rhetoric of autobiography I have described earlier to make its philosophical and metapoetic concerns blend unobtrusively into the real. But that blending is, of course, the topic of the poem as a whole!

26. On the sustained reversals of "prosaic" and "poetic" norms in this poem, see Scharf Gold, *Lo ka-brosh: Gilguley imajim ve-tavniyot be-shirat Yehuda Amichai*, 145–47. Her reading of these reversals, however, reiterates the modernist cliché about "language as an unsatisfactory instrument of communication" (ibid., 147), precisely the position Amichai is rejecting.

27. In his acceptance speech of the honorary doctorate from Tel Aviv University Amichai compares poetry to science: "Like science poetry must be precise even more than prose. . . . The determining factor is precision [*diyuk*], the immediate precision. . . . Like science poetry takes things out of context but then must return them . . . to a context that will have a future the way it had a past." In "Ha-shira hi sfat ha-nefesh" (Poetry Is the Language of the Soul), *Ha'aretz*, June 2, 1995.

28. In chapter 3 I discuss the reversal of the terms of this central romantic metaphor. And see also the poem "Imi hayta nevi'ah ve-lo yad'ah," in *"Melon Horay,"* #3, *Patu'ach sagur patu'ach*, 57; "My Mother Was a Prophet and Didn't Know It," in "My Parents' Lodging Place," #3, *Open Closed Open*, 57.

29. In an interview at our home, Berkeley, California, spring 1986.

30. See Sandbank, "Nof ha-nefesh: Rilke, Auden, Amichai," in *Shtey brek-hot ba-ya'ar*; "Amichai: ha-mischak ve-ha-shefa," in *Ha-shir ha-nakhon*; "'Mistovev, omed, mitmahameha': Rilke, Amichai ve-ha-mabat le-achor," in *Ha-kol hu ha-acher*.

31. Yehuda Amichai, "Mas'ot Binyamin ha-acharon mi-Tudela," *Akshav ba-ra'ash*, 97; "Travels of the Last Benjamin of Tudela," *Selected Poetry*, 60.

32. Pound's imagist "In a Station of the Metro" was first published in *Poetry* in 1913. On Amichai's preference for the simile, and on the role of juxtaposing initially distant semantic domains, see chapter 5.

33. In my final interview with him, at our home in Berkeley, California, in 1996.

Works Cited

Abramovitch, Shalom Ya'akov. *Kitzur mas'ot Binyamin ha-shlishi* (The Abbreviated Travels of Benjamin the Third). Odessa: Beylinson Press, 1896.

Abramovitch-Ratner, Tzila. "Beyn ha-mesaper le-veyn shiro: Le-sugiyat ha-korelatzya she-beyn shira le-veyn siporet" (Between the Storyteller and His Poem: On the Problem of Correlation between Poetry and Prose). In *Sefer Israel Levin*, ed. Re'uven Tzur and Tova Rosen, vol. 2, 227–46. Tel Aviv: Tel Aviv University, 1995.

Abramson, Glenda, ed. *The Experienced Soul: Studies in Amichai.* New York: Westview Press, 1997.

———. *The Writing of Yehuda Amichai: A Thematic Approach.* Albany: State University of New York Press, 1989.

Adorno, Theodor W. *Aesthetic Theory.* Trans. C. Lenhardt. London: Routledge and Kegan Paul, 1984.

———. *Negative Dialectics.* Trans. E. B. Ashton. 1966, reprint; New York: Seabury, 1973.

———. "Notes on Kafka." In *Prisms*, trans. Samuel and Shierry Weber, 243–71. Cambridge, MA: MIT Press, 1981.

———. *Notes to Literature.* Trans. Shierry Weber Nicholsen. Vol. 1. New York: Columbia University Press, 1991.

Agamben, Girogio. *Homo Sacer: Sovereign Power and Bare Life.* Trans. Daniel Heller-Roazen. Stanford: Stanford University Press, 1998.

———. *The State of Exception.* Trans. Kevin Attel. Chicago: University of Chicago Press, 2005.

Allen, Graham. *Intertextuality.* New Critical Idiom Series. London: Routledge, 2000.

Alter, Robert. *The Art of Biblical Narrative.* New York: Basic Books, 1981.

———. *The Five Books of Moses.* New York: W. W. Norton, 2004.

———. "Israel's Master Poet." *New York Times Magazine*, June 8, 1986.

———. "Mischak ve-chazon be-shirato shel Yehuda Amichai" (Play and Vision in the Poetry of Yehuda Amichai). Lecture delivered at the Jewish Theological Seminary, New York, NY, October 28, 1979.

357

———. "Only a Man." *New Republic*, December 31, 2008.

———. "The Untranslatable Amichai." *Modern Hebrew Literature* 13 (1994): 28–31.

———. *The Wisdom Books*. New York: W. W. Norton, 2010.

Althusser, Louis. "Ideology and Ideological State Apparatuses." In *Lenin and Philosophy and Other Essays*, 127–88. Trans. Ben Brewster. New York and London: Monthly Review Press, 1971.

Althusser, Louis, and Étienne Balibar. *Reading Capital*. London: New Left Books, 1970.

Amichai, Hana. "Al menat li-zkor: Yehuda Amichai, Natan Zach ve-uvdot she-ra'uy le-hatzig" (For the Sake of Remembering: Yehuda Amichai, Natan Zach, and Facts That Should be Presented). *Akhshav* 73–74 (2013–2014): 27–33.

———. "'Ruth ha-ktana hi Anna Frank pratit she-li'" ("Little Ruth Is My Own Private Anne Frank"). *Ha'aretz*, December 9, 2010.

———. "Shir mecha'a" (Protest Poem). Interview by Na'ama Lensky. *Israel ha-yom*, April 8, 2011.

Amichai, Yehuda. *Akhshav ba-ra'ash* (Now in the Earthquake). Tel Aviv: Schocken, 1969.

———. *Akhshav u-va-yamim ha-acherim* (Now and in Other Days). Tel Aviv: Likrat, 1955.

———. *Amen*. Trans. Yehuda Amichai and Ted Hughes. New York: Harper & Row, 1977.

———. "Ani navi ani she-chozer ba-tzohorayim ha-bayta" (I Am a Poor Prophet Who Returns Home for Lunch). Interview by Eilat Negev. In Eilat Negev, *Sichot intimiyot* (Intimate Conversations), 221–29. Tel Aviv: Yedi'ot Acharonot/ Chemed Books, 1995.

———. "Auden kore mi-shirav ha-acharonim" (Auden Reads from His Latest Poems). *La-Merchav/Masa*, December 2, 1955.

———. "Ba-aretz ha-lohetet ha-zot, milim tzrikhot li-hyot tzel" (In This Scorching Land, Words Must Provide Shade). Interview by Dan Omer. *Prosa* 25 (July 1978): 4.

———. *Ba-ru'ach ha-nora'a ha-zot* (In This Terrible Wind). Merchavya: Sifriyat Po'alim, 1961.

———. "Bikur be-nofo shel Dylan Thomas" (A Visit to the Landscape of Dylan Thomas). *La-Merchav/Masa*, October 14, 1955.

———. "Comments." In "Proceedings of a Meeting of the Hebrew Writers Union with a Group of Arab Writers, January 3, 1970." *Daf* 34 (March 1970): 13.

———. "Dorot ba-aretz" (Generations in the Land). Lecture delivered at the Writers' Association Conference, 1968. Published in *La-merchav*, May 3, 1968.

———. *The Early Books of Yehuda Amichai*. Trans. Harold Schimmel and Assia Guttmann. New York: Sheep Meadow Press, 1988.

———. *Even a Fist Was Once an Open Palm with Fingers*. Trans. Barbara Harshav and Benjamin Harshav. New York: Harper, 1991.

———. *Gam ha-egrof haya pa'am yad ptucha ve-etzba'ot* (Even the Fist Once Was an Open Hand and Fingers). Tel Aviv: Schocken, 1989.

———. "Ha-ani ha-lo ma'amin sheli" (My "Non-Credo"/My "I Do Not Believe"). Interview by Ya'akov Besser. In *Si'ach meshorerim al atzmam ve-al ktivatam* (Poets Talk about Themselves and Their Work), 50–53. Tel Aviv: Eked, 1971.

———. "Ha-shira hi sfat ha-nefesh" (Poetry Is the Language of the Soul). *Ha'aretz*, June 2, 1995.

———. *Ha-zman* (Time). Tel Aviv: Schocken, 1977.

———. "Irreverent Poet of Jerusalem." Interview by Laura Blumenthal. *International Herald Tribune*, October 26, 1995.

———. "Ktiva hi pri atzlanut nifla'a!" (Writing Is the Fruit of a Wondrous Laziness). Interview by Michael Miro. *Pi ha-aton* 18, no. 9 (1978): 6.

———. *Lo me-akhshav, lo mi-kan* (Not of This Time, Not of This Place). Tel Aviv: Schocken, 1963.

———. *Me-achorey kol ze mistater osher gadol (Behind All This a Great Happiness Is Hiding)*. Tel Aviv: Schocken, 1974.

———. *Me-adam ata ve-el adam tashuv* (From Man Thou Art and Unto Man Shalt Thou Return). Tel Aviv: Schocken, 1985.

———. "Mekave le-Nobel" (Hoping for the Nobel Prize). Interview by Dalia Karpel. *Ha-ir*, March 11, 1989.

———. "Meshorer le'umi? Ani?" (A National Poet? Me?). Interview by Edna Evron. *Ha'aretz*, October 22, 1999.

———. *Mi Yitneni malon* (Would I Had a Lodging Place). Tel Aviv: Bitan, 1971.

———. "Monolog shel ze'ev boded" (Monologue of a Lone Wolf). Interview in *Ha-olam ha-ze*, June 30, 1976.

———. *Not of This Time, Not of This Place*. Trans. Shlomo Katz. New York: Harper, 1968.

———. *Open Closed Open*. Trans. Chana Bloch and Chana Kronfeld. New York: Harcourt, 2000.

———. "Pa'amonim mevasrim ra'ot" (Ominous Bells). Interview by Arye Arad. *Ba-machane* 26, no. 9 (November 1971).

———. *Patu'ach sagur patu'ach* (*Open Closed Open*). Tel Aviv: Schocken, 1998.

———. *Poems by Yehuda Amichai*. Trans. Assia Gutmann. Intro. Michael Hamburger. New York: Harper & Row, 1968.

———. *The Poetry of Yehuda Amichai*. Ed. Robert Alter. New York: Farrar, Straus & Giroux, in press.

———. *The Selected Poetry of Yehuda Amichai*. Trans. Chana Bloch and Stephen Mitchell. Berkeley: University of California Press, 1996. First published by Harper & Row, 1986.

———. *Shalva Gdola: She'elot u-tshuvot* (A Great Tranquility: Questions and Answers). Tel Aviv: Schocken, 1980.

———. *She'at ha-chesed* (The Hour of Grace). Tel Aviv: Schocken, 1982.

———. *Shirey Yehuda Amichai* (The Poetry of Yehuda Amichai). 5 vols. Tel Aviv: Schocken, 2002–2004.

———. *Shirim 1948–1962* (Poems 1948–1962). Tel Aviv: Schocken, 1963.

———. *Shirim 1948–1962* (Poems 1948–1962). 3rd ed. Tel Aviv: Schocken, 1967.

———. "*Shirim al kfar natush*" (Poems on an Abandoned Village). *Yokhani* 1 (1961): 14–16.

———. "*Sicha im Yehuda Amichai*" (Conversation with Yehuda Amichai). Interview by Aviva Barzel. *Ha-Do'ar* 21 (1976): 325–27.

———. *Time: Poems by Yehuda Amichai*. New York: Harper & Row, 1979.

———. *Travels*. Trans. Ruth Nevo. New York: Sheep Meadow Press, 1986.

———. *Travels of a Latter-Day Benjamin of Tudela*. Trans. Ruth Nevo. Toronto: House of Exile, 1975.

———. *Ve-lo al menat li-zkor* (Not for the Sake of Remembering). Tel Aviv: Schocken, 1971.

———. *The World Is a Room and Other Stories by Yehuda Amichai*. Ed. and trans. Elinor Grumet et al. Philadelphia: Jewish Publication Society of America, 1984.

———. "Yehuda Amichai." Interview by David Montenegro. In David Montenegro, *Points of Departure: International Writers on Writing and Politics*. Ann Arbor: University of Michigan Press, 1991.

———. *Yehuda Amichai: A Life of Poetry, 1948–1994*. Trans. Benjamin Harshav and Barbara Harshav. New York: Harper, 1995.

———. "Yehuda Amichai: Eykh ata magi'a la-shir?" (Yehuda Amichai: How Do You Get to the Poem?). Interview by Hillit Yeshurun. *Hadarim* 6 (1987): 129–34.

———. *Yehuda Amichai: Selected Poems*. Ed. Ted Hughes and Daniel Weissbort. London: Faber & Faber, 2000.

———. "Yehuda Amichai: The Art of Poetry." Interview by Lawrence Joseph. *Paris Review* 122 (spring 1992): 212–51.

———. "Yoman" (Diary). *Moznayim* 29, no. 1 (1969): 18–23.

Apter, Emily. *The Translation Zone: The New Comparative Literature*. Princeton: Princeton University Press, 2006.

Aran, David. "Yehuda Amichai—be-shira u-vi-proza: Nisayon shel bikoret." (Yehuda Amichai—in Poetry and in Prose: An Attempt at a Critique). *Al ha-mishmar*, June 16, 1961.

———. "Yehuda Amichai—be-shira u-vi-proza (ma'amar sheni)" (Yehuda Amichai—in Poetry and in Prose (a Second Essay). *Al ha-mishmar*, June 23, 1961.

Arbell, Michal. "Abba Kovner: The Ritual Function of His Battle Missives (*Dapey krav*)." *Jewish Social Studies* 18, no. 3 (spring/summer 2012): 99–119.

Arpali, Boaz. "Amichai, Yehuda." In *The Encyclopedia Hebraica*. Supp. vol. 2. 1983.

———. *Ha-prachim ve-ha-agartal; shirat Amichai: mivne, mashmau't, po'etika* (The Flowers and the Urn: Amichai's Poetry 1948–1968). Tel Aviv: Siman kri'a /Ha-Kibbutz ha-Me'uchad, 1986.

———. "On the Political Significance of Amichai's Poetry." In *The Experienced

Soul: Studies in Amichai, ed. Glenda Abramson, 27–50. New York: Westview Press, 1997.

———. "Yerushalayim chatranit: Yerushalayim ke-tzomet mefarek mitosim be-shirat Yehuda Amichai" (Subversive Jerusalem: Jerusalem as a Myth-Busting Juncture in the Poetry of Yehuda Amichai). *Dapim le-mechkar be-sifrut* 14–15 (2006): 1–27.

Assman, Aleida. "The Curse and Blessing of Babel, or, Looking Back on Universalism." In *The Translatability of Cultures: Figuration of the Space Between*, ed. Sanford Budick and Wolfgang Iser, 85–100. Stanford: Stanford University Press, 1996.

Avidan, David. "Ha-shira ke-politika ve-ha-politika ke-shira: Rak al te'alem lanu, Yehuda" (Poetry as Politics and Politics as Poetry: Just Don't Disappear on Us, Yehuda). *Yedi'ot Acharonot*, November 22, 1985.

Bahat, Ya'akov, and Mordekhai Ron. *Ve-dayek* (Be Precise). Tel Aviv: Ha-Kibbutz ha-Me'uchad, 1960.

Bakhtin, Mikhail M. *The Dialogic Imagination: Four Essays*. Ed. and trans. Michael Holquist. Austin: University of Texas Press, 1981.

———. *Problems of Dostoevsky's Poetics*. Ed. and trans. Caryl Emerson. Minneapolis: University of Minnesota Press, 1984.

Balaban, Avraham. "Ha-mayim ve-ha-yayin" (The Water and the Wine). *Ma'ariv*, December 1, 1989.

Bardugo, Liron. "*Yehuda Amichai: Ha-mavet ha-yafe*" (Yehuda Amichai: The Beautiful Death). *e-mago*. Last modified October 5, 2005. www.e-mago.co.il/e-magazine/amichai.html.

Bargad, Warren. "Children and Lovers: On Yehuda Amichai's Poetic Works." *Midstream* 21 (1975): 50–58.

Bartana, Ortzion. "Amichai: She'elot u-tshuvot" (Amichai: Questions and Answers). *Yedi'ot Acharonot*, April 25, 1980.

———. *La-vo cheshbon* (Settling Accounts). Tel Aviv: Alef, 1985.

———. "Mahapekhan simpati: Yehuda Amichai—sikum beynayim" (A Likable Revolutionary: Yehuda Amichai—An Interim Summary). *Nativ* 6, no. 77 (November 2000): 107–11.

———. "Pninim ba-efer" (Pearls in the Ashes). *Ma'ariv*, November 23, 1989.

———. *Zehirut, sifrut eretzyisre'elit* (Watch Out, Land of Israel Literature). Tel Aviv: Papirus, 1989.

Barthes, Roland. *Camera Lucida*. Trans. Richard Howard. New York: Hill and Wang, 1981.

———. *Image-Music-Text*. Trans. Stephen Heath. London: Fontana, 1977.

———. *The Pleasures of the Text*. Trans. Richard Miller. New York: Hill and Wang, 1976.

Batchelor, Jennie, ed. "Beyond Influence." Special Issue, *Women's Writing* 20, no. 1 (March 2013).

Barzel, Hillel. *Meshorerey bsora* (Poets of Mission). Tel Aviv: Yachdav, 1983.

———. *Meshorerim bi-gdulatam* (Poets in Their Greatness). Tel Aviv: Yachdav, 1979.

———. "Yehuda Amichai: le-hakdim 'sof' la-'eynsof': Iyun bi-tfisat ha-shir shel ha-meshorer" (Yehuda Amichai: Putting 'End' before 'Endlessness': A Study of the Poet's Conception of the Poem). *Iton 77, nos.* 72–73 (1986): 20–23.

Bassan, Eyal. "Fictions of the Non-Conflictual." Ph.D. diss., University of California, Berkeley, forthcoming.

———. "Gnessin: Likrat sifrut minorit" (Gnessin: Toward a Minor Literature). Master's thesis, Tel Aviv University, 2010.

———. "Metaphorization vs. Interpellation: Reconsidering the Poetics and Politics of Yehuda Amichai's Fiction." Paper presented at the NAPH International Conference, Los Angeles, CA, June 2012.

Bassnett-McGuire, Susan. *Translation Studies.* London: Methuen, 1980.

Baxandall, Michael. *Patterns of Intention: On the Historical Explanation of Pictures.* New Haven: Yale University Press, 1985.

Be'er, Chaim. "Akhshav ba-ra'ash li-Yehuda Amichai" (Now in the Earthquake by Yehuda Amichai). *Ha'aretz,* March 21, 1969.

Ben, Menachem. "'Ki kol ha-adam edim'" ("For All Man Is Vapors"). *Yedi'ot Acharonot,* January 3, 1986.

"Benjamin II." In *Encyclopedia Judaica.* Vol. 4, 526–27. Jerusalem: Keter, 1971.

"Benjamin (Ben Jonah) of Tudela." In *Encyclopedia Judaica.* Vol. 4, 535–38. Jerusalem: Keter, 1971.

Benjamin, Walter. "The Task of the Translator." In *The Translation Studies Reader,* ed. Lawrence Venuti, trans. Harry Zohn, 1–23. London and New York: Routledge, 2000.

———. "The Task of the Translator." In *The Translation Studies Reader,* ed. Lawrence Venuti, trans. Steven Rendall, 43–63. London and New York: Routledge, 2012.

———. "Theses on the Philosophy of History." In *Illuminations: Essays and Reflections,* trans. Harry Zohn, intro. Hannah Arendt, 253–64. New York: Schocken, 1968.

Ben-Porat, Ziva. "Beyn-textualiyut retorit" (Rhetorical Intertextuality). *Ha-Sifrut* 34 (1985): 170–78.

———. "The Poetics of Literary Allusion." *PTL: A Journal for Descriptive Poetics and Theory of Literature* 1, no. 1 (1976): 105–28.

Ben-Porat, Ziva, et al. *Lirika ve-lahit* (Lyrical Poetry and the Lyrics of Pop). Tel Aviv: Porter Institute, 1989.

Bergonzi, Bernard, ed. *Innovations: Essays on Art and Ideas.* London: Macmillan, 1968.

Bermann, Sandra, and Michael Wood, eds. *Nation, Language, and the Ethics of Translation.* Princeton: Princeton University Press, 2005.

Bernard-Donals, Michael. "'If I Forget Thee, O Jerusalem': The Poetry of Forgetful Memory in Palestine." In *Forgetful Memory: Representations and Remem-*

brance in the Wake of the Holocaust, ed. Bernard-Donalds, 41–55. Albany: State University of New York Press, 2009.

Bernstein, Michael André. *Foregone Conclusions: Against Apocalyptic History.* Berkeley: University of California Press, 2006.

Bérubé, Michael. *Marginal Forces/Cultural Centers.* Ithaca, NY: Cornell University Press, 1992.

Bevis, William W. *Mind of Winter: Wallace Stevens, Meditation, and Literature.* Pittsburgh: University of Pittsburgh Press, 1988.

Bhabha, Homi K. *The Location of Culture.* London: Routledge, 1994.

Blanton, C. D. *Epic Negation: The Dialectical Poetics of Late Modernism.* Oxford: Oxford University Press, 2015.

Blatt, Avraham. "Shirat Amichai: Be-sha'ar Yerushalayim" (Amichai's Poetry: At the Gates of Jerusalem). *Ha-Tzofeh,* April 19, 1969.

Bloch, Chana. "Yehuda Amichai's 'O God Full of Mercy.'" In *Into English: An Anthology of Multiple Translations,* ed. Martha Collins and Kevin Prufer. Minneapolis: Graywolf, forthcoming.

Bloch, Chana, and Chana Kronfeld. "Amichai's Counter-Theology: Opening *Open Closed Open.*" *Judaism* 194, no. 49/2 (spring 2000): 153–67.

———. "On Translating Amichai's *Open Closed Open.*" *American Poetry Review* (March/April 2000): 15–19.

Bloom, Harold. *The Anxiety of Influence: A Theory of Poetry.* New York: Oxford University Press, 1973.

———. *A Map of Misreading.* New York: Oxford University Press, 1975.

Bourdieu, Pierre. *The Field of Cultural Production.* Ed. and Intro. Randal Johnson. New York: Columbia University Press, 1993.

———. *In Other Words: Essays Towards a Reflexive Sociology.* Trans. Matthew Adamson. Cambridge: Polity Press; Stanford: Stanford University Press, 1990.

Boyarin, Daniel. "The Eye in the Torah: Ocular Desire in the Midrashic Hermeneutic." *Critical Inquiry* 16, no. 3 (1990): 532–50.

———. *Intertextuality and the Reading of Midrash.* Bloomington: Indiana University Press, 1990.

———. *Socrates and the Fat Rabbis.* Chicago: University of Chicago Press, 2009.

Brecht, Bertolt. *The Trial of Lucullus.* In *The Collected Plays of Bertolt Brecht: Four,* ed. and trans. Tom Kuhn and John Willett. London: Methuen, 2003.

Brenner, Naomi. "Authorial Fiction: Literary and Public Personas in Modern Hebrew and Yiddish Literature." Ph.D. diss., University of California, Berkeley, 2008.

Brodsky, Joseph. "A Footnote to a Commentary." In *Rereading Russian Poetry,* trans. Jamey Gambrell and Alexander Sumerkin, ed. Stephanie Sandler, 183–201. New Haven: Yale University Press, 1999.

Brookman, Ari. "Yehuda Amichai." *Postcolonial Studies at Emory* (Fall 2001). https://scholarblogs.emory.edu/postcolonialstudies/2014/06/09/amichai-yehuda/.

Burnett, Leon. "Cultural Continuities?" In *Intertextuality and Modernism in*

Comparative Literature, ed. Emily Salines and Raynalle Udris, 39–65. Dublin: Philomel, 2002.

Butler, Judith. *Bodies That Matter: On the Discursive Limits of "Sex."* New York: Routledge, 1993.

———. *Excitable Speech: A Politics of the Performative.* London: Routledge, 1997.

———. *The Judith Butler Reader.* Ed. Sara Salih with Judith Butler. Oxford: Blackwell, 2004.

Chamberlain, Lori. "Gender Metaphorics in Translation." In *The Routledge Encyclopedia of Translation Studies*, ed. Mona Baker, 93–96. London and New York: Routledge, 1998.

Christian, Barbara. "The Race for Theory." *Feminist Studies* 14, no. 1 (1988): 67–79.

Çixous, Helene. "Sorties: Out and Out: Attacks/Ways Out/Forays." In *The Feminist Reader*, ed. C. Belsey and J. Moore, 101–16. London: Macmillan, 1989.

Clayton, Jay, and Eric Rothstein, eds. *Influence and Intertextuality in Literary History.* Madison: University of Wisconsin Press, 1991.

Cohen, Adir. *Ha-shira ha-ivrit ha-tze'ira* (Young Hebrew Poetry). Jerusalem: Mizrachi, 1963.

Cowart, David. "Tradition, Talent, and 'Stolentelling.'" In Cowart, *Literary Symbiosis: The Reconfigured Text in Twentieth Century Writing*, 1–26. Athens: University of Georgia Press, 1993.

Culler, Jonathan. "Presuppositions and Intertextuality." In *The Pursuit of Signs: Semiotics, Literature, Deconstruction*, 100–18. Ithaca, NY: Cornell University Press, 1981.

cummings, e. e. *Complete Poems 1913–1962.* 1972; reprint ed., New York and London: Harcourt Brace Jovanovich, 1980.

Dancygier, Barbara, and Eve Sweetser. *Figurative Language.* Cambridge: Cambridge University Press, 2014.

Darwish, Ali. *The Transfer Factor: Selected Essays on Translation and Cross-Cultural Communication.* Melbourne: Writescope, 2003.

Darwish, Mahmoud. "Le-zikhro shel Mahmoud Darwish" (Mahmoud Darwish, in Memoriam). Interview by Yosef Algazi. *Ha-gada ha-smalit: Bama bikortit le-chevra ve-tarbut* (The Left Bank: Critical Forum for Society and Culture). August 16, 2008. http://www.hagada.org.il/hagada/html/modules.php?name=News&file=print&sid=6108.

———. "A Love Story between an Arab Poet and His Land." Interview by Adam Shatz. *Journal of Palestine Studies*, 4, no. 31 (spring 2002): 67–78.

DeKoven Ezrahi, Sidra. "'Atem sho'alim keytzad ani kotev?': Dan Pagis ve-ha-proza shel ha-zikaron" ("You Ask How Do I Write?" Dan Pagis and the Prosaics of Memory). *Alpayim* 10 (1994): 94–110.

———. *Booking Passage: Exile and Homecoming in the Modern Jewish Imagination.* Berkeley: University of California Press, 2000.

———. *By Words Alone: The Holocaust in Literature*. Chicago: University of Chicago Press, 1980.

———. "From Auschwitz to Temple Mount: Binding and Unbinding the Israeli Narrative." In *After Testimony: The Ethics and Aesthetics of Holocaust Narrative*, ed. Susan Suleiman, Jakob Lothe, and James Phelan, 291–313. Columbus: Ohio State University Press, 2012.

———. "'To What Shall I Compare You?': Jerusalem as Ground Zero of the Hebrew Imagination." *PMLA* 122, no. 1 (2007): 220–34.

———. "'Tziyon ha-lo tish'ali': Yerushalayim ke-metafora nashit" ("Zion, Dost Thou Not Ask?": Jerusalem as a Female Metaphor). In *Rega shel huledet: Mechkarim be-sifrut ivrit u-ve-sifrut yiddish li-khvod Dan Miron* (A Moment of Birth: Studies in Hebrew and Yiddish Literature in Honor of Dan Miron), ed. Hannan Hever, 674–85. Jerusalem: Mosad Bialilk, 2007.

———. "Yehuda Amichai: paytan shel ha-yomyom" (Yehuda Amichai: Liturgical Poet of the Quotidian). *Mi-kan* 14 (2014): 143–67.

Deleuze, Gilles. *Essays Critical and Clinical*. Trans. Daniel W. Smith. Minneapolis: University of Minnesota Press, 1997.

de Man, Paul. *Allegories of Reading*. New Haven: Yale University Press, 1979.

———. "Shelley Disfigured." In *The Rhetoric of Romanticism*, 93–123. New York: Columbia University Press, 1984. Originally published in *Deconstruction and Criticism*, ed. Harold Bloom et al., 39–73. New York: Norton, 1979.

Ducrot, Oswald, and Tzvetan Todorov. *Encyclopedic Dictionary for the Sciences of Language*. Trans. Catherine Porter. Baltimore: Johns Hopkins University Press, 1979.

Eckstein, Lars. *Re-Membering Black Atlantic: On the Poetics and Politics of Memory*. Amsterdam: Rodopi, 2006.

Eco, Umberto. *Travels in Hyperreality*, trans. William Weaver. San Diego: Harcourt Brace Jovanovich, 1986.

Eliot, T. S. *The Sacred Wood: Essays on Poetry and Criticism*. 1920; reprint ed., London: Methuen, 1960.

Erlich, Victor. *Russian Formalism: History, Doctrine*. The Hague: Mouton, 1969.

Eshel, Amir. "Eternal Present: Poetic Figuration and Cultural Memory in the Poetry of Yehuda Amichai, Dan Pagis, and Tuvia Rübner." *Jewish Social Studies* 7, no.1 (fall 2000):141–66.

Eshel, Amir, Hannan Hever, and Vered Karti Shemtov, eds. "History and Responsibility: Hebrew Literature Facing 1948." Special issue, *Jewish Social Studies* 18, no. 3 (spring/summer 2012).

Eshel, Amir, and Todd Presner. "Introduction." In "Between Spontaneity and Reflection: Reconsidering Jewish Modernism." Special issue, *Modernism/Modernity* 13, no. 4 (2006): 607–14.

Even-Zohar, Itamar. "The Position of Translated Literature within the Literary Polysystem." In "Polysystem Studies." Special issue, *Poetics Today* 11, no. 1 (1990): 45–51.

———. "The Role of Russian and Yiddish in the Making of Modern Hebrew." In "Polysystem Studies." Special issue, *Poetics Today* 11, no. 1 (1990): 111–20.

Eyal, Nadav. "Za'aki eretz ahuva, girsat 1953" (Cry, the Beloved Country, the 1953 Version). *NRG.* February 2, 2010. http://www.nrg.co.il/online/1/ART2/048 /465.html.

Eysteinsson, Astradur. *The Concept of Modernism.* Ithaca, NY: Cornell University Press, 1990.

Feldman, Dina, Miriam Shlesinger, and Itta Shedletzky. "Five Hebrew Translations of Else Lasker-Schüler's Poem 'An Mein Kind.'" *Nashim* 19 (spring 2010): 176–98.

Feldman, Ziva. "The Metaphor of the Persona." In *The Experienced Soul: Studies in Amichai,* ed. Glenda Abramson, 71–75. New York: Westview Press, 1997.

Felstiner, John. "Writing Zion: An Exchange between Two Great Poets." *New Republic,* June 5, 2006.

Fishelov, David. "Yehuda Amichai: A Modern Metaphysical Poet." *Orbis Litteraum* 47 (1992): 178–91.

Fokkema, Douwe. *Literary History, Modernism and Postmodernism.* Amsterdam: John Benjamins, 1984.

François, Anne-Lise. *Open Secrets: The Literature of Uncounted Experience.* Stanford: Stanford University Press, 2008.

Frank, Joseph. *The Idea of Spatial Form.* New Brunswick, NJ: Rutgers University Press, 1991.

Friedman, Rivka. "Olam ha-dimuyim ve-ha-tadmiyot shel Yehuda Amichai: Iyun be-ba-ru'ach ha-nora'a ha-zot" (Yehuda Amichai's World of Similes and Imagery: A Study of *The World Is a Room*). *Ha-Do'ar* 55 (1976): 311–12.

Friedman, Susan Stanford. "Migration, Encounter, and Indigenisation: New Ways of Thinking about Intertextuality in Women's Writing." In *European Connection* 13, ed. Peter Collier, 215–71. Oxford: Peter Lang, 2005.

———. "Weavings: Intertextuality and the (Re)Birth of the Author." In *Influence and Intertextuality in Literary History,* ed. Jay Clayton and Eric Rothstein, 146–80. Madison: University of Wisconsin Press, 1991.

Funkenstein, Amos. "Intellectuals and Jews." The Bilgray Lecture, University of Arizona, 1989.

Gelber, Yoav. *Lama perku et ha-Palmach?* (Why Did They Dismantle the *Palmach?*). Tel Aviv: Schocken, 1986.

Geldman, Mordekhai. "'Tacharuyot nora'ot'" ("Terrible Competitions"). *Al-payim* 16 (1998): 121–25.

Gilbert, Sandra, and Susan Gubar. *The Madwoman in the Attic: The Woman Writer and the Nineteenth Century Literary Imagination.* New Haven: Yale University Press, 1979.

———. *No Man's Land: The Place of the Woman Writer in the 20th Century.* New Haven: Yale University Press, 1988.

Ginor, Tzvia. "Ha-mapal ha-pnimi shel ha-milim" (The Internal Cascade of Words). *Ha-Yom,* May 2, 1969.

Gluzman, Michael. "The Exclusion of Women from Hebrew Literary History." *Prooftexts* 11, no. 3 (1991): 259–78.

Gluzman, Michael. "'Le-ha'atzil alegantiyut la-sevel': al mekoma shel Dahlia Ravikovitch be-shirat dor ha-mdina" ("Endowing Suffering with Elegance": On Dahlia Ravikovitch's Place in the Poetry of the Statehood Generation). In *Kitmey Or: Chamishim shnot bikoret u-mechkar al yetsirata shel Dahlia Raviko-vitch* (Sparks of Light: Essays about Dahlia Ravikovitch's Oeuvre), ed. Hamutal Tsamir and Tamar S. Hess, 578–99. Tel Aviv: Ha-Kibbutz ha-Me'uchad, 2010.

———. "Mi-shirey ha-navi he-ani" (From the Poems of the Impoverished Prophet). *Ha'aretz,* November 4, 1998.

———. *The Politics of Canonicity: Lines of Resistance in Modernist Hebrew Poetry.* Stanford: Stanford University Press, 2003.

———. "Sovereignty and Melancholia: Israeli Poetry after 1948." *Jewish Social Studies* 18, no. 3 (2012): 164–79.

Gold, Nili Scharf. "The 'Feminine' in Yehuda Amichai's Poetics." In *The Experienced Soul: Studies in Amichai,* ed. Glenda Abramson, 77–92. New York: Westview Press, 1997.

———. "Images in Transformation in the Recent Poetry of Yehuda Amichai." *Prooftexts* 4 (1984): 141–52.

———. *Lo ka-brosh: gilguley imajim ve-tavniyot be-shirat Yehuda Amichai* (Not Like a Cypress: Transformations of Images and Patterns in Yehuda Amichai's Poetry). Jerusalem: Schocken, 1994.

———. *Yehuda Amichai: The Making of Israel's National Poet.* Waltham, MA: Brandeis University Press, 2008.

Goldberg, Leah. "Ad barzel" (Unto Iron). In *Ha-ometz le-chulin* (The Courage to be Secular), 217–19. Tel Aviv: Sifriyat Po'alim, 1975. First published in *Al Ha-Mishmar,* May 26, 1957.

———. "Gefen ha-yayin be-kharmey zarim" (A Wine Vine in Foreign Vineyards). In *Ha-ometz le-chulin* (The Courage to be Secular), 220–27. Tel Aviv: Sifriyat Po'alim, 1975. First published in *Al Ha-Mishmar,* July 10, 1957.

———. *Selected Poems.* Trans. Robert Friend. Foreword by Yehuda Amichai. Afterword by Gershom Scholem. London and San Francisco: Menard Press/Panjandrum Press, 1976.

Grice, H. Paul. "Meaning Revisited." In *Mutual Knowledge,* ed. N. V. Smith, 223–43. New York: Academic Press: 1982.

———. "Utterer's Meaning, Sentence Meaning, and Word-Meaning." *Foundations of Language* 4 (1968): 225–42.

Grossman, David. "Amichai va-anachnu" (Amichai and Us). Interview with David Grossman. *Ha'aretz,* October 22, 1999.

————. *Ayen erekh ahava* (See Under: Love). Tel Aviv: Ha-sifriya/Ha-Kibbutz ha-Me'uchad, 1986.

————. *Dvash arayot: Sipur Shimshon*. Tel Aviv: Pen/Yedi'ot Acharonot, 2005.

————. *Lion's Honey: The Myth of Samson*. Trans. Stuart Hoffman. Edinburgh: Canongate, 2006.

————. *See Under: Love*. Trans. Betsy Rosenberg. New York: Picador/ Farrar Straus & Giroux, 1989.

Guillén, Claudio. *The Challenge of Comparative Literature*. Cambridge, MA: Harvard University Press, 1993.

Gutknecht, Christoph, and Lutz J. Rölle. *Translating by Factors*. New York: State University of New York Press, 1996.

Guy, Hanoch. "Yehuda Amichai." In *Holocaust Literature: An Encyclopedia of Writers and Their Work,* ed. S. Lillian Kremer, 25. New York: Routledge, 2003.

Hallo, William. *Origins: The Ancient Near Eastern Background of Some Modern Western Institutions*. Leiden: Brill, 1996.

Harshav, Benjamin. *Explorations in Poetics*. Stanford: Stanford University Press, 2007.

————. "Hirhurim ishi'yim al Amichai: ha-shira ve-ha-mdina" (Personal Reflections on Amichai: Poetry and State). *Alpayim* 33 (2008): 121–37.

————. *The Meaning of Yiddish*. Berkeley: University of California Press, 1990. Reissued in the Contraversions Series. Stanford: Stanford University Press, 1999.

————. "On the Beginnings of Israeli Poetry and Yehuda Amichai's Quatrains: A Memoir." In *The Polyphony of Jewish Culture,* 175–85. Stanford: Stanford University Press, 2007.

Hartman, Geoffrey. "Poetics and Politics in Yehuda Amichai's World." Roundtable Discussion at the Yale Conference in Amichai's Memory. Yale University, October 21, 2007. Conference videos available at http://www.library.yale.edu/judaica/site/conferences/Amichai/.

Hendel, Ron, Chana Kronfeld, and Ilana Pardes. "Gender and Sexuality." In *Reading Genesis: Ten Methods,* ed. Ron Hendel, 71–91. Cambridge and New York: Cambridge University Press, 2010.

Herbert, Zbigniew. "Li-Yehuda Amichai." Trans. David Weinfeld. ["Bo ty jesteś? król a ja tylko książe."] *Ha'aretz,* May 13, 1994.

————. "To Yehuda Amichai." In *The Collected Poems 1956–1998,* trans. and ed. Alissa Valles, 489. New York: Harper Collins, 2007.

Hesse, Hermann. *Nedudim*. Trans. Yehuda Amichai. Jerusalem and Tel Aviv: Schocken, 1978.

Hever, Hannan. "'The Grey Historians of the Brain': Nativism in the Poetry of Moshe Dor." In *Nativism, Zionism, and Beyond,* 41–65. Syracuse: Syracuse University Press, 2014.

————. *Sifrut she-nikhtevet mi-kan: Kitzur ha-sifrut ha-Yisraelit* (Literature Written from Here: A Précis of Israeli Literature). Tel Aviv: Yedi'ot Acharonot, 1999.

Hirschfeld, Ariel. "Locus and Language: Hebrew Culture in Israel." In *Cultures of the Jews: A New History*, ed. David Biale, 1011–60. New York: Schocken, 2002.

———. "Ravikovitch acharey asor" (Ravikovitch after a Decade). *Yedi'ot Acharonot*, January 9, 1987.

Hochhuth, Rolf. *Memale ha-makom*. Trans. Yehuda Amichai. Jerusalem: Schocken, 1964.

Huss, Avraham. "Al shirat Amichai ve-Galay"(On the Poetry of Amichai and Galay). *Orot* 36 (1959): 45–48.

"International Books of the Year." *Times Literary Supplement*. December 5, 1997, 8–14.

Intrater, Roseline. "Yehuda Amichai and the Interelatedness of All Things." *Jewish Quarterly* 32, no. 3 (1985): 39–42.

Iser, Wolfgang. Foreword to *Memory and Literature: Intertextuality in Russian Modernism*, by Renate Lachmann, vii–xvii. Trans. Roy Sellars and Anthony Hall. Minneapolis: University of Minnesota Press, 1997.

Jacobson, David. *Does David Still Play before You: Israeli Poetry and the Bible*. Detroit: Wayne State University Press, 1997.

Jakobson, Roman. "On Linguistic Aspects of Translation." In *Language in Literature*, ed. Krystyna Pomorska and Stephen Rudy, 428–35. Cambridge, MA: Harvard University Press, 1987.

———. *Poetry of Grammar and Grammar of Poetry*. Vol. 3 of *Selected Writings*. Ed. Stephen Rudy. The Hague and New York: De Gruyter, 1981.

Jakobson, Roman, and Lawrence G. Jones. *Shakespeare's Verbal Art in "The Expense of Spirit."* The Hague: Mouton, 1970.

Johnson, Barbara. "Taking Fidelity Philosophically." In *Difference in Translation*, ed. Joseph F. Graham, 142–48. Ithaca, NY: Cornell University Press, 1985.

Juvan, Marko. *History and Poetics of Intertextuality*. Trans. Timothy Pogačar. West Lafayette, IN: Purdue University Press, 2008.

Kalderon, Nissim. "Hitraptut" (Becoming Worn Out). *Siman kri'ah* 1 (1972): 307–10.

———. *Yom sheni: Al shira ve-rok be-Israel acharey Yona Wallach* (A Second Day: On Poetry and Rock Music in Israel after Yona Wallach). Tel Aviv: Dvir, 2009.

Karmel, Ilona. *An Estate of Memory*. 1969; reprint ed., New York: Feminist Press, 1993.

Katznelson, Gid'on. *Le'an hem holkhim?* (Where Are They Going?). Tel Aviv: Alef, 1968.

Kaufman, Robert. *Negative Romanticism: Adornian Aesthetics in Keats, Shelley, and Modern Poetry*. Ithaca, NY: Cornell University Press, forthcoming.

———. "Poetry after 'Poetry after Auschwitz.'" In *Art and Aesthetics after Adorno*, ed. Jay M. Bernstein et al., 116–81. Berkeley: University of California Press, 2010.

Keynar, Gad. "Lo ka-brosh" (Not Like a Cypress). *Masa/La-merchav*, November 28, 1969.

Khayyám, Omar. *Meruba'im*. Translated into Hebrew by Ben-Tzion Ben-Shalom. Tel Aviv: Gazit Press, 1944.

Kluger, Ruth. *Landscapes of Memory*. London: Bloomsbury, 2004.

———. *Still Alive*. New York: Feminist Press, 2003.

Kolodny, Annette. "A Map for Misreading: Gender and the Interpretation of Literary Texts." In *The New Feminist Criticism: Essays on Women, Literature, and Theory*, ed. Elaine Showalter, 46–62. New York: Pantheon, 1985.

The Koren-Jeruslaem Bible. Bilingual edition. Jerusalem: Koren Publishing House, 1992.

Koren, Yehuda, and Eilat Negev. *Lover of Unreason: Assia Wevill, Sylvia Plath and Ted Hughes' Doomed Love*. Cambridge, MA: Da Capo Press, 2006.

Kramer, Shalom. *Re'alism u-shvirato: Al mesaprim ivriyim mi-Gnessin ad Applefeld* (Realism and Its Decline: On Hebrew Writers from Gnessin to Applefeld). Tel Aviv: Agudat ha-Sofrim be-Israel le-yad Hotza'at Masada, 1968.

Kristeva, Julia. *Desire in Language: A Semiotic Approach to Literature and Art*. Trans. Thomas Gora, Alice Jardine, and Leon R. Roudiez. Ed. Leon R. Roudiez. New York: Columbia University Press, 1980.

———. *Semeiotikè: Recherche pour une semanalyse*. 1966; reprint ed., Paris: Seuil, 1969.

Kronfeld, Chana. "Aspects of Poetic Metaphor." Ph.D. diss., University of California, Berkeley, 1983.

———. "Beyond Thematicism in the Historiography of Post-1948 Political Poetry." *Jewish Social Studies* 18, no. 3 (spring/summer 2012): 180–96.

———. "Ha-meshorer ki-metargem be-shirat Amichai" (The Poet as Translator in Amichai's Poetry). *Ot* 3 (2013): 5–20.

———. "Hyphenated States: Metaphor as Poetics of Survival in the Poetry of Yehuda Amichai." *Yearbook of Comparative and General Literature* 50 (2004): 23–44.

———. "The Joint Literary Historiography of Hebrew and Yiddish." In *Languages of Modern Jewish Culture: Comparative Perspectives*, ed. Joshua Miller and Anita Norich. Ann Arbor: University of Michigan Press, in press.

———. "Novel and Conventional Metaphors: A Matter of Methodology." *Poetics Today* 2, no. 1b (1981): 13–24.

———. *On the Margins of Modernism: Decentering Literary Dynamics*. Berkeley: University of California Press, 1996.

———. "Reading Amichai Reading." *Judaism* 179, no. 54:3 (summer 1996): 311–23.

———. "Sokhnut intertextualit" (Intertextual Agency). In *Intertextualiyut ba-sifrut u-va-tarbut: Sefer ha-yovel le-Ziva Ben-Porat* (Intertextuality in Literature and Culture: A Festschrift in Honor of Ziva Ben-Porat), ed. Michael Gluzman and Orly Lubin, 11–57. Tel Aviv: Ha-Kibbutz ha-Me'uchad, 2012.

———. "'The Wisdom of Camouflage': Between Rhetoric and Philosophy in Amichai's Poetic System." *Prooftexts* 10, no. 3 (1990): 469–91.

Kurzweil, Baruch. "*He'arot le-lo me-akhshav lo mi-kan*" (Remarks on Not of This

Time, Not of This Place). In *Chipus ha-sifrut ha-yisre'elit: Masot u-ma'amarim* (In Search of Israeli Literature: Essays and Criticism), ed. Zvi Luz and Yedidya Yitzchaki, 246–57. Ramat-Gan: Bar-Ilan University, 1982. First published in *Ha'aretz*, September 6, September 13, 1963.

———. "Shira otobiyographit 'ba-midbar ha-gadol'" (Autobiographical Poetry in "The Big Desert"). In *Yehuda Amichai: Mivchar ma'amarey bikoret al yetzirato* (Yehuda Amichai: A Selection of Critical Essays on His Writings), ed. Yehudit Tzvik, 79–94. Tel Aviv: Ha-Kibbutz ha-Me'uchad, 1988.

———. "Sipurey Yehuda Amichai" (The Stories of Yehuda Amichai). In *Chipus ha-sifrut ha-Isra'elit: Masot u-ma'amarim* (In Search of Israeli Literature: Essays and Criticism), ed. Zvi Luz and Yedidya Yitzchaki, 221–30. Ramat-Gan: Bar-Ilan University, 1982. First published in *Davar*, April 21, 1961.

Lachmann, Renate. *Memory and Literature: Intertextuality in Russian Modernism.* Trans. Roy Sellars and Anthony Wall. Minneapolis: University of Minnesota Press, 1997.

Lakoff, George. *Philosophy in the Flesh.* New York: Basic Books, 1999.

———. *Women, Fire and Dangerous Things: What Categories Reveal about the Mind.* Chicago: University of Chicago Press, 1987.

Lakoff, George, and Mark Johnson. *Metaphors We Live By.* Chicago: University of Chicago Press, 1980.

Lakoff, George, and Mark Turner. *More Than Cool Reason.* Chicago: University of Chicago Press, 1989.

Laor, Yitzhak. *Anu kotvim otakh moledet* (Narratives with No Natives). Tel Aviv: Ha-Kibbutz ha-Me'uchad, 1995.

———. "'Ha-shiva ha-nitzchit' shel Yehuda Amichai" (Yehuda Amichai's "Eternal Return"). *Ha'aretz*, August 13, 2004.

———. "*Ma she-rechem em mavti'ach ve-elohim lo*" (What a Mother's Womb Promises and God Doesn't). *Ha'aretz*, August 6, 2004.

———. "Preda min ha-sifrut ha-ivrit" (Farewell to Hebrew Literature). *Ha'aretz*, July 24, 2007.

Larkin, Margaret. "'Abd al-Wahhāb al-Bayātīs' 'Mawt al-Mutanabbī': A Case Study in Arabic Intertextuality." Forthcoming.

Lasker-Schüler, Else. *Selected Poems.* Trans. Audri Durchslag and Jeanette Litman-Demeestere. Foreword by Yehuda Amichai. Los Angeles and Copenhagen: Green Integer, 2002. Earlier edition published as *Hebrew Ballads and Other Poems.* Philadelphia: Jewish Publication Society, 1980.

———. *Shirim* (Poems). Trans. Yehuda Amichai. Tel Aviv: Eked, 1969.

———. *Ve-eynay tipot kvedot va-afelot* (And My Eyes Are Heavy and Dark Drops). Trans. Yehuda Amichai. Tel Aviv: Keshev Le-shira, 2008.

Lefevere, André. *Translating Literature: Practice and Theory in a Comparative Literature Framework.* New York: MLA, 1992.

———. *Translation, Rewriting, and the Manipulation of Literary Fame.* London and New York: Routledge, 1992.

Levin, Amos. *Bli Kav* (No Line). Tel Aviv: Ha-Kibbutz ha-Me'uchad, 1984.

Levy, Shimon. "Elements of Poetic Self-Awareness in Modern Hebrew Poetry." *Modern Hebrew Literature* 2, no. 3 (1976): 18–24.

Lewis, Bernard. *Middle East Mosaic: Fragments of Life, Letters, and History.* New York: Random House, 1999.

Likrat: Bita'on pnimi shel chug sofrim tze'irim (*Likrat:* Internal Mouthpiece of a Young Writers' Circle) 2. Mimeographed edition. Jerusalem, Av/August 1952.

Likrat: Bit'on chug sofrim tze'irim (*Likrat:* Mouthpiece of a Young Writers' Circle). First printed issue. Tel Aviv: Dov Guterman Press, 1953.

Lonsdale, Roger. "Gray and 'Allusion': The Poet as Debtor." *Studies in the Eighteenth Century.* Vol. 4. Canberra: Australian National University Press, 1979, 31–55.

Ma'ariv. "Poet Yehuda Amichai Translated into Many Languages." Online English edition. May 17, 1994.

Man, Rafi. "'Amichai hu meshorer metzuyan aval me'od mesukan'" ("Amichai Is an Excellent Poet, but Very Dangerous"). *Ha'aretz,* October 20, 2010.

Martz, Louis. *The Poetry of Meditation: A Study of English Religious Literature of the Seventeenth Century.* 1954; reprint ed., New Haven: Yale University Press, 1962.

Masiello, Francine. "Joyce in Buenos Aires (Talking Sexuality through Translation)." *Diacritics* 34, no. 3 (2006): 55–72.

Mattawa, Khaled. "When the Poet Is a Stranger: Poetry and Agency in Tagore, Walcott, and Darwish." Ph.D. diss., Duke University, 2009.

Meged, Eyal. "Yehuda Amichai: Li-krat ha-sof ata na'ase yoter pashut" (Yehuda Amichai: Towards the End You Become Simpler). *Yedi'ot Acharonot,* November 15, 1985.

Miller, Nancy K. "Changing the Subject: Authorship, Writing, and the Reader." In *Feminist Studies—Critical Studies,* ed. Teresa de Lauretis, 102–20. Bloomington: Indiana University Press, 1986.

Milner, Iris. *Ha-narativim shel sifrut ha-Shoah* (Narratives of Holocaust Literature). Bney Brak: Ha-Kibbutz ha-Me'uchad, 2008.

Miron, Dan. *Ha-tzad ha-afel bi-tzchoko shel Shalom Aleykhem* (The Dark Side of Sholem Aleichem's Laughter). Tel Aviv: Am Oved, 2004.

———. *Mul ha-ach ha-shotek: Iyunim be-shirat milchemet ha-atzma'ut* (Facing the Silent Brother: Studies in the Poetry of the War of Independence). Jerusalem: Keter, 1992.

———. "Patu'ach sagur patu'ach: Yehuda Amichai—ha-nusach ha-elegi" (*Open Closed Open:* Yehuda Amichai—the Elegiac Version). *Ha-Do'ar,* January 19, 2001.

———. "Yehuda Amichai: Mahapekhan im aba" (Yehuda Amichai: A Revolutionary with a Father). *Ha'aretz,* September 30, October 6, October 12, 2005.

———. "Yehuda Amichai: *Patu'ach sagur patu'ach*" (Yehuda Amichai: *Open Closed Open*). In *Ha-sifriya ha-iveret* (The Blind Library), 401–4. Tel Aviv: Yedi'ot Acharonot, 2005.

Moi, Toril. "Feminist Literary Criticism." In *Modern Literary Theory: A Comparative Introduction*, ed. Ann Jefferson and David Robey, 204–21. London: Batsford, 1982.

Moked, Gavriel. *Arba'a meshorerim* (Four Poets). Tel Aviv: Ministry of Defense Publications, 2006.

Morris, Benny. *The Birth of the Palestinian Refugee Problem 1947–1949*. Cambridge: Cambridge University Press, 1989.

Moynihan, Robert. *A Recent Imagining*. Hamden, CT.: Archon Books, 1986.

Murphy, John. "Jazz Improvisation: The Joy of Influence." *Black Perspective in Music* 18, no. 12 (1990): 7–19.

Nagid, Chayim. "Pney ha-sifrut nimchatzot ba-re'i" (The Face of Literature Squashed in the Mirror). *Moznayim* 56, no. 5 (1983): 41–42.

Naiman, Eric. "Shklovsky's Dog and Mulvey's Pleasure: The Secret Life of Defamiliarization." *Comparative Literature* 50, no. 4 (autumn 1998): 333–52.

Naveh, Hannah. *Bi-shvi ha-evel: ha-evel bi-r'i ha-sifrut ha-ivrit ha-chadasha* (Captives of Mourning: Mourning as Mirrored in Modern Hebrew literature). Tel Aviv: Ha-Kibbutz ha-Me'uchad, 1993.

Niranjana, Tejaswini. *Siting Translation: History, Post-Structuralism, and the Colonial Context*. Berkeley: University of California Press, 1992.

Nora, Pierre. "Between Memory and History: Les Lieux de Mémoire." In "Memory and Counter-Memory." Special issue, *Representations* 26 (spring 1989): 7–24.

Norich, Anita. "Under Whose Sign? Hebraism and Yiddishism as Paradigms of Modern Jewish Literary History." *PMLA* 125, no. 3 (2010): 774–84.

———. *Writing in Tongues: Translating Yiddish in the Twentieth Century*. Seattle and London: University of Washington Press, 2013.

Omer-Sherman, Ranen. "Yehuda Amichai's Exilic Jerusalem." *Prooftexts* 26 (2006): 212–39.

Ophir, Riki. "Why Read Poems in Such Hard Times? Sociopolitical History and Aesthetic Commitment in Modern Hebrew, Yiddish and German Poetry." Ph.D. diss., University of California, Berkeley, 2013.

Oppenheimer, Yochai. *Ha-Zkhut ha-gdola lomar lo: Shira politit be-Israel* (The Great Right to Say No: Political Poetry in Israel). Jerusalem: Magness Press, 2003.

Orr, Mary. *Intertextuality: Current Debates*. Cambridge: Polity Press, 2003.

Pagis, Dan. "Exercises in Practical Hebrew." In *Hebrew Writers on Writing*, ed. Peter Cole, trans. Peter Cole, 185–87. San Antonio: Trinity University Press, 2008.

———. *Kol Ha-shirim* (Collected Poems). Jerusalem: Ha-Kibbutz ha-Me'uchad/ Mosad Bialik, 1991.

Peckham, Morse. *Man's Rage for Chaos: Biology, Behavior and the Arts*. 1966. Reprint ed., New York: Schocken, 1967.

Pelli, Moshe. "Ha-nefesh ha-mefutzelet bi-mtzi'ut chatzuya le-achar ha-Shoah:

Iyun ba-roman shel Yehuda Amichai" (The Divided Soul in a Split Post-Shoah Reality: A Study of Yehuda Amichai's Novel). *Ha-Do'ar* 58 (1979): 492, 509.

Pound, Ezra. "A Few Don'ts by an Imagiste." *Poetry* (March 1911): 200–206.

———. "In a Station of the Metro." *Poetry* (April 1913): 12.

Pratt, Mary Louise. "Arts of the Contact Zone." In *Ways of Reading*, ed. David Bartholomae and Anthony Petrosky, 581–96. Bedford: St. Martins, 1999.

———. *Imperial Eyes: Travel Writing and Transculturation*. London: Routledge, 1992.

Rachel [Bluwshteyn]. *Flowers of Perhaps: Selected Poems of Ra'hel*. Trans. Robert Friend with Shimon Sandbank. London: Menard Press, 1994.

———. *Shirat Rachel* (Rachel's Poetry). 1935; reprint ed., Tel Aviv: Davar, 1961.

Ravikovitch, Dahlia. *Hovering at a Low Altitude: The Collected Poetry of Dahlia Ravikovitch*. Trans. Chana Bloch and Chana Kronfeld. New York: W. W. Norton, 2009.

Ravikovitch, Dahlia. *Kol ha-shirim* (Complete Poems). Ed. Giddon Ticotsky and Uzi Shavit. Tel Aviv: Ha-Kibbutz ha-Me'uchad, 2010.

———. "Od sefer: Ahava amitit" (Another Book: *True Love*). Interview by Dalia Karpel. *Ha-ir*, November 28, 1986.

Riffaterre, Michael. "Intertextual Representation: On Mimesis as Interpretive Discourse." *Critical Inquiry* 11, no. 1 (1984): 141–62.

———. "Syllepsis." *Critical Inquiry* 6, no. 4 (1980): 625–38.

Roberts, Michael, ed. *Faber Book of Modern Verse*. London: Faber & Faber, 1936.

Rogani, Haggai. *Mul ha-kfar she-charav: Ha-Shira ha-ivrit ve-ha-sikhsukh ha-yehudi-aravi 1929–1967* (Facing the Ruined Village: Hebrew Poetry and the Jewish-Arab Conflict 1929–1967). Haifa: Pardes Press, 2006.

Rokem, Na'ama. "German-Hebrew Encounters in the Poetry and Correspondence of Yehuda Amichai and Paul Celan." *Prooftexts* 30, no. 1 (winter 2010): 97–127.

Rosen, Tova. "'Kemo be-shir shel Shmuel Ha-Nagid': beyn Shmuel Ha-Nagid li-Yehuda Amichai" ("As in a Poem by Shmuel Ha-Nagid": Between Shmuel Ha-Nagid and Yehuda Amichai). *Mechkarey Yerushalayim be-sifrut ivrit* 15 (1995): 83–106.

Rosenberg, Joel. "Jeremiah and Ezekiel." In *The Literary Guide to the Bible*, ed. Robert Alter and Frank Kermode, 184–206. Cambridge, MA: Belknap/Harvard University Press, 1987.

Sachs, Arye. "Meshorer shel hitpa'alut" (A Poet of Amazement). *Ha'aretz*, November 29, 1985.

Sadan-Lovenstein, Nili. "Tavniyot imajistiyot be-shirat Amichai" (Image Patterns in the Poetry of Amichai). *Iton* 77, nos. 44/45 (1983): 45–46, and *Iton* 77, no. 46 (1983): 48–51.

Salih, Sara. "Introduction to 'The Lesbian Phallus and the Morphological Imaginary." In *The Judith Butler Reader*, ed. Sara Salih with Judith Butler, 138–43. Oxford: Blackwell, 2004.

Sandbank, Shimon. "Al shirey tzmadim u-modulariyut: Amichai ve-Else Lasker-

Schüler" (On Couplets and Modular Structures: Amichai and Else Lasker-Schüler). In Sandbank, *Ha-kol hu ha-acher* (The Voice Is the Other), 72–89. Jerusalem: Karmel, 2001.

———. "Amichai: ha-mischak ve-ha-shefa" (Amichai: The Play and the Abundance). In Sandbank, *Ha-shir ha-nakhon* (The True Poem), 81–91. Tel Aviv: Sifriyat Po'alim, 1982.

———. "Ha-ga'agu'im el ha-patu'ach" (The Longings for the Open). *Amot* 2, no. 8 (October–November 1963): 94–101.

———. "Li-she'elat ha-shir ha-kal" (On the Question of the Easy Poem). In *Ha-shir ha-nakhon* (The True Poem), 92–97. Tel Aviv: Sifriyat Po'alim, 1982. First published in *Siman Kri'a* 12–13 (1981): 331–34.

———. "'Mistovev, omed, mitmahmeha': Rilke, Amichai ve-ha-mabat le-achor" ("Turns Back, Stands, Lingers": Rilke, Amichai, and the Backwards Gaze). In Sandbank, *Ha-kol hu ha-acher* (The Voice Is the Other), 90–98. Jerusalem: Karmel, 2001.

———. "Nof ha-nefesh: Rilke, Auden, Amichai" (The Landscape of the Mind: Rilke, Auden, Amichai). In Sandbank, *Shtey brekhot ba-ya'ar* (Two Pools in the Forest), 173–214. Tel Aviv: Ha-Kibbutz ha-Me'uchad, 1976.

Sarna, Yigal. "Chay al ha-makaf. Yehuda Amichai" (He Lives on the Hyphen. Yehuda Amichai). *Yedi'ot Acharonot*, March 19, 2012.

Sas, Miryam. *Fault Lines: Cultural Memory and Japanese Surrealism*. Stanford: Stanford University Press, 2001.

Schachter, Allison. "A Lily among the Bullfrogs: Dahlia Ravikovitch and the Field of Hebrew Poetry." *Prooftexts* 28, no. 3 (2008): 310–34.

Schleiermacher, Friedrich. "On the Different Methods of Translating." In *The Translation Studies Reader*, ed. Lawrence Venuti, trans. Susan Bernofsky, 75–83. London and New York: Routledge, 2012.

Searle, John R. *Expression and Meaning: Studies in the Theory of Speech Acts*. Cambridge: Cambridge University Press, 1979.

———. *Speech Acts: An Essay in the Philosophy of Language*. Cambridge: Cambridge University Press, 1969.

Seidman, Naomi. *Faithful Renderings: Jewish-Christian Difference and the Politics of Translation*. Chicago: University of Chicago Press, 2006.

Setter, Shaul. "After the Fact: Potential Collectivities in Israel/Palestine" (Ph.D. dissertation, University of California, Berkeley, 2012).

———. "'Noshekh yonek mar'il lash motzetz madbik': al leshon ha-hitnagdut ha-ivrit be-shirato shel Yitzhak Laor" (On the Language of Resistance in the Poetry of Yitzhak Laor). *Ot* 1 (fall 2010): 163–90.

Shaked, Gershon. "Hoy dori ha-atzuv ve-ha-mukeh" (Oh, My Sad and Beaten Generation). In Shaked, *Gal chadash ba-siporet ha-ivrit* (A New Wave in Hebrew Fiction), 89–124. Tel Aviv: Sifri'yat Po'alim, 1971.

———. "Masa shel tachanot" (A Station Voyage). *Ha'aretz*, December 27, 1985.

Shalev, Meir. "Jerusalem, Jerusalem." *Yedi'ot Acharonot*, May 18, 2007.

Shamir, Ziva. "The Conceit as a Cardinal Style-Marker in Yehuda Amichai's Poetry." In *The Experienced Soul: Studies in Amichai*, ed. Glenda Abramson, 17–26. New York: Westview Press, 1997.

Shammas, Anton. *Arabeskot*. Tel Aviv: Am Oved, 1986.

———. *Arabesques*. New York: Harper & Row, 1988.

Sharpe, Peter. *The Ground of Our Beseeching: Metaphor and the Poetics of Meditation*. Selingsgrove, PA: Susquehanna University Press, 2004.

Shemtov, Vered Karti. "Between Perspectives of Space: A Reading in Yehuda Amichai's 'Jewish Travel' and 'Israeli Travel.'" *Jewish Social Studies* 11, no. 3 (spring/summer 2005): 141–61.

———. *Miktzavim mishtanim: Likrat te'oria shel prozodia be-heksher tarbuti* (Changing Rhythms: Towards a Theory of Prosody in Cultural Context). Ramat Gan: Bar Ilan University Press, 2012.

Shen, Yeshayahu. *Cognition and Figurative Language*. Tel-Aviv: TAU Porter Institute for Poetics and Semiotics, 1997.

———. "Cognition and Poetic Figures." In *The Cambridge Handbook of Metaphor and Thought*, ed. Raymond W. Gibbs Jr., 295–307. New York: Cambridge University Press, 2008.

———. "Metaphors and Categories." *Poetics Today* 13, no. 4 (1992): 771–94.

———. "Schemata, Categories and Metaphor Comprehension." *Poetics Today* 12, no. 1 (1991): 111–24.

Shklovsky, Viktor. *Knight's Move*. Trans. Richard Sheldon. London: Dalkey Archive Press, 2005.

Showalter, Elaine. "Feminism and Literature." In *Literary Theory Today*, ed. Peter Collier and Helga Geyer-Ryan, 179–202. Oxford: Polity Press, 1990.

Simic, Charles, and Mark Strand, eds. *Another Republic: 17 European and South American Writers*. New York: Ecco Press, 1976.

Sokoloff, Naomi B. "On Amichai's *El male rahamim*." *Prooftexts* 4 (1984): 127–40.

Someck, Ronny. "Be-derekh he-afar, be-shira shel tzavaron kachol" (On the Dirt Road, in Blue Collar Poetry). *Ynet*. September 22, 2000. www.ynet.co.il/articles/1,7340,L-130088,FF.html.

Sovran, Tamar. *Relational Semantics and the Anatomy of Abstraction*. New York: Routledge, 2013.

Spiegel, Shalom. *The Last Trial: On the Legends and Lore of the Command to Abraham to Offer Isaac as a Sacrifice: The Akedah*. 1967; reprint ed., Woodstock, VT: Jewish Lights Publishing, 1993.

Spivak, Gayatri Chakravorty. "The Politics of Translation." In *Outside in the Teaching Machine*, 179–200. New York: Routledge, 1993. Reprinted in Lawrence Venuti, ed., *The Translation Studies Reader*, 397–416. London and New York: Routledge, 2012.

Stahl, Nanette. *Law and Liminality in the Bible*. Sheffield, UK: Sheffield Press, 1995.

Stav, Shira. *Aba ani koveshet: Avot u-vanot ba-shira ha-ivrit ha-chadasha* (Reconstructing Daddy: Fathers and Daughters in Modern Hebrew Poetry). Or Ye-huda: Dvir/Heksherim, Ben Gurion University, 2014.

Stevens, Wallace. *Opus Posthumous*. Ed. Samuel French Morse. London: Vintage, 1957.

———. *The Palm at the End of the Mind: Selected Poems and a Play*. Ed. Holly Stevens. 1967; reprint ed., New York: Vintage Books, 1972.

Stewart, Susan. "The Pickpocket: A Study in Tradition and Allusion." *Modern Language Notes* 95, no. 5 (December 1980): 1127–54.

Sullivan, Karen, and Eve Sweetser. "Is 'Generic Is Specific' a Metaphor?" In *Meaning, Form and Body*, ed. Fey Perrill, Vera Tobin, and Mark Turner, 309–27. Stanford: CSLI Publications, 2009.

Sweetser, Eve. *From Etymology to Pragmatics: Metaphorical and Cultural Aspects of Semantic Structure*. Cambridge: Cambridge University Press, 1990.

———. "Regular Metaphoricity in Gesture: Bodily-Based Models of Speech Interaction." *Actes du 16e congrès internationale des linguists*. Elsviere, 1998. CD-ROM.

———. "'The Suburbs of Your Good Pleasure': Cognition, Culture, and the Bases of Metaphoric Structure." In *The Shakespearean International Year Book*, vol. 4, ed. G. Bradshaw, T. Bishop, and M. Turner, 24–55. Aldershot, UK: Ashgate, 2004.

Szobel, Ilana. "'La-chasof et ha-avel be-makom she-hu kayam': Edut, ashma ve-acharayut ba-shira ha-politit shel Ravikovitch" ("Unearthing Wrongdoing Wherever It Exists": Testimony, Guilt, and Responsibility in Ravikovitch's Political Poetry). In *Kitmey Or: Chamishim shnot bikoret u-mechkar al yetsirata shel Dahlia Ravikovitch* (Sparks of Light: Essays about Dahlia Ravikovitch's Oeuvre), ed. Hamutal Tsamir and Tamar S. Hess, 444–69. Tel Aviv: Ha-Kibbutz ha-Me'uchad, 2010.

Teres-Tzukerman, Rachel. "Al shir echad shel Yehuda Amichai" (On One Poem by Yehuda Amichai). *Proza* 4, nos. 58–59 (1982): 25–26.

Teutch, David (Rabbi), ed. *Kol Ha-neshama: Machzor la-yamim ha-nora'im* (Kol haneshamah: Prayerbook for the Days of Awe). Elkins Park, PA: Reconstructionist Press, 1999.

Ticotsky, Giddon. "'Be-ozvi et chayay, karati bo, va-tov li': Yehuda Amichai ha-tza'ir kotev le-Leah Goldberg" ("When I Left My Life, I'd Read It, and All Was Good": The Young Yehuda Amichai Writes to Leah Goldberg). *Ot* 1 (fall 2010): 215–26.

Todorov, Tzvetan. *The Fantastic: A Structural Approach to a Literary Genre*. Ithaca, NY: Cornell University Press, 1975.

Toury, Gideon. *Descriptive Translation Studies and Beyond*. Amsterdam/Philadelphia: John Benjamins, 1995.

———. *In Search of a Theory of Translation*. Tel Aviv: Porter Institute for Poetics and Semiotics, 1980.

Tranquille, Danielle, and Soorya Nirisimloo-Gayan, eds. *Rencontres: Translation Studies*. Moka: Mahatma Gandhi Institute, 2000.

Tsamir, Hamutal. *Be-shem ha-nof: le'umiyut, migdar ve-subyektiviyut ba-shira ha-yisre'elit bi-shnot ha-chamishim ve-ha-shishim* (In the Name of the Land: Nationalism, Subjectivity, and Gender in Israeli Poetry of the Statehood Generation). Jerusalem/Be'er Sheva: Keter/Heksherim, 2006.

Tsamir, Hamutal, and Tamar S. Hess, eds. *Kitmey Or: Chamishim shnot bikoret u-mechkar al yetsirata shel Dahlia Ravikovitch* (Sparks of Light: Essays about Dahlia Ravikovitch's Oeuvre). Tel Aviv: Ha-Kibbutz ha-Me'uchad, 2010.

Turner, Mark. *The Literary Mind: The Origins of Thought and Language*. Oxford: Oxford University Press, 1996.

Tzemach, Shlomo. "Matzevet ve-shalakhta." In *Shti va-erev* (Woof and Warp), 216–35. Tel Aviv: Am Oved, 1959. First published in *Davar*, June 28, 1957.

Tzvik, Yehudit. "Ba-derekh el ha-shalva ha-gdola" (En Route to the Great Tranquility). In *Yehuda Amichai: Mivchar ma'amarey bikoret al yetzirato* (Yehuda Amichai: A Selection of Critical Essays on His Writings), ed. Yehudit Tzvik, 95–104. Tel Aviv: Ha-Kibbutz ha-Me'uchad, 1988.

———. "Li-vchinata shel ha-intertextualiyut be-shirat Amichai: ha-tavnit ha-makifa" (On the Question of Intertextuality in the Poetry of Yehuda Amichai: The Comprehensive Pattern). *Aley si'ach* 37 (summer 1996): 57–68.

———, ed. *Yehuda Amichai: mivchar ma'amarey bikoret al yetzirato* (Yehuda Amichai: A Selection of Critical Essays on His Writing). Tel Aviv: Ha-Kibbutz ha-Me'uchad, 1988.

———. "Yetzirat Amichai bi-r'i ha-bikoret" (Amichai's Oeuvre in the Mirror of Its Criticism). In *Yehuda Amichai: Mivchar ma'amarey bikoret al yetzirato* (Yehuda Amichai: A Selection of Critical Essays on His Writings), ed. Yehudit Tzvik, 7–60. Tel Aviv: Ha-Kibbutz ha-Me'uchad, 1988.

Venuti, Lawrence. *Rethinking Translation: Discourse, Subjectivity, Ideology*. London and New York: Routledge, 1992.

———. *The Translator's Invisibility: A History of Translation*. London and New York: Routledge, 1995.

———, ed. *The Translation Studies Reader*. 2000; reprint ed., London and New York: Routledge, 2012.

Wallach, Yona. "Hebrew." In *The Defiant Muse: Hebrew Feminist Prose from Antiquity to the Present*, ed. Shirley Kaufman et al., trans. Lisa Katz, 189–91. New York: Feminist Press, 1999.

———. *Tzurot*. Tel Aviv: Sifrey Siman Kri'a, 1985.

Weisman, Anat. "Zman u-tnu'a be-shirat David Avidan" (Time and Movement in the Poetry of David Avidan). Ph.D. diss., Hebrew University, 2005.

Weissbrod, Rachel. *Ba-yamim ha-acherim: tmurot ba-shira ha-ivrit beyn tasha"ch le-tashka"ch* (In Other Days: Shifts in Hebrew Poetry between 1948–1967). Tel Aviv: Open University, 2002.

Wolf, Diane. *Beyond Anne Frank: Hidden Children and Postwar Families in Holland*. Berkeley: University of California Press, 2007.

Yaniv, Shlomo. "Beyn tzura u-mahut" (Between Form and Essence). *Aley si'ach* 15–16 (1982): 139–44.

Yeats, W. B. *The Collected Poems of W. B. Yeats*. Ed. Richard J. Finneran. New York: Simon & Schuster, 1989.

Zach, Natan. "Daf chadash" (New Page). *Ha-olam ha-ze*, March 14, 1986.

———. *Kol he-chalav ve-ha-dvash* (All the Milk and Honey). Tel Aviv: Am Oved, 1966.

———. "Le-akliman ha-signoni shel shnot ha-chamishim ve-ha-shishim be-shiratenu" (On the Stylistic Climate of the 1950s and 1960s in Our Poetry). *Ha'aretz*, July 29, 1966, 10, 13.

———. *Shirim shonim* (Various Poems). Tel Aviv: Alef, 1960.

———. "Sipurav ha-shiriyim shel Yehuda Amichai" (The Poetic Stories of Yehuda Amichai). In *Ha-shira she-me'ever la-milim: Te'orya u-vikoret 1954–1973* (Poetry beyond Words: Theory and Criticism 1954–1973), 331–36. Bney Brak: Ha-Kibbutz ha-Me'uchad, 2011. First published in *Yokhani* 2 (August 1961): 26–30.

Zertal, Idith. *Ha-umah ve-ha-mavet* (Death and the Nation). Or Yehuda: Dvir, 2002.

———. *Israel's Holocaust and the Politics of Nationhood*. Trans. Chaya Galai. Cambridge, MA: Cambridge University Press, 2005.

Index